The Performance of American Government

Checks and Minuses

Gerald M. Pomper

AND

Badi G. Foster
Charles E. Jacob
Wilson C. McWilliams
Alan Rosenthal
Jay A. Sigler
Rutgers University

THE FREE PRESS NEW YORK
Collier-Macmillan Limited London

printing number
1   2   3   4   5   6   7   8   9   10

CONTENTS

TABLES

FIGURES

PREFACE

This volume is a cooperative effort of six members of the political science faculty of Rutgers University. Our teaching responsibilities place us on different campuses—Badi Foster, Wilson McWilliams, and myself at Livingston College, Charles Jacob at Rutgers College, Alan Rosenthal at the Eagleton Institute of Politics, and Jay Sigler at the College of South Jersey. The common institutional structure and intellectual emphasis of the University, however, have stimulated our combined efforts. We are happy to acknowledge these contributions of Rutgers.

There are many individual and joint services we would like to recognize here. The Rutgers University Research Council has provided financial aid, and its Center for Computer Services has provided computing time. Professor James Rosenau originally suggested this effort, and David Harrop of The Free Press has been a consistently helpful and understanding editor. Manuscripts have been carefully typed by Joyce Crossland, Pat DeCandia, Karen Osowski, Margaret Ryan, Melva Sanzon, and Roberta Weber. We have benefited greatly from the comments and challenges of our students and colleagues at Rutgers.

As general editor of the volume, I have incurred some special debts. Miss Bess Handaly has not only typed much of the manuscript, but has also coordinated the effort. Judson James and Kathleen Frankovic made useful comments. Thomas O'Donnell was very helpful as a research aide, doing many of the calculations in chapter 2. My wife and children have often reminded me of the true priorities of life. The greatest contributions, of course, have been made by my fellow authors, whose work now follows.

G.M.P.

INTRODUCTION

by Gerald M. Pomper

That American government is in crisis has become a cliché. It is also a fact.

The authors of the following chapters concur in the existence of the crisis. Our common purpose is to analyze its causes, consequences, and possible resolutions. To promote this purpose, we discuss six aspects of the performance of American government, and describe its formal institutions. While we use some similar theoretical constructs, we are more fully agreed on our concerns than our concepts.

What is the crisis? Outward manifestations of political decay[1] are no more distant than the daily newspaper, as evidence accumulates of the inability of the United States to achieve its declared objectives. After more than a decade, the nation continues to fight a war contrary to its proudest moral purposes and beyond its mighty military power. Racism and discrimination continue after decades of governmental programs dedicated to equality for its Black citizens. Poverty persists despite governmental spending greater than the total income of virtually every nation on the earth. Technological development, stimulated by government subsidy and management, brings unwanted consequences of environmental decay, unemployment, and inflation.

As governmental policies fail to achieve their objectives, government itself loses its popular authority. Presidents are reviled, Congress is seen as ineffective, movements are begun to impeach members of the Supreme Court, and traditional loyalties to the political parties are discarded. The symbols of allegiance lose their appeal, as the Constitution is neglected, policemen are vilified, the flag is desecrated, and the military code of duty and obedience is seen as a rationalization for the atrocities of My Lai. Blacks particularly have indicated their alienation from the political system in a series of urban ghetto riots and rebellions.

Explanations for each of these problems are readily available. The morass of Vietnam can be attributed to the deficiencies of the State Department, for example, or the disrespect for government to the agita-

1. See Samuel P. Huntington, *Political Order in Changing Societies* (Yale University Press, 1968), chap. 1 for a seminal discussion of political order and political decay.

tion of violent radicals. Social scientists distrust such explanations, for we seek general causes of general behavior. The indications of political disorder are not isolated but widespread throughout the society. All institutions are affected. To explain and react to the problems, we must attempt broad-range and theoretical analysis.

In our view, the present crisis consists essentially of the limited effectiveness and responsiveness of American government. But the political institutions of the United States are designed to achieve these very two goals or, in Madison's words, to "enable the government to control the governed; and in the next place oblige it to control itself." [2] To promote effectiveness, the government has been provided with increasing powers over the economy, an articulated structure, military force, and iternational standing. To promote responsiveness, a variety of institutions and processes have evolved through American history, including popular elections, interest groups, judicial review, and the panoply of checks and balances between executive and legislative branches.

American government, we argue, is not accomplishing these ends of effectiveness and responsiveness. As the earlier examples indicate, contemporary actions of national agencies are inadequate to the great purposes of the Constitution: "to form a more perfect Union, establish Justice, insure domestic Tranquility, provide for the common defense, promote the general Welfare, and secure the blessings of Liberty." These deficiencies are closely related to a lack of governmental responsiveness. The expressed needs and wants of the citizenry are not heard, or insufficiently heeded, or considered only long after they are expressed.

The problem is evident in the particular aspects of American politics which will be analyzed in the following chapters. A constitution based on a mechanistic theory of politics does not meet the demand for organic communities. A decaying party system does not provide a means for the transmission of popular preferences. Congressional control over policy declines with the increased stress on technical expertise and the need for rapid action, particularly in foreign policy. The president becomes increasingly isolated from political controls, while he is also increasingly handicapped in implementing his own policies. The judiciary is overwhelmed by demands for societal leadership, demands unmanageable through the accustomed adjudication of individual cases. Blacks seek the redress of historical grievances from an unresponsive nation.

Inadequacies in governmental performance are not due to the malevolence of individual men and women, although malevolent persons exist. They are due to defects in a more general system, and to the new expressions of politics with which the system must cope. New institu-

2. *The Federalist, No. 51* (Modern Library ed., 1941), p. 337.

tions and processes must be devised, or old ones reconstituted, to meet these new needs.

The basic defect in the system, we believe, is that American politics and political institutions conflict. American politics is rapidly developing new forms of participation and new demands for popular control. American political institutions, on the other hand, favor incremental rather than rapid change, limited participation, and only indirect popular control.

New and extended political participation is evident in the expansion of the franchise to the young and to ethnic minorities, street demonstrations, citizen movements within the political parties, interest-group litigation, public opinion polls and television, and even in overt violence. The rapidity with which participation is now expanding is illustrated by the growth in the eligible electorate. Close to twenty-five million persons will be able to vote for president for their first time in 1972. This *new* group of voters is greater than the *total* electorate in any contest before 1920.

Increased participation has been accompanied by innovative demands and actions, such as community control of local schools, revenue-sharing between federal and state governments, consumer lawsuits, abolition of the electoral college, restrictions upon the war-making power of the president, Congressional reform, and local vetoes of federal executive and judicial orders. This is a diverse group of programs, but they have a common feature. All are expressions of the general demand for increased popular control. All reflect an underlying belief that current institutions are insufficiently responsive, or inadequately controlled, or potentially dangerous. Significantly, these programs to assert popular control draw support from widely disparate factions, ranging from the libertarian right to the left-wing advocates of "participatory democracy." [3]

The established institutions of the United States, however, are not presently equipped to cope with increased participation and new demands. The Constitution was partially intended to limit direct mass influence, on the assumption that "the public voice, pronounced by the representatives of the people, will be more consonant to the public good than if pronounced by the people themselves." [4] The numerous checks and balances within and between the parties, Congress, and the president together function to maintain existing power relationships, not to transform them. The common law, the foundation of American justice, assumes and reinforces the marginal character of social development. These institutions are well designed for indirect, restricted, and incre-

3. On the problems of decentralization and participation, see the discussion of Robert A. Dahl, *After the Revolution?* (Yale University Press, 1971).
4. Madison, *The Federalist*, No. 10, p. 59.

mental democracy. They do not perform well when participation quickly expands and when the demands, as in the problem of racism and discrimination, are for rapid, sustained, and extensive change.

New demands and new forms of participation are expressions of the political modernization of the United States.[5] A mass democracy is taking shape in the land in which the ideal of democracy was first given legitimacy. It remains to be seen if the institutions of America, designed in a pre-democratic era, are adequate in this new period. We will argue that the performance of American government is in fact mixed, one in which ratings must include approving checks and critical minuses.

Finally, however, we should note some hopeful trends. There are indications of party realignment. Congress has begun its own reform, and controls are being attempted over the extensive power of the national executive. The courts have responded to social needs in areas such as criminal justice and the suffrage. Individuals, from Ralph Nader to the suburban housewife, are increasingly aware and involved. The Black community has asserted its right to full participation in American life. These changes are disturbing at times, but they indicate the basic vigor of the nation. An active citizenry is not always a comfort to government, but it is comforting to a democracy. We will analyze these varying trends more fully in the following chapters.

THE ANALYSIS

The authors of this book admittedly have their own opinions, and we do not seek to disguise them. We believe our scholarly obligation is not to deny our points of view, but to admit to them explicitly and to support them with the fullest and fairest evidence we can marshal. We do not fulfill our responsibilities by assuming a false posture of detachment from the problems of our time and nation. Rather, we seek honestly to confront all of the data available, and to do so in an open manner which allows others to test our assumptions, methods, and reasoning.

In acknowledging our own biases we also recognize that we may be wrong. We invite all readers to dispute our ideas and to develop their own interpretations of American politics. To facilitate their independent thought we have attempted to separate our own analyses from basic factual and statistical data upon which interpretation can be built. Our individual interpretations are found in six long essays dealing with the Constitution, the parties, the Congress, the President, the courts, and the

5. See the discussion in Huntington, pp. 32-39, and chap. 2, and in chap. 2 below.

condition of Afro-Americans. While these essays obviously include factual material, their emphasis is on the meaning of these facts and their consequences for the performance of American government. We hope the reader will find these essays challenging and, conversely, that he will indeed challenge them, either in a group or privately.

Sound reasoning depends in part on a knowledge of basic and relevant information. One cannot interpret the Constitution if he has not read it, for example. To facilitate individual interpretation, we seek to provide the necessary factual base. In separate sections of the four chapters dealing with the institutions of American government, we provide crucial details on the structure and processes of the parties, Congress, the executive branch, and the Courts. Obviously, facts cannot be presented without some criteria of relevance and, therefore, some interpretation. The emphasis in these sections, however, is on presenting the essential data that the reader will need to understand the institutions and to confront the interpretative essays.

We believe this separation of material into two different, but related, forms of presentation is advantageous to our readers. Those who want to obtain basic information on governmental institutions need read only the supplementary sections, without being forced to accept the authors' particular interpretation. Those who are already well-versed in this material can immediately read the essays, without being required to endure another repetition of familiar information. Readers thus can select and combine those sections most appropriate to their interests and level. For the authors, this separation has made it possible for us to develop our own thoughts without being burdened by a mass of data or the constant necessity to move to new topics. We have then been able to present the basic material without feeling that this data inhibited our thinking or was burdensome to the reader.

This organizational scheme is one of the unifying elements of this book. Theory is a second unifying element. This volume is not meant to be a theoretical work, nor do we seek rigidly to adhere to a deductive model of the political system. We are more concerned with discussing the political institutions of the United States and their adequacy in meeting current policy problems. We do attempt, however, to write within the same general framework and to use similar central concepts. A brief discussion of these concepts here may illuminate the reading of the essays.

Political institutions are regarded not as independent social entities, but as a specialized set of interactions within the general social system of the United States. They derive their character from the general society and influence that society in turn. In this interrelationship we can designate the specialized activity of political institutions as "the authoritative allocation of values." Following David Easton, what we mean by this activity is that political institutions make decisions which are generally enforceable and acceptable (i.e. authoritative) on the distribution of scarce resources such as power, wealth, and life chances (i.e. the allocation of values).[6]

In allocating values, political institutions are affected by, and affect in turn, the general society. There is a flow to the political system of inputs, comprised of demands and supports. Demands are expressions of needs by individuals and groups, articulation of wants, ethical restraints, and the like. Demands can be as narrow and specific as the petition of a judicial litigant or as broad and general as the insurrection of Black ghetto residents. The environment also provides positive and negative supports for the political system. Supports are underlying sentiments of loyalty or disloyalty toward the system. While the pledge of allegiance to the flag represents positive support for the system, the burning of that flag is a negative support.

The political system reacts to the inputs in various ways, not necessarily satisfactorily. Illustratively, demands can be recognized, ignored, compromised, and repressed. Supports may be strengthened or weakened. The eventual result is the formulation of outputs, which may be specific statutes or decisions, ceremonial actions such as a presidential tour, or maintenance of the status quo. Whatever their content, political outputs become new influences on the society, in turn giving rise to changes in the political demands and supports. There is then a continuous, circular pattern of interaction. In this sense, the political system can be defined as the agency for the conversion of inputs into outputs. The manner in which this conversion takes place constitutes the political institutions.

Activity by the political institutions and political figures obviously has consequences for the society. These consequences are known as the functions of the institution. To be precise, when we speak of the function of an institution, we generally mean the consequences which that activity has for the society. Illustratively, we often say that the Supreme Court issues binding decisions. We mean by this that the function or consequence of Supreme Court activity is the establishment of binding decisions. The latter formulation is clumsy language, so we often use the former form of expression, but we are still referring implicitly to the functional explanation. Most generally, when we refer to the political system as authoritatively allocating values, we mean that the consequences

6. See David Easton, *A Framework for Political Analysis* (Wiley, 1965), chap. 1.

of its activity is that scarce resources are distributed in generally acceptable ways.[7]

There are many analytical advantages to thinking in functional terms.
We avoid reifying institutions, for we no longer think of Congress as
"making" laws, in the same way a carpenter "makes" furniture. Institutions are seen as secondary, as particular structures to perform a function,
but by no means the only way it could be done. We are then intellectually free to speculate on and discover other ways in which the
function could be performed. For example, we might agree that in every
society there will be laws, general rules for the allocation of values.
If we look for the function of rule-making (i.e., activity which has
the consequence that rules are made), rather than for a legislative body,
our vision is less restricted. We can recognize that rule-making occurs
not only in legislative bodies, but through bureaucracies, consultations
with oracles, street gangs, and so on. We can also become sensitive to
change and breakdown in institutions. The consequences of political
action can be detrimental as well as beneficial. The function of the
stamp tax imposed on the American colonies can be seen as diminishing
support for the British government. In contrast, a focus on the institution
of Parliament would be more likely to lead to a conclusion that the
Stamp Tax was a revenue-raising law.

The theoretical usefulness of this form of analysis is not universally
accepted in the social sciences. There are problems in specifying functions, in demonstrating the connection between a particular structure
or institution and its functions, and in eliminating ideological bias.
While this controversy is important—for sound theory is basic to an
understanding of society—we do not intend to pursue the discussion in
this volume. We use the general scheme because it provides a focus for
our essays. We do not presume to be offering a general theory of American politics, much less of the political system. For our purposes in
discussing and illuminating the character and crisis of American politics,
functional analysis provides useful concepts. We ask no more at this
point.

Throughout these essays there is continuing reference to the political
problems and status of Black Americans. The nation's institutions, we
agree, have not met their needs. In conceptual terms, their demands have
not been heard, their support has decreased, and outputs relevant to them
have been unsatisfactory. This dominant problem deserves special treatment, both intellectually and politically. In the last essay, therefore, the
focus of analysis is reversed. We look not at the institutions directly,
but at their outputs. In assessing the historical and contemporary condi-

7. On functional analysis, see Robert Merton, *Social Theory and Social Structure*
(Free Press, 1968), pp. 104-108.

tion of Afro-Americans we can reach a judgment on the adequacy of the political institutions of the United States.

The reader may wish to consider several analytic questions as he reviews these essays. These include: What are the functions of each institution? How do the consequences of one political action affect the consequences of others? Does the performance of the functions in the contemporary United States contribute to stability or change? Are there means of improving the functional performance? What alternative structures could be devised to perform the function better and lead to more socially desirable consequences? We will consider these questions in our own essays, hoping to promote further thought by our readers.

Ultimately, our hope is to stimulate concern and action. To be meaningful, concern and action must be based on analytical ability and grasp of factual information, which we seek to promote through this volume. Analysis and knowledge are insufficient, however, in a time of crisis for our country. Informed and insightful involvement is needed. Hope for improved performance by American government essentially depends on an improved political performance by Americans.

THE AMERICAN

CONSTITUTIONS

by Wilson C. McWilliams

CONSTITUTIONS AND CONSTITUTIONALISM

Asked to describe their government, most Americans would probably refer to the Constitution and might add that the United States is a "government of laws and not of men." Yet Americans know that words written on paper can "govern" only through men. In movies and television the rule of law is inseparable from the skill and bravery of sheriffs, policemen, and federal agents, themselves assisted by the Colt .44, the Thompson sub-machine gun, and modern devices like computers and chemistry laboratories. We know, in other words, that the law can rule only when enough men believe in it or accept it and are willing, if need be, to enforce the law's commands on those who are unwilling to obey. Americans have little doubt that Thomas Hobbes was right when he declared that "convenants, without the sword, are but words." [1]

Still, we Americans often view the Constitution as politically neutral and "above" politics. Civics classes teach us to see the Constitution as a set of rules and procedures by which men play the "great game of politics," [2] and political scientists sometimes echo that teaching. The Constitution defines a series of ways in which private citizens and officials are allowed to act (the "freedom of speech" or the "powers of Congress") and establishes other ways in which we must act in order to win whatever prize we want from the political game ("how a bill becomes a law" or "the due process of law"). The Constitution, in this view, differs from a game of "Monopoly" only in that the rules, rather than the chance of the dice, determine when we are told to "Go to Jail."

1. Thomas Hobbes, *Leviathan*, ed. C. B. Macpherson (Penguin, 1968), p. 223.
2. The phrase is taken from Frank Kent, *The Great Game of Politics* (Doubleday Doran, 1935).

No set of procedures is "neutral," however. All procedures are methods by which we hope to achieve results, means for reaching ends, and constitutional procedures are no different. (The rules of "Monopoly," for example, are based on the assumption that we want to win by driving all other players "out of business"). "All associations," Aristotle wrote, "are instituted for the purpose of attaining some good—for men do all their acts with a view to achieving something which is, in their eyes, good." [3] At least implicitly, all constitutions begin with an idea of what is necessary, desirable, and good for the people they are to govern. Some values and goals, derived from a conception of human nature, are thought to be truly valuable, parts of the public good and the good life. And by implication, other possible goals are considered to be less important or even undesirable.

Many conservative political thinkers, for example, have argued that a hereditary nobility and an established church are valuable as sources of stability, reverence, and security; but our Constitution specifically rejects both institutions.[4] Many socialists and radicals have urged the economically deprived to "expropriate the expropriators," but the Fifth Amendment requires that property holders be paid "just compensation" for any property taken from them.

Founded on some notion of desirable ends (or "outputs"), constitutions are also based on ideas of the ways in which human beings will behave (or "inputs"). To get to whatever destination we aim at, we must know where we are at the moment, our strengths and weaknesses, and the obstructions which may lie between us and our goal. The idea of human nature which underlies a constitution's theory of value is also important because it predicts which things men will demand and support, which they will resist, and how they will translate such feelings into action. Too, constitutions are based on convictions about the specific nature of the people who are to be governed, as distinct from the nature of men generally. If we believe that peace is good, but think that men have strong warlike impulses, we will design one kind of institutions; if we think that our citizens, by habit, training or genetic inheritance are peace-loving, we might want a radically different kind of institutions for them than we would prescribe for other men.[5]

Constitutions also involve some estimate of the environment, both human and natural. Constitutions and statutes in the arid states of America often make elaborate provisions for the "authoritative allocation" of

3. Aristotle, *The Politics of Aristotle*, ed. Ernest Barker (Clarendon Press, 1952), p. 1.

4. Article I, section 9 and the First Amendment.

5. *Politics of Aristotle*, pp. 154-156.

water;[6] in states with adequate rainfall, such institutions would seem pointless (or wrong-headed: in the English Common Law, rivers are partly regarded as a means for carrying water *off* the land). If Americans had felt themselves to be, or expected to become, desperately poor, we might have been less willing to protect private property.[7] If we had guessed that other nations would become more friendly or less warlike, we might have fixed a limit to the size of the army or prohibited the waging of offensive war (both proposals were made in 1787).[8]

Finally, constitutions also involve some prediction of the ways in which present-day decisions will affect political behavior in the future. The Framers, for example, believed that if the Articles of Confederation were not changed, the American states would become more divided with the passing of time.[9] They were equally convinced that the Constitution would produce results which would gradually increase feelings of national unity.

Constitutions, in other words, are *theories of government*, if only by implication. They are not "above" politics; each constitution describes and hopes to establish a specific *kind* of politics. Obviously, most constitutions have political consequences which were not intended. An error in understanding human nature, a misperception of the political environment, a failure to foresee change: all of these can result in institutions which have "unanticipated consequences." The Whig revolutionaries in England, who established some of Britain's most important constitutional institutions in 1689, would have been horrified to see them result in universal suffrage, utilitarianism, and eventually, in a government guided by vaguely socialistic principles.[10] The authors of our own Constitution would have disliked the mass political party and certainly hoped to prevent conflicts like the Civil War. And the supporters of the Fourteenth Amendment, mostly men concerned to wipe out the heritage of slavery, did not design the amendment as a device to prevent the regulation of business.[11] All of this, of course, only reminds us that human wisdom is never perfect.

But even without such unintended developments, constitutions work

6. Carey McWilliams, *California: the Great Exception* (Wyn, 1949).
7. David Potter, *People of Plenty* (University of Chicago Press, 1959), argues that abundance has been the chief factor shaping the American character.
8. *The Federalist*, ed. Max Beloff (Blackwell, 1948), pp. 158-163, 115-124.
9. Ibid., pp. 20-31.
10. Edmund Burke was horrified before the event. See *An Appeal from the New to the Old Whigs* (Bobbs Merrill, 1962).
11. Jacobus Ten Broek, *The Anti-Slavery Origins of the Fourteenth Amendment* (University of California Press, 1951); the amendment was used to aid business by means of the doctrine, discussed later, that the corporation as a "legal person" could not be deprived of "due process" by the states.

to the advantage of some men and interests and to the disadvantage of others. That, after all, is their aim. If we hope to encourage virtue, we plan to discourage vice; if we desire to promote "enterprise," we must devalue leisure; if we ordain economic equality, we must prevent the acquisition of wealth. In both intended and unanticipated consequences, constitutions help to determine "who gets what, when and how" and, by implication, to decide who does not.[12]

In general, we may prefer a "government of laws" and advocate constitutionalism, but the value of any specific constitution depends on what laws are involved. To understand any constitution, we must discover the political theory it embodies; to evaluate it, we need a political theory of our own.

Mechanistic and Organic Theories

Americans tend to take their own Constitution for granted, when they are not engaged in "Constitution-worship." The power of habit, the influence of early rearing, and our formal education about politics combine to give us emotional and intellectual blind spots where the Constitution is concerned. We do not see that the Constitution involves a theory because we have been trained to think in the terms of the very theory which the Constitution embodies. This acculturation, however, blinds us to the meaning of many issues in American politics—and often to much about ourselves.

If an American is asked to define "the Constitution," for example, he will almost certainly refer to the formal, written document that describes our governmental institutions. Yet even that definition is based on a theory; it reflects a *mechanistic* theory of politics rather than an *organic* theory. And the conflict between these two varieties of political and constitutional theory is central to much of American culture and political life.

Mechanistic theories, as the term implies, see governments and constitutions alike as "machines," devices which men construct consciously to enable them to fulfill their individual desires. The desires of men are taken as givens, starting-points established "by nature," goals which men have a "right" to further. Logically, if not historically, men exist "before" governments and create them only because they find it difficult or impossible to achieve their goals by themselves. Many mechanistic theorists, like Hobbes and Locke, portrayed men in pre-political "state of nature," in which individuals, seeking to preserve their lives and acquire goods, were constantly in danger of being killed or dispossessed by others. Men might accept enslavement in order to stay alive, but

12. The phrase is from Harold Lasswell, *Politics: Who Gets What, When, How?* (McGraw-Hill, 1936).

such despotism was fundamentally illegitimate. Legitimate government resulted from a decision by a given body of men to escape the "state of war" by agreeing to a "social contract" and creating a government to enforce order and protect life, liberty and property.[13]

Though mechanistic theorists differ greatly in the ways in which they describe this process and in the purposes for which they believe men founded governments, certain principles are common to all of them. First, while men "give up" certain rights to government—such as the right to decide when it is legitimate to kill someone else—they "retain" other rights. (The Ninth Amendment makes this point quite specifically.) Government is not only limited to certain purposes; it is excluded from interfering with others. The political order is divided into a *public* sphere in which government may act and a *private* sphere in which it may not. Sometimes called the distinction between "state" and "society," this theoretical separation is the foundation of mechanistic constitutionalism.[14]

In mechanistic constitutions like the written Constitution of the United States, many institutions—the Bill of Rights is the obvious example—are designed to keep the distinction intact, preventing public government from encroaching on private freedoms. Other institutions are intended to guarantee that "the state" serves the purposes of "society." Periodic voting is, of course, one such device; but many qualifications have been attached to the principle of majority rule in one constitution or another to protect the rights of minorities or to prevent the government from being seized by a "faction" within society. The "check-and-balance" mechanism of our Constitution is one such device; "proportional representation," designed to insure minority representation and to check the "tyranny of the majority," has been adopted in many foreign governments and in several cities in the United States.[15] In all cases, however, mechanistic constitutionalism sees the goals of public action as rightly determined by private motives. Constitutions exist to translate private desires into efficient and rational public policy, but the public order is the servant and private man the master.

Organic theories, by contrast, begin with the premise that man is "by nature" a social and political animal. This is in part a reflection of the fact that man is born and to a considerable extent remains a

13. For a discussion of this aspect of mechanistic theory, see J. W. Gough, *The Social Contract* (Clarendon Press, 1957).

14. John H. Schaar, "Some Ways of Thinking About Equality," *Journal of Politics*, 26 (1964), pp. 884 f.

15. One of the strongest advocates of proportional representation was John Stuart Mill. See *Utilitarianism, Liberty and Representative Government* (Dutton, 1951) and Henry Magid, "John Stuart Mill," in Leo Strauss and Joseph Cropsey, eds., *History of Political Philosophy* (Rand McNally, 1963), pp. 688-691.

dependent and weak being, who could scarcely survive at all without the help of others. But in organic theory, political society is more than a tool for men. It exists *before* and to some degree *above* men, and decisively affects their personalities and characters.

It is necessary to emphasize that, for organic theorists, this shaping of the human personality is *natural*. Mechanistic theories imagine that men act "naturally" only to the extent that they have not been molded and trained by society. Organic theory argues that such behavior, even if we can conceive of it, would be unnatural or less than natural. Man begins, organic theory contends, as little more than a bundle of potentials, and beyond a few "instincts" (a term organic theorists avoid far more than their mechanistic counterparts do), man does not even know what he wants. Human beings need the protection, emotional support, and education provided by political society in order to develop and discover the "self" of each individual, in order to *realize* their nature. "Nurture," in other words, is a part of human "nature," for without society human beings would remain abortive and incomplete. Aristotle summed up this aspect of organic theory when he declared that an isolated man "must either be a beast or a god," for he could not be human.[16]

Of course, an organic theorist will concede, many (or most) societies do their work very imperfectly or very badly. Sometimes this failure is due to a lack of resources: we would not expect many men to develop a concern for ultimate truth if they lived in a desert where all their waking hours had to be spent looking for food and water. But also a political society may have what are, for any given organic theorist, incomplete or erroneous ideas about what is truly natural and valuable in men. Perverse values and bad institutions can distort or misuse some of the most valuable qualities in human beings. In the nineteenth century, Americans were instructed that, since the "survival of the fittest" was the law of history, ruthless competition was the best way to serve humanity; they were also taught that reason required men to accept the "scientific" belief in "inferior races." [17] (Many Americans still believe and teach such doctrines; they are, however, far less characteristic of the society than they were in the past.) Rationality and the desire to serve were thus twisted to the purposes of racism, cutthroat competition, and imperialism.

It follows, for organic theorists, that men are likely to realize their nature only when they live in the right kind of state in the right sort of environment, and only such states are "natural" for men. Aristotle asserted, for example, that man is "by nature an animal intended to live

16. *Politics of Aristotle*, p. 6.
17. Richard Hofstadter, *Social Darwinism in American Thought* (Beacon, 1955).

in a *polis*" (a city-state like those of ancient Greece).[18] And the organic theorist argues that all less perfectly natural states should, to the extent that they can, try to approximate the natural ideal.

Ideals aside, however, organic theory insists that whether we like it or not, political societies do shape the character and personality of the individual, if only by neglect. Thus when Jean Jacques Rousseau contended (against mechanistic ideas) that men must give up *all* their rights to the political community, he meant that they must do so in fact, whatever theorists might say or men might prefer.[19] It follows that, in organic theory, there is no separation of public and private spheres, no distinction between state and society. If my character and personality are affected by the kind of relations I have with my friends, with my wife, or with God, by how much money I have or whether I like my work, then all of these matters are political concerns which will be crucial to the kind of political society which exists in my country.

The organic theorist is arguing, in other words, that the *real* constitution of a state is not just its formal laws and institutions of government; in fact, those laws and institutions may not be very important. The constitution of a country is like the "constitution" of a man: it includes all those things, resources, customs, beliefs and relationships which make the citizens of the country what they are and which make the country, in turn, what it is. Thus Alexis de Tocqueville observed that, although the Mexican Constitution of 1824 was almost a copy of the American document, Mexican government had rapidly fallen into dictatorship. The customs of the American people, Tocqueville concluded, were more important than formal laws in establishing and maintaining the real character and the true constitution of American democracy.[20] Men, organic theory contends, are the real "empowerers" of government and the real limitations on it.

Organic theory, in other words, has little confidence in paper constitutions and in procedural limitations on government. Procedure is the essence of mechanistic constitutionalism, since mechanical theorists hope that the free choices of private men can be turned into desirable public action by determining the ways in which men pursue their goals. Organic constitutionalism is more concerned with substantive limitations; it is

18. *Politics of Aristotle*, p. 5. Aristotle made powerful arguments to support this contention, so powerful that most political theorists until comparatively modern times were likely to accept them; today the argument may be coming back into fashion.

19. Ernest Barker, ed., *The Social Contract* (Oxford University Press, 1953), pp. 256-257, 262-263.

20. Alexis de Tocqueville, *Democracy in America* (Schocken, 1961), Vol. I, pp. 379-383.

interested in *what* men want and *what* government does, rather than *how* these ends and policies are determined.

A mechanistic theorist would argue, for example, that if the president has acted according to the procedures and within the powers fixed for him by the Constitution in waging war in Vietnam, then his action is constitutional. Many Americans, however, make what amounts to an organic argument against this proposition. They argue that peace is good for men and that wars should only be fought when absolutely necessary, or that America is a country devoted to democracy. They go on to contend that the war in Vietnam is unnecessary or undemocratic, and consequently that the war is unjust and immoral. If an organic theorist agreed with this argument, he would add "and therefore, unconstitutional."

Nor, the organic theorist would insist, is this way of understanding constitutions a mere spinning of words. To the extent that certain values and institutions, standards of right conduct, and beliefs about proper procedure become embedded in the lives and minds of a people, they will insist that government (and their fellow citizens) live up to the principles involved. They may not have to insist, for the rulers may share those standards and values with the ruled. But apart from such an "organic" relation to people's lives and values, laws and procedures have no importance at all.

Laws and statutes in the United States might proclaim racial equality, for example, but racism made (and makes) many of them unenforceable. Section 2 of the Fourteenth Amendment provides that any state which denies men over twenty-one the right to vote shall have its representation in the House of Representatives reduced; but despite that clear constitutional "commandment," Southern states were always allowed full representation provided the means they used to restrict the vote were sufficiently devious and informal. And even the enforcement of formally equal laws cannot create equality where economic and social inequality, educational deprivation, and habit combine to make Whites feel that Blacks are "inferior" and leave Blacks without pride. The demand for "Black Power" is, even in the most limited sense, an insistence on those things which will make equality "real," and necessarily involves an organic conception of the constitution and politics.[21] In the same sense, although the British Parliament has, theoretically, almost limitless power, provided that the Queen consents to its actions, the current Conservative majority would no more think of outlawing the Labor Party (or, for that matter, the Communist Party) than the Queen would think of using

21. For an early example, see W. E. B. DuBois, "The Immediate Program for the American Negro," *The Crisis*, 9, (April 1915), pp. 310-312; see also Stokely Carmichael and Charles Hamilton, *Black Power* (Random House, 1967), pp. 2-57.

her "power" to veto a bill if it did. Custom and ideas like "fair play" limit the government far more strictly than any formal restrictions could ever do.

Organic theory regards real constitutions (as opposed to formal institutions of government) as very hard to change at all. In a bad political society, even the discontented have been shaped by the polity they detest; a people long accustomed to despotism has not been trained to be free. And in a reasonably good system, tampering with workable institutions and beliefs may only make matters worse if those who make the changes do not understand the real forces at work which limit the possibilities for change. Plato wrote that when he was a young man, recognizing that all governments were radically corrupt, he had been eager for social reform, but he had learned with the years that it was difficult if not impossible to set matters right.[22] More than once Black Americans have despaired of ever being able to change the human blindness of White America; separatism and emigration have been closely connected to the belief that racism is irrevocably a part of the constitution of White society.

Because it emphasizes the difficulty of fundamental change, organic theory is often appealing to conservatives (or leads to conservatism). Obviously, revolutionary change (from above or from below) is much easier if constitutions are something men make and if they can be transformed by a sweeping program of legislation. Organic theorists regard that attitude as superficial. Edmund Burke, for example, denounced the revolutionaries in France for believing that by "theoretic dogma" they could remake a long-established society.[23] In the same spirit, American conservatives sometimes argue that racial equality cannot be "legislated" because real change comes only from the "heart." [24]

But one cannot push this ideological association too far. Many revolutions have been based on organic doctrines. The English revolutionaries of 1689 argued it was they, not the king, who upheld the "immemorial law" of England. Black radicals and important elements of the white New Left today speak of American politics in organic terms. And Karl Marx combined both organic and mechanistic ideas. Marx believed that men would, after the proletarian revolution, be able to make their own institutions. He argued, however, that such a revolution could take place only after a long period of economic and social change had prepared the way for it by changing the "consciousness" of workers. Before such developments had matured, any hope for revolutionary change was a romantic illusion; even major changes in the formal institutions of gov-

---

22. Plato, *Epistles* (Bobbs Merrill, 1962), pp. 215-217.
23. Edmund Burke, *Reflections on the French Revolution* (Dent, 1955).
24. Barry Goldwater, *The Conscience of a Majority* (Prentice-Hall, 1970), p. 63.

ernment would not change the real nature (or, in organic terms, the "constitution") of capitalist society.[25]

As different as the two theories of constitutionalism are, both share a common premise. They agree that "limited government" is preferable to other kinds of regimes. Unlimited rule provides great opportunities, but it involves gigantic risks, and both organic and mechanistic constitutionalists agree that the former should be sacrificed in order to avoid the latter. In this sense, all constitutionalist theories value stability and security and all have an element of conservatism.

In every political society some laws and policies must change with circumstances and with changes in what we think and desire. In war we cannot have "business as usual," and the taxes which financed our government in 1800 would pay only a tiny fraction of its expenses today. Constitutionalism asserts, however, that some institutions should not change, whatever circumstances may seem to dictate and whatever we may think at the time. Even if we thought it would advance racial harmony to silence Governor Wallace or Huey Newton, the Constitution forbids us to do so, just as it prohibits "cruel and unusual punishment" even if it seemed that torture would enable us to "fight crime" more effectively. Constitutionalism makes a separation between *policies*, means for reaching ends which must be allowed to change from time to time, and *institutions*, procedures which are so inseparable from our goals as to require that they be changed only in slow and difficult ways if at all.

Constitutionalists, in other words, always believe in a "higher" or "fundamental" law which overrides all lesser laws.[26] Whether they see that higher law is embodied in written rules and mechanisms of government, or whether they find it in the beliefs and customs of a people, constitutionalists assert that the convictions of the moment must yield when they conflict with the more permanent wisdom of the "constitution." All constitutionalist doctrines, as this suggests, are based on the proposition that the rulers of a country, whether these are an elite or the people as a whole, often do or are tempted to make mistakes about the political good. The preference for a "government of laws and not of men" rests on the belief that the "disembodied reason of the law" is less likely to err than is the fleshly reason of living men, that the law understands what is good for men more surely than they do themselves.

Implicitly or explicitly, constitutionalism divides the human mind into

25. Lewis Feuer, ed., *Marx and Engels* (Doubleday, 1959), pp. 1-41, 246-261.
26. Alan Grimes, *American Political Thought* (Holt, Rinehart and Winston, 1955), p. 98. See chapter on the judicial institution, pp. 292 ff.

two parts. In their immediate beliefs and decisions, their "apparent will," men are likely to be influenced by irrationality and temporary surges of passion, by lack of information, and by perceptions too parochial in space (arising out of their own local experience) or in time (because, living in the present, they fail to learn from the past and do not care enough about the future). But, constitutionalists argue, men truly desire what is good for them even when they make mistakes about how to get it, or even when they err in deciding what it is. Hence their "true will" is sometimes quite different from what they want at the moment; the "true will" is what they would want if they were accurately informed, reasonable, and able to see things as a whole. A fat man on a diet may be overcome by his passionate desire for chocolate, but he will regret his decision and wish that someone had reinforced his "real" desire to abstain. Constitutionalism applies the same principle to politics. A constitution is designed to enable the "true will" of men to prevail over their "apparent will," whether the constitution is thought to embody the real will or only to contain checks and procedures which will force men to go slowly, deliberate with others, and think matters through until, hopefully, the "true will" or something more like it emerges.[27]

Constitutionalism is, to that extent, "undemocratic." And of course, constitutions need not be democratic at all; any political system can be constitutional. "Constitutional" is an adjective which modifies and limits the noun to which it is attached. To the simple principle of monarchy ("rule by one man"), of aristocracy ("rule by the best men") or of democracy ("rule by the people"), constitutionalism adds the qualifying phrase "according to the law." Constitutionalism is partly undemocratic because it is partly "unmonarchic" and "unaristocratic"; it distrusts *all* doctrines and forms of government because it is founded on distrust of men and of human thought. (And obviously, if a constitution matters, it will frustrate some and possibly all of the people it governs, even if they think that such frustration is good for them.)

There are as many kinds of constitutional democracy as there are definitions of democracy. At least three, for example, have had powerful advocates in recent American politics. Our Constitution provides for a fairly equal suffrage and defines men as equal "before the law," but it makes no provision for economic and social equality. Quite the contrary, the Constitution places large areas of life in a private sphere

27. Alexander Hamilton wrote, "It is a just observation that the people commonly *intend* the public good. . . . But their good sense would despise the adulator who should pretend that they always *reason right* about the means of promoting it." (*The Federalist*, p. 366). For an organic view, see Rousseau's argument in Barker, ed., *The Social Contract*, pp. 261-262.

from which government is debarred and gives private property considerable protection. Conservative Supreme Courts in the past construed those limitations in extreme ways. In the nineteenth century, it ruled that corporations were "legal persons" possessed of all the rights the Constitution gave to the individual [28] and, by accepting the doctrine of "separate but equal," it excluded any claim that social inequality destroyed the meaning of legal equality.[29] Though such opinions have been overruled or modified, many conservative Americans regret the fact or, at least, want to stop any further incursions of the notion of equality into the economic and social sphere.

For years, however, other Americans have argued that economic inequality creates differences of power so great as to make political democracy a sham.[30] Accepting the Democratic nomination in 1936, Franklin D. Roosevelt claimed that the time had come for Americans, who had overthrown political monarchy in 1776, to banish the "economic royalists" whose power corrupted democracy. Most Americans then seemed to agree (Roosevelt carried every state except Maine and Vermont), and today probably an even larger majority would agree that the New Deal made an important contribution to democracy in advancing economic security and "equality of opportunity." But of course the United States is very far from economic equality, and demands for a more equal "piece of the pie" continue to play a central role in American politics.

A new source of conflict, however, resulted from the fact that the New Deal dealt only marginally and indirectly with the kind of social inequality suffered by racial minorities and women. Movements which demand that such inequities be eliminated often meet resistance from those who feel their basic needs were (or can be) met within the structure of New Deal reforms. To protesters, however, a "social oligarchy" of Whites (or men) is as much a contradiction of democracy as "economic royalism."

The New Deal, in fact, was a kind of halfway house between conservative mechanistic constitutionalism and the more organic ideas of recent critics. Similarly it combined two ideas of equality. Movements of protest today, against the mechanistic notion that all men are originally ("born") equal, argue the organic creed that although men are often born into inequality they are equal "by nature" and can become equally valuable human beings. The first (mechanistic) belief implies that the

28. *Santa Clara County vs. Southern Pacific R.R.*, 118 U.S. 394, 396 (1886).

29. *Plessy vs. Ferguson*, 163 U.S. 537, 552, (1896). For an excellent discussion of the Court's ideas in this period, see Robert G. McCloskey, *American Conservatism in the Age of Enterprise* (Harvard University Press, 1951), pp. 72-126.

30. For an early example of such criticism by a political scientist, see J. Allen Smith, *The Spirit of American Government* (Macmillan, 1912).

law should treat all men the same way; the second (organic) suggests that the aim of policy should be to enable men to realize their equality and, consequently, that it should give special advantages to those who "start behind." [31]

To take a less familiar case, the Soviet Union has a variety of constitutionalism which at least claims to be democratic. It may seem strange to refer to the U.S.S.R. as "constitutional" in any sense, since the written constitution of the Soviet Union is often violated and at best means very little. But in the first place, Marxian theory regards political institutions as little more than a "superstructure" on the real, economic basis of life, so it is not surprising if Soviet leaders are rather cavalier with written political rules. Second, the formal government of the Soviet Union is very limited indeed; it is "checked" and controlled by the Communist Party at almost every point. Government officials and even the people at large, Marxist-Leninism declares, may very well have a "false consciousness," an "apparent will," at odds with their "true will." The Party, because its members are versed in Marxian science and under the discipline of their fellows, is far more likely to have a "true consciousness." The Party, then, must be the "vanguard of the proletariat," a guide for and a limitation on government and people, a constitution, and a supreme court—rolled up in one institution.[32]

There are many problems in this theory, not the least of them the fact that the very human members of the Communist Party are themselves unlimited. Nonetheless, Soviet theory and practice is a kind of constitutionalism. That only emphasizes the proposition that constitutions and constitutionalism are not political panaceas; they are and reflect theories about politics. No constitution is better than the theory on which it is based, and theory is the test of any constitutional order, including our own.

CONSTITUTIONALISM IN AMERICA

"Americans," Alan Grimes writes, "accepted constitutionalism long before they ratified the Constitution of 1787." [33] Puritans wrote "covenants" before they even ventured off the ships which brought them to New England, and the history of Colonial America is largely a record of struggles over charters and the rights granted in them.

31. G. K. Chesterton regarded this organic creed, "the pure classical conception that no man must aspire to be more than a citizen and that no man shall endure to be anything less," as the moral center of American politics. R. T. Bond, ed., *The Man Who Was Chesterton* (Doubleday, 1960), pp. 132-133.

32. For a Soviet discussion, see Andrei Vyshinsky, *The Law of the Soviet State*, trans. H. Babb, (Macmillan, 1948).

33. *American Political Thought*, p. 98.

Religion was one major source of constitutionalism, for it necessarily involved the conviction that a "higher law" existed above and beyond the decisions of men. Those who read the Bible seriously were often convinced that the Second Commandment, by forbidding idolatry, required believers to suspect all states and governments, lest patriotism become an idol. Even if they believed in a duty to "render unto Caesar that which is Caesar's," Christians and Jews were convinced that in any conflict, Divine Law took precedence over that of the state.

Religious constitutionalism was an organic theory. Though there was a wide variation in political ideas, and though Protestant (and especially Calvinistic) ideas were more influential in America, Christian and Jewish theory generally agreed in the seventeenth and eighteenth centuries that the organization of the family, the conduct of economic life, the use of leisure, and even what men ate and drank were critical to the development of men, and hence of concern to the community.

To an important extent religious theory was also substantive, more interested that justice be done than in the ways by which it was accomplished. This was, of course, more noticeable in Christian creeds which portrayed Jesus as struggling against a narrow legalism and arguing that even generally good laws had to be set aside when they conflicted with right conduct. ("The Sabbath is made for man, not man for the Sabbath.") [34] But if Jews were more cautious—and that is debatable—they had long recognized the same principle. Certainly all the lesser rules of men had either to change or to have exceptions when they came into conflict with the Law of God.

Religious ideas had also influenced and become entwined with medieval constitutionalism, although medieval thought had independent roots in local custom, classical philosophy, and Roman Law. Medieval law and thought influenced all who came to America, especially because so many came from rural or traditional communities. (Blacks brought a similar, non-European tradition drawn from the law of African states and affected by medieval Islam.) But obviously, American political history was most deeply affected by the fact that habit, experience, and theory had encouraged English immigrants to think of the Common Law as "immemorial," so ancient as to be almost part of the flesh and blood of Englishmen.[35]

By the eighteenth century English legal theorists had rejected the idea, put forward in *Cavendish's Case* in 1587, that the "law of the land"

34. *Mark* 2:27.
35. J. G. A. Pocock, *The Ancient Constitution and the Feudal Law* (Cambridge University Press, 1957). See the chapter on the judicial institution, pp. 71 ff.

took precedence over the decrees of government; Americans generally continued to accept it. The Framers, very modern men for their times, also spurned a great deal of traditional and medieval theory. But the older ideas were an integral part of the values and personalities of Americans generally; they could not be weeded out and have continued to play a vital role in American politics.[36]

Theories of constitutionalism, in medieval thought, were based on a belief in the natural law, an organic idea which conceived of the whole world as governed by a law written into the being of men and things. Men, more than animals or inanimate nature, could violate that law, but unlike more human laws, the natural law could not be broken without penalty. If a man refused to eat, he would die of starvation; if he committed murder, he would pay the penalty in spiritual anguish and self-hatred.

But the natural law was not a rigid code of ethical rules. All rules, in fact, might have exceptions. It might seem wise for an eldest son to inherit all of his father's property, but not if it resulted in his sister's starving. It might be a general rule that I can decide who may and who may not cross my land, but if I have allowed men to cross it for years and have encouraged them to make plans based on being allowed to cross, it would be arbitrary and unreasonable for me suddenly to put up a fence. Medieval theories were, for this reason, obliged to create a sphere of law called "equity," which allowed men to plead that justice required that in their particular case an exception be made to the rule.

As this suggests, medieval natural law denied almost altogether the right of men to act arbitrarily and according to their "will," even if the rules of procedure seemed to allow it. It was, as Ewart Lewis put it, "not primarily a theory of natural rights but of what, under given circumstances, was naturally right." [37] And that natural rightness took precedence over all human laws.

As might be expected, given such an organic idea of law, medieval constitutionalism also regarded the political community as essential for men and part of their nature. In critical respects the community created and took precedence over all merely "private" rights. Thus, for example, all property could be taken from individuals by the community if the public good required it. In the language of the law, the community possessed "eminent domain," the highest form of ownership. That doctrine finds its way into our own Constitution, for the Constitution

36. Edward S. Corwin, The "Higher Law" Background of American Constitutional Law (Cornell University Press, 1955).

37. Ewart K. Lewis, "The Contribution of Medieval Thought to the American Political Tradition," American Political Science Review, Vol. 50 (1956), pp. 462-474, at p. 467.

does not create a "right of property" except as a qualification on "eminent domain": the government may not take property from individuals except by "due process of law" and after paying "just compensation," but it can take property once those conditions are met. And, of course, it can tax us at any time.

In the same sense, medieval constitutionalism did not regard man as having a "right" to his own life. The community had made that life possible and had helped make a man what he was; consequently, it had a claim on him. It could prevent him from taking his life; suicide was a crime and citizens and officials had a right to prevent it (as they do today). It could also require him to risk his life, or even to lose it, when the community was under attack or in danger.

But partly because it deprecated the notion of private rights, medieval constitutional theory developed a very important sphere of public rights. Since the political community was vital to all men, they had a right to be consulted about public policy. "What touches all," medieval constitutionalists declared, "must be approved by all." It was the duty of a king to consult with representatives of his subjects. Rulers were morally obliged to give reasons to the ruled and to hear counter-arguments. Yet although representatives could refuse their consent if the king could not make a rationally compelling case for his policies, they were morally obliged to agree to those policies if he did make such a case. Representatives were not supposed to reflect the "will" of their constituents in any simple sense; they were under an obligation to reflect the rational (or "true") will of those they represented. Parliament was, in a sense, a *court* rather than a legislature, concerned with applying the law of nature to the shifting situation of men; it could no more refuse a king arbitrarily than a jury could arbitrarily find a prisoner guilty.[38] Medieval constitutionalism denied the arbitrary power of kings because it denied all arbitrary rights, whether of rulers, representatives or ruled.

Of course, medieval thinkers knew perfectly well that kings, subjects, and representatives might very well refuse to be reasonable. They argued, however, that the chances for rationality would be greater if men were obliged to discuss policies and give reasons for their views (even if, in modern language, these were only "rationalizations"), partly because such a requirement would appeal to the rational element of man's nature. Given that, the natural law allowed different peoples to design procedures appropriate to their circumstances which might maximize the chances for just policy.

In the last analysis, men were under no obligation to obey—and might have a duty to disobey—unjust policies and laws. The most that could

38. C. H. McIlwain, *The High Court of Parliament* (Yale University Press, 1910).

be required was that a citizen give his government every chance to act reasonably (and vice versa). Citizens judging their government were under the same obligation that bound it, when they were accused of crimes, to prove guilt "beyond a reasonable doubt." When that had been said, however, the medieval constitutionalist insisted that human prudence could and ought to do no more. Ultimately, he declared, all constitutions and all law must come down to the decisions and devotion of men.

Constitutionalism and the Framers

This dependence on public virtue and rationality was, for the Framers of our Constitution, a major weakness which encouraged them to reject religious and medieval theories of constitutionalism. Traditional organic theory, the Framers felt, did not provide adequate safeguards for a political order, especially in the long term. If good rulers and citizens were the only protection of a constitutional order, they reasoned, it would forever be in danger from force and at best would depend on the accidents of individual character and personality.

They turned instead to the "new science of politics" which, the Framers believed, made it possible to reduce the extent to which a constitutional system depended on human virtue almost to the vanishing point. Derived partly from liberal political theories, like those of John Locke, and partly from the mechanistic ideas then current in natural science, the new doctrine promised that men could create a political machine which would be "self-regulating," one which could transform even the worst human "inputs" into desirable "outputs." [39]

The desire for predictability and reliability over the long term and the hope to contrive a constitutional system which would work even if men were at their worst encouraged the authors of *The Federalist* to slight the amiable and admirable qualities they saw in men. (It helped that the opponents of the new Constitution, though they often adhered to a very different political theory, were even more suspicious of human nature.) [40]

"It is in vain to say," James Madison declared, "that enlightened statesmen will be able to adjust . . . clashing interests and render them subservient to the public good. Enlightened statesmen will not always be at the helm. . . ." Enlightened citizens were, if anything, even less likely. "In a nation of philosophers . . .," Madison jibed, "a reverence for the laws would be sufficiently inculcated by the voice of enlightened reason. But a nation of philosophers is as little to be expected as the philosophical race of kings wished for by Plato." Hamilton reminded Americans that

---

39. *The Federalist*, p. 37. Hamilton argues that whatever the faults of the "new science," it is more reliable than men (p. 148).
40. Cecilia Kenyon, ed., *The Anti-Federalists* (Bobbs Merrill, 1966).

"We, as well as the other inhabitants of the globe, are yet remote from the happy empire of perfect wisdom and perfect virtue." [41] Madison summed up the case:

> If men were angels, no government would be necessary. If angels were to govern men, neither external war nor internal controls over government would be necessary. In framing a government which is to be administered by men over men, the great difficulty lies in this: You must first enable the government to control the governed; and in the next place, oblige it to control itself. A dependence on the people is, no doubt, the primary control on the government, but experience has taught mankind the necessity of auxiliary precautions.[42]

But that emphasis on the worst in mankind also corresponded to the Framers' belief that men are and ought to be free "by nature," and that while government may be necessary to control or influence individual behavior, it ought not to concern itself with attempts to mold or educate character and personality. Madison doubted whether it would be possible to make all men into public-spirited citizens, but he insisted that even if it were possible, such a course would be undesirable. The protection of the diverse, individual faculties of men, he argued, is the "first object of government." Man, as the Framers saw him, was by nature a private, individualized being concerned with the fulfillment of his own desires and especially with his own survival. "The great principle of self-preservation" was one which Madison equated with both "absolute necessity" and "the transcendent law of nature and of nature's God," a law man followed by necessity and by right.[43]

At least until they won mastery over nature, however, men's desires (particularly their desire to survive) were sure to be frustrated. The world was a place of scarcity whose first teaching was "not enough." Necessarily and by right, man was a power-seeking animal involved in a war with nature, driven to struggle for ever-greater resources in his quest for safety and gratification. And since other men either possessed or were rivals for those resources and goods, man's war with nature involved him in a war with men.

The liberal theory from which this picture of the "state of nature" was derived, however, also postulated that human reason, the "servant of the passions," led them to see that the constant insecurity and destructiveness of the "state of war" was unproductive. As mentioned earlier, this doctrine asserted that reason led men to enter a "social contract" with one another, in which they "gave up" certain rights in order to

41. *The Federalist*, pp. 44, 258, 248.
42. Ibid., p. 265.
43. Ibid., pp. 42, 225.

enjoy those they retained more effectively. Society was an instrument designed to enhance the satisfactions of private man; it was, moreover, a military alliance. Agreeing to let their fellow citizens alone in the exercise of certain rights, and setting up procedures for the adjustment of conflicts, men were able to combine their efforts in the war against nature and against other men.

Since the political order was only a tool for the fulfillment of certain private desires, the state aimed, like the men who had "constituted" it, to acquire and safeguard power. Power enabled men and states to do as they wished; it was, in the terms of this theory, the *sine qua non* of liberty. Since men are "ambitious, vindictive and rapacious," Hamilton contended, it is the "uniform course of human events" for states to conflict with one another.[44] Even a rational state, which sought to avoid the destructiveness of war, had to seek non-destructive means of acquiring power. (Notably, one of the duties given Congress in Article I of the Constitution is the obligation to "promote the progress of science and the useful arts.")

In the mechanistic constitutionalism of the Framers, private men would be made (or forced to be) free from communities. Individuals, factions, and branches of government would be rendered comparatively weak and insecure, and forced to pursue their own separate interests. Competition would then be endemic, preventing any person, group or government agency from tyrannizing others. But at the same time, as the Framers knew, competition would lead the system as a whole to increase its power. Insecurity would lead men and groups to feel that they never "had enough," and competition would work to the same end.

The growth of human power was equivalent to the growth of human mastery over nature. In seeking power, provided they acted rationally rather than destructively, states and men were not only forwarding their own self-interest: they were advancing human progress. A strong union, Hamilton declared, would make "an active commerce, an extensive navigation, a flourishing marine . . . the inevitable offspring of moral and physical necessity," and would enable America to defy domestic and foreign politicians who attempted "to control or vary the irresistible and unchangeable course of nature." [45]

The Framers' "Science of Politics"

These very broad principles and goals are the core of the basic theory of the American Constitution. Many political analysts have tried to explain the Constitution in narrower terms. Professor Charles A. Beard, in 1913, described the Constitution as little more than a reflection

44. Ibid., p. 20.
45. Ibid., pp. 50-51.

of the economic interests of the men who wrote it, and Senator Albert J. Beveridge, who admired the Constitution, agreed that it was written to "enforce order, facilitate business and safeguard property" in the interest of the well-to-do.[46]

There is an element of truth in such explanations; the Framers never posed as ardent democrats or economic equalitarians. But the Beard-Beveridge thesis is incomplete, as much so as those arguments which refer to the Framers as "conservatives" without adding that they were conservative *revolutionaries*. The "economic interpretation of the Constitution" errs because the "self-interest" of the Framers made even *greater* claims than Beard, Beveridge or their imitators imagine. The pride and ambition of the Framers was more expansive than a concern for bank balances. They aimed to establish, as the Great Seal of the United States declares, a "new order of the ages," hoping to revolutionize all human history by setting the United States on a scientific foundation.[47] To leave out their zeal for "scientific" political theory is as serious an omission as it would be to explain the Soviet Union in terms of the "economic interests" of Lenin and Trotsky while saying nothing about Marxism.

The principal defect of "unscientific" politics, and hence the major danger the Framers sought to avoid in America, arose, they believed, from a conflict between human *interests* and human *affections*. Man's interests, his rational and true will, required him to pursue power and to struggle with nature because short of the mastery of nature man could have no complete satisfaction, and his life, more or less, would be only a record of frustration. But his affections desired immediate rather than long-term satisfactions and yearned for comfort, relaxation, and ease. There was nothing wrong about such desires as goals, but they tempted men to settle for too little, to accept a level of resources which frustrated too many other desires.

Moreover, men also developed an intense affection for the local groups into which they were born and in which they lived, especially because they emotionally associated such groups with the satisfaction of their basic needs for food, shelter and protection. Such local affections, however, made men oblivious to the fact that their interests would be better satisfied by larger, more efficient, and more powerful political and social units. Men defended the family and its interests against the state, the interests of the state against those of the union, and so on, blind to the fact that by so doing they were hurting themselves. The affections of

46. Albert J. Beveridge, *Life of John Marshall* (Houghton Mifflin, 1916), Vol. 1, p. 312; Charles A. Beard, *Economic Interpretation of the Constitution*, (Macmillan, 1913).

47. Hannah Arendt, *On Revolution* (Viking, 1963).

men, parochial in time and space, warred with their interests and even more with the long-term logic of human progress and the interests of humanity.

The affections were, as the Framers saw them, even more dangerous in America than elsewhere. America was a rich country and was distant from foreign enemies. In other countries the hold of the affections on men was likely to be broken by war and poverty, events which both freed men from the affections and forced them to follow the path of their interest; temporarily at least, America was largely exempt from want and danger. At the same time, Americans had what the Framers felt were unrealistic ideas about the extent to which citizens and states would devote themselves voluntarily to the general interest of the union. The war for independence and resentment against the British system of government had combined to create a common enemy and object of hostility that had, for the moment, "repressed the passions most unfriendly to order and concord," but such unity could not be expected to last.[48] Thus, although the authors of *The Federalist* spent much time in warning Americans of foreign dangers which seemed likely to arise in the future, they were as worried about the domestic conflicts which might develop if such foreign perils failed to materialize. And the problem of the affections in America was made worse by the likelihood that "perverted demagogues" and "ambitious politicians" would appeal to parochial affections in order to advance their own interests and power.

All of these principles and concerns found expression in the Constitution. There were, of course, many differences of opinion among the Framers, and these resulted in the famous compromises of the Constitution: the provisions for representation in the House and Senate, the decision that a slave would count as three-fifths of a man for the purpose of representation, and the creation of an "electoral college" to select a president rather than having him elected by the House. But these disagreements and compromises should never cause us to neglect the "scientific" doctrines which were common to almost all of the Framers and which shaped our institutions in fundamental ways.

First of all, the Framers were agreed that the large size of the Union was an advantage rather than a defect. Classical political theory, with which many of the Anti-Federalists agreed, had held that a good state —and certainly a free republic—had to be small, so that citizens might participate in government and so that men's emotions as well as their reason would tie them to the common good. The Framers argued, however, that small states had two serious defects: (1) they were too small to be powerful and hence were contrary to men's interests, and

48. *The Federalist*, p. 259.

(2) the very sense of importance which classical theory had believed a citizen of a small state would feel, the fact that individuals and small groups mattered a great deal in small communities, made small states liable to "faction." Small, intense and homogeneous groups of citizens could hope to seize the state and use it for their own purposes and to the disadvantage of their fellow citizens. The small state, in other words, strengthened rather than weakened the parochiality of affection by seeming to unite it to interest.

The advantage of a large state, Madison argued, was that such small and homogeneous groups would be too small and too weak to seize power by themselves. The only group sufficiently large to take power would have to be a coalition with many internal differences; it could agree only on very limited goals and could hardly form a scheme to oppress everyone else. In other words, groups which could be *effective* would be so large and diffuse that they would have little emotional meaning to the individual and *vice versa*. The size of the union would be an advantage because it lessened the danger of rule by faction, but also because it would force the individual to make a sharp distinction between his interest and his affections, and thus weaken the hold of parochial groups over him.[49]

Second, the Framers agreed on the principle of the *division of powers*, which parcelled powers out between the states and the federal government. The advantages of the division of powers were similar to and supplemented the advantages of size. Classical political theory, following the same organic principles as had led it to favor small states, argued that a federation should be a union of *states* alone. That is, it had contended that the federal government should be composed of the delegates of state governments and that federal authority should speak to citizens only through the mouth of state governments. A federation, in this view, looked structurally rather like the United Nations today.

Most Anti-Federalists adhered to this view, and though many wanted a stronger central government than that provided for by the Articles of Confederation, they wanted it strengthened within the framework of the Articles. The Federalists, on the other hand, argued that giving the central government greater powers in this way would only be writing words on paper and relying on the rationality and patriotism of state governments which, given the nature of political societies, was untrustworthy.

The central government, to have real authority, would need to win the affections, prejudices and feelings of citizens themselves. "It must stand in need of no intermediate legislations . . .," Hamilton wrote: "The

49. Ibid., pp. 36-40, 44-48.

government of the union, like that of each state, must be able to address itself immediately to the hopes and fears of individuals; and to attract to its support those passions which have the strongest influence upon the human heart." [50]

Hence the Constitution does more than give some powers to the federal government and some to the states exclusively, leaving the rest to be shared. By giving "exclusive" powers to the central government, the Constitution provides that in these areas the federal regime *and it alone* may speak for and to the citizen. As against classical federalism, this institution *establishes a division of loyalty in the citizen*. In classic federalism, he need only obey his state; in American federalism, his allegiance is split. And, of course, the two jurisdictions are not neatly separable. In some areas, states and the federal government share power; in others, the exclusive powers of one may conflict with the exclusive powers of another. If the federal government goes to war, it drastically affects the ways in which state government can operate; before the Civil War, it was clear that if the federal government refused to return fugitive slaves to their owners, it would greatly weaken slavery, while if it did return them, it would threaten the ability of "free states" to stay free.

Whenever conflicts exist, two courses of action are open to the citizen. He can let the courts decide, and in the American Constitution the federal courts have the ultimate authority. The Framers had every reason to believe that the federal courts would tend to expand federal power. But if the citizen rejects the courts, he must himself make the decision as to which government he will obey. The Framers stress that state governments will be protected by being always closer to the affections of their people. But Madison and Hamilton are at some pains to contend that the federal regime will be better administered and that its powers are more important than those of the states. The Framers were confident that the federal regime would, by meeting the needs and interests of citizens, gradually win their allegiance away from the states.[51] But in any case, the division of powers is designed to break the hold of the affections on the individual and to weaken his loyalty to parochial communities.

The size of the state and the division of powers combined would serve to decrease the loyalty felt by the individual citizen for any group or "faction." And this, the Framers believed, would serve several purposes. It would free the individual from control by his affections and by the group, liberating him to pursue his interests. It would, at the same time,

50. Ibid., pp. 76-77.
51. Ibid., p. 240; see also pp. 132, 136.

make him more, rather than less, governable, and make it easier to channel his energies in productive directions. "The reason of man, like man himself," Madison wrote, "is timid and cautious when left alone; and acquires firmness and confidence in proportion to the number with which it is associated." Dividing man's loyalty left him more or less alone, and made him a careful and prudent self-seeker; if he acquired firmness and confidence at all, it would be as a citizen of the United States as a whole. And though the Framers disagreed about the ways in which patriotism should express itself, few would have disagreed with Hamilton's goals.

> . . . Europe, by her arms and by her negotiations, by force and by fraud, has, in different degrees, extended her dominion over . . . Africa, Asia and America. . . . The superiority she has long maintained has tempted her to plume herself as the mistress of the world, and to consider the rest of mankind as created for her benefit. . . . Facts have too long supported these arrogant pretensions of the European. It belongs to us to vindicate the honor of the human race and to teach that assuming brother moderation. Union will enable us to do it. Disunion will add another victim to his triumphs. Let Americans disdain to be the instruments of European greatness! [52]

Of course the Framers went further than the division of powers, establishing the *separation of powers* which creates three somewhat overlapping spheres of executive, legislative, and judicial power within the federal government. Recently James MacGregor Burns has argued that the Framers were right in presuming that the diversity of factions in a large state effectively eliminated the possibility of tyranny by any one of them. But, Burns contends, the separation of powers adds, to a political system where agreement would always have been difficult, an *artificial* barrier which creates a "deadlock of democracy" and prevents the enactment of needed policies.[53]

This position is not new in America. Among the reasons Patrick Henry gave for opposing the Constitution was his belief that the separation of powers was a "visionary" scheme which would divide the community.[54] But the Framers would have answered that without the "check-and-balance" system the federal government would itself be a danger. Gathered together in the capital, federal officials might become another parochial, local community—a faction more dangerous because it would be at the center of things, while other factions would be dispersed. The Framers knew too much about "court politics"—in which

52. Ibid., p. 53; for Madison's comment on human reason, see p. 258.
53. James MacGregor Burns, *The Deadlock of Democracy* (Prentice-Hall, 1963).
54. Raymond Gettel, *History of American Political Thought* (Appleton-Century, 1928), p. 130.

officials around the king played political games of their own and neglected more general interests—for them to leave that possibility open in
America. Competition between the branches of government was the
means by which government would be obliged to "control itself."

> Ambition must be made to counteract ambition. The interest of the man
> must be connected with the constitutional rights of the place. It may be a
> reflection on human nature that such devices should be needed to control
> the abuses of government. But what is government itself but the greatest
> of all reflections on human nature? [55]

The Framers believed that they understood the "true interest" of
men, their "natural" desire to be free and power-seeking animals, for
whom government was only a device adopted for protection and to
further private interests. They designed a constitution that would make
men so, whatever their apparent will. And there are few Americans who
do not see some aspect of the success of that design around them,
and feel its impact in themselves.

ORGANIC CONSTITUTIONALISM
IN THE AMERICAN TRADITION

Yet the Framers did not foresee everything. Nor, as an organic constitutionalist would point out, are old traditions and values easily eliminated,
and those traditions, in turn, lead to political movements and claims on
the public order. The Constitution was adopted only after a bitter
debate in which its opponents relied on arguments drawn from traditional theory, and almost certainly would have been defeated if its
supporters had not conceded that the federal government would at once
amend the Constitution by adding a Bill of Rights.[56]

There were many reasons why the Framers had omitted a Bill of
Rights from the original document. Many believed it was needless, since
men only granted to any government those of their "natural rights"
they explicitly "gave up." Since the Constitution gave no power to
regulate the freedom of speech, the people must have retained that
right. And to suggest that a Bill of Rights "granted" certain rights to
the people was to imply that government could *deny* rights which
belonged to men "by nature." In a similar vein, Hamilton argued that
stating rights like "the freedom of the press" allows government to
engage in interpreting the meaning of such phrases, and added, "Who
can give it any definition which will not leave the utmost latitude for

---

55. *The Federalist*, p. 265.
56. For the debate on the Constitution, see John D. Lewis, ed., *Federalists vs.
Anti-Federalists* (Chandler, 1967).

evasion?" In fact, Hamilton went on, the desire for a Bill of Rights is based only on "verbal and nominal" considerations rather than real political security. A Bill of Rights might lessen the watchfulness of the people; the real security of the Constitution lay in the watchful insecurity inherent in the mechanisms of competition it embodied.[57]

Against such mechanistic arguments, those who favored a Bill of Rights, like Jefferson, developed their own arguments in organic terms. A written Bill of Rights was necessary and desirable because it would teach and remind the people, especially in future generations, what their rights were. Proponents of a Bill of Rights remembered the importance of royal charters in instilling in Englishmen a sense of what had been promised them and was, hence, their right. To this extent, advocates of a Bill of Rights were suspicious of the theory of "natural right," for though they believed such rights existed, they did not feel that men knew spontaneously what their rights were. Society had to provide means for *teaching* men what was theirs "by nature."

It was in the same spirit that Jeffersonians argued for what later came to be called "strict construction" of the Constitution. Nowadays, that term is only a political slogan. President Nixon appeals to it, but though he is "strict" in protecting states, he is "loose" in relation to civil rights and liberties; Mr. Justice Douglas is strict in the latter case and loose in the former. Jeffersonians tried to be more consistent. Strict construction was desirable because it enabled the people to read the Constitution and understand it. Loose construction implied interpretation, and interpretation required citizens to turn to lawyers and to experts in constitutional law. Creating confusion in the mind of the people, loose construction would make them dependent on such experts to determine the meaning of the Constitution. (As, of course, it has over the years.) Strict construction was a technique of teaching which enabled and encouraged the people to learn and to have confidence in their own judgment.

Most of us have felt a shock when we realized that some of our "rights" granted in the Constitution seemed to be violated in practice. Protests against compulsory chapel in private schools and colleges, for example, are almost certainly the result of a belief that Americans possess the "right" of "freedom of religion." While in strict procedural and mechanical terms, that "right" does not apply to private associations, the belief that it is an "American right" does apply in political terms. And it is such beliefs that are the center of organic theory. In the same sense, almost all Americans would feel that it would violate the "freedom of religion" of Friends to deprive them of the privilege

57. *The Federalist*, pp. 440-441.

of "conscientious objection." Again, though in mechanical terms there is no such "right," there is a real right because of the organic, political support for it in the community.

Other institutions have been part of the American constitution, as an organic theorist would define it, without being mentioned in the written document at all. The agencies of "socialization," which help to shape the values and personality of the citizen, are critical; the family, of course, is preeminent, but schools, churches and ethnic groups are also deeply significant. Such institutions teach men their substantive values, the things they will demand, those they will support, and those they will fight to keep or to acquire from and in government. Without them constitutional procedures would be only a shell; had they been different, American government might have been unrecognizable.

Historically such groups were especially important because they taught a theory of man and morality radically different from that which is embodied in the written Constitution. In the churches and families, but also in most ethnic groups, loyalty, compassion, and sacrifice for the good of the community were human obligations; the groups which engaged the affections of a citizen were those to which he owed high, if not the highest, duties, and "sticking by your own" was a central principle. These "private" groups, in other words, taught and embodied an older constitutional order than that advocated by the Framers, an organic tradition which was sometimes directly in conflict with, and always different from, the mechanistic theory of the written Constitution.

Religion, as Tocqueville realized, was particularly critical in teaching the principle of equality. When we compare one man with another in secular terms, we cannot help noticing their differences of appearance, intelligence or virtue; if we see the same men as God might see them, those differences pale in relation to the common qualities and failings of humankind. The movements against slavery owed much, for example, to such evangelists as the nineteenth-century preachers, Charles G. Finney and Theodore D. Weld. And whatever faults may be charged to them, without the Negro churches the survival of the idea of racial equality would have been much more difficult. Frederick Douglass, for example, often appealed to the Scripture against the "scientific" racism of the nineteenth century, and when W. E. B. DuBois conceded that equality was only a "belief," he was able to add that "a pious belief outweighs an impious belief." And, of course, the belief in equality has been a vital—though not always determining—force in American political life.[58]

Many instances might be given of the organic impact of the agencies

58. Howard Brotz, ed., *Negro Social and Political Thought* (Basic Books, 1966), pp. 230-231, 242-243, 317; and W. E. B. DuBois, *Dusk of Dawn* (Schocken, 1968), p. 146.

of socialization on the American Constitution, but one more should suffice. The shrewd political tactics and pressure politics of the Anti-Saloon League and other temperance groups succeeded in making Prohibition part of the "supreme law of the land." [59] But such groups were dominantly White, middle class, Protestant, and concentrated in the Middle West and the South. Other groups, but especially Catholics and minority ethnic groups, never accepted the legitimacy of the Eighteenth Amendment; that is, they denied the right of the government to legislate about drinking habits, and many Protestants agreed in regarding drinking as a "private" matter. So many Americans were opposed to the amendment on principle that it was a dead letter. The organic constitution of America had successfully resisted the written Constitution; the repeal of Prohibition was only a belated acknowledgment of the fact.

Parties and Organic Constitutionalism

Perhaps the most obvious organic institution in America is the political party. Parties are nowhere mentioned in the Constitution, and there is every reason to suppose that the Framers regarded them with hostility as dangerous "factions." Initially parties were little more than coalitions of leaders who met at the national capital or who corresponded with one another and who held similar views about public policy. But as economic and social change and the policies of government drew citizens into contact with the larger society and shattered the autonomy of local communities (the process of social mobilization), more and more citizens felt the need for some vehicle to make the government understand and respond to their needs. And at the same time they became aware of others across the country who shared their concerns. Political parties developed rapidly and assumed something like their present form by the 1840s.

It should be understood that one important "need" that parties served was psychological. Parties gave men the confidence that at least some of their rulers were "men like ourselves." Even if the policies of the pre-partisan government had been ably designed to satisfy the material interests of the people at large, there would have been a psychological distance, an "estrangement," between rulers and ruled. And with distance would have came public suspicion and resistance on one hand, and a similar suspicion of the public on the part of officials on the other.

Both Jefferson's embryonic party and Jackson's more mature one began as "state's rights" movements suspicious of federal authority and concerned to confine government to the narrowest possible sphere. Success, however, brought "our man" and "our party" to power and reduced or

59. Peter Odegard, *Pressure Politics* (Columbia University Press, 1928).

eliminated the very suspicions which had been the core of the party program. Jefferson's purchase of Louisiana or his imposition of an embargo on trade with states involved in the Napoleonic Wars were based on a very "loose" interpretation of the Constitution and an expanded sense of federal responsibility that would have outraged Jeffersonians had they been invoked by anyone but Jefferson himself. Jackson, of course, was even more assertive, and the Jacksonians, eventually, changed from a party suspicious of government to one which made a mystique of the Union and its "Manifest Destiny."

This is a way of saying that parties were instruments for organic constitutionalism. People were less suspicious of the "powers" of government when they were confident that what government would *do* with those powers was likely to be in conformity with their own values and feelings. Procedural limitations seemed less important when one trusted the character of those in power; parties, in other words, made the United States less of a "government of laws" and more of a "government by men."

This was, as the Tammany Hall leader George Washington Plunkitt knew, especially critical when it came to immigrants and other minorities whose traditional organic ideas clashed sharply with the individualistic and impersonal norms embodied in formal laws. Party "machines" bent the law, building alongside the legal structure of government a chain of reciprocal loyalty and allegiance which enabled the citizen to substitute personal bonds for impersonal rules. He could expect a sympathetic hearing from rulers who at least understood, and quite possibly shared, his own culture. To Protestants, the practice of holding political meetings in churchyards savored of irreverence; to the Irish, it was part of a traditional culture shaped by the fact that the British had allowed Irishmen to meet in large groups only in and around churches. And when the "machine" came to power, laws forbidding such meetings were quietly allowed to drop. Similarly, welfare and employment did not require a man to ask "charity" or to be dealt with as a kind of cipher by an impersonal bureaucracy. They were things he could ask for as part of the obligations of friendship and reciprocal allegiance.

All these things, obviously, built emotional bonds between citizens and their government. This is what Plunkitt had in mind when he declared that "the parties built this great country." They had made patriots, he asserted, out of newcomers and strangers. Of course, they had twisted or even broken many laws, even the Constitution, sometimes. But, as another Tammany leader had asked in the spirit of organic constitutionalism, "What's the Constitution between friends?" [60]

60. William Riordan, *Plunkitt of Tammany Hall* (Dutton, 1963), p. 13. See the essay on political parties, p. 97 ff.

Today party machines have lapsed in favor of public service bureaucracy for the most part, and it can be argued that party identification
is growing weaker for most Americans. But even so, most Americans
"feel better" when government is in the hands of their party; party
still helps to close the gap between rulers and ruled when "we" are in
power. Of course, sometimes we are "out." That, however, indicates the
fact that party rule modifies and partly replaces the mechanical "checks
and balances" of the Constitution with an organic rule of check and
balance, the conflict of "ins" and "outs." Republicans, long suspicious
of presidential power, have been much more likely to urge Americans
to "support the president" since Richard Nixon took office; liberal
Democrats, once the major assailants of the Supreme Court ("the nine
old men") have been the major defenders of the court's recent activism.
Our view of the Constitution, in other words, depends partly on whose
Constitution we think it is.

Parties have other important constitutional consequences. The requirements of organization and the peculiarities of the electoral college
(which makes "carrying" a *state* the key to campaign strategy) have
made our parties, organizationally, into state and local bodies. Our national parties are coalitions of fifty state parties (and those parties are
themselves often coalitions of local parties). Political parties, in other
words, are important organic supports for federalism and local government in American politics.

Finally, by controlling the alternatives that are available to the voters,
parties effectively control the substantive meaning of the election.
Except in extreme cases, voters hate to "waste" their vote on third party
candidates (and such candidates find it difficult even to get on the ballot,
let alone to finance and organize a campaign). And in states and localities
where one party is overwhelmingly dominant, party nominations may
be tantamount to election. In this sense, American government is a milder
form of what Italians call *partitocrazia*, rule by parties.

This vital organic role has made parties the object of many political
movements concerned to guarantee that parties were responsive to voters
rather than instruments for dominating them. The Progressive movement,
for example, emphasized the direct primary as a means of control; some
of the same concern has been evident in the efforts of liberal Democrats
to reform the party's convention mechanisms after 1968. Such concerns
reflect a recognition that political parties, though theoretically "private"
and voluntary associations, are actually institutions of the government
and parts of the Constitution no less important than the Congress and
the presidency.

This constitutional role of the political parties was clearly recognized in cases involving the "white primary," in which Southern Democratic parties barred Negroes from participation in primary elections—and in effect from any real role is elections at all, since at that time there was no effective alternative in Southern one-party systems.[61] The Supreme Court had decided in 1932 that parties which were given their authority by the state legislature could not bar Negroes without violating the "equal protection" clause of the Fourteenth Amendment. But when the executive committee of the Democratic Party of Texas adopted such a rule on its own, without legislative authority, the Court ruled in 1935 that parties were "voluntary associations for political action" and outside the scope of the amendment. This decision in *Grovey vs. Townsend* faithfully followed the principles of mechanistic constitutionalism, but like that theory, the Court's decision flew in the face of the real nature of American politics. By 1944, in *Smith vs. Allwright*, the Court had reversed itself, declaring that since primaries were an "integral part" of the election procedure, political parties could not exclude Negroes. In 1953 the Court went even further. In one Texas county, the Jaybird Democratic Association, a private political club, conducted a "straw vote" before the primary. Negroes could vote in the primary itself, but this right was academic since, in practice, the Jaybird candidate always won and the club excluded Blacks. In order to protect effective suffrage, the Court was forced to rule that this "private" pre-primary was also a "public" institution governed by the Fourteenth Amendment.

In relation to parties, in other words, the Supreme Court was forced to recognize that the distinction between "public" and "private" spheres, one of the basic principles of mechanistic constitutionalism, was simply invalid. Parties were organically part of the Constitution, whatever the written document might say or leave unsaid. The implications of these decisions and others like them are, obviously, far-reaching, and they reflect a serious and growing crisis in American constitutionalism.

CONSTITUTIONALISM IN CONTEMPORARY POLITICS

Since the end of the nineteenth century it has been evident to a growing number of political observers that the Constitution no longer described much of what took place in American politics. Political science has become less and less "institutional" in its approach to politics, presuming a sharp distinction between formal law and the "real world."

61. *Nixon vs. Condon*, 286 U.S. 73, (1932); *Grovey vs. Townsend*, 295 U.S. 45, (1935); *Smith vs. Allwright*, 321 U.S. 649, (1944); *Terry vs. Adams*, 345 U.S. 506, 1953.

Few political scientists, however, have been willing to go to the logical extreme and argue that the idea of "constitutional government" in the United States is no more than a political myth. Such hesitation is probably justified, but contemporary social science testifies that the great constitutional machine designed by the Framers has broken down in decisive respects.

Decline of Checks and Balances

The division of powers has long been in decay. The growth of a national and international economy, and with it the development of great private organizations independent of any particular locality, has deprived state and local governments of any real ability to "govern" economic life. Mobility has weakened the attachment of Americans to home and place; for increasing numbers of us, a state or city is only a location where one happens to live at the moment. States and cities are almost constantly in "crisis," lacking the resources to deal with problems and looking to Washington to provide relief. Localities which attempt to "check" the federal regime are rare indeed; even Southern political leaders look eagerly to the federal government for defense contracts and other expenditures. Probably the Framers would be neither surprised nor unhappy with this development, but it does suggest a change from the traditional picture of the Constitution of the United States.

The Supreme Court, certainly, was reluctant to abandon the old image. It once distinguished between "manufacture," an activity subject to state and local control, and "interstate commerce," subject to federal authority. The Court was soon forced to concede that as a "practical matter" there was no such distinction, that industrial plants were not isolated and local but parts of a "flow of commerce" that connected primary producer, manufacturer and consumer in a single process.[62] But the Court clung to the idea that some activities were local by nature and affected commerce only "indirectly," whatever might seem to be the case in practice. Obviously, a strike could paralyze "interstate commerce," but the Court insisted that labor relations were a local matter with which the federal government could not interfere. Justice Sutherland declared in 1936 that labor conflicts and problems

. . . are local controversies and evils affecting local work undertaken to accomplish [a] local result. Such effect as they may have upon commerce . . . is secondary and indirect. An increase in the greatness of the effect adds to its importance. It does not alter its character.[63]

62. *U.S. vs E. C. Knight*, 156 U.S. 1, (1895); *Swift and Company vs. U.S.*, 196 U.S. 375, (1905).
63. *Carter vs. Carter Coal Co.*, 298 U.S. 238, 308, (1936).

By the next year, however, the Court had reversed itself.[64] Partly, it was responding to political pressures, but no one, in the middle of the Depression, could really believe that labor conditions were "local." Nor could one think of great corporations as only so many local plants. A long line of decisions has rendered almost all of the economy open to direct federal intervention and regulation. Lawyers and courts were more wedded than political leaders and movements to the mechanistic procedures of the Constitution, but eventually even they were compelled to acknowledge the organic facts. The Court, as Robert Stern writes, no longer requires "a division for governmental purposes of what is in fact inseparable." [65]

Similarly, although welfare has traditionally been a local function, states and localities today look to the federal government to standardize or assume the burden of welfare. As travel has become easier, the poor and the unemployed have found it simpler to move from one section of the country to another. Poor and less liberal states lose population to wealthier and more liberal areas; these, in turn, feel they are being imposed upon but cannot constitutionally prevent such migration.[66] Poverty, too, has become a national problem, beyond effective control by localities, and as local areas cease to be "communities," becoming more and more merely collections of people, local citizens feel no particular obligation to care for others who are no more than strangers. All this indicates how far we have come from the original division of powers.

The separation of powers, moreover, has also been breaking down. Very early, political scientists like Woodrow Wilson observed that the importance of Congress was declining within the federal government.[67] Congress was too slow and statute law was too rigid to deal with the rapidly changing world of modern industrialism. The complexity of the world left Congressmen no more than intelligent amateurs, dependent on the executive or perhaps favorite experts of their own for information. Finally, Congress is an impersonal institution which is forced by its nature to make many "deals" and compromises in public. Citizens find it easier to identify with the president, whom they can see as a human being (however inaccurately they perceive him) and

64. *N.L.R.B. vs. Jones and Laughlin*, 301 U.S. 1, (1937).

65. Robert L. Stern, "Problems of Yesteryear: Commerce and Due Process," in Robert G. McCloskey, ed., *Essays in Constitutional Law* (Random House, 1957), p. 178.

66. *Edwards vs. California*, 314 U.S. 160, (1941).

67. Woodrow Wilson, *Constitutional Government in the United States* (1908), p. 73; this revised Wilson's earlier belief in legislative dominance, *The State* (Heath, 1889), pp. 581-583.

who seems "above" dealing because he speaks to the public only after his bargains have been struck.[68]

It has only added to the problem—however greatly—that Congress has very few powers in the area of foreign affairs, which has necessarily weakened its position in a time of growing international involvement. Even the powers Congress has, like "the power of the purse," tend to be negative; if used, such powers seem to be "obstructing" the president's policy and may even appear unpatriotic. In a famous case Congress was reluctant to give Theodore Roosevelt the funds to send the Navy around the world, but T.R. discovered that he had enough to send it halfway and left Congress to decide whether it would appropriate the funds to bring it back. In cases where national interests or survival are more seriously involved, Congress is in a still more difficult position. Even the long debate about the role of Congress which has developed in relation to Vietnam has not yet made Congress willing to force the president to withdraw all American troops by some fixed date.

All of these developments have led to an increasing concentration of power in "the presidency." But so many powers and duties have been given to the president that he cannot possibly exercise or even supervise more than a few of them. More and more authority and discretion is vested in administrators, the great majority of them career civil servants. Even where the president makes the decision himself, he is critically dependent on administrative officials to advise him and to interpret and carry out his policy. This has been most subject to comment and criticism in the case of the military, but the problem is general rather than specific. The president finds it very difficult to avoid being controlled by "his" machinery; a "fourth branch of government" has developed outside the framework of the Constitution.[69]

To be sure, the Supreme Court has tried to oversee such developments. But the Court works slowly and can only hear a limited number of cases. It can act at all only when there is a "case or controversy," which means that it depends on citizens to test laws, and to "test" the constitutionality of a law one must break it, with the risk of suffering the penalty if the Court decides the law was constitutional after all. Worse, the Court can hear a case only after the fact, which makes it relatively powerless to *prevent* unconstitutional actions. In the last century, when few acts could have literally disastrous consequences, this was a tolerable defect. The tremendous dangers of twentieth-century life have changed all that, especially in matters of foreign policy.

68. Bertrand de Jouvenel, *The Evolution of the Forms of Government* (Sedeis, 1963), pp. 25-33. But see essay on the Presidency, p. 236 ff.
69. Edward S. Corwin, *The President: Office and Powers* (New York University Press, 1957), pp. 300-304.

The Court's recognition of such limitations has been partly responsible for recent judicial "activism," especially the willingness to enunciate broad principles not required to deal with a specific case but which help to establish the law before the event. The Court has also extended some protection to pressure groups which hope to bring cases before the Supreme Court. And it has also been suspicious of administrative power. In one case, the Court even ruled that if an individual lies in one part of a citizenship questionnaire, but covertly tells the truth in another (about membership in subversive organizations), it is up to immigration officials to find it out, and he cannot be deprived of citizenship later if they make a mistake.[70]

But such decisions only emphasize the limitations of the Court. The Court has done little or nothing to limit the president's conduct of foreign affairs, for example. The justices have recognized that not to allow the president discretion, or to judge his actions with the aid of hindsight, might encourage a dangerous hesitancy or rigidity in an area where flexibility is necessary and where some decisions must be made quickly. The major doctrine of restraint, the requirement that decisions be those that a "reasonable man" might have made, is vague indeed at a time when life and politics have become so confusing that the most reasonable of men is likely to feel that his decisions are only stabs in the dark. And in any case, any restrictions the Court may seek to impose will be effective only if they are accepted by a broad section of the public and when at least some citizens are willing to take the responsibility of seeing that they are carried out.[71]

Decline of the Organic Constitution

The American citizen, however, has problems of his own. Some of his difficulties are those the Jeffersonians predicted if America abandoned —as she surely has—the principle of "strict construction." Many of our citizens, especially the poor, do not see law as their protection. The law seems (and often is) arbitrary and incomprehensible, an alien and threatening force, a weapon in the hands of those who interpret and enforce it. Even if we are neither poor nor uneducated, most of us feel helpless and frustrated when we encounter the jargon of lawyers and administrative officials, the tangle of precedents and procedures that stand between us and understanding. Administrative discretion and judicial interpretation may be necessary, but they are forms of power

70. *Chaunt vs. U.S.*, 364 U.S. 350, (1960).
71. On the limitations of the court, see Glendon Schubert, *The Presidency in the Courts* (University of Minnesota Press, 1957) and Loren P. Beth, "The Supreme Court Reconsidered: Opposition and Judicial Review in the United States," *Political Studies*, 16 (1968), pp. 243-249.

which stand between the citizen and his government. They tend to make us suspicious of the law and fearful of government. They create in us a desire to stay uninvolved, and such attitudes have serious consequences for the organic constitution of the United States.

In fact the disordered state of the "checks-and-balances" mechanism might not matter much were it not for the disintegration of the distinction between "public" and "private" spheres. As our economy and society have become national, we have become dependent on great private organizations which control much of our life; as the world has "grown smaller," we have been forced to rely on mass media which supply us with information necessary to us as citizens and even as private men. Though these "private" organizations sometimes compete with one another, they are few enough in number to be able to reach agreements which reduce competition to a minimum. And while we may have some "choice" between them—we can decide which channel to watch or which corporation to buy an automobile from—we can neither do without them nor create alternatives to them. The media, trade unions and private corporations are, in an important sense, *governments* over men; they are no more "voluntary associations" than states or local governments, and, in fact, we have more "choice" between localities than between these "private" regimes.[72]

Trying to maintain the traditional distinction between public and private spheres, the Supreme Court at the beginning of the century gave great emphasis to the "freedom of contract," a private right with which government could not interfere. This led the Court to strike down legislation prescribing minimum wages and maximum hours, a position it held down to the years of the New Deal. Eventually economic and political events made it clear that whatever the legal and mechanistic doctrines might say, the "individual employee" and the "individual corporation" were not equally free members of a private sphere, and that the former might need governmental assistance if he were to avoid a hopeless dependence.[73]

In the same sense, the Court argued in the *Civil Rights Cases* of 1883 that the fourteenth Amendment gave the federal government no authority to deal with racial discrimination by "private" persons. It became clearer and clearer, however (especially as racism became less respectable), that such a distinction was untenable. Private rights were often critically dependent on state recognition and support, while to

---

72. Grant McConnell, *Private Power and American Democracy* (Knopf, 1966).
73. *Lochner vs. N.Y.*, 198 U.S. 45, (1905), *Adkins vs. Children's Hospital*, 261 U.S. 525 (1923), and *Adair vs. U.S.* 236 U.S. 1 (1915), give the traditional view. See, by contrast, *West Coast Hotel vs. Parrish*, 300 U.S., 379, (1937) and *Virginian Ry. vs. System Federation*, 300 U.S. 515, (1937).

deny a man access to a job, facilities for travel, or access to commercial business was to deny him any effective public equality. Recent decisions have consistently expanded federal authority to prevent "private" racial discrimination, whatever the cost to the traditional doctrine.[74]

But the effort to regulate "private governments" by public standards creates problems itself. Aside from the growth of administrative power that regulation entails, the power of private governments is such that the regulated often become the regulators, acquiring effective control over the public agencies set up to "control" them and using public authority to support their own ends.[75]

In general, it is clear that individuals find themselves unable to control their "own business." Skill and hard work did not prevent millions from losing their jobs during the Depression; saving has not protected older Americans against inflation. Technological and social change constantly threatens mature people with obsolescence (one reason why the generation gap creates so much anxiety), and decisions by men we neither know nor control, at home and abroad, can set at nought all our best-laid plans. Dependence, weakness, and insecurity are the hallmarks of the time.

Acts which we seemingly *can* control—like driving automobiles that pollute the air or refusing to live next to members of other racial groups —have important public consequences. But we feel, rightly, that the actions of one individual do not matter much. Even if I am concerned about such consequences, I am likely to fear that if I sell my car or live in an integrated area, I will suffer without changing anything, and so I may fall back on "taking care of number one." (Many discontented students, obviously, have followed this pattern in their own way). Private weakness decreases public spirit.

As the Supreme Court recognized in *Wickard vs. Filburn*, many "unimportant" individual decisions taken together become vital matters of policy. In this case, a farmer raised twenty-three acres of wheat which he fed to his own livestock; this action was found to be "inter-state commerce" because by raising and consuming his own wheat, Filburn had affected the supply and price of wheat nationally. Admittedly, he had not done so very much, but the Court argued that the "trivial" quality of his action did not matter: "his contribution, taken

74. *Civil Rights Cases*, 109 U.S. 3, (1883), *Heart of Atlanta Motel vs. U.S.*, 379 U.S. 241, (1964) and *Katzenbach vs. McClung*, 379 U.S. 294 (1964). In the last case, students of the commerce power are interested that the Court gave the federal government authority to act wherever the effect on commerce is "substantial *or harmful*" (my italics). For an excellent discussion of the theoretical problem, see Robert L. Hale, *Freedom Through Law* (Columbia University Press, 1952).

75. McConnell, *Private Power;* also Walter Adams and Horace Gray, *Monopoly in America: the Government as Promoter* (Macmillan, 1955).

together with that of many others similarly situated, is far from trivial." [76] It would be too much to expect that, in such situations, the citizen would act on the basis of abstract principle. Governmental action becomes essential in areas once thought to be "private" because the individual lacks the practical means—even if he has the will—to advance public values and interests.

This kind of governmental expansion has also been encouraged by the decline of the older communities and social groups which once protected Americans. Churches, ethnic groups and families rarely if ever have sufficient resources; local communities—especially in cases like the Depression—have been subject to the same problems as the individual himself. Those older communities have also been undermined by change and mobility. The family, in its present form, is an intense but tiny unit of parents and children, highly mobile but unable to do much more than adapt to social forces. The other traditional communities and groups are increasingly weak, partly undermined by the intensity of family loyalties. As such groups lost the ability to protect the individual against catastrophe or to provide him with necessary services, he has been forced to turn to private and public governments. But such governments do not give the individual the sense that he matters, the psychological security which was part of the older order of things. Even when they help him (and sometimes they are hostile or incomprehensible to the average citizen), private and public bureaucracies are impersonal, lying outside the sphere of the individual's knowledge and control.[77]

Organizations which are large enough to affect public policy in important ways are so gigantic that all but a small fraction of their members feel unimportant.[78] But it is not clear how much it would help to feel "in control" of government. The magnitude of immediate crises demands that we concentrate our attention on them, but we know from experience that this leads us to ignore or overlook developing problems until they too reach crisis proportion. Vietnam might have been solved with relative ease in 1945, 1954, or 1961; at those times, however, we were rightly concerned with other things. Now that we are centering attention on Vietnam, we ought to suspect that other problems are developing behind our backs. In the same sense, we have ignored pollution until the water and air are seriously poisoned. But even if we could foresee the future consequences of present events, today's crisis

76. *Wickard vs. Filburn*, 317 U.S. 111, 127-128 (1942).

77. John Dewey, *The Public and its Problems* (Holt, 1927) and Henry S. Kariel, *The Decline of American Pluralism* (Stanford University Press, 1961).

78. Karl Mannheim, *Man and Society in an Age of Reconstruction* (Harcourt Brace, 1951).

cannot be "put off." Politics seems like a constant race to plug holes in the dike, forever "behind" events, at best a response to problems which have developed almost of themselves.

All of these developments encourage what Lord Bryce long ago called "the fatalism of the multitude," the sense of being prisoners of great impersonal forces beyond our control.[79] This has serious constitutional consequences; as we lose the sense of being able to control the government, we become less willing to trust it; to the extent that we feel we do not matter to government—and even more, if we suspect that *it* does not matter—we will not give government our support. To reverse Madison: now that the government no longer seems to "control itself," it finds it difficult to "control the governed" except as an alien force in their lives.

Most important, perhaps, is the fact that all these things have undermined the moral basis of constitutionalism among rulers and ruled alike. Intellectual and political leaders have articulated and taught a widely held belief that the better part of political wisdom consists in "adapting" or "adjusting" oneself to events, in understanding that "all things are relative" and that institutions must "evolve." Extreme pragmatism of this sort undermines the very idea of a "fundamental law," attacking the conviction that some things ought not to change and destroying the constitutionalist's distinction between institutions and policies. Even the notion that there is a moral law seems unsophisticated and *passé*. (Increasingly those who appeal to morality speak of it as a private feeling or intuition rather than as part of a public and discoverable order.) Government, given such a theory, should be "by forces" rather than "by laws" or even "by men." [80]

The Revival of Constitutionalism

Americans have been unwilling to give up constitutionalism. At least two major theories of constitutional government have developed in recent years. Pluralism, which has dominated much thinking in political science, asserts that man is a group animal and that politics is the "struggle between groups." Formal institutions, in this theory, matter less than the "structure of group competition" and are chiefly important in giving "access" to different groups. (Minorities, for example, often turn to the Supreme Court, hoping for greater advantages than they could win elsewhere.) Groups become the critical "representative" bodies,

79. James Bryce, *The American Commonwealth* (Commonwealth, 1908), Vol. 2, pp. 358-368.
80. De Jouvenel, *Forms of Government*, pp. 33-42.

and government is important principally as a "broker" which arranges compromises between conflicting groups.[81]

Obviously this theory differs in important respects from that of the Framers, especially in deprecating formal institutions of government. In another sense, however, it is merely a restatement of mechanistic theory. Pluralist constitutionalism believes that, where there is a wide variety of interest groups and comparative freedom to form new ones, the political "process" becomes virtually "self-regulating." Groups are prevented from making extreme claims by the "countervailing power" of others. They compete with each other for the allegiance of citizens, especially when the individuals concerned are members of more than one organization, which forces groups to represent the interests and desires of their members. Even unorganized interests are "virtually represented," if for no other reason than to keep them unorganized.[82]

There have been many criticisms of this theory, especially in recent years. It has been pointed out that group "competition" is highly limited and that major groups reach implicit or explicit agreements to respect each other's "sphere of influence," with conflict occurring only in marginal areas. Also, research has suggested that the number of unorganized persons and interests is far greater than was believed, and that it is extremely doubtful whether groups can be said "to represent" their members in a true meaning of the word. Government, moreover, does not seem to be simply a neutral broker; in some cases, it has created the supposedly "voluntary" groups that "pressure" it, while in others, as has been indicated, groups have captured important sectors of the government itself. Finally, political scientists like Grant McConnell and Theodore Lowi have argued that the competition of narrow private constituencies neglects broader public interests of concern to a wide but diffuse section of the American people.[83]

Even on its own terms, one aspect of pluralist theory deserves special attention. Pluralists have never denied that leaders of groups and active citizens have very different political attitudes and ideas from the mass of members and unaffiliated citizens. These active citizens, generally drawn from the better educated and more affluent sections of society, pluralist theory declares, are more characterized than members-at-large

81. Two important pluralist texts are David Truman, *The Governmental Process*, (Knopf, 1951) and Robert A. Dahl, *Pluralist Democracy in the United States* (Rand McNally, 1967).

82. For an example of such arguments, see John Kenneth Galbraith, *American Capitalism: the Concept of Countervailing Power* (Houghton Mifflin, 1952).

83. Representative critiques include McConnell, *Private Power;* Theodore Lowi, *The End of Liberalism* (Norton, 1969); and Sanford Levinson and Phillip Green, eds., *Power and Community* (Pantheon, 1970).

and citizens-in-general by allegiance to the "rules of the game," the norms and procedures of American constitutionalism.[84] On the whole, too, pluralists have regarded such elites as more rational, better informed and more far-sighted than citizens at large. The distinction between elites and masses, even the assertion that "democracy is a choice between competing elites," does not disturb pluralists; the power of elites is the guarantee that constitutional norms will be upheld.

Two aspects of this doctrine should be observed. First, pluralists do not see any serious differences of *value* between elites and masses because, in the mechanistic tradition of the Framers, they regard all men as power-seeking animals. The only distinction is, presumably, sophistication of method and means. Second, the whole argument tends to make active citizens and group leaders into the *embodiment of the true will* of the American people. They, rather than the laws or the people at large become the "constitution" of the United States. This does not force pluralists to revise the view that the political system is "self-regulating," for most of them regard the attitudes of elites as a by-product of the group "process." Firmly in the mechanistic tradition, pluralists are more doubtful of the constitutional machine and probably even more fearful of the mass public than were the Framers themselves.[85]

Many organic theories, by contrast, have been asserted in contradiction of pluralist ideas. In general such counter-theories have argued that America is a "sick society," that its "constitution" is diseased and in need of therapy. Obviously, this argument is concerned more with the organic than the formal constitution, and most of those who make it have been concerned with the lack of community, security, and personal meaning which they see in America. Where pluralism seeks to compensate for the shortcomings of the mass of Americans, its opponents seek to mitigate or remove those limitations. Hence, for example, the growing concern among critics of American politics for "community control," for new and warmer social forms and for institutions which encourage participation. Also related are the various attempts to destroy those aspects of American culture which make citizens feel worthless, degraded, and powerless, such as racism and discrimination against women. Diverse as such theories and movements are (and often violently opposed to each other), they share a central theme, the desire

84. For a good example, see Herbert J. McClosky, "Consensus and Ideology in American Politics," *American Political Science Review*, Vol. LVIII (1964), pp. 361-382.

85. Michael Paul Rogin, *The Intellectuals and McCarthy: the Radical Specter*, (M.I.T. Press, 1967), and Peter Bachrach, *The Theory of Democratic Elitism* (Little Brown, 1967).

to *reconstitute* some sort of organic communities which can be set against the gigantic organizations and massive forces of the time.[86]

Changes in constitutional ideas and attempts to preserve constitutional government in some form can be seen in a wide variety of movements and policies. For example, in *Baker vs. Carr* and subsequent cases, the Supreme Court has departed from the traditional idea that legislative apportionment was a "political question" and has required that states apportion legislative and Congressional seats based on equal population.[87] The movement to abolish the electoral college and substitute "one man, one vote" is obviously related. Both of these doctrines, however, are extreme cases of mechanistic thinking. Districts with equal population may or may not be "fair" and representative; gerrymandering, for example, is still possible provided that it is not too grotesque. (However, the Court has begun to deal with cases that involve gerrymandering designed to prevent racial equality.) More important, while "one man, one vote" is mechanically "just," it does not even address the organic inequalities between man and man. By accident, the electoral college *does*, and provides racial and religious minorities with a political advantage which partly compensates for their weakness in numbers, money, and social position. The mechanical rule of equality might, in fact, result in lessening political equality in America.

The Court has also, like many Americans, been concerned to protect what remains of the "private sphere" from governmental invasion. Hence, in *Griswold vs. Connecticut*, the Court resurrected the ninth Amendment to find a state and anti-birth control law invalid because it violated the "zone of privacy" which surrounded all the Bill of Rights like a "penumbra." [88] The law, it declared, violated the "fundamental" and "deeply rooted" right of privacy in marriage.

In this case, obviously, the Court was concerned to protect an organic institution, the family, from excessive state control. It has been equally sensitive in the case of religion, striking down even bland non-denominational school prayers.[89] In both cases, however, the Court appealed to the individualistic language of mechanistic theory, speaking of privacy and private rights. In the prayer decision especially, the Court aroused a storm of protest because it was, in the eyes of its critics, striking at the ability of the community to *protect* its organic institutions, weakening

86. For some examples, see Mitchell Cohen and Dennis Hale, eds., *The New Student Left* (Beacon, 1966); Erich Fromm, *The Sane Society* (Rinehart, 1965); and Eldridge Cleaver, *Soul on Ice* (Dell, 1968). Carmichael and Hamilton, *Black Power*, is interesting in merging organic and pluralist theories.

87. *Baker vs. Carr*, 369 U.S. 186 (1962), and *Reynolds vs. Simms*, 377 U.S. 533 (1964).

88. *Griswold vs. Connecticut*, 381 U.S. 479 (1965).

89. *Engel vs. Vitale*, 370 U.S. 421 (1962).

what Connecticut had taken, in the *Griswold* case, to be one basis of the family, and in the prayer decisions, limiting the community's ability to protect religion against secularism. To such critics the Court, whatever its aim, had contributed to those trends which fragment society and isolate the individual.[90]

Even if we think such attacks unwise or unjust, those who make them have a point. Especially in its language the Court reinforced the tendency, already powerful in America, for people to define their discontents in terms of a lack of individual freedom and private rights. This has been evident, of course, in all those movements concerned to secure one form of "liberation" or another. The case of feminists, for example, is impossible to refute; women *have* suffered serious formal and informal discrimination in America. But the argument that abortion should be legalized because woman has a "property" in her body (whatever the merits of legalized abortion), or Kate Millet's suggestion that the conjugal family yield in favor of child-rearing by expert technicians, surely reflect a privatism and a mechanistic ideology in no way necessary to women's claims to equality.[91]

A very different kind of constitutional argument is involved in the whole line of civil rights cases beginning with *Brown vs. Board of Education*, which struck down school segregation.[92] That case involved the rejection of mechanistic doctrine, the rule of "separate but equal," in favor of an analysis which considered the psychological and social impact of discrimination on the individual. Implicitly the Court was adopting organic theory, concerning itself with the ways in which institutions shape and affect individual personality, arguing that if formally "equal" institutions produced feelings of inferiority, the law has not afforded "equal protection." On similar grounds the Court has recently declared that localities must provide equal public services to all their citizens and has also effectively required all states to maintain some sort of public school system.

Blacks and other racial minorities have gone further, demanding not only "open admission" to colleges and other institutions of higher education, but insisting that school curricula reflect the history and culture of racial minorities, and that institutions respond to the needs of the individual for personal understanding, recognition, and dignity. Similarly, such movements have often been militant in urging new forms by which it is possible for communities to control their own schools, police, and development within an urban context, revitalizing the concern for

---

90. On the related problem of censorship, see Walter Berns, et al., "Pornography vs. Democracy," *Public Interest*, 22 (Winter 1971), pp. 3-44.
91. Kate Millet, *Sexual Politics* (Doubleday, 1970).
92. *Brown vs. Board of Education*, 347 U.S. 483 (1954).

participation and for the idea that a man's peers are his proper judges. All these demands appeal to the conviction that man is a political animal, that community—contrary to mechanistic doctrine—is a need inherent in man's nature; and they reaffirm, if only implicitly, a tradition of constitutionalism which is older in America than that embodied in the formal Constitution.

In cases like *Miranda vs. Arizona*, the Court has demonstrated a growing concern to check and limit administrative power, insisting that an individual accused of any crime be informed of his right to remain silent and to consult a lawyer, and requiring that a lawyer be appointed if he is unable to secure one for himself.[93] The decision also, however, involved a recognition that "consent" cannot be presumed because an individual does not protest. Isolated man, the Court conceded, is neither rational nor free; he is fearful and weak, and his suspicion of others is no protection (it only adds to the problem if he lacks education). Man, contrary to mechanistic theory, is free only with the explicit assistance of law and counsel. The fortunate and the well-to-do in America have not been alone, and the Court's decision has therefore had its greatest effect on the poor. But *Miranda* has implications for all Americans in a society where increasing isolation has seemed an inevitable political process.

But there are constitutional problems with which no court can deal. Courts cannot, for example, create their own "test cases"; they can only encourage citizens to disobey laws and authorities by hinting that a favorable ruling will result if a test is provided. More importantly, courts cannot cure the public's blindness, ignorance, or indifference toward political problems, nor can they overcome the sense of many Americans, whose interests are neglected, that they are hopelessly alone. Finally, courts cannot resolve problems which require immediate solutions or which cannot be solved except by legislation—the great substantive issues like war and peace or racial inequality.

Civil disobedience, banished to a political limbo by mechanistic theory, becomes a necessary part of the constitutional system when the "self-regulating" institutions have become visibly defective and when older organic restraints decline. Some men must disobey rules they believe to be contrary to the substantive and procedural values of America, if only to call such issues to the attention of the more apathetic and indifferent, and to avoid the danger that the great organized groups will allow such issues to pass unnoticed, from folly or design. Tyranny, as John Locke knew, can develop whenever citizens are politically absent-minded, and even more when they feel isolated and afraid.[94] To be

93. *Miranda vs. Arizona*, 384 U.S. 436 (1966).
94. Barker, ed., *Social Contract*, pp. 174-175, 186-187.

sure, civil disobedients take the law "into their own hands." But the law is always in someone's hands, and citizens have an official responsibility to their fellows and to themselves.[95]

It is a sad fact that violence may be part of this process. Yet violence has often been necessary for men to call attention to *themselves* as human beings. Loneliness and feelings of unimportance breed violence which is senseless and tragically destructive—a desperate effort to matter to someone, somehow. We can respond to violence by a greater violence, invoking repression against the crime and physical violence we fear. But we can also recognize that violence need not be a physical attack, that can be expressed in political clashes where the weapons are words and votes, and such "non-violent" violence goes hand in hand with the sense that one is neither helpless nor alone. That knowledge, more than more recent conceits, is a permanent foundation of democracy.[96]

Perhaps the old laws are dead. But organic theory felt that they were never alive except as they moved as values in our minds, for it saw a more fundamental law in the nature of man. When more elaborate devices and machines fail, one comes back to that law and to man with all his present weakness and his hope for virtue. The "constitution" of man makes him a political animal, one who needs to rule and be ruled in turn, from which all the vitality of democracy derives. And it is on the basis of that "constitution" that we may hope to build a new and possibly a better Constitution for the threatening future.

95. See my essay, "Civil Disobedience and Contemporary Constitutionalism," *Comparative Politics*, Vol. 1 (1969), pp. 211-227.
96. See H. L. Nieburg, *Political Violence* (St. Martin's, 1969) and W. C. McWilliams, "On Violence and Legitimacy," *Yale Law Journal*, Vol. 79 (1970), pp. 623-646.

2

PARTY FUNCTIONS

AND PARTY FAILURES

by Gerald M. Pomper

The current crisis in American government is a failure of its political parties.

Historically, the political development of the United States has been closely related to the growth and strength of its parties. Political and social democracy came with the rise of the Democratic-Republican party of Andrew Jackson, freedom for the slaves followed the emergence of Lincoln Republicanism, and the welfare state was developed by Franklin Roosevelt's Democratic coalition. Strong parties promoted responsive government.

If the parties are weak, major force for the development of the nation is absent. There is considerable evidence of the decay of American parties. To question the viability of the parties is, in turn, to question the viability of American democracy. If our institutions are to demonstrate responsiveness and effectiveness, a basic prerequisite is a party system able to perform necessary functions. The capacity of the parties can be assessed through analysis of six functions attributed to them. After examining the performance and conditions of the parties, we can proceed to projections of the future.

FUNCTIONS OF AMERICAN PARTIES

We shall deal with six related functions of the parties: (1) Aggregation of demands upon the political system; (2) Conciliation of groups in the society; (3) Staffing the government; (4) Coordination of government institutions; (5) Political socialization; and (6) Promotion of stability. This list of party functions is not exhaustive, for parties have additional consequences for the society. Nor is the list exclusive, for agencies other than parties perform some of these same functions. However, these six functions do comprise some of the most significant consequences of party activity. Each of them merits separate consideration.

Aggregation of Demands

"It is the party system," writes Almond, "which is the distinctively modern structure of political aggregation and which in the modern, developed, democratic political system 'regulates' or gives order to the performance of the aggregative function by the other structures." [1] By aggregation is meant the various processes by which different demands are advanced, eliminated and ordered, resulting in an agreed set of policies pressed upon the formal institutions of government. From the varied, even conflicting, demands of individuals groups, classes, sections, and races, the party creates and presents a combined program.

As an aggregator of demands upon the government, the party can be seen as a voting coalition. The party's program evolves from the demands of the groups included in its voting coalition. Its ideology is not explicit and philosophically defined. It is a "silent ideology" comprised of the demands of its constituent groups.[2] The character of party is illustrated well by the coalition most recently evident in American electoral politics, the New Deal Democrats.

Before the 1930s the Democratic party was clearly a weak aggregator. It had won the presidency only four times since the onset of the Civil War, and never convincingly. It particularly represented the declining areas of the nation, such as the South. Its policy positions emphasized dated controversies, such as the silver question, or imitated the beliefs of the dominant Republic party, as in the sacred defense of balanced budgets.

The Great Depression, beginning in 1929, transformed the party. As the viable alternative to the incumbent Republicans, it became the focus of the demands of all estranged groups. Its attraction was not due to the quality of its programs for, in 1932, Democrats pledged federal budget and state, not federal, unemployment insurance. The party was transformed not because of its ideology, but through the demands of the various groups which turned to Roosevelt. These demands led to new governmental programs and to a new voting coalition.

Urbanites have been a major component of the electoral alliance.

---

1. Gabriel Almond, "A Functional Approach to Comparative Politics," in Almond and James S. Coleman, eds., *The Politics of the Developing Areas* (Princeton University Press, 1960), p. 40.

2. The concept of "silent ideology" is taken from Frank Sorauf, *Political Parties in the American System* (Little, Brown, 1964), p. 63.

The urban vote had been Republican in the past, and was a major support of the pre-New Deal G.O.P. majority. Gradually, then rapidly, this
vote shifted toward the Democrats. The movement began, in fact,
before the Depression, based on the higher birth rate of Catholic
ethnic groups, and it was stimulated by the candidacy of Al Smith
in 1928. The conclusive shift came with the Depression and New Deal,
as seen in Table 2.1. Where the major cities had previously been Republican or marginal in their voting, they now become overwhelming Democratic.[3]

Table 2.1. Urban Voting for Democratic Candidates, 1920-1940
(in percentages)

Democratic Percentage of Two-Party Vote

City	1920	1924	1928	1932	1936	1940
New York	30.5	43.9	62.1	71.4	75.2	56.2
Cook County (Chicago)	23.7	24.7	46.9	57.1	64.1	55.5
Philadelphia	32.7	13.5	39.7	44.0	62.1	60.0
Los Angeles	23.8	10.1	29.0	59.7	67.9	58.9
Wayne County (Detroit)	19.0	8.1	37.1	59.4	67.9	62.0

Source: Richard M. Scammon, ed. *America at the Polls* (University of Pittsburgh
Press, 1965).

Urban support of the Democrats overlapped that of the economically
underprivileged. American politics became more oriented to social class
differences. The change was dramatically illustrated by the famous pre-
election poll of the *Literary Digest*, a mass circulation magazine of the
time. On the basis of a massive survey of telephone subscribers, the
same method used successfully in the past, the *Digest* predicted a Republican victory in 1936. However, the vote was now divided on class
lines; the Republican sympathies of those wealthy enough to have tele-
phones in the midst of the Depression was a poor index to general sentiment, as demonstrated by the overwhelming Democratic victory. The
change to class politics could also be found outside of cities. Harlan
County, Kentucky, was the storied scene of violent clashes over union
organization of coalminers. Always a poor area, it had voted Republican
until the Depression and the political upsurge of the United Mine Workers. An area which had given eighty-two precent of its vote to the Republicans in 1920 became two-thirds Democratic in a score of years.

The Democrats also gained disproportionate support from minority
groups. Negroes, steadfast Republicans since the Civil War, became
strong Democrats. Black urban areas in the North, which had once re-

3. See Samuel Lubell, *The Future of American Politics* (Doubleday, 1956), Chaps.
3, 4.

turned eighty percent majorities for the G.O.P., now voted for the Democrats in equivalent proportions. A similar transformation of historic loyalties occurred among Jews. Youth was a minority group of a different sort, and it too strongly supported the Democrats. Fully ninety-three percent of the new voters in 1932 voted for Roosevelt that year, as did some three-fourths of the voting novices in the next two elections. This high Democratic vote of first-timers contrasted severely with the bare fifth of these young people who voted for the party in 1924.[4] At the same time, the party retained much of its traditional support in the South and other areas.

The new Democratic majority was an expression of the demands of various groups. In the policies of the New Deal the party demonstrated its ability to meet the demands of these groups and to perform the aggregative function. Program of relief, public works, and housing were directed toward the cities. The economically underprivileged benefitted from union recognition, social security, and minimum wages. Minority groups were aided by these welfare measures, as well as by specific programs such as the establishment of federal fair employment practices. A Civilian Conservation Corps and National Youth Administration attempted to aid the young. Southern support for the party was rewarded by the establishment of the Tennessee Valley Authority and farm stabilization programs.

The New Deal programs did not all work, and their utility and desirability in many cases remain open to question. For example, economically these programs did not resolve the existence of widespread unemployment, which lasted until the intense demands of the Second World War appeared. Politically, however, they certainly worked. The Democratic party did aggregate demands and did establish a majority coalition. The several and separate wants of the cities, the underprivileged, the South, and so on, could not have been achieved through isolated action. By combining their demands into a common expression of support for the Democrats, these groups were able to achieve some considerable part of their objectives. The New Deal provided the means for the conversion of group inputs to policy outputs.

Conciliation of Groups

American political parties have been diverse bodies. open to all groups, and inclusive of some portion of virtually every significant social group. The parties have provided a location for the meeting and conciliation of the diverse interests of the nation. "Party politics is not a matter of mobilizing one great homogeneous group against another homogeneous group. Even more important, it is not a matter of mobilizing one aggre-

4. Angus Campbell, et. al., *The American Voter* (Wiley, 1969), p. 155.

gate of solid blocks against another aggregate of equally solid blocks of voters. The collision of parties is cushioned by the fact that there are no solid blocks. . . . The hospitality of the parties to all interested is one of their most pronounced characteristics." [5]

Diversity within the parties promotes internal conciliation of different interests. Group differences are not settled simply through conflict between the parties, or through formal governmental actions. Some of the differences can be reconciled within the parties, as different groups and interests seek common ground, party unity, and party victory. "Common loyalty to an organization is no small factor in bringing men of contrary interests together. This straddle presumably can stretch only so far; but before the breaking point is reached, concessions are often made out of loyalty to the organization which both sides value." [6]

The conciliation of groups can be see in various internal processes of the parties. Diverse social groups are represented among the organizational personnel of each party. In Detroit, illustratively, the local party is depicted as "a very eclectic recruiter. . . . Within the Republican party precinct cadre were large proportions of Catholics, Negroes, union members, low-income workers, even Irish and Poles. A similar picture exists on the Democratic side. The Democrats had invaded such traditional 'Republican' social groups as the upper occupational and income classes, those with a German or English background, whether Catholic or Protestant." [7] With all significant groups represented in the organization, conciliation is promoted.

Integration of diverse groups is also promoted on the electoral level through the traditional device of the "balanced ticket," in which the party deliberately seeks to include persons of different social backgrounds on its slate. The practice is often deplored by self-styled idealists who argue that the "best man" should be nominated regardless of his group identity, but this argument implicitly presumes that there are unlikely to be "good men" from all groups, a subtle expression of prejudice. The parties, seeking broad support, have used the balanced ticket to attract votes from all groups. In New York state, for example, the parties have attempted to nominate for state-wide positions at least one person from each of New York City, its suburbs, and the upstate area, and to designate at least one Protestant, one Irish Catholic, one Italian Catholic, and one Jew. As the Black vote has become more important in the state, the requirement of the balanced ticket is beginning to mandate

5. E. E. Schattschneider, *Party Government* (Holt, Rinehart and Winston, 1942), pp. 87-88.

6. E. Pendleton Herring, *The Politics of Democracy* (Norton, 1940), p. 131.

7. Samuel J. Eldersveld, *Political Parties: A Behavioral Analysis* (Rand McNally, 1964), pp. 59-60.

the nomination of one Black, at least on the Democratic slate. The same process has been evident in national nominations. Traditionally, persons from different sections were nominated for president and vice-president. Similarly, since 1960, a Catholic has been nominated for a balancing position on one of the party tickets.

Parties have also attempted to reconcile the policy demands of different groups. The method used has sometimes been simple evasion. The party may refuse to take a stand or adopt a contradictory position, as in the apocryphal tale of a local party's resolution on a Sunday closing law. The party pledged to enact a law requiring all businesses to be closed on Sunday, and also pledged not to enforce the law, thereby satisfying all groups. In party platforms condemnation of the opposition or pleas for party loyalty have often been substituted for a resolution of policy conflict.

At other times policy differences are compromised in order to promote the common goal of party unity. Northern liberals compromised their advocacy of school desegregation in 1956 in order to retain the support of the South for the Democratic party. Republican conservatives agreed to liberal planks on social security in the platform of 1960 in order to win the support of Nelson Rockefeller and his faction. Both parties in 1968 called for the gradual withdrawal of American troops from Vietnam, in attempts to win the favor of both 'hawks' and 'doves'. These positions were not clearly logical or necessarily defensible. They do illustrate the conciliation of groups within the party. "The accomplishment of party government has been in its demonstrated ability for reducing warring interests and conflicting classes to cooperative terms." [8]

Staffing the Government

American political parties function to staff both the elected and appointed offices of government. Their task is particularly important in filling elected offices, where they drastically simplify the choice offered to voters, limiting the number of alternatives to no more than a handful and usually to only two serious candidates for any particular position.

Party action makes a rational choice possible for the voters, but it also excludes many alternatives. The 1968 nominations of Humphrey, Nixon, and Wallace presented the voters with a manageable number of options. In offering this choice, however, the parties were also denying voters the chance to elect McCarthy or Rockefeller.

Nominating candidates is perhaps the distinctive feature of parties. Other agencies engage in policy disputes and affect government policy.

8. Herring, *Politics of Democracy*, p. 132.

In nominations, by contrast, the parties have been dominant and rarely challenged. While other groups attempt to influence nominations—such as financial contributors and labor unions—their actions are typically within the parties, not in rivalry with them.

The nominating function is particularly critical in the United States. Traditional beliefs in direct democracy have led us to elect a vast number of government officials, over half a million in all. Not only chief executives and legislators, such as the state governors and members of state legislatures, are elected. The ballot is also used to choose state cabinet members, judges, local administrators, school boards, and even such presumed experts as coroners. The sheer volume of the task of filling offices would be overwhelming for an unguided electorate. Moreover, in some cases the parties go beyond nomination of candidates actively seeking office, by recruiting individuals, bringing men and women into public service who might otherwise refrain from political activity. Recruitment of new peronnel is particularly evident for lesser positions and in situations in which the party finds itself in a minority.

After the nominations have been made, the parties remain important in the candidates' campaign for office. The most important asset a candidate has is his party label, which will automatically bring him large numbers of votes, regardless of his individual qualities. His designation as the party nominee provides access to public political meetings, to "equal time" in the mass media in many instances, and to important sources of funds, as well as to the long-standing organizational strength of his party. The important role of parties in campaigns was demonstrated as early as 1800 when Aaron Burr organized a massive voting campaign on behalf of the Republican national ticket. "He himself harangued in the city's taverns, guided an active finance committee, amassed an index of voters and their political histories, organized ward and precinct meetings, and worked at the polls." [9] As we shall see later, few partisans today have Burr's energy. Nevertheless, the party remains a principal agent for the campaign.

The parties also function as staffing agencies for non-elective positions. One of the primary motives for political activity in the United States has been patronage, the achievement of public office for faithful party work. "To the victors belong the spoils" has been a prevailing political axiom for extensive periods of our history. Conversely, many reform movements have centered their efforts on the elimination of patronage and the substitution of non-partisan or "merit" appointments.

The defects of the spoils system as an administrative technique have been widely described. Persons appointed on the basis of their party

9. William N. Chambers, *Political Parties in a New Nation* (Oxford, 1963), p. 155.

work have rarely possessed the technical skills needed in a bureaucratic position. Favoritism and corruption were likely when the tenure of an officeholder was destined to be short and was dependent on the favor of party leaders. An emphasis on patronage goals tended to minimize concern for policy questions.

Whatever its defects, party patronage has served the function of staffing the government. Other structures obviously can perform the same function, as evidenced by civil service systems. Now that the number of jobs open to patronage has been sharply reduced, it should be noted, however, that there were some desirable aspects to patronage. Election turnovers did guarantee that new men and some new ideas would periodically be introduced to the bureaucracy. Furthermore, the patronage system recruited officials eager to carry out the policies of their elected superiors and to conform to the program of the party which had won popular support. Their partisan loyalty provided a means, albeit imperfect, of making the government responsive to public opinion.

Political interference with the bureaucracy had some advantages, as well as its more publicized and obvious defects. Individual circumstances were more likely to be considered, and not only the application of abstract rules. Given political interference, a policeman might be more willing to disregard a minor charge against one of the party's constituents. Protected by civil service tenure, the same policeman might be more insistent on rigid interpretations of the law. Public order might well be better preserved and loyalty to the system more fully reinforced in the first case. Political interference permitted a certain degree of human warmth to melt the icy formality of bureaucracy. At the cost of possible favoritism, the individual voter might gain some feeling of control over his immediate political environment. Few voters now have such feelings in dealing with impersonal and "objective" bureaucracies, unless they are able to get help from their Congressman—a new form of political interference.[10]

Coordination of Governmental Institutions

A widely acknowledged function of political parties is to coordinate divided national, state, and local institutions. Nationally, parties bridge the separation of the president and Congress. In a classic work, Henry Jones Ford argued that "party organization continues to be the sole efficient means of administrative union between the executive and legislative branches of the government; and that whatever tends to maintain and perfect that union makes for orderly politics and consti-

10. See essay on Congress, pp. 163 ff., and essay on the Constitution, p. 1 ff.

tutional progress; while whatever tends to impair that union disturbs the constitutional poise of the government, obstructs its functions, and introduces an archaic condition of affairs full of danger to all social interests. This is the cardinal principle of American politics." [11]

The checks and balances established by the Constitution are well known. They are so extensive that they carry the potential for deadlock unless some means is available to overcome the inertia they contribute to American government. Parties have functioned to break deadlocks, bridge divisions, and provide a means of unified action. Particularly in periods of innovation in American history, parties have been the means by which coherent programs of public policy have been adopted. The aggregation of interests at the electoral level has thus become aggregation at the governmental level.

One example of this use of party was during Jefferson's presidency. The first Republican president did not adhere to a rigid separation of institutions, but rather sought "to embody himself with the House of Representatives . . . and become leader of that party." Congressmen sympathetic to Jefferson's program were installed in the critical positions of Speaker and chairman of the Ways and Means Committee. Legislative proposals were discussed in the party caucus and on the floor before being sent to committee for polishing. When they emerged, they were passed through party votes, often stimulated by the personal lobbying of Jefferson from an office near the House chamber.[12] Through organized party action, the branches were coordinated and a clear party program was enacted.

Party government since has rarely been as evident and disciplined as in Jefferson's period, but there have been somewhat similar eras in the first quarter of this century, under Republican Speaker Joseph Cannon and Democratic President Woodrow Wilson. Franklin Roosevelt met more resistance, but could still use his position as party leader to win the acceptance of the broad policy reforms constituting the New Deal. The most long-lasting changes in public policy came in the "second hundred days" in 1935, when Congress passed the National Labor Relations Act, social security, the public utility act, work relief, and reorganization of the Tennessee Valley Authority. Resistance to these measures was strong even among Democrats. The importance of party as a means of coordinating institutions and implementing policy, however, was shown in the Congressional votes on these measures. On the average, Roosevelt received the support of 94% of the Democrats,

11. Henry Jones Ford, *The Rise and Growth of American Politics* (Macmillan, 1914), p. 356.
12. James M. Burns, *The Deadlock of Democracy*, (Prentice-Hall, 1963), pp. 35-38.

compared to half of the Republicans.[13] Party unity enacted a party program.

The American polity is divided not only at the national level. Federalism introduces another cleavage into government, separating federal, state, and local institutions. Party has provided a means of bringing some coherence and cooperation into these relationships. Individual politicians promote union as they follow career-lines up and down the governmental ladder. Thus legislators seek governships, governors seek Senate seats, senators seek the presidency.[14] Personal ambitions connect the separate levels of government.

Nominations provide another means of cementing the cracks of federalism. All elected federal officials are nominated through state and local processes. Congressmen and senators, though they deal with national problems, must first satisfy the demands of their local party organization and local electorates. They must concern themselves not only with broad national policies, but also with the new county post office, local opinion on civil rights, and subsidies to the district's industries.

Presidential nominations are also closely tied to state and local politics. Delegates to the national nominating conventions traditionally have been primarily the representatives of decentralized party organizations. Their principal concerns have been the advancement of their local interests. They have sought the adoption of policies favored by their constituents, the designation of candidates popular at home, the aid of party standard-bearers in the election of local candidates, and promises of national favors to their separate party organizations.

Delegates have not brought much concern with national problems to the conventions, but their focus was appropriate. For much of American history, national politics essentially involved the conciliation and accommodation of the demands of different sections or geographical interests, such as slave and free states, or wheat and cotton groups. In bringing state and local party considerations to bear on the national platform and nominations, the conventions were providing a suitable mechanism for the aggregation of demands and the coordination of sub-national and federal institutions.

The nomination of Abraham Lincoln in 1860 provides a good illustration of the process. Lincoln was nominated primarily because the party believed he could win the presidency through the satisfaction of diverse local interests. His Western origin and support of free land was seen as attractive to the frontier states. Identified as a moderate on the slavery issue, he was believed to have some appeal to the Border states. Bargains

13. Compiled from roll calls in *The New York Times*.
14. See Joseph Schlesinger, *Ambition and Politics* (Rand McNally, 1966).

with individual state leaders brought him the support of the crucial delegations of Pennsylvania and Ohio. Ultimately Lincoln's nomination represented a national coalition of divergent state interests sufficiently cohesive to win the election and conduct the war.

The political parties' coordinating function has also been demonstrated in the less benign institution of the urban machine. The machines flourished during the half century following the Civil War. This was a period of large-scale immigration, urban growth, the development of industrial capitalism, and widespread poverty. These led to demands for governmental action. The informal political structure of the machine developed in response to these demands.[15]

The emergence of political machines was not inevitable; other means could have evolved to meet the needs of the time. The problems of poor immigrants, for example, conceivably could have been dealt with by a welfare state rather than by the precinct captain. The emergence of the machine was directly related to the lack of coordination of urban government. Management of the city was not in the hands of municipal governments alone, but was divided between city, state, and independent authorities. Within the municipal government, power was divided among plural executives, multichambered legislative bodies, and administrative boards. Large areas of activity were removed from government completely, reflecting the nineteenth-century distrust of political power. The checks, restraints, and controls on formal government were so great that no important action could be taken unless some informal means for the coordination of government were developed. The machine performed this function.

Where a machine took root, the power to govern was restored. To gain a transit franchise or protection of gambling, the businessman followed the simple procedure of persuading or corrupting the machine's boss. While no more honorable than convincing or bribing a host of official agencies, the procedure was at least more efficient. The immigrant seeking citizenship and a job could achieve both by a visit to the local clubhouse, rather than attempting to cope with unfriendly administrators or employers speaking an unfamiliar language. The long-term work of developing the modern metropolis—building its transportation system, creating its parks, lighting its streets—was facilitated by the centralized structure of the machine. The boss saw profit in public works, so he marshalled the necessary political power to develop the city. "He united the elements in a divided society in the only manner in which they could be united: by paying them off." [16]

15. See Robert Merton's classic analysis, "Some Functions of the Political Machine," in *Social Theory and Social Structure*, enlarged ed. (Free Press, 1968), pp. 126-136.
16. Seymour J. Mandelbaum, *Boss Tweed's New York* (Wiley, 1965), p. 67.

In time the machines helped to make municipal government itself more rational. George B. Cox, Republican boss of Cincinnati at the turn of the century, was credited with introducing order into chaotic politics. He "cooperated in securing a series of state laws designed to provide the city with a stable and centralized government. These statutes replaced the bicameral legislative body with a single board of legislation. The mayor's term was extended to three years and the office endowed with additional appointive powers." Cox centralized power under a board of administration which eventually "enjoyed concurrent power with the board of legislation in granting franchises and contracts and possessed the sole authority to extend franchises. Gradually, more and more departments were placed under its control. By 1896 it ruled every administrative field which commanded extensive patronage." [17]

The machine need not be romanticized, for it performed its coordinating function at great cost. Bosses were often dishonest, not necessarily benevolent, difficult to control democratically, and neglectful of many vital urban problems. Broad considerations of social welfare and broad approaches, such as minimum wage laws, were neglected. The machine instead concentrated on aid to individuals, not groups, and on the effects rather than the causes of urban development. The costs of machine rule were ultimately paid by the poor, whom it claimed to represent. The Christmas basket for the immigrant widow was scanty compensation for the loss of a breadwinner who died for lack of public health facilities. To acknowledge the functions performed by the machine is not to praise it.

Political Socialization

In every polity, a critical function is socialization—the transmission, to members of the society, of knowledge and emotion concerning the actors and objects of politics. Political socialization occurs through many structures, predominantly in the family and schools. Parties also are involved in the process. A party can be a symbol for the expression of loyalty or aversion. It can be a short course in the issues and ideology of the times. Through this organization individuals can also learn about the processes and structures of formal institutions, and become trained in the acquisition and use of political power.

The urban machine illustrates the socializing function of parties. At the time of large-scale immigration to America, other mechanisms of socialization were ineffective. Families of foreign birth and traditions could not teach their children about the strange political customs of the United States. Schools attempted "citizenship" training, but educa-

17. Zane L. Miller, *Boss Cox's Cincinnati* (Oxford, 1968), pp. 93-94.

tion was not universal, particularly beyond the primary grades. Moreover, the schools could influence only the youngest newcomers or the native-born generation, not adult immigrants. The party machines, however, did socialize the new Americans. Machine workers met passenger ships at the docks, it was said, and helped the immigrant to do the following, in order: to get a job, to fill out citizenship papers and, only then, to get off the boat. If not literally true, the description at least indicates the close connection made by the parties between service to the new Americans and the reward to the parties for that service.

The machine, acting in its own self-interest, taught the immigrant basic political facts: how to become a citizen, where and how (and, sometimes, how often) to cast a ballot, the names of the parties and of the candidates. More complex political learning followed quickly as the immigrants learned how to obtain a government job outside of civil service, how to avoid the rigors of the law, what the relative advantages of a vote for Democrats or Republicans were, and how to organize political action.

Immigrant groups soon began using the political parties for their own advancement. The Irish, the first immigrants active in urban politics, later organized groups along ethnic lines, recruiting and training their leaders from the parent group. As Ford patronizingly noted, "It is a matter of common observation in the politics of our great cities that a surprising amount of intimacy and association between people of different nationalities is thereby brought about. In the district headquarters of a party organization, one may perchance see an Irish ward captain patting on the back some Italian ward worker who can hardly speak intelligible English, but whose pride and zeal in the success of his efforts to bring his compatriots 'in line with the party' are blazoned upon his face." [18] Having learned from the Irish, newer immigrant groups soon began to move ahead on their own, to contest for power, and eventually to gain control in many areas. In New Haven Italians began to be elected to minor offices in 1890 and to major offices in the decade beginning in 1910. A large growth in the local power of Italian-Americans began after 1930, and was capped by the election of a member of the group as mayor in 1945.[19] Other groups followed a similar pattern of political socialization. From tutelage by another group they progressed to a cooperative position and then to independent power.

Aside from immigrants, the parties have sought to socialize other new voters. As the suffrage has been extended throughout American history,

18. Ford, *The Rise and Growth of American Politics*, p. 307.
19. Robert A. Dahl, *Who Governs?* (Yale University Press, 1961), pp. 43-44.

the parties have solicited the new electors for their support. As early as 1800 Aaron Burr vigorously registered new voters. "He cracked the problem of disfranchisement for many city workmen under the state's property test for suffrage, by arranging for joint land tenancies which made each participant a legal owner." [20] The establishment of White manhood suffrage in the Jacksonian period was accompanied by the elaboration of formal party machinery to mobilize the new mass electorate. After the Civil War the freed slaves were brought into the electorate through the Fifteenth Amendment to the Constitution and Southern Reconstruction. Radical Republicans particularly were eager to enroll Black voters as a means of assuring national supremacy for their party. Massive socialization was accomplished through the party, as millions of new voters received biased but effective teaching about American politics.[21] With the adoption of woman suffrage, the parties added special divisions to appeal to the new female voters and reserved offices in the party hierarchy for women. Each extension of the vote has thus brought an extension of party socializing effort.

The parties serve as an object of political socialization, as well as its means. The political learning which occurs in families is partially oriented toward parties. Gilbert and Sullivan observed:

> *That nature always does contrive*
> *That every boy and every gal*
> *That's born into the world alive*
> *Is either a little Liberal*
> *Or else a little Conservative!*

Children learn of parties through their families, long before they understand anything about party loyalty. One study found that six of ten children in fourth grade already expressed an identification with one of the major parties; only afterward are the party labels invested with more specific meaning.[22]

For the most part, children adopt the partisanship of their parents. Between generations, only 7 percent are in the opposite party from their parents, and three-fifths are in the identical grouping. As new citizens enter the political world, they have been socialized to retain the basic partisan predispositions of their parents. Furthermore, party loyalty is the most important political attitude transmitted between generations. Children learn their partisanship at home, though there can be considerable differences between the generations on other issues and opinions.

20. Chambers, *Political Parties*, p. 155.
21. See Kenneth Stamp, *The Era of Reconstruction* (Knopf, 1966), pp. 120-167.
22. Fred Greenstein, *Children and Politics* (Yale University Press, 1965), pp. 71-75.

Party loyalty is thus one of the most vital means by which the nation reproduces itself politically.[23]

Promotion of Stability

The most general function of American parties has been to promote the integration and stability of American society. In effect, the party system has been a conservative influence, both in the sense that it has helped to preserve the American political system and in the sense that it has retarded change within that system.

Huntington has seen parties as critical for the stability of a society, particularly in periods of economic growth, social modernization, and the expansion of mass political participation. "The principal institutional means for organizing the expansion of political participation are political parties and the party system. A society which develops reasonably well-organized political parties while the level of political participation is still relatively low (as was largely the case in . . . the United States) is likely to have a less destabilizing expansion of political participation than a society where parties are organized later in the process of modernization." [24] As the United States industrialized, became a world power, and expanded popular influence, established parties were available as a channel for the expression of demands and a focus of supports.

Performance of the other functions attributed to parties is one means of conserving the political system. The parties have been relatively successful in aggregating demands, conciliating groups, staffing the government, coordinating institutions, and socializing emerging electorates. A general consequence of their activity has been that demands have drawn responses, and that support has been forthcoming. By promoting incremental change they have deterred radical action.

The performance of the parties in absorbing social protest illuminates their conserving function. The history of American politics has not evidenced placidity and universal agreement. There have been many periods of widespread and extreme protest, such as marked the abolitionist movement and the industrial expansion of the late nineteenth century. In responding to protest, it has been common for the parties to absorb some of the program of the dissenting group, and thereby to curtail its appeal. The program of the Free Soil party was eventually incorporated within that of the new Republican party. The Populists, born of the agricultural depressions of the 1880s, advocated an extensive

23. M. Kent Jennings and Richard G. Niemi, "The Transmission of Political Values from Parent to Child," *American Political Science Review*, 62 (March, 1968), pp. 172-175.

24. Samuel Huntington, *Political Order in Changing Societies* (Yale University Press, 1968), p. 398.

program of government intervention in the economy, and received 8.5 percent of the presidential vote in 1892. Recognizing the appeal of the third party, the Democrats in 1896 appropriated the most dramatic part of the Populist program, unlimited coinage of silver, while abandoning more radical planks, such as government ownership of the railroads. One electoral result was the rapid disappearance of the Populists. In the early years of the Depression, protests included Huey Long's "share-the wealth" taxation scheme and the leftist programs of Socialists, who received nearly a million votes in 1932, and Communists, who received over one hundred thousand. The actions of the New Deal, including enactment of progressive taxation, social security, and public welfare, sharply curtailed these movements. By the 1936 election left-wing parties won only a quarter of their 1932 votes, while Huey Long's threat died with his assassination. Limited social change promoted systemic stability.

A major conserving influence has been the loyalty of voters to the principal parties. Protest movements have found it difficult to arouse support contrary to established loyalties. Significantly, the largest third-party movements have been those formed from the fission of a major party, in which dissidents could still lay some claim to be the "legitimate" heirs to the party label. Thus Theodore Roosevelt in 1912 or Robert LaFollette in 1924, and even George Wallace in the South in 1968, benefitted by their professed adherence to "true" party principles. Those who have forthrightly sought to establish new ideological directions, from Marxists to Conservatives, have had little success.

The inhibiting influence of party loyalty has been a source of anguish to ideologues and demagogues, but also a source of stability for the general system. In the period 1950-1954, many were concerned about the influence of Senator Joseph McCarthy. His destructive investigations of alleged communist influence in American life were presumed to be highly popular with the voters. Careful anlaysis revealed, however, that support of McCarthy was closely associated with party loyalty. Republicans generally supported him and Democrats were likely to be opposed. His electoral influence was limited, independent of party.[25]

Another illustration of the inhibiting effect of party loyalty is found in the support of the most prominent contemporary demagogue, George Wallace. When support of Wallace is analyzed by age, older voters are seen to regard him more highly than younger voters. Despite this appeal, however, when it comes to the actual vote Wallace draws a *lower* percentage from the older citizens. The explanation is that the older voters are more loyal to the established parties, and therefore

25. Nelson Polsby, "Towards an Explanation of McCarthyism," *Political Studies*, 8 (October, 1960), pp. 250-271.

less willing to foresake that loyalty in the polling place.[26] Similar reasons account for Wallace's better showing in primaries or opinion polls than in formal elections. In primaries and polls the voter is uninhibited by party loyalties. Thus Wallace was able to win nearly a majority in the Maryland Democratic primary of 1964, and to receive over a fifth of the preferences expressed in national polls during the 1968 campaign. In the actual election his share of the vote dropped to 13 percent nationally and 15 percent in Maryland.

Party leadership also promotes stability. Social movements require organization, but the loyalties and interests of established personalities in the existing parties restrict potential defections. While searching for leadership, protest movements may wither. The Vietnam protest movement of 1968 was thus severely handicapped by the reluctance of Robert Kennedy and other Democrats to challenge the party leadership of Lyndon Johnson. Even Southern segregationists, constituting a large body of opinion, have been hampered by the reluctance of aspiring politicians to lead a new segregationist faction. Loyalty to the national Democratic party has restricted leadership among Southern dissidents largely to those who have no possibility of advancement within that party (e.g., Mississippi Governor John Williams, disciplined by the House Democrats), those near the end of their political life (Senator Strom Thurmond), or at the very beginning of their careers (the new Republican organizations). Most party leaders continue to have emotional as well as material stakes in party loyalty, and such stakes help to maintain the established system.

American parties are conservative in another sense—that of limiting change to incremental development. The emphasis in American parties has been on conciliation and moderation, not on complete programs or deliberate social reform. This characteristic is evident in the way in which the parties have performed their various functions. Aggregation of demands has been accomplished by joining disparate, even conflicting, groups together in a common pursuit of power. Most commonly, alliances have been formed on negative programs—against the Federalists, against Jackson, against Depression, against Roosevelt—rather than on behalf of an agreed ideology. Conciliation of groups has meant that social conflicts are moderated within the party, rather than sharpened for resolution in clear electoral conflicts. Structures such as the urban machine sought limited, divisible, and tangible goals such as patronage, rather than attempting reconstruction of urban life. The ethnic base of the machine was useful in socializing new citizens, but it also perpetuated

26. Philip Converse, et al, "Continuity and Change in American Politics," *American Political Science Review*, 63 (December, 1969), pp. 1103-4.

and even emphasized division among the voters. The mass energy for policy change which might have been organized on a class basis was dissipated by concentration on limited ethnic advances. Instead of attempting, for example, to change the distribution of wealth, the machine won allegiance by providing each ethnic group with a place on a balanced ticket.

The conservative character of American parties has not been due to any organized conspiracy or evil design. The constitutional checks and institutional restraints have made such parties almost inevitable. The relative security and prosperity of the United States permitted the luxury of slack politics. A general consensus existed, favoring capitalism, restricted international involvement, and a conditional ethnic pluralism. Within these restraints, parties performed their limited functions, usually to the satisfaction of the active citizenry. Disadvantaged groups were gradually admitted to political power, as were the White immigrants; compensated by economic prosperity, as were the industrial workers; or essentially ignored, as were the Blacks.

In 1972 it is difficult to believe the traditional parties will suffice. Mounting problems of industrialization, of war, and, preeminently of race, require change in the parties. As Herring noted, "There is much that is not heroic in our system. The heroic mold has seemed ill suited to the peaceful routine of minding one's own business and working for a living. If we are approaching more dangerous times we will have less use for . . . our easygoing, rough-and-tumble politics of compromise and barter." [27] Clearly we are in more dangerous times. It is a moot question, however, whether our parties can be cast in a more heroic mold, and can be made adequate for the problems of the time. The evidence, rather, is that the parties are increasingly inadequate to the contemporary challenges of American life.

THE DECAY OF AMERICAN PARTIES?

To this point we have discussed six functions of the parties. In this section it will be argued that the parties are decreasingly capable of performing their tasks. Paralleling the previous six sections, we shall attempt to demonstrate the following propositions: (1) The Democratic party majority is rapidly dissolving; (2) The parties are less able to conciliate disparate groups; (3) The parties have lost substantial control over nominations, campaigns, and patronage; (4) Party ties are of decreased significance in coordinating governmental institutions; (5) Political socialization of groups, particularly Blacks and youth, is inadequate;

27. Herring, *Politics of Democracy*, p. 238.

and, consequently, (6) American politics is highly unstable, due to rapid political modernization. Each of these propositions requires supporting evidence.

Decline of the Democratic Party

The evidence for the decline of the New Deal Democratic party majority consists of several strands of data. Most obvious are the gross returns from presidential elections. The period of Democratic supremacy was the five consecutive national victories from 1932 to 1948. In the five succeeding elections, the Democrats have won a majority of the popular vote for president only in 1964, and have lost the presidency itself on three of the five occasions.

Other indications of change are found in peculiar features of these elections. Two of these ballotings (1956 and 1968) resulted in the historically-odd election of a president and Congress of different parties, and two (1956 and 1960) brought a decline in the Congressional representation of the party winning the presidency. Moreover, of the last five Congressional elections, three (1962, 1968 and 1970) brought historically limited change in the distribution of seats between the parties.

Recent national campaigns show strange characteristics. The South has become a major area of competition, in contrast to previous assumptions of its solid Democratic loyalty. In fact, every one of the eleven Confederate states has voted against the Democrats at least once in recent presidential elections. In 1964, in the Goldwater-Johnson contest, an ideological emphasis was evident that was in sharp contrast to typical American politics. The Arizona senator particularly sought to wage the campaign on broad philosophical themes. He succeeded in raising the ideological consciousness of the voters,[28] while aiding President Johnson in a triumph comparable to Roosevelt's in 1936. Completing these developments were the peculiar events of 1968: the forced retirement of an incumbent president, the rise of domestic violence to political significance, and the advent of George Wallace as leader of one of the most popular third parties in American history.

The evidence of change is dramatically evident on this descriptive level. Confirmation of change can also be found in various quantitative measures. These relate to the pattern of party identification, particularly among groups in the New Deal coalition; to the factions in national conventions; and to the geographical distribution of party support.

---

28. Two articles report similar developments in 1964: J. O. Field and R. E. Anderson, "Ideology and the Public's Conceptualization of the 1964 Election," *Public Opinion Quarterly*, 33 (Fall, 1969), pp. 380-398; John G. Pierce, "Party Identification and the Changing Role of Ideology in American Politics," *Midwest Journal of Political Science*, 14 (February, 1970), pp. 25-42.

Party identification is the voter's long-term, underlying feeling of allegiance to a particular party. Repeated studies have shown that regardless of the outcome of particular elections, the basic partisanship of the electorate is highly stable. However, greater volatility is evident in recent years. Data on this point are available for presidential election years since 1940 from the Gallup poll and, since 1952, from the more sophisticated studies of the Survey Research Center of the University of Michigan. These sources show a similar trend. In 1940 the Democrats enjoyed a slight advantage in party identification. The Democratic margin increased over the next two decades, at a slow average rate or less than 1 percent a year. Change came more rapidly in the 1960s. The Democrats first gained a huge advantage in 1964, leading the Republicans by 53-25 percent. Since then, there has been a marked decline in Democratic support and a marked increase in self-identified Independents. Until 1964 a steady fifth of the voters considered themselves nonaffiliated. Since that year the group has increased to 30 percent of the electorate, and more voters now identify as Independents than as Republicans. The trend is illustrated in Figure 2.1.[29]

Detailed analysis of these changes in party identification point to the dissolution of the Democratic party majority. One important indication of the party's decline is found in the composition of the vote for George Wallace in 1968. Wallace did not have a neutral effect on the party balance; he did not draw equally from both parties. His vote was almost entirely from Democrats, who contributed 46 percent of his total, and from Independents, who provided 41 percent, leaving only 13 percent gained from the Republicans. Wallace's vote among the Independents was disproportionately from those who had left the Democratic party. Three times as many former Democrats as former Republicans supported the Alabama governor.

The decline in the Democratic coalition is also shown in the social composition of the Wallace vote. Wallace drew his greatest strength in the South, among manual workers, the young, grade-school and high-school graduates, and non-professional workers. These are precisely the groups that formed vital elements of the New Deal coalition, but deserted the party of Franklin Roosevelt in 1968.[30]

The Wallace vote is not likely to be just a temporary phenomenon, regardless of the individual fate of the governor. There are many indications that the vote he attracted is permanently lost to the party. Wallace

29. Figure 2.1 is derived from Everett C. Ladd, Jr., Charles D. Hadley and Lauriston R. King, "The American Party Coalitions: Social Change and Partisan Alignments, 1935-1970," a paper presented at the 1970 meeting of the American Political Science Association.

30. *Congressional Quarterly Weekly Report*, 26 (1968), p. 1815.

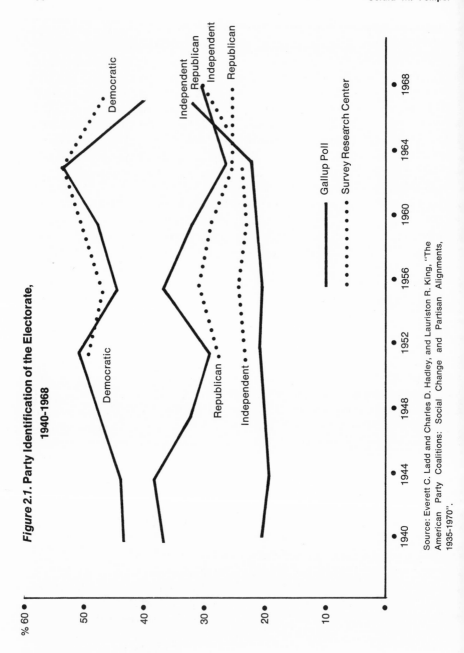

Figure 2.1. Party Identification of the Electorate,
1940–1968

Source: Everett C. Ladd and Charles D. Hadley, and Lauriston R. King, "The
American Party Coalitions: Social Change and Partisan Alignments,
1935–1970".

voters in 1968 were far more favorable to Nixon than to Humphrey, and their positions on issues were closer to those they attributed to the Republican than the Democratic candidate.[31] Moreover, Wallace voters of 1968 now seem ready to vote for the Republicans. Three-fourths said they would vote Republican if the Alabama governor were not a candidate in 1972. A Gallup poll on the Congressional elections of 1970 also found that two-thirds of the Northern Wallace voters expected to vote for Republican congressional candidates. Even in the more traditional South, the Republicans were likely to receive a slight 7-6 congressional majority from the Wallace group.[32]

Another indication of the weakened Democratic majority is found in changes in party identification. If we compare loyalty toward the Democrats among several population groups in 1960 and 1968, we find some important changes. The total percentage of Democratic support has dropped slightly during this period. More significant are the changes within particular groups, as detailed in Table 2.2. The decline in Democratic support is particularly great in such groups as white Southerners, manual workers, white urban residents, and the young.[33] As the Wallace vote previously indicated, the Democratic losses are especially severe in the groups constituting the previous majority coalition.

The changes in Democratic support are not accidental. They reflect the inherent internal strains of the old coalition as well as the onset of new problems. The most evident strains in the coalition have centered around the unacknowledged issue of race. The New Deal was not consciously designed to benefit Blacks. White and southern prejudices were often accepted, as in the exclusion from minimum wage laws of occupations in which Negroes were concentrated, such as farming and domestic work. Moreover, most of the reform programs of the 1930s did not change the status of the poorest groups. Legislation to insure bank deposits or to support farm prices were of little help to those too poor to acquire savings or raise cash crops.

Without conscious purpose in many cases, however, Democratic policies did have some benefits for non-whites. Programs to relieve poverty inevitably aided the many poor Blacks. Some specific actions

31. On a "feeling thermometer," in which candidates were ranked from 0 to 100, Nixon's median rating was ten points higher than Humphrey's among Wallace voters. On the issue of urban unrest, Wallace voters clustered toward the "tough" end of a 7-point scale, a majority being at points 6 and 7. They perceived Nixon as occupying point 4 on this scale, Humphrey at point 2, and Wallace, their preferred candidate at 7. For related evidence, see Converse, "Continuity and Change in American Politics," pp. 1090-92.

32. *New York Times*, 22 March 1970, p. 71; 16 November 1969, p. 55.

33. Compare with Samuel Lubell, *The Hidden Crisis in American Politics* (Norton, 1970).

Table 2.2. Party Identification, 1952 to 1968
(in percentages) *

	1952	1956	1960	1964	1968
Strong Democrats	23	22	21	27	20
Weak Democrats	26	24	26	25	26
Independents	23	24	23	23	29
Weak Republicans	14	14	14	14	15
Strong Republicans	14	18	16	11	10

* Apolitical and unclassified responses are omitted.

Changes in Party Identification of Population Groups, 1960 to 1968
(percentages add horizontally to 100% for each year) *

	1960					1960				
	SD	WD	Ind	WR	SR	SD	WD	Ind	WR	SR
Region and Race										
White, North	18	21	25	17	19	15	24	30	19	13
Black, North	32	14	42	12	0	48	30	19	1	1
White, South	25	36	18	9	12	20	29	36	10	5
Black, South	26	30	20	8	16	67	30	3	0	1
Education										
Elementary	24	27	22	12	14	33	30	18	11	8
High School	22	28	25	15	11	24	30	25	13	7
Some College	17	22	23	16	22	15	25	36	15	9
College Graduate	13	20	27	16	23	12	17	35	21	16
Age										
Under 28	16	28	27	12	17	12	23	46	14	5
29-38	20	30	27	12	11	22	30	28	14	6
39-48	20	25	25	14	16	20	26	29	18	7
49-58	22	26	23	16	12	23	24	26	16	10
59-68	22	23	17	15	23	28	24	21	13	14
Over 68	27	16	15	17	25	23	28	13	14	22
Occupation										
Professional	12	22	28	18	20	12	18	37	20	13
Managerial	18	25	19	19	18	17	22	34	17	9
Clerical, Sales	16	33	23	10	18	15	24	32	18	11
Craftsmen	24	27	32	10	7	14	30	32	16	8
Operatives	26	29	28	10	7	24	30	29	9	7
Service Workers	23	20	24	20	12	30	29	29	5	8
Laborers	14	34	20	9	22	41	24	19	9	7
Farmers	18	18	19	23	22	26	27	11	23	12
Not Employed	27	20	14	15	24	29	28	20	11	12
Religion and Race										
White Protestant	18	24	22	16	21	14	24	30	19	13
White Catholic	29	33	21	10	6	22	30	32	10	6

Table 2.2 (Continued)

	1960					1968				
	SR	WD	Ind	WR	SR	SR	WD	Ind	WR	SR
Jewish	21	28	47	5	0	33	19	43	5	0
Black	29	22	31	10	8	59	30	9	1	1
Residence and Race										
Large Cities, White	24	25	23	10	18	16	22	40	12	9
Large Cities, Black	28	25	37	8	1	59	27	11	1	1
Suburbs, White	15	25	24	18	17	17	24	31	17	11
Suburbs, Black	34	25	22	12	6	58	34	8	0	0
Rural, White	26	26	20	12	15	16	28	26	20	11
Rural, Black	25	14	30	11	20	52	32	12	0	4

* Some rows do not add precisely to 100% because of rounding.

were undertaken on behalf of Negroes, such as the establishment of the principle of fair-employment practices. The ideological thrust of the Democratic program was toward equality, and the logic of inclusion of Blacks could not be evaded completely. Moreover, political logic supplemented ideology. The growing Black vote in Northern cities became an important element in winning the critical industrial states. In 1944, 1948, and 1960 Democratic victories for president were built on narrow margins in the states with large blocks of electoral votes, and the margins could be attributed to the Negro balance of power.[34]

Black equality and Southern segregation were inherently contradictory. The strains became evident as early as 1936, when South Carolina Senator Ed Smith left the Democratic convention to protest a speech by a Negro congressman, Arthur Mitchell. As the party became more committed to a civil rights program, the racist elements in the party were increasingly uncomfortable, leading to the Dixiecrat rebellion in 1948, limited defections to the Republicans in the 1950s, the independent elector movement of Mississippi Governor Ross Barnett in 1960, the Goldwater sweep of the Deep South in 1964, and ultimately to the Wallace movement.

By 1965 segregation was legally ended, but race became a more salient issue as it affected new interests. The demands of Blacks came to focus not on the elimination of overt bias but on real equality of results, as defined by schooling, jobs, and power. Demands shifted from proclamations of desegregation to the elimination of low reading scores, entrance into closed occupations, and political control of Black communities. The interests threatened by these goals were no longer the benighted

34. As it was in Henry Lee Moon's book, *Balance of Power: The Negro Vote* (Doubleday, 1948).

Snopeses of the South, but the suburban parent, the union craftsman, and the Democratic ward committeeman.

The New Deal coalition had been based most generally on class interests, the combined votes of lower social and economic groups. Racial conflicts, never absent in America, had been partially subordinated to common class goals within interracial organizations such as unions and the Democratic party. Race now disrupts these alliances, as the critical conflicts occur between Blacks of lower economic position and Whites of only relatively better position. The neighborhoods, jobs, and political power around which conflict occurs are those previously controlled by the White working class. Groups once united in the party are now divided among themselves and thereby divide the previously dominant majority.

The coalition has also been disrupted by the emergence of new issues of foreign policy. The New Deal was created primarily to deal with a domestic crisis. There was no coherent foreign policy inherent in its program. Circumstances, individual leadership, and international necessity brought the evolution of a policy of collective security and anti-communism; but the lack of any clear relationship to the basic party program was revealed by the similarity of Republican policies and by the doctrine of a "bipartisan foreign policy." As international issues moved to the fore politically, therefore, the Democratic coalition lost its binding force. Vietnam decisively demonstrated the instability of the coalition on issues of foreign policy, but the war was only the precipitating agent for a supersaturated political mixture.

National Convention voting provides further evidence of the change in party coalitions. Until 1964 consistent factional alignments existed in conventions of both parties. State delegations could be clearly classified as conservative or liberal; a state voting for a given conservative candidate in one year could be predicted to vote for another candidate of the same ideological character in another convention.[35]

In the 1968 conventions we find a change. To illustrate the new patterns in the Republican party we can divide the states into five groups, ordered from conservative to liberal. In Table 2.3 we find that Robert A. Taft, at one time the standard power of conservatism, won majorities only in states in the three more conservative categories. In 1964, when conservatism triumphed in the party with Barry Goldwater, the historical pattern held, but the candidate's support had now been extended into the fourth grouping. Nixon, however, disrupted the pattern. Although

---

35. This argument is a development of that presented by Frank Munger and James Blackhurst, "Factionalism in the National Conventions, 1940-1964: An Analysis of Ideological Consistency in State Delegation Voting," *Journal of Politics*, 27 (May, 1965), pp. 375-394.

he was particularly strong in the conservative faction (despite the challenge on the right from Ronald Reagan), and his support resembled Goldwater's, it was more dispersed. Nixon failed to win majorities in six state delegations carried by Goldwater, while he added five states lost by the Arizona Senator.

Table 2.3. Convention Candidates: Distribution of Votes for Selected Candidates, (as percentages of total votes for the candidate *)

Republican Candidates	Factional Category					
	I	II	III	IV	V	N
Eisenhower for President (1952)	8.3	6.7	8.3	16.8	59.9	590
Taft for President (1952)	31.2	20.6	30.5	6.6	11.1	485
Goldwater for President (1964)	28.0	17.1	25.0	22.4	7.5	879
Nixon for President (1968)	27.0	17.2	25.3	12.6	17.9	673

Democratic Candidates	Factional Category						
	I	II	III	IV	V	VI	N
Humphrey for Vice-President (1956)	46.6	19.9	6.2	0.4	26.8	0.0	128
Kennedy for President (1960)	28.9	24.5	19.3	25.4	0.5	1.4	685
Johnson for President (1960)	3.0	3.2	5.0	2.5	16.3	70.0	402
Humphrey for President (1968)	15.1	14.7	12.3	18.9	12.9	26.1	1689

* All votes are calculated from the first ballot, before shifts. District of Columbia, Alaska, Hawaii and the territories are excluded from all votes.
Source for 1952-64 data: Frank Munger and James Blackhurst, "Factionalism in the National Conventions, 1940-1964: An Analysis of Ideological Consistency in State Delegation Voting," Journal of Politics, 27 (May, 1965), pp. 375-394.

Further indications of party change are found in the Democratic party, in which six factions, arranged from liberal to conservative, can be identified. Unlike any candidate of the party since the creation of the New Deal majority, Humphrey's nomination in 1968 was based on the support of the most conservative of the six state groupings. However, even this pattern was not consistent, for the vice-president drew some backing from states in all groupings. In contrast to the 1960 nomination, he lost eleven states carried by liberals, and won seventeen others. The Minnesotan's support at the convention fit better the pattern of Lyndon Johnson in 1960, for Humphrey lost only one of the Texan's states, while winning nineteen new ones. The new states, however, were scattered through all of the ideological groupings previously evident in the party. Both Nixon's and Humphrey's nominations thus indicate new directions within the major parties.

Geographical distributions of party support are a third indication of change in national coalitions. Areas once securely Democratic or Republican have become competitive, or have even come to be bastions of the erstwhile opposition. Under the New Deal coalition, the South was solidly Democratic, while upper New England and the Plains states were reliably Republican. We have already noticed the shift in the Southern presidential vote. This change has been reflected not only at this level, but in balloting for lower offices. In recent years Republicans have elected five senators, 26 representatives, four governors, and a tenth of the state legislators in six Southern states. In the vote for Congress, perhaps the best single indicator of basic party support, the party received a third of the ballots in the former Confederacy. Conversely, the Democrats have invaded former Republican territory. Significantly, three of the leading possibilities for the 1972 Democratic nomination for president—Senators Muskie, McGovern and Hughes—come from states previously considered off-limits to the party.

A statistical indication of the change is provided by state-by-state correlations of the Presidential vote. A high and positive correlation indicates the persistence of the basic voting alignments in the nation, while lower or negative figures show a change in the party lines. Thus the persistence of the New Deal coalition can be seen in correlations between the elections of 1932 and 1944 close to .90, where 1.0 would be a perfect relationship. A marked change is evident, however, when we correlate the elections of 1964 and 1968 with the New Deal contests. These correlations are all negative, and strongly in this direction. The vote for Johnson shows approximately −.70 correlation to the New Deal elections, and the vote for Humphrey correlates with that for Roosevelt in the range of −.54 to −.69. There has evidently been a strong shift in the territorial base of the party, paralleling the demographic changes discussed earlier.[36] Similar changes can be found within states, by analyzing the relative Democratic vote in individual counties.[37] The result is a definite shift of the base of the Democratic party toward the Northeast, and a contrary movement of the Republican party toward a territorial base in the South and West. Neither party, however, has yet secured the stable majority coalition needed for effective political action.

Party Conflict

A second major indication of the decay of the parties is their decreased ability to conciliate diverse groups. Performance of this function has become more difficult for two reasons: greater homogeneity of party membership and weakened mechanisms for achieving agreement.

36. For further description, see my article, "Controls and Influence in American Elections (Even 1968)," *American Behavioral Scientist*, 13 (November-December 1969), pp. 215-230.
37. Walter Dean Burnham, "American Voting Behavior and the 1964 Election," *Midwest Journal of Political Science*, 12 (February, 1968), pp. 1-40.

The parties have become less diverse in composition. When each party contains a mixture of all social groups in the nation, it provides a locus for the reconciliation of differences. Conversely, when groups are separated into different parties, partisan conflicts reinforce social discords. Thomas Jefferson foresaw the difficulty when he warned, "A geographical line, coinciding with a marked principle, moral and political, once conceived and held up to the angry passions of men, will never be obliterated." [38] His fears were confirmed by the Civil War. In modern times, two defenders of American parties worried: "The day some major element completely deserts one party in favor of the other, the stage will have been set for the kind of conflict that leads to actual civil war, and our parties will have failed to maintain our kind of consensus." [39] As we have seen, Blacks have now completely deserted the Republican party, and other groups are potential defectors from both parties.

A related trend is toward greater ideological homogeneity within the parties. It is less true than in the past that there are similar distributions of "liberals" and "conservatives" within each party. In the past decade ideological awareness has increased in the electorate. As voters have sorted themselves between the parties, Democrats have become more clearly liberal and Republicans more identifiably conservative. An indication of this development can be found in the replies to six policy questions asked of national samples of voters in 1956 and 1968. In Table 2.4, the percentage favoring increased federal action on these six issues is detailed by party identification. In 1956 there was very little relationship between a liberal policy stance and partisanship, with Strong Republicans, for example, almost as prone to support federal aid to education as Strong Democrats (68 percent as opposed to 81 percent). By 1968 there is a much closer relationship. The Strong Democratis are four to five times more likely to support this program than Strong Republicans. The same development is evident in questions dealing with federal provision of medical care, guarantee of full employment, non-discrimination laws in employment, enforcement of racial integration in the schools, and economic aid to foreign nations.[40]

38. Cited in Allan Nevin and Henry S. Commager, *America: The Story of a Free People*, (Little, Brown, 1943), p. 178.
39. Austin Ranney and Willmoore Kendall, *Democracy and the American Party System*, (Harcourt, Brace, 1956), p. 509.
40. The data are computed from the 1956 and 1968 surveys of the Michigan Survey Research Center. The questions used are, by deck and column numbers, in 1956: 3/12, 3/18, 3/21, 3/24, 3/33, 3/54; in 1968: 4/54, 4/58, 4/60, 4/74, 4/76, 5/29. These are the only questions dealing with specific policies which are essentially repeated in the two surveys. The *gamma* coefficient, included in the last line of the table, is a statistical indication of the association between two variables. Its maximum value is 1.0.

Table 2.4. *Party Identification and Policy Position, 1956-1968*
(in percentages supporting "liberal" position)

Party Identification	Aid to Education				Medical Care				Job Guarantee			
	'56	'60	'64	'68	'56	'60	'64	'68	'56	'60	'64	'68
Strong Democrat	80.0	66.8	51.0	53.6	74.2	74.5	78.2	81.3	75.6	71.2	52.6	53.1
Weak Democrat	78.1	59.0	44.1	38.3	67.3	60.2	65.2	72.1	64.0	62.4	38.4	39.7
Independent	71.0	53.2	39.3	32.9	55.8	56.7	57.2	55.3	55.0	56.6	31.0	27.0
Weak Republican	68.7	39.1	21.5	22.5	51.4	47.5	43.5	39.3	59.5	43.9	25.9	24.9
Strong Republican	67.7	44.5	15.5	12.0	45.9	54.2	23.6	42.7	51.5	52.7	16.1	25.4
Gamma	.15	.20	.34	.36	.24	.18	.45	.41	.19	.16	.31	.25

Party Identification	Fair Employment				School Integration				Foreign Aid			
	'56	'60	'64	'68	'56	'60	'64	'68	'56	'60	'64	'68
Strong Democrat	73.3	63.0	56.3	61.9	38.7	39.8	53.7	58.9	49.5	51.4	64.7	51.3
Weak Democrat	71.3	63.1	42.9	43.5	44.4	37.5	43.2	44.6	55.4	48.8	59.2	45.8
Independent	66.6	65.4	50.3	37.7	48.8	47.1	49.0	37.3	49.9	53.2	57.5	42.7
Weak Republican	70.8	62.7	36.3	37.8	49.3	43.0	50.5	37.4	48.2	54.0	56.6	47.0
Strong Republican	66.8	65.9	20.6	31.3	38.8	41.5	34.8	31.5	51.4	61.5	49.7	41.8
Gamma	.04	-.02	.22	.24	.04	-.01	.08	.43	.01	-.03	.08	.04

These changes make the parties resemble more closely than in the past the "responsible parties" advocated by many observers. If each party is relatively united on its policy positions, then the choice between parties can also be a choice of program. This development contributes to visible public control over policy. At the same time, however, it reduces the capacity of the party internally to reconcile ideological differences. Conflict is escalated from a settling of differences within the partisan family to a public contest between warring clans.

Parties today also have fewer available methods to resolve their internal quarrels. The parties have changed from armies of combat to arenas of combat. They are not disciplined bodies, with identifiable and respected leaders, efficient cadres and loyal troops. To a great and increasing extent they are paper forces whose greatest asset is their title and the legitimacy it confers, not the force they command.

A party army requires a high measure of unity within its leadership, or at least means to achieve agreement among the leaders. American parties have occasionally used hierarchical discipline, in true military fashion, to achieve such unity. The political machine best exemplified the practice. More often, they used bargaining techniques to bring cohesion among autonomous warlords. To a great extent, however, neither set of techniques is employed today. Attempts to impose discipline are rarely made, and the political machine is severely limited in scope. Where discipline is attempted, as in the Lyndon Johnson's control of the 1968 Democratic convention, its results are detrimental, bringing disaffection and defeat.

The more common techniques of unity through bargaining are also disappearing. The horse-trading and negotiations once typical of national conventions had many objectionable features, morally as well as politically. Their virtue was that they resulted in a high degree of agreement within the party, enabling it to enter a campaign as a combined force, even if its martial tunes were somewhat discordant and its uniforms frayed. National conventions no longer provide a location for this kind of bargaining. They are simply the arenas in which one faction seals its temporary capture of the party name and tradition.

There has been no clear instance of a negotiated Presidential nomination since the Republicans chose Alfred M. Landon in 1936. The patterns instead have become those of a victory by an individual leader of a selective faction, such as Goldwater in 1964, or the inheritance of party leadership by some member of the inner circle, such as Humphrey in 1968.[41] The decline of bargaining is also evident in the virtual extinction of the multiple ballots once typical of party conclaves.

41. Paul David, et al., *The Politics of National Party Conventions*, (Brookings Institution, 1960), chap. 6.

The decline of party discipline is evident in local nominations as well, perhaps the single most important locus for power within the parties. The direct primary was introduced into all states over the last half-century in an effort to destroy the control of party chieftains over the selection of candidates. While it has not totally removed their influence it has certainly weakened it. A "balanced ticket," appealing to different factions within the party and different voter constituencies, is unlikely in the absence of an institutionalized means of negotiation. The result can be seen in the 1970 Democratic nominations in New York state. A party attempting to appeal to an electorate which is 80 percent Christian, 90 percent White, and 60 percent outside of New York City was presented, via the primary, with a ticket which included four Jews and one Black, all of whom lived or worked primarily in New York City. By contrast the Republicans, who maintained party discipline, were able to nominate a balanced ticket. Subsequently, all but one of the Democrats lost the election.

Our political parties are not organized for combat. Their organizational cadres are very poorly developed. According to legend, the parties were once hierarchical organizations built on thousands of precinct workers and extending upward to professional state and national leadership. The contemporary facts are quite opposite. Many precincts —perhaps a fourth in all—are uncovered by even a single worker for one or both parties. In the Republican case, over three-fourths of the party organizations in the major cities in 1960 did not have all of their districts named. Even where they exist, most precinct workers do not work very hard for the party. The busy partisan who visited his constitutents, intervened with the authorities, and provided free advice and friendship, has apparently passed from the scene. In fact, by 1964 only a fifth of the electorate was even personally solicited for its vote by each party.[42] Organization is limited at the higher levels as well. Over a tenth of the counties have been reported without party chairmen. Even state chairmen, who might be considered key figures in any coherent organization, tend to be unpaid and part-time.[43]

Underlying these changes is the decline in emotional attachment to the party. As in all social organizations, including armies, sentimental attachment has been at least as important as narrow self-interest in creating cohesion. The devotion to the party as such appears to be

42. John Kessel, The Goldwater Coalition (Bobbs-Merrill, 1968), p. 263.
43. V. O. Key, Politics, Parties and Pressure Groups, 5th ed. (Crowell, 1964); Republican National Committee, Report of the Committee on Big City Politics (1961); Samuel J. Eldersveld, Political Parties: A Behavioral Analysis (Rand McNally, 1964), chap. 13; Charles W. Wiggins and William L. Turk, "State Party Chairman: A Profile," Western Political Quarterly, 23 (June, 1970), p. 327 f.

weakening as it becomes the vehicle for individual ambitions rather than collective efforts. The Massachusetts party thus becomes the Kennedy organization, and the California Republican party the Reagan faction. Even on the presidential level, candidates are more disposed to ignore the party. There has been "an increasing tendency to stray outside the party machinery for political assistance even in campaign years. . . . It also means that a successful candidate is unlikely to regard the party machinery as something to which he should pay attention after he is in office." [44]

Loyalties are redirected toward individuals. Defeated aspirants for party nominations or unsuccessful advocates of policy positions do not feel the traditional compulsion to stay "regular." Democrat Arthur J. Goldberg can support former Republican John V. Lindsay for mayor of New York City, Lindsay can reciprocate when Goldberg runs for governor, and both will be praised for their independence of party. The old feudal system of the parties, in which prescribed rules governed an ordered set of relationships, has been replaced by a "bastard feudalism," in which leaders command individual loyalties in battles for personal advancement. These actions reveal "a new reality: the party not as a broad coalition or even as an alliance between factions, but as a political kingdom to be disputed by private armies owing their allegiance not to some local machine, but to a nationally puissant family or individual." [45]

The decline of loyalty to the parties is also evident among the party troops, its loyal partisans who vote for candidates simply because they display the party emblem. In the periods of greatest partisan feeling in American history, it was common for all candidates on the party ticket to receive almost identical votes, with the differential between the most popular and the least preferred candidate being less than 2 percent.[46] Parties can no longer achieve this level of loyalty. It is taken as a sign of intelligence and insight for voters to split their tickets—selecting, cafeteria-style, candidates of different parties for different offices. Split-ticket voting is evident in 10 percent of ballots, and general electoral instability, or voting independent of party loyalty, had become evident among half of the voters by 1964.[47] Moreover, the increased proportion of independents in the electorate indicates that instability will become even more evident in the future.

44. George Reedy, The Twilight of the Presidency (World, 1970), pp. 120-121.
45. Lewis Chester, Godfrey Hodgson, and Bruce Page, An American Melodrama (Dell, 1969), p. 231, and pp. 231-236.
46. Walter Dean Burnham, "The Changing Shape of the American Political Universe," American Political Science Review, 59 (March, 1965), pp. 7-28.
47. Richard M. Merelman, "Electoral Instability and the American Party System," Journal of Politics, 32 (February, 1970), p. 127.

Parties and Personnel

Parties evidence less effectiveness in staffing the government. Many important public officials no longer come from party ranks. Less than half of the chief executives of major cities are elected directly. Even where elections are still employed, partisan ballots are used in only a third of the communities.[48]

While many organizations remain active, they have lost exclusive control over their most unique function, that of nominating candidates. The direct primary has largely accomplished its work of abridging the influence of parties and of weakening the party structure.[49] Informal attempts to circumvent the intent of the primary system through party endorsements are limited in effect. Party endorsements do not prevent primary challenges, and non-endorsed candidates can often gain votes by a campaign against alleged party "bosses." Party organizations which have used pre-primary endorsements, in such states as Massachusetts, New York, New Jersey, and California, are abandoning them as un-enforceable. Nominating decisions will instead be influenced by the reputation of incumbents, the attractions of personality, money, and the intervention of non-party interests.

The parties also have a decreased role in the other aspect of electoral selection, campaigning. American parties were designed for electioneering among a relatively small electorate, which was partisanly and geographically stable, and could be effectively reached through face-to-face contact. The precinct captain was an effective campaigner when his constituency consisted of persons he had known for years and who would respond to his personal and partisan appeals. Even where he continues to try, he cannot be as effective in a suburban nation, where neighbors are transients, where political independence is praised, and where the potential electorate is well over a hundred million.

Fast, high-density, impersonal campaigning is needed. The place of the party worker is taken over by new specialists with different skills, as different structures perform an old function. For the face-to-face contact of the party, the advertiser substitutes the televised spot. For the intuitive feel for trends and issues of the experienced politician, the pollster substitutes random samples and statistical test. For the candidate's decisions on strategy, the public relations specialist substitutes a marketing campaign. The displacement of parties has proceeded to the point that one of the most successful public relations firms, Whitaker

48. Eugene C. Lee, "City Elections: A Statistical Profile," *Municipal Yearbook, 1963* (International City Managers' Association, 1963), pp. 74-84.
49. See V. O. Key, *American State Politics* (Knopf, 1956), chaps. 4-6.

and Baxter, insisted on exclusive control of a campaign without interference by the candidate or the party.[50] More recently another huckster
has gone even further, insisting that the candidate remain mute throughout "his" campaign. The increasing participation of non-politicians
in campaigns, such as athletes and entertainment celebrities, is a related
phenomenon.

Changes in campaigning may not be detrimental to either the candidate
or the public. Candidates are better served by accurate public opinion
surveys than by clubhouse comments. The quality of campaign rhetoric
is not necessarily lower because it is composed by advertisers instead
of city councilmen. The voter may be gaining a more accurate impression of a candidate from a television commercial than he did from
a precinct captain. These changes are important, then, not because
they clearly debase the electoral process. They are noteworthy because they diminish the party's role in staffing the government, thereby
further decreasing its functional significance. The deficiency of the new
agencies is not that they are more deceptive than the parties, but that
they are less visible and therefore less accessible. The precinct worker
or the office-holder could be approached and rewarded or punished
for his conduct, in campaigns and in power. The new campaigners
work largely for profit, not for power. The citizen cannot vote them
out of office, and their jobs are not dependent on their political fortunes. Popular control is thereby diminished.

The parties have also lost their effectiveness in staffing the non-elective
positions of government. The inexorable trend is to remove all positions
in administrative agencies from the realm of party politics. The attractive
slogans of "merit systems" and "professionalism" are employed to in-
sulate bureaucracies from outside intervention. At the federal level,
Presidents have fewer than two thousand discretionary appointments,
and the conversion of the Post Office to an independent agency has
eliminated what was once the greatest source of patronage. Similar
changes have occurred in most states and large cities, partially because
of federal laws requiring merit systems of appointment in programs
receiving national funds.

The process of partisan exclusion from the civil service has now
gone beyond the elimination of the spoils system. In place of the old
party machines have arisen the civil service machines seeking complete
control over entrance, promotion, and leadership of their agencies. Not
only technical or specialized positions come to be defined in "professional" terms, but even the chief executive positions. In New York City

50. Stanley Kelley, Jr., *Professional Public Relations and Political Power* (Johns
Hopkins Press, 1956), chap. 2.

the pattern is particularly evident. Mayor Lindsay has faced continuing opposition (and deliberate obstruction) from the bureaucracy because he has not followed past practice mandating that the head of the police department be a former policeman, the head of sanitation be a former garbage-collector, and so on. Each agency vigorously seeks to make itself "self-perpetuating and not readily subject to the controls of any higher authority." These attempts often succeed, because of the assumed undesirability of "political interference," which is understood to include not only corruption, but even policy-making by the elected chief executive of the city.[51]

Where patronage still exists, detailed studies indicate that the parties have not been effective in its administration. Even for the low-skill jobs, the party does not want to antagonize incumbent workers, and it is likely to retain most appointees. For high-skill jobs, it is difficult to find appropriate party members to reward, and the resistance of "professional" interests seeking to monopolize access to the position is formidable. In all positions there is a common tendency for affected groups to define the jobs of interest to them as "non-political," thereby excluding party intervention. Increasingly they succeed, further diminishing the party function.[52]

The recruitment system of parties is thoroughly inadequate. They do not maintain personnel files or have any regular system for matching party work to governmental reward. Positions are filled by a non-rational combination of demands by aggressive party leaders, limited bargaining, and considerable recruiting outside of the party organization. John Kennedy's experience is illuminating. Upon his election in 1960 the Democrats had been out of the White House for eight years. One would expect that the party would have many persons desirous and qualified for appointments. Yet Kennedy, himself well-acquainted with party personnel, found himself despairing of finding the right persons for his administration. "People, people, people! I don't know any people. I only know voters. How am I going to fill these 1,200 jobs," he complained. Ultimately, he resorted not to the party, but to government agencies and informal advisers such as Clark Clifford.[53] The victors could not effectively possess the spoils.

51. Theodore J. Lowi, "Machine Politics—Old and New," *The Public Interest*, 9 (Fall, 1967), pp. 83-92. Quotation from p. 87.

52. See Frank Sorauf, "State Patronage in a Rural County," *American Political Science Review*, 50 (December, 1956), pp. 1046-56; and Daniel P. Moynihan and James Q. Wilson, "Patronage in New York State 1955-1959," *American Political Science Review*, 58 (June, 1964), pp. 286-301.

53. Arthur M. Schlesinger, Jr., *A Thousand Days* (Houghton Mifflin, 1965), p. 127.

Falling Bridges

Parties have functioned as bridges between the separated institutions of American politics. These bridges appear to be falling—nationally, between state and federal governments, and locally.

The decline in effectiveness is evident in the relations of the president and Congress. The president leads Congress, but he does not employ party as the principal means of his leadership. The quality of executive leadership is particularly notable in regard to foreign policy, where the president employs techniques of persuasion outside of the party system, such as meetings with committees, public appeals, and the doctrine of nonpartisanship, or bipartisanship. This doctrine frees the president, for he can claim immunity from partisan criticism by an appeal to alleged overriding national interests. Bipartisanship does not subject the president to the control of either his own party or that of the opposition. "Its only practical effect has been to increase the strength of some presidents under some circumstances." [54]

The decreased importance of party can be seen in Congressional roll call votes. In the times of party control, floor votes reflected differences between Republicans and Democrats. In the early twentieth century 90 percent of the parties took opposing positions on as many as half the roll calls.[55] In the period since 1950, by contrast, almost no roll calls showed such strong division. In fact, even half of the parties have been opposed less than two-thirds of the time. Moreover, over the course of the last two decades, even by this modest test, the frequency of partisan division has generally declined, so that the factions now take opposing positions only about one-third of the time.[56] As seen in Figure 2.2, the proportion of such roll calls has declined by an average of 2 percent a year. Legislation is not commonly passed by action of a visible agency, the party, which can be held accountable by the voters. It is more often passed by shifting and unidentifiable coalitions, whose existence cannot be understood by the electorate and whose power therefore cannot be controlled.

The decreased influence of party can also be seen in the higher seg-

54. Reedy, *Twilight of the Presidency*, p. 127.
55. A. Lawrence Lowell, "The Influence of Party Upon Legislation in England and America," *Report of American Historical Association* (1901), pt. I, pp. 540-541.
56. The data are computed from the annual volumes of *Congressional Quarterly Almanac*, beginning in 1949. Figures for individual sessions are combined to give a composite figure for the entire Congress ending in the year indicated on the chart. The party unity index is the proportion of all roll calls in the House or Senate in which a majority of Republicans vote in opposition to a majority of Democrats. Lowell's index was much more severe, measuring those roll calls in which 90 percent of each party were opposed.

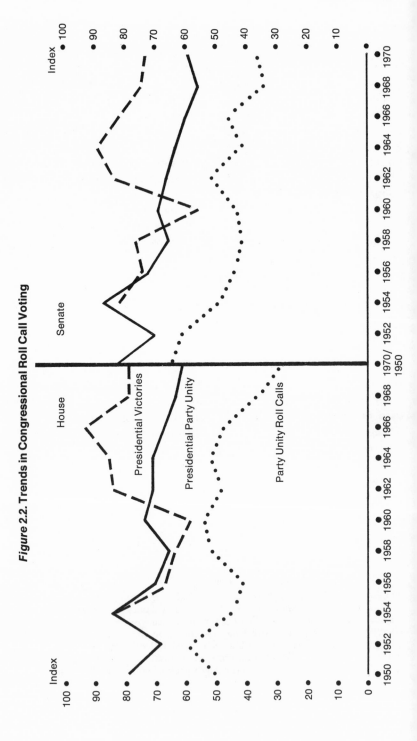

Figure 2.2. Trends in Congressional Roll Call Voting

ment of Figure 2.2. Two indexes are graphed in this section: unity within the president's party, and presidential legislative victories. Party unity gradually declines at an annual rate of 2 percent. The proportion of presidential victories, however, actually increases slightly. We can see that the president's success in achieving his legislative program has become independent of the unity of his party. Statistically, the independence of the two characteristics is shown by the low correlation (.05 for both Chambers, .03 for the Senate, .07 for House) between presidential victories and party unity. There is a greater relationship if we compare the president's success with another measure, the support for the president's program within his own party. The correlation here is still weak, but meaningful, at .28 (-.18 for the Senate but .70 for the House).[57] If party were an effective bridge, the president's success on roll calls dealing with his program should be closely related to the unity of his party and to his party's support on roll calls, in both chambers dealing with that program. Instead, we see there is limited and inconsistent correlation. Party no longer functions to unite the two branches.

A particular instance of the decline of party is provided by the passage of President Johnson's "Great Society" policies in 1965. This program of legislation, including such innovations as Medicare, Federal Aid to Education, and the Voting Rights Act, has often been compared to the outpouring of New Deal statutes. However, the impact of party was less in the Johnson period. Compared to the "second hundred days," the important Johnson bills were passed despite relatively low Democratic cohesion, reaching as low as 55 percent in the Senate and 38 percent in the House. The Johnson program was not passed because of party unity, but because the Democratic margin was sufficiently large to tolerate defections, and because it was aided by some Republican votes.

Party as a tie between institutions depends largely on electoral necessities. Republican congressmen would be likely to cooperate with a Republican president, for example, if their fates at the polls were tied together. It would be in the interest of members of the House to support the president's program if, in so doing, they increased their own chances

---

57. Unity within the party is the average party-unity score by members of the president's party, whether Republican or Democratic. This score signifies the percentage of times on which the average member of the party voted with his party, when majorities of the two parties were opposed. The proportion of presidential victories is the percentage of roll calls dealing with the president's program in which the president's position was victorious. The presidential support score is the proportion of such roll calls on which the average member of his party supported the president's position. All scores are derived from the annual volumes of *Congressional Quarterly Almanac*.

of re-election. Increasingly, however, presidential and congressional results are disparate. Congressional incumbents have become highly likely
to win elections, regardless of the presidential results, and therefore owe
little to the party leader's alleged "coattails." [58] Split-ticket voting further
fosters independence, as voters are more willing to vote for individual
congressmen regardless of party. An index of the increasing political
separation between the two branches are the number of districts won
by a presidential candidate of one party and a congressman of the
opposition. These results have been more frequent in recent times. While
"split-district" results occurred in one-sixth of all elections since 1920,
they appeared in one quarter of the contests in 1960, and one third in
1964 and 1968.[59]

Electoral ties between the state and national governments have also
weakened. These ties are particularly crucial in regard to state governors.
If governors and presidents are elected at the same time, the common
partisan judgment of the electorate is likely to bring some degreee of
coordination. Concurrent election was the practice in past years, such
as 1944, when most of the governors (32 of 48, and 27 of 37 outside
the South) were elected on the same ballot as the president. In the past
decades, however, state constitutions have been greatly changed. The
two elections have been separated, by providing four-year gubernatorial terms beginning in the middle of a president's tenure. The result is that, by 1972, only 19 of the 50 state executives and 17 non-
Southerns, will be chosen in that presidential year.[60] Only a seventh
of major cities hold elections concurrently with state or national balloting.[61]

The most important party tie between state and national institutions
has been the national convention. There the demands of state and local
factions were reconciled through the platform and the choice of candidates. The system was kept responsive to public needs by the desire
of all organizations to nominate a winning candidate. As political folk
humor prescribed, a successful presidential candidate would be the
"ferryboat" who dragged along all the "garbage" of the party's state
and local candidates. To protect their own parochial interests, the
various factions would seek a candidate of nationwide appeal.

Nominating conventions can no longer function adequately. State

58. Nelson W. Polsby, "The Institutionalization of the U. S. House of Representatives," *American Political Science Review*, 52 (March, 1968), p. 146.
59. Data for the period through 1964 are from Milton C. Cummings, Jr., *Congressmen and the Electorate* (Free Press, 1966), chap. 2. For 1968, from *Congressional
Quarterly Weekly Report*, 27 (June 6, 1969), pp. 884-921.
60. *Book of the States, 1945-46* (Council of State Governments, 1943), p. 560;
Book of the States, 1970-71 (1970), p. 145.
61. Lee, *City Elections*, pp. 74-84.

and national political concerns have become disassociated, for the president's tasks are no longer encompassed by state or country borders. Problems of civil rights or economics are national in scope. Resolving the clash of Blacks and construction unions is different from resolving the clash of the Ohio and Texas factions. Interests of dispersed groups such as Blacks, students, women, and workers are not easily represented in a geographical distribution of power. Furthermore, the president's foreign constituency is completely unrepresented. The most important tasks facing him are those of international relations. The problems of nuclear arms and diplomacy are completely outside the ken of the local partisans who decide nominations. Able to choose a domestic broker, they are irrelevant in the selection of an international politician.

The constraints on the nominating convention have also weakened. It is no longer crucial for state and local organizations to respond to public opinion. In terms of narrow self-interest, their political futures are increasingly separate from that of the president. As the merit system is extended throughout the federal bureaucracy, he has little patronage to offer them. As voters become more independent, the electoral fate of the president becomes distinct from that of local tickets. Local parties may thrive while the presidential candidate falls, as southern Republicans did during the Goldwater debacle and as Chicago's Mayor Richard Daley did during Humphrey's defeat. The garbage still floats to shore while the ferryboat sinks.

In this situation the choice of a nominating convention may represent only the personal preferences of the delegates, not their calculated choice of a qualified candidate likely to capture the spoils of victory. The party tie between state organizations and the national leadership has been damaged. The national convention retains the power to make nominations, but that power is less responsible because it is less constrained by political controls.

On the local level as well, parties are less able to coordinate governmental institutions. Urban machines have been largely displaced. Their welfare functions to a great extent have been assumed by bureaucracies, which provide much greater and more efficient aid, even while they are less compassionate. Business interests have fewer favors to ask of municipal governments, and therefore less need to corrupt politicians. The formal institutions of government have become more centralized, as in "strong mayor" systems, decreasing the importance of informal coordination by the machine. These new institutions, however, are not under party control.

Where parties still remain in close contact with their constituents, they are reduced to aiding them to find their way through the bureaucratic maze. The need for political intervention is real. Demands for the protection of individuals by ombudsmen system and civilian review boards, as well as the popularity of walking tours by mayors, indicate that existing channels are inadequate for the expression of citizen grievances. Functioning local parties could provide direct, regular, and effective channels, but few urban organizations are now adequate to the task.

Political Socialization

Political socialization of new citizens remains necessary in American society, but the parties are not fully successful in performing this function. Their deficiency is evident in regard to Blacks, who have only recently been enfranchised in practical terms, although their constitutional right to the ballot has existed since Emancipation. When the massive Negro migrations to the north began with the First World War, the parties were presented with the opportunity to socialize this new "immigrant" group. In political terms, Blacks shared many of the characteristics of the White ethnic groups. They were poor and unfamiliar with urban life and therefore needed the services of a welfare organization such as the machine. Group characteristics were highly visible, and networks of social communication such as the churches existed, so political organization was feasible. Moreover, being native-born, the Blacks were citizens and had no language barrier. Given these characteristics, we might reasonably haxe expected the rapid mobilization of Negro voters.

In fact, the parties have been slow to respond. Black registration and voting has tended to lag behind that of whites, typically being 10 percent below the average participation in northern industrial cities.[62] Even half a century after the beginning of large-scale migration to the big cities, Negroes had disproportionately low proportions of political nominations, patronage positions, and public offices.[63] Their movement into political power was considerably slower than that of White immigrant groups.

Political socialization of the new urban residents might be expected particularly of the Democratic organizations, since Blacks had become strong supporters of the party after the New Deal. However, the urban machines had been weakened by the decline in their resources and attacks by good-government reformers. Furthermore, local parties sometimes actively opposed voter registration, and more commonly simply neglected to act. Weak, disinterested, or hostile party groups sought to protect their own position. Registering large numbers of Black voters might aid the national ticket, but it might also mean the displacement of faltering White leadership. Inertia by the parties eventually led to

62. Oscar Glantz, "The Negro Voter in Northern Industrial Cities," *Western Political Quarterly*, 13 (December, 1960), pp. 999-1010.
63. Chuck Stone, *Black Political Power in America* (Bobbs-Merrill, 1968), chap. 5.

registration figures so low that some northern counties became subject to the Voting Rights Act of 1970, which activated federal registration of voters when less than half of the adult population was registered.

The failure of the parties to mobilize the new Black vote has been evident in the recent movements toward Black political power in cities. Of the three most prominent Negro mayors, only Carl Stokes in Cleveland received a significant measure of party support. Andrew Hatcher, after winning the Democratic nomination for mayor of Gary, Indiana found virtually the entire party organization, including the county chairman, actively supporting his Republican opponent. Kenneth Gibson in Newark, New Jersey, won election in a nominally nonpartisan contest in which much of the Democratic organization campaigned for his Italian opponent.

Political agencies, including the parties, have succeeded better in creating loyalty to the system among the masses of Blacks than in promoting their active participation. Blacks overwhelming identify with one of the established parties, the Democrats, and tend to believe in the efficacy of political action. There are many signs, however, of Black alienation. The most obvious are the ghetto insurrections of the past six years. A less forceful indication is the relatively large proportion of Blacks who feel alienated from America. According to the Harris poll, over half of Blacks believe "the people running the country don't really care what happens to people like ourselves." Only about a fourth of Whites hold this feeling. These sentiments of alienation, moreover, have increased in recent years and are more evident among younger Negroes.[64]

Decreased effectiveness in supportive socialization is also evident among youth. The younger voters are increasingly likely to reject both political parties and instead to identify as Independents. While youth has always shown this tendency, it is more marked at the present time. In 1956 32 percent of the youngest group, aged 30 and below, were Independents, compared to an enlarged proportion, 46 percent, of the same age group in 1968. Even greater disaffection from the parties is evident among the critical college population. Here among future leaders an actual majority call themselves Independent, and this category has attracted new adherents at an accelerating rate.[65]

The lack of partisan loyalty among younger voters is paralleled by

64. *New York Times*, 16 April 1968, p. 23. For similar results, see David O. Sears, "Black Attitudes Toward the Political System in the Aftermath of the Watts Insurrection," *Midwest Journal of Political Science*, 13 (November, 1969), pp. 515-544.

65. The Gallup Poll, reported in the *New York Times*, 14 December 1969, p. 55. In 1966, 39 percent of college students were Independents. Six months before the last poll, 44 percent were in this category.

other indications of decreasing commitmen, although the total level
of positive support for the system remains high. While young people,
like their elders, generally support such action as Chicago's police
repression of demonstrations at the 1968 Democratic convention, they
are more likely to believe that excessive force was employed,[66] and
more willing to use non-electoral means of political action. The young
are not, on the whole, ready to revolt, but they have not been fully
incorporated into electoral politics by the parties.

Finally, and most obviously, we can note the incomplete socialization
evident in the relatively low turnout of American voters. The most
elementary form of mobilization by the parties is to bring the voters
to the polls, yet the percentage of adults who cast ballots is actually
quite small. In a presidential election, which draws the most voters, the
highest turnout in the twentieth century was the 63.8 percent who
voted in the Kennedy-Nixon contest of 1960. Congressional elections
typically draw only about half of the adult population, and local elections
often do far worse.

These results, far below the 80 to 90 percent turnouts achieved in
other nations, indicate that the parties have failed to bring substantial
elements of the population into active participation in the political
system. Much of the non-voting, moreover, is due not to the alleged
apathy of the voter, but to barriers to participation, such as discrimination, residence and registration laws, and inconvenient polling practices.
The parties have not been sufficiently concerned with the activation of
the electorate to take the necessary actions to change these laws. The
effect of these barriers is to exclude many groups, particularly the disadvantaged, from political power, reserving it for an oligarchy of some
seventy million voters. "It is the largest, most broadly based ruling
oligarchy in the world, but it is not as inclusive and as broadly based
as some other systems." [67]

Unstable Politics

Given the decline of their other functions, the parties cannot perform
their most general function: promoting integration and stability in the
society. The loss of stability and moderation is readily apparent, as extremists ranging from Wallace to Weathermen gain significant support
and publicity. The methods of political action have been extended far
beyond the accustomed bargaining and the restrained combat of the

66. John P. Robinson, "Public Reaction to Political Protest: Chicago, 1968," *Public
Opinion Quarterly*, 34 (Spring, 1970), pp. 1-9.
67. E. E. Schattschneider, *The Semi-Sovereign People* (Holt, Rinehart and Winston, 1960), p. 109. Also see Walter D. Burnham, *Critical Elections and the Main-
springs of American Politics* (Norton, 1970), chaps. 4, 5.

parties. Assassination has become a political fact, bombing a political tactic, looting a political message, and assault an expression of patriotism. Party politics, it is said, substitutes ballots for bullets in the resolution of social conflict. An increasing number of Americans seem prepared to reintroduce bullets.

Decline of the parties is neither the primary cause of social instability nor an isolated trend. The underlying cause of our current instability is the absence of modern political institutions in the United States —in a time of rapid political modernization of the population. Modern political institutions would include a unified national government, complex and disciplined administrative hierarchies, and party agencies promoting mass participation. While the United States is economically the most developed nation in the world, political institutions have not progressed, as Huntington argues, beyond the stage of the "Tudor polity" of Elizabethan England. Where the genuinely modern state has rationalized centralized authority, power in the United States is deliberately fractured, checked, and limited. Where we find in the modern state specialized structures of authority, we find in America separated institutions and shared powers. Where modern parties attempt to mobilize the entire population, Democratic and Republican organizations have only limited effect on most citizens' lives. "The United States thus combines the world's most modern society with one of the world's most antique polities." [68]

Despite its underdeveloped political institutions, the United States historically was able to accommodate early and rapid expansion of popular participation in politics, and to avoid most of the disruptions typical of economic growth. Stability was possible because of the restricted role of government. No severe foreign threats existed. Dominant values left economic expansion to individual capitalists and the capricious movements of the invisible hand of free enterprise. If government were not to direct society, rationalized authority and specialized structures were unnecessary. If the power of government was not to be employed by an aroused electorate, popular participation could be safely permitted.

These conditions no longer exist. International involvement cannot be avoided in the age of intercontinental missles. A mature economy requires government direction. The citizenry is making new demands on the government. In sum, the United States is now undergoing political modernization, but the parties and other institutions are not yet able to control or respond to new demands. The modernizing process is evident in four trends: increased political participation, the loss of traditional authority, national integration, and the growth of ideology.

68. Huntington, *Political Order in Changing Societies*, chap. 2, and p. 129.

Increased participation is one of the signs of modernization. It is evident even in the relatively privileged middle class, which is turning to politics as a new form of leisure activity and social service. But new involvement is more marked among those who previously have been excluded from sustained political action. Although they have not been socialized into the parties, large numbers of Blacks, the poor, and the young have been brought into politics. Their political action is not always through the electoral process, but demonstrations, takeover of buildings, and deliberate violence can be even more potent political acts. Student seizure of campuses, burning of brassieres, or construction workers' marches function to politicize large numbers of person who previously abstained from significant acts affecting the distribution of power. The United States today bears the marks of a society in which large numbers are rapidly entering the political system and making demands on it, though not through the established organizations. As our present experience and that of other nations shows, the results are not necessarily peaceful, stabilizing, or desirable.

Modernization also involves the loss of traditional authority and prestige, and this feature is also notably visible in contemporary America. The destruction of the Southern racial code by Blacks insistent on equality, criticisms of college faculties by students and Spiro Agnew, the castigation of male chauvinists by women's liberation advocates, the disregard for legal restraints in the smoking of marijuana, and the beating of college students by policemen—these diverse phenomena are alike in being attacks on past authority or previously privileged groups. Those previously subordinate in status no longer accept the legitimacy of the traditional hierarchy. Independence from traditional partisan loyalties is one element of a general release from accepted patterns of deference.

A third major feature of the current political modernization is the movement toward the nationalization of American society. This development is not new, but it represents a clear source of the current tensions. The United States is now economically centralized by its mature capitalist industries. The issues we face are now *national* issues: race, war, pollution, urban life. Through television, universal education, and residential mobility, we have developed a common political discourse in an increasingly homogeneous society. Even our formal governmental institutions evidence the beginning of centralization, notably in the growth of unchecked presidential power and the national bureaucracy. What is lacking is a political means of employing and directing this national power. The parties have traditionally been organized on a local and geographically dispensed basis. They are not organized to deal with national demands.

Lastly, in a period of modernization the type of political demand changes. Particularistic claims—such as individual's demand for a patronage position—become less dominant. The stress comes to be more on group demands. As group consciousness heightens, ideologies develop, functioning to present a unified explanation of the political world to group members, to increase the solidarity of the group, and to make wide-ranging demands on the polity.[69] The movement to Black unity is probably the clearest contemporary example. From individualistic politics, including corruption and stress on individual mobility, there has been a change to group politics, involving bloc voting, economic boycotts, and mass demonstrations. Accompanying the new emphasis on group action has been the development of ideologies of "Black power." Demands of the group change from particular to universal, from tangible to ideological, and from material to moral.

This form of political modernization is also evident in other groups. A new awareness of identity is evident among other non-white minorities —among students (who, with the 18-year vote, will have considerable political potential); among women; among more conservative groups as Italians, construction workers, and even the steoreotyped elite group of the White Anglo-Saxon Protestants.

Group consciousness often means the escalation of political conflict, because demands are phrased in collective, ideological, moralistic—and therefore non-negotiable—terms. The redefinition of political disputes is now evident in the United States, where conflicts seem to involve very basic values rather than merely opposing interests. The polarization of hawks and doves is not only a question of specific policy in Vietnam; it is a difference over the values of patriotism, anti-communism, and military involvement. The dispute between young and old is not on policy issues, where there is actually relatively little difference of opinion; the conflict, where it exists, is over life styles. The conflict over race is not only, perhaps not primarily, over integrating a suburban school or ending discrimination in construction. It involves issues of the meaning of equality, of the differences between achievement and ascriptive criteria, and of the personal psychological defenses involved in racism.

American parties are not able to handle value conflicts. Indeed, American government itself has been based on an assumption of a value consensus. The parties have been bargaining, brokerage agencies. They can deal well with personal ambitions or with issues which involve tangible and divisible benefits. The pork barrel of public works or the economic haggling between labor and business over a minimum wage

69. See James C. Scott, "Corruption, Machine Politics, and Political Change," *American Political Science Review*, 63 (December, 1969), pp. 1142-58.

law is within their ken. They can manage ethnic clashes when they can be reduced to individualistic terms, such as the allocation of slots on a balanced ticket, or to tangible benefits, such as the distribution of school funds. They have not been capable of dealing with large questions of ultimate values, of universalistic ideologies, and of morality. Their genius has been in generally avoiding such questions, aided by favorable conditions of the American environment. The one period in which they could not avoid such issues culminated in the Civil War.

Value questions cannot be ignored today, but can they be resolved? At the present time the United States critically needs means of defining its national objectives and of mobilizing the social and political power to accomplish these goals. In a phrase, it needs modernized political institutions. "Without strong political institutions, society lacks the means to define and to realize its common interests. The capacity to create political institutions is the capacity to create public interests." [70] The parties might become the vehicle of modernization, the means to redefine values, integrate the nation, establish legitimate authority, and fulfill the demands of new political participants. Yet their capacity for the task is doubtful.

Having viewed our present difficulties, we can now attempt to predict the future directions of American politics.

FUTURE DIRECTIONS

Two distinct possibilities in the development of American parties can be forecast. The first is their continued decay, contributing to the emergence of a "mass society." The alternative is party realignment leading to the development of a new, cohesive majority coalition prepared to cope with the critical issues of American democracy. Definitive evidence is lacking to resolve the question. Hence in this last section we can but speculate on the two possibilities.

The simplest prediction to make is to extrapolate present trends. The long process of party dissolution can easily continue, and confirming evidence can be found in every election. Defection of voters from traditional partisanship, abandonment of past loyalties by party leaders, increasing control of campaign management by technicians, growth of uncontrolled bureaucracies, alienation from the parties—these phenomena are easily documented. It is possible to imagine—even presently to describe—American politics as being nothing more than a contest between

70. Huntington, *Political Order in Changing Societies*, p. 24.

unprincipled personalities, each with manipulated "images," conducting campaigns to win temporary popular fancy without any coherent program or capacity for sustained governmental action. The game of politics then becomes only a game, with no greater social import than the outcome of the Little League World Series.

Yet the decline of parties would have more serious consequences. Parties provide the most vital linkage between the public and its government. They are the critical means by which those of relatively little individual power can combine their efforts to accomplish social goals. The decay and disappearance of parties thus would serve to strengthen the position of those with established economic or social power, while it weakened the position of those who must rely on political resources.

The decay of party linkages could eventually result in the emergence of a "mass society," in which there are no significant intermediate groups between elites, those dominant in the society, and the mass of the population. There are no mediating groups—parties, voluntary associations, regional groupings, and the like—to create relationships and mutual controls between the two groups. In such a society, as analyzed by Kornhauser, the critical characteristic is that elites and mass are accessible to, or open to manipulation by, each other. Elites are influenced not by organized group activity, but by direct action, such as violence and demonstrations. The mass is atomized and unstructured, characterized by "strong feelings of alienation and anxiety, and therefore the disposition to engage in extreme behavior to escape from these tensions. In a mass society there is a heightened readiness to form hyper-attachments to symbols and leaders. . . . Total loyalty is the psychological basis for total domination." [71] In such contexts participation swings between intense emotional involvement for short periods and apathetic resignation for longer periods. Unanchored by a comprehensible group life, opinions change rapidly, through elite manipulation of remote events and symbols.

Some characteristics of mass society are evident in the United States today. Violence is used successfully to gain political ends, such as poverty funds, which are not obtained through voting and lobbying. The tactic indicates both the limitations of traditional methods and the accessibility of elites to direct threats. The decline of intermediate associations is evident in decreased union membership, weakened family structure, and residential mobility. The increased power of the presidency, bureaucracies, and corporations make the mass more accessible for manipulation, and television and opinion research provide the means. Recent politics, particularly the Wallace movement, fits the model of

71. William Kornhauser, *The Politics of Mass Society* (Free Press, 1959), p. 32.

a mass society in many respects: the attraction to a charismatic leader, an ideological focus on remote threats, attacks on established authority, and rapid changes of mood from emotional commitment to bitter resignation.

Stable parties do not exist in mass society, but non-party politics cannot meaningfully solve existing problems, for it does not provide sustained power and support for coherent government action. Elections can become more cleverly managed, but also less meaningful. Sudden voting shifts, increased personality appeals, and the development of pseudo-ideologies are likely. Politics comes to consist of spasmodic, conflictful and unstable episodes. A mass society can deal only with immediate threats and demands. Ghetto rebellions in this situation will result in some minimum palliatives, and in maximum force to soothe aroused fears. Tensions will not be resolved, however, as rebellion and repression reinforce each other. Ultimately force prevails.

A mass society and repressive government is possible in the United States but not, in our view, probable. The symptoms described above do not clearly portend the death of the patient. Public opinion is highly stable on most issues—perhaps, indeed, too stable. Manipulation through the mass media may sell beer, but it does not indisputably sell candidates. Americans are sometimes disturbed by social trends, but are more often intelligently unmoved by contemporary Cassandras.[72] While it is disturbing that Wallace received 13 percent of the vote in 1968, we should remember that he was rejected by 87 percent of the electorate. The expansion of political participation and questioning of political values now occurring is destablizing, but it also constitutes a healthy democratic ferment.

Alternatively, the future may see the development of revived parties after a period of party realignment. Party reorganization is being stimulated by two diverse influences. In the Republican party, centralization and efficient campaign management is being furthered by the demands of technology, financing, and presidential leadership. The Democratic party is changing in a different direction, that of a mass-based organization. Its direction is evidenced by the reforms in party structure and convention selection fostered by the McGovern commission; by reliance on small financial contributors, alliances with labor unions and "cause" groups; and by expanded use of volunteer campaigners.[73] Although quite different in their directions, both parties are responding to the demands of modernization, the Republicans evidencing the national-

72. See V. O. Key, Jr., *Public Opinion and American Democracy*, (Knopf, 1961), esp. chap. 10.
73. See John S. Saloma, "Developments in American Party Structure," a paper presented to the 1970 meeting of the American Political Science Association.

izing influences, the Democrats responding to demands for increased participation.

Changes are evident in the party organization of Congress as well. Control of the institution has passed from the small oligarchical group of seniority leaders that once constituted the Establishment. Reforms in congressional procedures have been enacted into law, and both Republican and Democratic groups have instituted important modifications of the seniority tradition to make chairmen responsive to their party. Moreover, a majority in both parties, including majorities of incumbents, now favor changes in this procedure.[74]

There has also been increased policy consensus within the parties. Party leaders have been distinct in their views for some time, and have fulfilled many of the conditions necessary for a "responsible party system." [75] As we have seen, in recent years there has been a marked increase in the policy consciousness of voters and an increasing correspondence between party loyalties and policy position. Much of the movement between the parties is not simply decay, but a more coherent sorting of leaders and followers. As liberals such as John Lindsay leave the Republican party, and conservatives such as Strom Thurmond enter, the parties become more ideologically coherent. With increased coherence they may become able to contend with the value questions raised with modernization.

Lastly, new voting coalitions may be in the offing. As evidence accumulates of the dissolution of the old loyalties, many scan the horizon for the shape of the new alignment. Republicans see an emerging but "silent majority" combining Whites of the South, working class, and suburbanites, along with traditional business support.[76] Democrats hope for an alliance built on economic issues which unites Blacks, workers and the middle class.[77] The most thoughtful analysis is that of Burnham, who sees the possibility of "a top-bottom alliance against the 'great middle'," of polarization of "black against white, peripheral regions against the center, 'parochials' against 'cosmopolitans,' blue-collar whites against both blacks and affluent liberals, the American 'great middle,' with its strong attachment to the values of the traditional American political

74. *Congressional Quarterly Weekly Report*, 28 (October 16, 1970), 2569. See essay on Congress, pp. 00-00.

75. See Herbert McClosky, et. al., "Issue Conflict and Consensus Among Party Leaders and Followers," *American Political Science Review*, 54 (June, 1960), pp. 406-427; James L. Sundquist, *Politics and Policy: The Eisenhower, Kennedy and Johnson Years* (The Brookings Institution, 1968).

76. Kevin Phillips, *The Emerging Republican Majority* (Arlington, 1969).

77. Richard Scammon and Ben Wattenberg, *The Real Majority* (Coward McMann, 1970).

formula, against urban cosmopolitans, intellectuals, and students who have largely left that old credo behind." [78]

We cannot be certain which of these coalitions will eventually come to domniate American politics. Instead, no majority coalition may appear. The trends to political independence and partisan decay may continue, and a mass society may eventuate. If we are to meet the nation's accumulated problems, however, we need a reconstructed party system to mobilize popular support for vigorous and sustained governmental action. There are signs of party development, but they are not yet convincing. Effective action will come from the deliberate activity of sensitive and knowledgeable citizens. A political revival is necessary, but it must be gained through deeds, not faith. As Herbert Muller observed in viewing the ruins of another civilization, the Byzantine empire: "Our only possible hope lies not in prayer but in more thought and in more earnest, responsible endeavor. The plainest lesson I get from the history of St. Sophia is that men cannot count on miracles." [79]

78. Burnham, *Critical Elections,* pp. 165, 169. In chaps. 5 and 6 of his book, Burnham deals with the ideas of this last section in a far more thorough and insightful manner than I have been able to do.

79. Herbert J. Muller, *The Uses of the Past* (Mentor, 1952), p. 32.

THE PARTY INSTITUTION

Although unmentioned in the Constitution, political parties in fact constitute one of the major institutions of American political life. The behavior of voters and politicians exhibits a predictable regularity that is characteristic of members of any institution. This section presents basic factual information on the party institution under three headings: the partisan government, party environment, and electoral behavior.

THE ENVIRONMENT

The parties have been shaped by two critical environmental factors, their history and legal institutions. We shall consider each briefly, although fuller accounts are available elsewhere.[1]

Party Development

American party history has consisted of a succession of two-party systems, each of them ending with a period of party realignment and the stabilization of a new order. The dominant party consistently sets the tone of each period, while the other party is available as a focus of discontent. After a time these discontents accumulate to promote change.

The first party system emerged soon after the adoption of the Constitution. While party lines were not evident in the first election of George Washington as president, John Adams as vice-president, and the new Congress, they were discernable by 1792, when a contest over the

1. The best general histories of American parties are Wilfred Binkley, *American Political Parties*, 4th ed. (Knopf, 1962) and Eugene Roseboom, *A History of Presidential Elections* (Macmillan, 1959). Two of the best textbooks are V. O. Key, Jr., *Politics, Parties and Pressure Groups*, 5th ed. (Crowell, 1964) and Frank Sorauf, *Party Politics in America* (Little, Brown, 1968).

vice-presidency developed between Adams and George Clinton, the caucus candidates of the developing Federalist and Republican factions. Conflict centered around such issues as Alexander Hamilton's program of nationalistic economic development, the power of the federal government, and the Napoleonic wars in Europe.

The party system was fully established by 1800, when Jefferson was elected president. Party discipline in the electoral college was so strong that Jefferson and his intended running-mate Aaron Burr received identical electoral votes, and the final choice was made by the House of Representatives. For a time the Federalists offered competition to the Republicans, but continued defeats and the attempt at secession by some Federalist leaders in New England brought about the death of the party. The Republicans had meanwhile forged a unified party, characterized by presidential leadership, party voting in Congress, and the choice of presidential nominees in the congressional caucus. By 1820 James Monroe was re-elected president without opposition.

One-party politics is inherently unstable in a free society, however, and the Republicans quickly began dividing. The confused election of 1824 was followed by the clear choice of 1828, when Andrew Jackson was elected as the candidate of the coalition of Democratic Republicans, based principally in the West and South. Jackson's election came at the time of the expansion of political democracy and economic opportunity in the nation. Property qualifications for the vote were virtually eliminated, the spoils system of patronage was legitimized, and the number of elected offices was rapidly expanded. Democratization and institutionalization of the parties followed, with the establishment of national conventions and national committees. Those opposed to Jackson's policies of low tariffs, easy money, and Western development consolidated in the Whig party, under the leadership and occasional presidential candidacy of Henry Clay.

This second party system continued until the Civil War. It was closely competitive, with both parties organized in all sections, alternating in office, and winning elections by bare margins. Because each party was a truly national amalgam of different sections, however, they were particularly prone to disturbance by sectional issues. Slavery was a fundamental issue involving economic, sectional, and moral differences which could not be accommodated by the system.

The North and South became increasingly different in their economies, their values, and eventually their party politics. The decline of this second party system was evidenced by the development of third parties. By 1854 the Whig party could no longer hold together. It was quickly replaced by the Republican party, which arose as a strictly sectional party opposed to the expansion of slavery into the western territories.

By 1860 the Democrats, too, could not contain the division of the nation, splitting into separate southern and northern factions. And the war came.

The aftermath of the Civil War brought the third party system into being. The Republicans first were able to capture national control through the combination of Northern votes and Southern Reconstructionist governments. After the passing of Southern states under White Redeemer control, a close balance was established at the national level, with Republican votes based on memories of the war, business support and homesteaders, balanced by Democratic votes from the South, emerging urban political machines, and traditional areas of support. After Reconstruction no party was able to win a convincing presidential majority, and control of Congress shifted frequently.

The close party balance ended as the nineteenth century waned. Major social economic changes were occurring at this time, including the closing of the frontier, the rise of corporate capitalism, and the overseas expansion of the nation. Political change was indicated by the advent of new parties, such as the Populists. An economic crisis, the depression of 1893, precipitated a new party alignment. In the presidential election of 1896 massive shifts of voters occurred, to the net advantage of the Republican candidate, William McKinley. The Republican party was changed and strengthened. Its sectional strength derived from the Civil War was broadened into a national coalition of farmers, laborers, and business. After this election competition and popular participation rapidly declined, leading to the establishment of one-party Republican dominance in the North and West, and one-party Democratic dominance in the South. This fourth party system, dominated by the Republicans, lasted until the upheavals of the Depression and New Deal. These events brought the fifth party system, which we will discuss more fully below.[2]

The Legal Environment

Legal factors also constitute part of the environment of the parties. The existence and persistence of only two major parties has resulted from historical and cultural factors, but the two-party mold has also been strengthened by laws. Access to the ballot has been generally restricted to parties which have received a prescribed minimum of votes in previous elections, whereas new groups have been required to submit petitions signed by large numbers of voters—nearly half a million in the case of Ohio. The effect of these requirements has been to place the major parties on the ballot automatically, while raising barriers to new factions. The barriers could be overcome, however, as demonstrated by

2. For fuller analyses of the significance of these changes, see William N. Chambers and Walter D. Burnham, *The American Party Systems* (Oxford University Press, 1967).

George Wallace's ability to win a place on the ballot of all fifty states in 1968. In the course of his campaign Wallace also successfully challenged restrictive laws. Winning the aid of the Supreme Court he had often attacked, Wallace saw the Ohio law declared unconstitutional. In the process access to the ballot has been eased considerably.

The electoral system, however, still favors a two-party pattern. The important offices in America are single executives, such as governors—not multiple executives, such as cabinets. Power cannot be shared among coalitions. Moreover, almost all major contests in the United States are decided on the basis of a plurality, or "first-past-the post" method. This means that the candidate with the most votes, even if less than a numerical majority, wins the office contested. There is no procedure for a second, run-off election, for the shifting of votes between candidates once cast, or for proportional representation. The effect of such a system is to consolidate factions into only two opposing parties to avoid dividing their strength and thereby electing a common enemy. The necessity of union has been clearly demonstrated in recent years in New York. In 1969 John V. Lindsay was re-elected as mayor only because the opposition divided its votes between two candidates. The following year James Buckley was elected senator only because liberals divided their votes between the regular Democratic and Republican nominees—both liberals.

The choice of a president is not decided by direct popular election, but through the electoral college, where a successful candidate must win an absolute majority of the 538 votes. By state law and practice, but not by constiutional requirement, each state (except Maine in 1972) casts all of its votes for the candidate who receives a plurality of the popular votes among its voters. This "winner-take-all" system promotes a two-party system within each state. The necessity to win a national majority promotes unity among state parties.

The legal framework also defines the membership and organization of parties. Entrance to the primary election at which nominees and party officials are chosen is governed by state law, not by the parties themselves. Voters become legally recognized as Republicans or Democrats simply by declaring their affiliation. No test of loyalty is demanded and no organizational commitment is required. Financial contributions are not obligatory, and most voters do not in fact contribute to "their" political faction. Given a secret election ballot, moreover, there is no assurance that self-identified partisans even support the party's candidates.

The easy entrance of voters to the parties is demonstrated in the nominating process. Professional politicians do not control the selection of the party leaders and candidates. These decisions are made in primaries potentially open to all who choose to participate. Most states use the "closed primary" system, restricted to those who have indicated their party preference at some time before they enter the voting booth. The time at which this preference must be indicated varies considerably, however. In some cases, no choice must be made until the voter appears at the polls, and the primary is "closed" only in the most nominal way. In other cases the restriction is more meaningful. In New Jersey, for example, those wishing to change parties must wait for two years. In six states the primary is formally "open" to all. Each elector receives lists of both parties' aspirants and can choose either. In Washington and Alaska's "blanket primary," the voter can play hopscotch, selecting candidates of different parties for different offices. Under such conditions party membership is unlikely to be stable. Ideological or organizational coherence among the members is largely fortuitous.

A third area in which legal constraints are important is that of finance.[3] "Money is the mother's milk of politics," but the laws provide sparse nutrition. In a national election total spending is probably close to $300 million, but there is no statutory encouragement to fund-raising, no meaningful controls over spending, and no accurate reporting of the funds spent. The results are that parties must devote considerable effort to raising funds, that candidates of moderate means are excluded or handicapped, and that large contributors to the parties are potentially able to exercise disproportionate influence in politics. That money alone does not win elections was repeatedly demonstrated by Franklin Roosevelt's victories over better-financed candidates. That money is important is demonstrated by the increasing tendency for party nominations to be sought and elections won by those with independent sources of wealth, such as Governors Nelson Rockefeller of New York and Milton Schapp of Pennsylvania.

The importance of laws with regard to financing campaigns is largely that of negative influence. Neither the states nor the federal government provide any financial support of candidates, except for minor aids such as Oregon's voter pamphlet, distributed at state expense to the electorate, in which candidates can present their platforms. Repeated suggestions for government subsidy of the parties, or for allowing contributions to be tax-deductible, have been just as repeatedly defeated. The federal government could aid candidates indirectly through its regulation of television. Suspension or abolition of "equal-time" provisions of the law would permit free debates between major-party candidates without the intrusion of a host of miniscule parties such as Vegetarians and Socialist Workers. The government could also require television networks to provide free or inexpensive time to candidates. Except in 1960, however,

3. For fuller analyses, see Alexander Heard, *The Costs of Democracy* (Doubleday, 1962) and the extensive publications of the Citizens' Research Foundation.

these proposals have been defeated as a result of partisan presidential maneuvering. President Johnson in 1964 opposed debates in a race in which he was clearly in the lead. President Nixon vetoed a bill to restrict spending to 7¢ a voter, because it would eliminate the huge financial advantage now held by the Republicans.

In the absence of such federal assistance, candidates must seek funds where they can. In both parties there is a heavy reliance on large contributors, those providing $500 or more. Many of these donors are officials of companies doing defense and aero-space business with the federal government, who contributed a reported one and one-quarter million dollars in 1968. Although the Democrats were in office that year, Republicans received six times as much money as the incumbents.[4] Other sources of money include party dinners, direct-mail campaigns, particularly in the Republican party, and labor unions and "cause" groups, particularly among Democrats.

The laws also provide no inviolate restrictions over the amounts raised or spent. Federal laws ostensibly control finances, by limiting the amount a candidate can spend on his own behalf, ($25,000 for the Senate, $5,000 for the House), restricting individual contributions to a political committee to $5,000, holding expenditures by any national committee to $3 million, and prohibiting contributions and expenditures by corporations and unions. Similar state laws are widespread, but none of these statutes has any practical effect. The limitations on candidates are evaded by contributions by his family. Restrictions on individual contributions are rendered meaningless by gifts to many committees supporting the same candidate, such as Doctors or Chiropractors or Osteopaths for one or the other candidate. Overall spending limits are overcome by the same practice of proliferating committees. Business contributions are still made, but in the name of the corporation's executives (who may subsequently be given an equivalent "bonus"). Union spending is concentrated on "non-partisan" activities such as registration and "educational" campaigns, while direct contributions are made through a separate Committee on Political Education.

The effect of the finance laws is to disperse fund-raising and spending, but not to limit it. Given this dispersal, reporting cannot be accurate. Moreover, reporting requirements often do not cover such vitally important activities as primary campaigns, convention electioneering costs, or the activities of non-party or intra-state groups. Statutes governing political finance neither prevent corruption nor assure equality between the parties. Rather, they make corruption more difficult to discover and leave the parties more open to the pressures of the economic market.

4. *New York Times*, September 20, 1970, p. 52.

Politically the principal result of these laws is to decentralize power within the parties and to limit their ability to respond to a large electorate of limited means.

PARTY ORGANIZATION

Formal party organization is regulated in detail by state laws, but is virtually unnoticed by federal statutes. Alongside, and often in reaction to, the formal regulations, there are many informal practices.

Formal and Informal Structure

In outward structure the major American parties are highly democratic organizations, responsible to the rank-and-file members. The base of the party structure is the voting district, often called the precinct, consisting of between five hundred and a thousand voters in most instances. Typically those voters who have declared their membership in a party elect in an annual primary a committeeman and committeewoman to represent the district within the party. These committeemen are envisaged by the law as the grass-roots representatives of the voters. They are often charged with responsibility for filling higher party office. For example, all of the committeemen in a city ward may convene to select the ward chairman, as all of the committeemen in a county together select the county chairman. They often act formally or informally to designate party candidates for public office, and to fill vacancies on the party ticket. In legendary accounts of the efficient party machine, these committeemen also serve as precinct captains, charged with getting out the vote, registering new voters, and acting as a grievance and patronage center for the neighborhood.

The contemporary fact, however, is that these grass roots have withered. Many committee positions are simply vacant. To fill them often requires an effort by higher party officials to recruit persons willing to do little more than have their names on the ballot. Competition for the positions, is rare, so voters do not have much choice or control. Voters themselves do not take much of an interest in these elections, which are often won with as few as fifty ballots gathered from relatives and friends. Apathy and inactivity are far more common than machine efficiency.

The position of committeeman is not widely attractive because it carries little direct power. No nominations for public office and no policy decisions are made at the precinct level. Influence within the party can come only in concert with other precinct committeemen, but the great number of these positions (as many as three thousand in one county in New York) makes a coordinated drive difficult. There are also relatively few direct incentives for activity at the precinct level. Only in the most well-organized parties, such as Mayor Daley's in Chicago, can precinct leaders expect patronage rewards. For most persons material gains will come from politics only if they move up the hierarchy. If they remain as precinct leaders, they must be satisfied with limited recognition, a modicum of influence over party decisions, and, probably most important, the excitement of engagement in the political struggle.

The effect of this dispersed party structure is to make the party easily penetrable by those who are willing to seek the lowly precinct positions. Reform movements, such as the amateur Democrats of New York and California, or ideological groups, such as the Goldwater and McCarthy factions, have found it relatively simple to enter the party. But after winning initial battles they find it more difficult to win the war. The fact of the large number of precincts requires a continuing series of small victories, which must be repeated every year or two. To win the important strongholds, such as the control of a county or an entire state, requires widespread and continuing effort to gain the allegiance of voters who, not unreasonably, are largely uninformed and disinterested in the complexities of election law.

In practice, power within the power is most likely to be held by the county chairman. Formally chosen by the county committeemen, he is more likely to recruit and select these functionaries than to be controlled by them. While the chairman does not control the party, he does have resources which enable him to exercise influence. In some cases he may be able to devote full-time to the position or, more normally, to combine his politics with a closely related occupation, such as law, real estate, or construction. The county, moreover, is an active political unit in most states, with its government machinery entailing jobs, nominations, legal favors, and public expenditures, and with greater significance for its policies.

Direction of state parties varies. The members of the state committee sometimes are elected by the voters directly, or may comprise the county chairmen, and sometimes are chosen by state conventions comprised of directly elected delegates. The state committee in turn selects its chairman. The state chairman has few substantial powers unless he is supported by a governor of his party. In most cases he must rely for support on shifting and uncertain coalitions of local leaders, particularly county chairmen.

The national committee of each party, formally the apex of the party structure, has been more aptly termed the locus of "politics without power." Consisting of two or three persons from each state, the national committee nominally directs the party between conventions; but its members are actually selected variously by the delegates from each state, a state convention, the state committee, or the voters in the primary. It chooses its own chairman, normally following the preference of the party's presidential candidate. The committee's duties are primarily administrative, and its effective power is limited to organizing the next convention, generating publicity, and providing service to the state and local organizations. Nominations of public officials are regulated by state law. Policy-making is in the hands of congressional leaders and the president, candidates, and the writers of convention platforms. No important patronage is held by the national committee, which must depend, even for its budget, largely on contributions from state parties, although both parties are now developing individual low-cost memberships.

The party structure by no means constitutes a military chain of command. Its coherence is dependent not on hierarchy but on the common interests of the various elements of the party, particularly the basic interest in winning elections. Ideology, personality, and the shared experience of political combat provide intangible ties, supplemented by the occasional material links of patronage, contracts, and office. Another means of cohesion is supplied by the overlapping of offices. In some cases the same individual may occupy different positions, providing a personal unification. Carmine DeSapio, probably the last strong leader of New York's Tammany Hall, provides a good example. DeSapio was a precinct commiteeman from a small Italian neighborhood in Greenwich Village. His fellow precinct committeemen selected him as ward chairman, and a majority of the ward chairmen in Manhattan chose him as county leader. Under a Democratic governor of New York, he became secretary of state and *de facto* leader of the state party, and was later named the national committeeman for the state as well. Gradually he lost all of these positions, but he was not finally retired from politics until he lost an election among his neighbors for precinct committeeman. The accumulation of county, state, and national party power ultimately depended on opinion in the espresso cafes and small groceries of a few city blocks.

The openness, fluidity—perhaps shapelessness—of American parties is further demonstrated in the ease of entrance. There are no formal rites of initiation or tests of acceptability. Candidates commonly earn the Democratic or Republican label simply by winning the nomination of the party in a primary election. In some cases this freedom is slightly restricted by legal requirements that a party candidate must be a registered member or certify his loyalty, but these are hardly onerous limitations.

In recent years there have been slight movements to establish meaningful standards of party loyalty within the organizations. Since 1952 the Democrats have required of national convention delegates a pledge that they will support the presidential candidate of the convention, and will seek to have that candidate placed on their state ballots under the Democratic label. Disloyalty to the national ticket was punished in particularly outrageous cases by denying congressional seniority to two Southern "Democrats" who supported Barry Goldwater for President in 1964 and one who supported Wallace in 1968. A stricter adherence to party philosophy has also been demanded in the Republican party of late. In 1970 Vice-President Spiro Agnew successfully opposed the re-election bid of New York's incumbent Republican Senator, Charles Goodell, characterizing him as one who "consistently opposes a president of his own party [and] who makes public opposition to all his party stands for a major article of his political faith." In the same year other liberal Republican candidates were reported to be receiving very limited financial aid from national Republican fund-raising groups. The official attitude toward partisan loyalty remains, however, that of the party's former national chairman, Rogers Morton. Commenting on Senator Goodell's party orthodoxy, he declared, "If he's a Republican in New York, he's a Republican with me." [5]

Party organizations can no longer control the selection of their candidates, for nominations through primaries are now virtually universal in the United States. Two of the last holdouts were New York and Connecticut, which previously provided for nominations by state conventions or committees. In 1970, for the first time, primaries were held in both states, and some of the convention's choices were overruled by the voters. In other states the organization has been more successful in turning back challenges. The party choice may receive a preferred place on the ballot, be identified as the endorsed aspirant, or receive the benefit of party funds and manpower.

National Conventions

Presidential and vice-presidential nominations remain formally in the hands of the parties, in the persons of delegates to the national conventions held every four years. Since the initiation of conventions in 1831, they have become highly-structured institutions, with formal rules, elaborate ceremonies, and major tasks—selection of national candidates, construction of the party platform, and general government of the federal party.

Delegates to the conventions are chosen by one of two principal methods. In upwards of twenty states (the exact number is changing as

5. *New York Times*, October 1, 1970, p. 1.

the 1972 presidential campaign begins), the voters choose delegates in direct primaries. In most of these cases the voters can also affect he presidential nomination at the same time, by choosing delegates with announced candidate preferences, or by separately indicating a presidential choice which is binding on the elected delegates. In the remaining states the delegates to the national conventions are chosen through party processes, which vary considerably in their responsiveness to the rank-and-file. National convention delegates may be chosen directly by a state committee, in which case there is no direct input by the voters. The more common pattern is for voters to choose local delegates, through informal meetings or elections, who then proceed to conventions at higher levels, such as the county, congressional district, and state. Delegates to the national convention are then chosen at these higher levels. They may be bound in their presidential preference by action of these party meetings, or by a separate state-wide vote of the party electorate.

The number of delegates from each state is decided by the national committees and is based primarily on the state's population, as reflected in congressional representation, and on the party vote. In the Republican party distribution by population is modified by additional delegates alloted to those states giving most support to its candidates. In the 1972 Democratic convention, approximately equal weight will be given to population and the states' presidential vote in the last three elections.

Important proposals for reform of convention procedures have been instituted in the Democratic party. Responding to the extreme divisiveness of the 1968 convention in Chicago, two reform groups were established by direction of the convention itself and further action of the national committee. A large number of reforms have been urged by these groups, the Commission on Party Structure and Delegate Selection, chaired by Senator George McGovern, and the Commission on Rules, chaired by Congressman James O'Hara.

The recommendations of the McGovern Commission are designed to increase popular participation in the party. It prohibited delegate selection before the calendar year of the convention, selection of more than a tenth of the delegation by committee systems, unit rules, fees above ten dollars, proxy votes, and secret caucuses. It also called for apportionment of delegates on the basis of a combination of party strength and population, the adoption of publicized rules of procedure in all state parties, and reasonably proportionate representation of young people, racial minorities, and women in every delegation. The O'Hara group devised a new system of delegate apportionment, made committee representation more equitable, and established standards to insure procedural fairness. Ultimate enforcement of these standards will be the responsibility of the 1972 convention, but a considerable amount of change has already occurred in most states, and the new standards have already been adopted by the national committee, indicating that the next Democratic conclave will be a more open and representative body.[6]

Through these varied procedures, the Democrats ultimately select over three thousand delegates (some with only half a vote), and the Republicans approximately fifteen hundred. Groups of this size are suitable as campaign rallies, but cannot act as deliberative bodies. Important decisions on credentials, platform, and party government are therefore referred to committees. On most occasions the general desire for party unity and presidential victory results in compromises agreeable to all, but divisive issues can be brought to the convention floor for the ultimate test of strength. In the Democratic convention of 1968, for example, these tests brought the adoption of new party rules, the replacement of the segregated Mississippi delegation by an integrated group, and the adoption of a platform on Vietnam largely supporting the policies of President Johnson.

Selection of a presidential candidate also involves negotiation—in this case between candidate factions, state blocs, interests groups, and prominent individuals. In the past this decision meant involved bargaining, prolonged balloting, and compromise selections. The typical victor was the governor of a large state, who controlled large numbers of delegates and who was not conspicuously identified with any contentious national policies. In recent decades the pattern has changed radically. Presidential candidates now win their nominations by bringing external pressure to bear on the convention, through their victories in primary contests, their standing in public opinion polls, and their prominence in the mass media. Decisions are typically foreclosed before the convention meets, or are rapidly decided. No convention since 1952 has required more than one nominating ballot, and only four since 1928 have gone beyond the minimum. Proposals to increase popular control of the process, such as those of the McGovern Commission, are likely to speed this conversion. After the nomination of the presidential candidate, the choice of a running mate is decided by the nominee in consultation with other party leaders and then ratified by the entire convention. Even widely unpopular choices, such as that of Spiro Agnew, will be accepted by almost all factions in the party.

6. See Democratic National Committee, Commission on Party Structure and Delegate Selection, *Mandate for Reform* (1970); Eli Segal, "Delegate Selection Standards: The Democratic Party's Experience," *George Washington Law Review,* 38 (July, 1970), pp. 873-891; and *Congressional Quarterly Weekly Report,* 29 (February 26, 1971), p. 449.

ELECTORAL BEHAVIOR

Votes are probably the most important acts affecting political parties. In understanding voting it is useful to conceive of the electoral process as a funnel. Various influences flow through the funnel, the result at the narrow bottom being the vote itself. The height of the funnel is measured, in this analogy, not lineally in inches, but temporally, in weeks, years, and generations.

Party Loyalty

Some of the influences on a given election, such as the presidential contest of 1972, originate even before the birth of contemporary voters. Vital historical events have affected the perceptions and loyalties of the population. These sentiments have resulted in attachment to a party, its leaders and programs, and in the transmission of these loyalties from one generation to the next.

Two events in American history have clearly had this massive impact —the Civil War and the Great Depression that began in 1929. The Civil War was probably the most traumatic event of American history. Its immediate effects—the death of six hundred thousand persons, the emancipation of the slaves, and the immense growth in national governmental power—were great in themselves. Yet the long-term effects continue to be operative more than a century later. The Republican party, created only six years before the War, was transformed from a minority to the majority party. Until the Depression it won all but four of eighteen Presidential elections, and was never decisively defeated. The residue of these century-old loyalties is still evident, although it is finally being eroded. The traditional Republicanism of upper New England, of small towns and farm areas, and of the Plains states stems symbolically from the loyalties created at Gettysburg, just as the traditional support of the Democrats in the White South stems from Sherman's burning of Atlanta. While the United States quadrupled in population from 1860 to 1930, Republican dominance was maintained by the transmission of party allegiance from generation to generation.

The party's hegemony was ended by the Depression. Population trends were already undermining the G.O.P. position, particularly the growth of urban, immigrant, and Catholic groups. What the economic and social dislocations of 1929 did was to bring more rapid and more complete change. With over one-fourth of the labor force out of work, traditional loyalties were overthrown. The industrial states, the working classes of these states, and Negroes abandoned their past ties to the Republicans and became predominantly Democratic. The conflict between the parties was restructured from one based on sections to one based primarily on economic class. The urban vote shifted to the Democrats, as seen in Table 2.1 above, so much so as to become a mainstay of the new party coalition.

Class voting persisted through the New Deal period. By 1940 the hightide of the Democrats had receded, but the defections revealed even more clearly the class character of their coalition. In 1940, for example, the Democrats lost 35 percent of the business and professional voters who had supported Franklin Roosevelt in 1936. Only 15 percent of unskilled workers deserted the party. As new voters entered politics, they reinforced the pattern. A minority of new business and professional voters voted Democratic in the elections from 1940 to 1948, in contrast to 59 percent to 75 percent of the new working class voters.[7] Our politics today still broadly reflects the alignments and issues derived from the era of the Depression and New Deal, although the old issues are losing their potency with new voters.

Historical events are linked to the ultimate voting act through the identification of the citizen with a particular party. As the Civil War made a great majority of our voters Republican, the Depression made many of their descendants Democrats. Once established, party loyalty has great persistence, both within generations and across generations. Few voters change their party loyalty during their lifetime, even though they may vote for the opposition on occasion. Fewer than a fifth of today's voters report that their party loyalty was different at some time in the past.

In any given election, over 80 percent will vote for the same party as in most recent contest. Over the course of an entire lifetime, moreover, about half of the voters have never voted for the opposition candidate for president. The depth of party loyalty is also evident in straight-ticket voting. While the number of voters who will vote for men of different parties for different offices is increasing, it is still characteristic of only a minority of the electorate. Because of the great stability of individual party identifications, the distribution of party loyalties across the entire population is also stable. As Table 2.2 showed, the proportion of Democrats, Independents and Republicans changed only marginally until recent years.

The persistence and transmission of party loyalty are often considered evidences of the lack of discrimination of the electorate. Americans tend to be ashamed to admit their partisanship, claiming that they "vote for the man, not the party"—even when their "man" curiously comes always from the same party. In some cases, to be sure, loyalty is based on

7. V. O. Key, *The Responsible Electorate* (Harvard University Press, 1966), pp. 37-39.

nothing more than tradition and habit. In many more cases, however, there are discernable reasons in the social characteristics and policy preferences of the voter for his political preference. Party identification is closely—although not perfectly—related to these characteristics. It is grounded in a social reality, not only in inheritance and traditional prejudice.

The connection between these characteristics and party loyalty is the basic reason for the high transmission of party loyalty across generations. Most children occupy a social status similar to that of their parents. They derive their ideas and opinions—about politics as well as other matters—in considerable part from their families. Coming from the same root stock, being similar in basic social and psychological ways, it is not surprising that they are similar in the party preference which is derived from these characteristics. Significantly, children who are different from their parents psychologically and socially are also more likely to convert politically.[8]

Voters and Issues

Further along the temporal funnel, in the present generation party loyalties are related to the political opinions of the voter. These opinions have been classified by the Survey Research Center into four categories. A small percentage of the voters was found in 1956 to evaluate the parties in terms of their presumed ideological positions, such as liberalism and conservatism. The largest percentage assessed the Democrats and Republicans on the basis of the group interests which the parties were regarded as supporting or opposing. Democrats were liked by these respondents, for example, because they were seen as being pro-labor, while Republicans might be credited with friendship for farmers. Another large group judged the parties by "the nature of the times," tending to praise the incumbents, whatever their label, in a period of peace and prosperity, and to blame them during times of conflict and recession. Only a relatively small proportion viewed the parties completely without any issue-content. The full distribution of responses is presented in Table 2.5.

There is some evidence of an increase in the ideological awareness of the electorate. One study of the 1964 campaign, in which Republican candidate Barry Goldwater made a conscious ideological appeal, finds that a third of the voters could now be classified in this first category. The increase is shown in Table 2.6. Loyalty to parties is now related to particular policy positions as well.

Party loyalty is related also to the social characteristics of the voter. The pattern of Democratic and Republican support is not identical, but

8. Arthur J. Goldberg, "Social Determinism and Rationality as Bases of Party Identification," *American Political Science Review*, 63 (March, 1969), pp. 5-26.

Table 2.5. Levels of Conceptualization of 1956 Voters

Level	Proportion of Total Sample	Proportion of Voters
A. Ideology		
I. Ideology	9½%	3½%
II. Near-Ideology	9	12
B. Group Benefits		
I. Perception of Conflict	14	16
Single-Group Interest	17	18
II. Shallow Group Benefit Responses	11	11
C. Nature of the Times	24	23
D. No Issue Content		
I. Party Orientation	4	3½
II. Candidate Orientation	9	7
III. No Content	5	3
IV. Unclassified	4½	4
	100 %	100 %

Source: The American Voter, p. 249.

varies by region, race, class, age, education and residence. Details of these patterns are provided in Table 2.2 above. Because of historical circumstances and voter perceptions of the parties' position, along with the

Table 2.6. Ideological Awareness in 1956 and 1964

Conceptual Level	Strong Democrat	Weak Democrat	Independent	Weak Republican	Strong Republican
1956					
Ideologue	10%	9%	13%	16%	19%
Group Interest	65	50	38	31	29
Nature of Times	16	20	24	28	39
No Issue Content	9	21	25	25	21
Total	100%	100%	100%	100%	100%
N	(363)	(401)	(412)	(247)	(261)
1964					
Ideologue	22%	19%	28%	35%	41%
Group Interest	42	33	21	13	10
Nature of Times	20	20	22	20	16
No Issue Content	16	18	30	33	32
Total	100%	100%	101%	100%	100%
N	(417)	(384)	(353)	(209)	(201)

Source: John C. Pierce, "Party Identification and the Changing Role of Ideology in American Politics," Midwest Journal of Political Science, 14 (February, 1970), p. 35.

reinforcement of tradition and political inheritance, we find that a Democrat is more likely than a Republican to be working class, young, urban, a high-school graduate, Catholic or Jewish, and Black. As the previous discussion and table also indicate, these patterns are being modified.

Votes are also affected by short-term factors. Voters do desert the party, sometimes permanently in a switch in affiliations, but more often temporarily for a given election. While partisanship constitutes a "standing decision" in a favor of one camp, this decision can be changed by attractive individual candidates or the impact of particular issues. Thus nearly a fourth of self-identified Democrats deserted their party to vote for Dwight Eisenhower in 1952 and 1956, while about a fifth of Republicans left the G.O.P. temporarily in 1964, when it nominated Goldwater.

Voters also respond to particular issues. An analysis of the 1968 election by Richard Boyd shows a marked deviation from the "expected" or traditional Democratic vote among those discontented with policy on Vietnam, urban unrest, and the performance of President Johnson in office. The Democratic vote was down a slight 8 percent from expectations among those who took a "dove" position on Vietnam, but was 25 percent below the normal level among "hawks." It was only 3 percent short among those who viewed the solution to urban unrest as lying in correcting problems of poverty and unemployment, while it was 30 percent below expectations among those who emphasized the use of force. Among those who considered that Johnson had done a good job, the actual Democratic vote was almost identical to that predictable on the basis of party identification. Among those who judged he had done a poor job, the vote was 34 percentage points below expectations.[9] Voters clearly did not simply follow party tradition. They were considerably influenced by the issues of the time.

The funnel of electoral causation narrows as we approach the individual campaign. Not many votes are actually decided by the events of particular contests. The historical heritage of decades, or the impact of a four-year administration, cannot be overcome by party maneuvering over a few months. The vast majority of voters, typically between two-thirds and three-fourths, acknowledge that they make their electoral decisions no later than the time candidates are nominated. For many of those remaining, the campaign's purpose is only to reinforce or activate their existing partisan loyalty. It is relatively uncommon for voters to be converted

9. Richard Boyd, "Popular Control of Public Policy: A Normal Vote Analysis of the 1968 Election," forthcoming, Figures 3, 4 and 9. I have combined the percentages given in this manuscript for the two categories at the extreme of each scale employed.

through campaign propagandizing, or for the outcome of the election itself to be changed. In over half a century, probably only in 1948 and 1960 did the campaign change the outcome from what would have occurred if the balloting had been held in August rather than November. The 1968 campaign almost represented a third case, but its most remarkable feature may have been the stability of Nixon's support, which held at about 43 percent from convention polls through the official balloting.

If the effect of campaigns is marginal, they are still important, for most elections are won by rather small margins, and even a 5 percent shift can change the result. Campaigns affect the turnout, by arousing or or deadening the interest of voters. They define the issues, making some of the voters' multiple social characteristics and varied opinions more salient than others. They provide a test of the candidates' individual abilities, and an opportunity for them to win votes on the basis of their personal attractiveness. It is possible to "snatch defeat from the jaws of victory," as the Republicans did in 1948, and to win by coming from behind, as John F. Kennedy did in 1960. The techniques of victory, however, are not well-understood.[10]

The Voting Act

The end of the causal chain is the voting act itself. Election day turnout is likely to be crucial in party contests.[11] Voting participation is affected by a number of factors, which can be grouped as social and psychological, political, and legal. The available literature on the subject indicates complex relationships among these factors, which we will not attempt to explicate. Socially, voting is more frequent among the more educated, those of middle-age rather than the very young or elderly, among middle-class occupations, Whites, men, and urban residents. It is more common among those in voluntary associations, and those with access to political information through social groups or the mass media. Psychologically, voting tends to increase among those who are personally more secure and those free from cross-pressures in different partisan directions.

Political factors and perceptions are also important. Participation

10. See Karl Lamb and Paul Smith, *Campaign Decision-Making* (Wadsworth, 1968).

11. The more important works on this subject include: Lester Milbraith, *Political Participation* (Rand-McNally, 1965); Robert Lane, *Political Life* (Free Press, 1959); Seymour Lipset, *Political Man* (Doubleday, 1960), chap. 6; *The American Voter*, chaps. 5, 11; Donald Matthews and James Prothro, *Negroes and the New Southern Politics* (Harcourt, Brace and World, 1966); *Report* of the President's Commission on Registration and Voting Participation (1963); Morris Rosenberg, "Some Determinants of Political Apathy," *Public Opinion Quartery*, 18 (Fall, 1954), pp. 349-366; Stanley Kelley, et. al, "Registration and Voting: Putting First Things First," *American Political Science Review*, 61 (June, 1967), pp. 359-379.

increases when voters perceive a personal relevance to government policies or a close election, and when they are strongly identified with the political parties. Turnout is higher when differences between the parties and candidates are magnified, and higher for national offices than for state and local positions.

Perhaps the most critical factors are the legal barriers to voting participation. The United States probably places more obstacles in the way of the citizen seeking to cast his ballot than any other democracy. Personal registration is required in almost all states, and often must be periodically renewed. The procedures involved are inefficient, and the rolls close long before election. Residence requirements of a year exist in thirty-three states, and often apply even to presidential voting. Poll taxes, literacy tests, and other devices designed to limit Negro voting have been outlawed only in the last five years, and their heritage continues to depress turnout among Blacks and even White Southerners.

The process of balloting is also poorly administered. Paper ballots are still widely used, and defective voting machines are common. Election day is not a holiday for most voters, and the polls are frequently closed by the time many voters return from work. A presidential commission in 1963 found, in fact, that only five states met all of its standards of desirable voting procedures. Turnout could probably be improved most rapidly simply by removing legal barriers, rather than the more common practice of exhorting voters "to do their duty."

The voting age has become a significant issue in recent years. Until 1943 the minimum age for voting in all states was 21. By 1970 Alaska, Georgia, and Kentucky allowed 18-year-olds to vote, the minimum age was lowered to 19 in Montana and Massachusetts, and stood at 20 in Hawaii, Maine and Nebraska. However, Congress in 1971 proposed a constitutional amendment to establish a universal voting age of 18, and the states quickly ratified the Twenty-sixth Amendment more than a year before the 1972 presidential election. The effects of adding ten to fifteen million new voters to the electorate are incalculable, but certainly will be significant.

3

THE EFFECTIVENESS

OF CONGRESS

by Alan Rosenthal

Only the blind, the impervious, and the few blithe spirits can fail
to be concerned with the challenges facing the United States today.
"Crisis" is an overused word; yet it aptly characterizes the situation
American political institutions now confront. Our governments and our
politics are undergoing severe trials, not because society is changing,
but because so much is happening all at once.

Participation is expanding. More and more people are organizing, no
longer willing to make their views felt through periodic elections but
insistent on exercising influence continuously. Protest and violence are
new methods, and anyone, anywhere, who acts dramatically can come
alive with the help of television and the other mass media. Expectations
and demands are rising. Citizens expect and want more from government and politics—certainly more than they have received in the past
and probably more than they can realize in the future. Impatience and
intolerance are growing. There is no delaying satisfaction, and there is
no abiding opposition.

The pace of political processes is too slow to meet multiple and
intense demands. Disintegrating forces in American society are strong.
Groups appear to be polarized—the young against the old, one race
against another, women against men. Integrating forces are weak. Students
and Blacks reject the system, and the White working classes feel rejected
by it. Just as the natural environment may be undergoing irreversible
deterioration, American society may be in the process of irreparable
cleavage.

Not so long ago political institutions served to bring Americans
together, or at least to engage their attention and command their respect.
But today, public opinion polls tell us, government and politics are in
low esteem. People feel that big government is becoming a threat to

the country; they believe that corruption in Washington is increasing; they think that our present leadership in politics is worse than in the past. Not too surprisingly, perhaps the only governmental agency that continues to command widespread approval is the F.B.I., whom seven persons out of ten rate very favorably. But even the F.B.I. during recent years has lost the support of 13 percent of the population. If such a sacred institution is losing favor, there can be little doubt that significant change in American attitudes is indeed taking place.

This is the environment in which the United States Congress finds itself. It is little wonder that, like other political institutions, the legislature is also declining in public esteem. A demonstration of this decline can be seen in the figures below, which present public evaluations of congressional performance according to surveys conducted by Louis Harris and Associates:

Table 3.1. Popular Evaluations of Congress

	Percentages Rating the Job Done by Congress		
Year	*Positive*	*Not Sure*	*Negative*
1965	64	10	26
1966	49	9	42
1967	38	7	55
1968	46	8	46
1969	34	12	54
1970	34	12	54
1971	26	11	63

While support is diminishing, criticism of Congress is increasing. Critics are intense. According to them, Congress should be doing much, but is in fact doing little. It neither attends to its own problems nor to the nation's. It is not performing well; it is not responsive to the people. Congress is no help; it is an obstacle. Consequently, the critics conclude, it must be changed radically and revitalized. This is the time, if we are to reconstruct American life, for institutional renewal of a legislature confronting institutional crisis.

To call for better performance, greater responsiveness, and institutional renewal is easier, of course, than to say what all of this adds up to. What are the critics talking about? What do we mean by an effective Congress? Unfortunately there is no definitive model, no ideal construct, no convenient measuring sticks to tell us what Congress should be doing and how well Congress is doing it. The best we can do is to apply our judgments to the evidence at hand.

In evaluating Congress, it is useful to explore three principal questions, which are necessarily interrelated. First, what major tasks does Congress undertake, and how adequately does it perform them? Second, what difference should and does Congress make in the political system, particularly with respect to governmental power and governmental response? Third, how does the congressional institution—that is, the internal characteristics of Congress itself—affect congressional performance and determine what difference it makes? If we can shed some light on these questions, then we should have a good idea of how effective Congress is and how effective it might become.

THE TASKS CONGRESS UNDERTAKES

Congress performs a variety of services for constituents and constituencies. It enacts laws. It organizes and reorganizes agencies of the executive branch. It raises revenues and appropriates funds. It advises on foreign policy, ratifies treaties, and confirms executive appointments. It initiates constitutional amendments. But to start evaluating Congress we need to focus on its principal tasks: policy making, review and evaluation, and public education. Then our question is: how well does Congress perform these tasks?

Policy Making

There is no getting around the fact that the president plays the major policy role in American government. Congress participates in making policy, but it does not carry the main burden for the initiation of policy. It is not constituted to exercise initiative broadly or regularly; nor can it be without sacrificing too much else.

The president normally initiates. It is in the executive branch that campaign promises are drafted into concrete proposals, departmental programs screened and coordinated, priorities established, and the agenda for the legislative process determined. Congress normally responds to executive impulses, questions presidential priorities, and rearranges the agenda. In doing this it takes proposals, examines them in the light of alternatives, and then renders its judgment. It can accelerate, retard, or deflect; it can accept, expand, limit, modify, or reject.

There was a time when Congress played the predominant role in the policy-making process. In the early 1880s, writing about the American system in the twenty years between the death of Lincoln and the emergence of Cleveland, Woodrow Wilson bemoaned that checks and balances were no longer effective. His book was titled *Congressional Government*. Between the time of his writing and the end of the first decade of the twentieth century, the legislative role continued to be strong. One study shows that during this period Congress had a preponderant influence in shaping over half the major laws enacted. The balance shifted shortly thereafter. The period from 1933 to 1940 saw congressional influence decline markedly, with only two of twenty-four major laws attributable mainly to its work.[1] During the administration of Franklin D. Roosevelt bureaucracy developed, the executive office of the president was established, and the era of "executive-centered" government was underway. By the 1960s most observers of the national scene could agree not only that initiation was virtually the exclusive prerogative of the executive, but also that the executive dominated the policy-making process and Congress was little more than an obstacle.

Such an assessment is too simple, however. There are a number of ways in which Congress has played an extremely potent role. As is well known, Congress can reject executive proposals. It has never been reluctant to say no, and has been criticized repeatedly for obstructionism. It did not subscribe to everything Roosevelt wanted during his first administration; it became more disagreeable during his second. Harry S. Truman had difficulty with his domestic legislative programs, as his epithet, "Do Nothing 80th Congress," graphically attests. Presidents Eisenhower, Kennedy, and Johnson had their share of troubles on Capitol Hill. Among them they made 4,515 requests for legislation to the 83rd through the 90th Congresses during 1953–1968. A majority—about 51 per cent—were not granted.

Familiar as we are with congressional rejections, we are probably less acquainted with some other congressional activities with respect to policy making. When executive leadership is not forthcoming, the legislature can fill the vacuum—not across the board, but within particular policy domains. It can and does initiate selectively, filling in gaps overlooked by the administration. It can and does initiate on the periphery, in areas not covered by administration programs, but where substantial numbers of people either want action or will feel its effects.

Congressional activity in policy making is especially important during the tenure of unaggressive presidents. The Eisenhower years were a period of congressional creativity in a number of policy areas where the president did not choose to lead. The White House, the Bureau of the Budget, and department heads were either hesitant, divided, or simply opposed to certain policies; it was Congress that showed the initiative and took command in developing them. It assumed major responsibility for aid to airports, food stamps, urban mass transit, air and water pollution, and other programs. Congress, of course, was not without assistance. It received help from key professionals in the executive agencies that were concerned with one matter or another. There were also the interest groups that wanted things done. The AFL-CIO and

---

1. Lawrence H. Chamberlain, *The President, Congress, and Legislation* (Columbia University Press, 1946), pp. 450–452.

liberal congressmen together pushed Medicare. The National Education Association and congressional Democrats together pressed for federal aid to the public schools. Area redevelopment, aid to higher education, and manpower development and training programs all involved the efforts of groups outside and of individuals within Congress.[2]

Even during the tenure of aggressive presidents, congressional participation in policy making is important. Sometimes, it is true, a determined president or circumstances, or both, excludes Congress from taking any real part in the development of certain policies. This happened during the first hundred days of Roosevelt's New Deal. The country was in crisis, FDR had won a smashing victory at the polls and had the chance to exert his mastery. In three months after his 1933 inauguration he sent fifteen messages to Congress and steered fifteen major laws to enactment. Congress did little but say yes. Its attitude was expressed by the Republican floor leader in the House, who during the brief debate on the Emergency Banking Act, said: "The house is burning down and the President of the United States says this is the way to put out the fire."

Sometimes presidential pressure and legislative party loyalty combine to render Congress impotent. This happened on a few occasions during the Johnson administration. Although debated in one form or another for several years, the Elementary and Secondary Education Act of 1965 was passed by Congress hastily and with no significant change. The war on poverty also found Congress virtually excluded from the legislative process. Although a momentous departure, the Economic Opportunity Act of 1964 was cursorily considered and quickly ratified with only the most minor alterations.

It is exceptional, however, for even the aggressive executive to so completely dominate the policy-making process and for Congress to act as a "rubber stamp." During the first New Deal, when presidential leadership was strong and governmental power was shifting to the executive, Congress still asserted itself in a number of areas. It impelled the executive to turn its attention to industrial recovery and a federal works program; it took the lead in developing labor legislation, a federal deposit insurance system, and public housing programs.

After Eisenhower, legislative leadership centered in the White House. Nonetheless, Congress played a role. Much of what Presidents Kennedy and Johnson proposed and achieved could be attributed to Congress. First, there was the historical contribution. Preceding the 1960 election, congressional Democrats, allied with interest groups and the Democratic

2. These examples, as well as others, are presented in Frederic N. Cleaveland and associates, *Congress and Urban Problems* (The Bookings Institution, 1969), and James L. Sundquist, *Politics and Policy: The Eisenhower, Kennedy, and Johnson Years* (The Brookings Institution, 1968).

Advisory Council, developed a domestic program which became the core of Kennedy's campaign. James L. Sundquist, who served as administrative aide to a Democratic senator and later as a high official in the Kennedy and Johnson administrations, put it this way: "The platform writers and the presidential nominee contributed emphasis, style, and form, but the substance of the program had been written with unusual precision and clarity during the eight years out of power. . . ." [3] Second, there was the indirect contribution. Kennedy and later Johnson preempted with their own initiative a number of programs on which Congress itself was ready to proceed. On other matters individual congressmen injected their own ideas into administration bills and advanced their own proposals on the ladder of presidential priorities. Third, there was the direct contribution. In some areas—such as air and water pollution—Congress continued to lead and the executive continued to follow. In other areas Congress left its own unmistakable imprint: it recast the accelerated public works and manpower development and training programs, and it was responsible for major sections of the civil rights acts of 1964 and 1965.

Let us examine issue-domains for a moment. Congressional participation varies from one to another of these domains, and can be stable or vacillating in each. In some, congressional dominance is fairly well established: immigration policy has long been largely the product of the legislative branch. In others, responsibility has been rather equally shared: tax and revenue policy provide an example. Ordinarily congressional committees depend on executive expertise as the starting point for their consideration of legislation. This is illustrated by the statement to an administration witness by a senior chairman of a major House committee. "Don't expect us to start from scratch on what you people want," he admonished. "That's not the way we do things here—*you* draft the bills and *we* work them over." [4] The House Ways and Means Committee operates differently. Although it takes into account recommendations of the administration and the Treasury Department, it is not guided by their draft bills. The tax bill it reports, and almost always passes in identical form on the House floor, is the product—not the start —of the committee's work. In this area the policy input of Congress is surely as important as that of the administration.

There are some domains where overall initiative resides with the executive, but where the legislature is more than a mere onlooker. With regard to the space program, Congress has played an important role in

3. Ibid., p. 415.
4. Quoted in Richard E. Neustadt, "Presidency and Legislation: Planning the President's Program," in Aaron Wildavsky, ed., *The Presidency* (Little, Brown, 1969), p. 594.

deciding how much money to allocate and in broadening the geographic and institutional bases of spending and facility location. With regard to the atomic energy program, Congress—or at least its Joint Committee on Atomic Energy—has exercised sustained and substantial influence on national policy.[5]

In two most significant domains the executive has traditionally been in almost complete control of the determination of policy. Foreign affairs and defense have in the past witnessed only spasmodic and generally ineffective congressional participation. Although always advantaged by constitutional precedent, since the period of the Second World War the executive's dominance in areas involving national power and national security has increased tremendously.

The president has surely dominated American foreign policy, wielding unquestioned primacy while Congress acted as the passive, concurring, junior partner when its approval was needed. In the decade from 1949 through 1958, for instance, Congress initiated quantitatively more foreign-policy proposals than the executive; yet its influence was on marginal and relatively unimportant matters. If one examines twenty-two major cases from the neutrality legislation of the 1930s to the intervention by the United States in Cuba in 1961, executive initiation is visible in nineteen and executive influence is predominant in sixteen. Of the seven cases where violence was at stake, the executive dominated in six.[6] Seldom was Congress consulted in anticipation of a crisis situation, where violence was likely to occur. President Eisenhower's request in 1955 to use force, if necessary, to defend Formosa was quickly approved by Congress. Resolutions on Berlin and Cuba, providing legitimacy for virtually any exercise of executive power, were hastily ratified in 1962.

The past impact of Congress on military and defense policy has also been slight. Effective decision has rested with the executive branch. Throughout the period since the Second World War, Congress simply accepted the strategic programs, force-level recommendations, and major weapons systems proposed by the administration in power. Year after year, tremendous military spending bills passed both chambers, often with only a single day of debate and sometimes without a single floor amendment proposed. The legislative branch, and particularly the Armed Services committees and the Defense Appropriations subcommittees, concerned itself with the detailed administrative aspects of policy. But it took little account of how defense and military policies might affect

5. On tax and revenue policy, see John F. Manley, *The Politics of Finance* (Little, Brown, 1970); on space policy, see Vernon Van Dyke, *Pride and Power* (University of Illinois Press, 1964); on atomic energy, see Harold P. Green and Alan Rosenthal, *Government of the Atom* (Atherton, 1963).

6. James A. Robinson, *Congress and Foreign Policy-Making* (Dorsey Press, 1962).

relations between the United States and the Soviet Union, China, and the communist and the uncommitted nations of the world. When they were dealt with by Congress, military requirements were evaluated in isolation from other significant policy considerations. Congressional participation in this domain had little meaning at all for natonal or international political objectives or for the troubling problems our country had to face and try to resolve.[7]

Since 1967 a remarkable change has taken place. Due to America's involvement in Vietnam specifically and Indochina generally, the national legislature has begun to reassert the authority over foreign and military policies that it had previously surrendered. A few years ago Senator William Fulbright, chairman of the Foreign Relations Committee, maintained that the Senate should not deal with day-to-day policy making, but rather with the more basic problems of international relations, providing a forum for their examination. At that time little was done. But recently Congress, and especially the Senate, has questioned administration foreign and defense policies. It has probed relentlessly, publicized constantly, debated thoroughly. It has not been reluctant to question conventional wisdom, to oppose the president, to offer alternatives.

In the domains of foreign and defense policy, congressional power is inherently negative, partly because of the constitutional advantages of the presidency and partly because of the organization of Congress itself. Congress cannot speak with one authoritative voice; still, it has begun to exercise a critical check on how the administration develops and conducts foreign and defense policy.

The 91st Congress witnessed the most severe challenge to the executive's prerogatives and the most vigorous assertion of congressional power in decades. The Gulf of Tonkin resolution, which President Johnson cited as a legislative mandate supporting his decision to intervene with American combat forces in the Vietnam war, had been rushed through the committees and both chambers of Congress in two days during 1964. After months of debate, in 1970 Congress repealed the resolution. It also enacted an amendment to a foreign aid bill, prohibiting the intervention of U.S. ground forces in Cambodia, Laos, and Thailand, in an attempt to prevent a large-scale expansion of the war without congressional assent. It made an effort as well to require the administration to withdraw all American troops from Vietnam by the end of 1971. The

7. Lewis Anthony Dexter, "Congressmen and the Making of Military Policy," in Robert L. Peabody and Nelson W. Polsby, eds., *New Perspectives on the House of Representatives*, 2nd ed. (Rand McNally, 1969), pp. 175-194; Samuel P. Huntington, *The Common Defense* (Columbia University Press, 1961); Edward A. Kolodziej, *The Uncommon Defense and Congress, 1945-1963* (Ohio State University Press, 1966).

amendment failed in the Senate, but the outcome could hardly be considered a vote to continue the war. Instead, it was a close decision to allow the president to reduce American participation at a pace of his own choosing.

On these issues of foreign policy, major initiatives have come from the Senate, and particularly the Committee on Foreign Relations. This committee has operated on the twin premises that a marked imbalance exists between the executive and legislative branches of government, and that Congress should reassert its authority in the domain of foreign policy. During the 91st Congress the committee undertook the most searching and broad-ranging examination of this nation's foreign policy since the Second World War. In addition to its persistent challenges to the war in Indochina, the Foreign Relations Committee established a subcommittee to conduct an investigation of the international military commitments of the United States and their relationships to foreign policy. The subcommittee's work has led to further controversy between Congress and the administration.

The House of Representatives has been more inclined than the Senate to leave American foreign policy in the hands of the president. Its Committee on Foreign Affairs, having become comfortable in a subordinate role, has seen its responsibility as giving bipartisan support to the foreign policy established in the executive. But even in the House and the Foreign Affairs Committee there are increasing signs of independence. During the 91st Congress a subcommittee drafted a resolution requiring the president to seek, whenever feasible, appropriate consultation with Congress before involving American forces in armed conflict abroad. The resolution passed the House.

The net effect of all this has not been to force the president to adopt a particular position. It has been unmistakably to signal to the administration the dissatisfaction of Congress with the substance and process of foreign policy. A majority in Congress is agreed on a larger measure of legislative control; but there is still disagreement as to how control should be achieved and for what specific purposes it should be exercised.

Linked to recent assertiveness in foreign policy has been sharp congressional criticism of defense policy. As recently as 1968 one liberal senator introduced a number of amendments to curtail or eliminate certain weapons and spending programs. He received little support and his amendments were unsuccessful. Then the climate changed. During the first year of the 91st Congress heated debate took place on the administration's program for an antiballistic missile (ABM) system. One roll call on the issue, which the administration won narrowly, was the closest vote on a major matter of national security policy in more than a quarter of a century. Another battle occurred the following year. The administration again prevailed, but only after its program had been substantially curtailed.

Meanwhile both liberals and conservatives in Congress teamed up to challenge the high level of spending on the military. Even the Armed Services and Defense Appropriations subcommittees of the two houses, traditionally bulwarks for aggressive defense, became more economy-minded in reviewing what had previously been seen as routine military bills. Most direct attempts to cut the defense budget were defeated during the 91st Congress. But the battle on spending had significant indirect effects. The administration delayed some programs, altered others, cut a few more. As a result of prodding by Congress, it reduced defense spending by several billions of dollars, bringing the percentage of the federal budget spent on the military to the lowest point in twenty years.

It is hard to assess fully the import of recent congressional activity on foreign and defense policy. Certainly the administration has lost fewer battles than it has won. But participation by Congress is being felt. A senator like Majority Leader Mike Mansfield produces an effect just by keeping before the Senate his resolution calling for a substantial decrease in the number of American troops in Europe. A senator like Fulbright has an effect just by perservering—constantly pushing the administration toward the ratification of a non-proliferation treaty, the opening of strategic arms limitations talks, and the scaling down of United States commitments abroad. One group of senators has an effect by indicating the breadth and depth of national weariness with the Vietnam war, impelling the president to steadily withdraw American forces from Southeast Asia. Another overlapping group has an effect by challenging military spending, causing the administration to reexamine its premises, modify its defense programs, and reduce its requests for military funds. Still another group moves to assert congressional prerogatives by introducing legislation to regulate the exercise of the president's constitutional powers to commit the nation to war. There can be little doubt, as the National Committee for an Effective Congress stated toward the end of 1971, that the Senate and even the House have broken with the past and are beginning to assert influence over foreign and military policy.

This new congressional assertiveness in foreign and defense affairs has affected other areas as well. It is not only that Congress is controlled by the party in opposition to the president; but more congressmen —both Democrats and Republicans—are questioning administration priorities and administration judgments. In the 91st Congress 152 of 381 presidential requests were enacted. The rejection rate was 60 percent, higher than the average of the previous fifteen years. During the course of American history the Senate approved 108 presidential nominations for the Supreme Court and failed to approve only 26. In the first years of the Nixon administration, however, two of four presidential candidates for the Court were rejected after the most intensive debate. Eisenhower's tenure in office, which included Congress controlled by the opposition for six of his eight years, saw only two of 181 presidential vetoes overridden. The administrations of Kennedy and Johnson saw no presidential vetoes overriden by Democratic Congresses. In his first two years in office, President Nixon vetoed only nine bills (a few by "pocket vetoes" in the last days of the 91st Congress); but two of his vetoes were overridden.

In the domestic area relationships between Congress and the Nixon administration have been marked by both cooperation and conflict. On some important measures Congress went along. It tightened controls on the emission of pollutant materials into the air and established liability for the cleanup costs of oil spills; it expanded the unemployment insurance system; it established a comprehensive occupational health and safety program; it converted the Post Office Department into a government-owned corporation; and it enacted a number of crime bills. On some important measures Congress balked at administration proposals. It did not agree to the funding requested for the supersonic transport airplane (SST); it questioned the president's family assistance plan; and it showed no desire to rush headlong into a program of revenue sharing. On other measures Congress took the lead or went further than the administration desired, and met with presidential opposition and occasional vetoes. It insisted on allocating more funds to education, health, and poverty programs; it approved an extension of a Voting Rights Act, which had enfranchised almost a million southern Negroes; it enacted a provision granting the vote to 18-year-olds; it required the automotive industry to drastically reduce pollutants emitted by new cars; it passed a manpower training bill, providing among other things for public service jobs; and it adopted a measure imposing limits on spending for television time during election campaigns.

As far as policy making is concerned, the contemporary Congress has not been reluctant to participate or hesitant to challenge the executive. It may not be completely sure of what methods to take to achieve the goals it wants to achieve, so it debates long and hard the national problems of welfare, health insurance, and revenue sharing. The formulation of new policy is not easy, in part because it is so difficult to determine what will succeed.

The capacity of our governmental machinery to establish new domestic programs has apparently outrun its capacity to make them work. Imaginative policies do not always achieve their intended effects.

The federal bureaucracy, for example, is not able to put congressional policy against racial discrimination completely into effect. Some of the civil rights laws work well—particularly those dealing with voting and public accommodations. But others—such as those concerned with employment, housing, and federal grants—demonstrate a wide gap between policy declaration and policy enforcement. Local educational authorities accept federal funding designed by Title I of the 1965 Elementary and Secondary Education Act to further the education of disadvantaged children. But these funds often are spread too thin, spent inadequately, or devoted to the schooling of all children rather than to just that of the intended recipients. Consequently they do not measurably help poor children. State governments respond to congressional enactments with less than dispatch. Only one-third meet the deadline for compliance with a 1967 law requiring federally certified meat inspection programs, even though the deadline had been extended for a year. The welfare systems of nearly four-fifths of the states fail to comply with federal standards. Federal programs come into conflict one with another, or simply have too little impact. Aid to highways discourages urban mass transport and leads to even greater pollution of the environment. Food assistance plans are incapable of meeting the problems of malnutrition.

The list could be extended. But what all this strongly suggests is that a legislature cannot be content with sharing in determination of policy. It must ensure that policy is appropriate, that it is competently administered, and that it makes a positive difference. Probably the most challenging task of Congress today is policy review and evaluation.

Only the urgency for improved congressional review and evaluation is new. Since passage of the Legislative Reorganization Act of 1946, Congress has concerned itself with the task, recognizing the need for continuous review of administration or "legislative oversight." Its purposes have been to check dishonesty and waste, to guard against harsh or mistaken administration, to invigorate entrenched administrative routines, and to assure compliance with legislative intent as embodied in law.

Congressional techniques and resources to perform legislative oversight are many and of a rich variety. Congress grants agencies the right to exist and to perform certain functions. It can determine an agency's administrative structure. By virtue of its participation in the enactment of new programs, Congress inevitably examines existing ones. It authorizes funds and appropriates annually, and these processes offer opportunities for review and guidance. Congress demands special or periodic reports from departments and agencies; it provides for a legislative veto of certain action by the executive; and it sometimes requires committee clearance of administrative decisions. Standing committees hold hearings and conduct investigations; they criticize and direct administration officials by means of their written reports. As an arm of the Congress, the General Accounting Office audits the operations of departments and agencies. Individual members and staff maintain contact with personnel from the executive branch, issuing informal instructions for administrative behavior. And virtually every congressman intervenes with an administrative agency from time to time on behalf of a constituent.

Intervention on behalf of constituents is part of a congressman's service as a representative of his constituency. It entails responding to mail, furnishing information, and processing requests for help in which personal problems are involved. It means listening to constituents, trying to satisfy their individual demands and meet their particular grievances. Service, and particularly what congressmen refer to as "case work" involving specific assistance to people, is important for several reasons. It also has implications for legislative review and evaluation. On the one hand, by attending to people's requests and complaints, congressmen learn something about policy and administration, how things are actually working, and what needs revision and improvement. On the other hand, the very knowledge that some congressman is sure to look into a matter affecting his constituents helps keep administrators on their toes and deters to some extent bureaucratic indifference to the problems of individual clients.

Case work has relevance to the behavior of both congressmen and constituents. This aspect of a congressman's service to his constituents may be potentially valuable to congressional review and evalution of administration and its programs. But the potential is unrealized by a system in which 535 representatives and a thousand staff employees act as ombudsmen for citizens. It is necessary for the information that results from case work to be aggregated and used in a more systematic and coordinated fashion. This in effect would place major responsibility for the translation of citizen requests and complaints into generally revised programs and administrative procedures with the standing committees of Congress.

The standing committees are the principal work groups of the House and Senate. The effectiveness of legislative review and evaluation must hinge on their efforts. Congress recognizes this, and in the Legislative Reorganization Act of 1946 provided that:

To assist Congress in appraising the administration of the laws and in developing such amendments or related legislation as it may deem necessary, each standing committee shall exercise continuous watchfulness of the execution by the administrative agencies concerned of any laws, the subject matter of which is within the jurisdiction of such committee. . . .

Though this provision has made some difference, it has not really achieved the result desired and it must essentially be termed a failure.

Most important of the several reasons for this failure are the orientations of congressmen. In their committee work, most congressmen are oriented toward legislation: they tend to think in terms of the introduction and the passage of bills. There is little fascination in the workings of existing programs; enacted programs sustain no ongoing interest to the legislative mind. Perhaps therefore congressmen tend to regard agency operations as elusive and program effects as unfathomable—all too difficult and time-consuming to understand, and virtually impossible to evaluate. One senator, for example, speculated that the lack of oversight by committees ". . . may be due to the fact that it is that non-glamorous, nose-to-the-grindstone work." By contrast, members and their committees can derive satisfaction and reputation from attending to their policy-making tasks, and trusting that what they do will have worthwhile consequences.

There are also political factors which discourage serious oversight activity. Partisan loyalty to a president conflicts with a close examination of agencies that are part of his administration. But whatever the partisan situation, there is always the possibility that a committee and an agency will form a mutually rewarding partnership, with the committee adopting the agency and then protecting it. This has happened frequently with committees of the Senate and House. In addition, there is the reluctance of committee members to be critical of an agency's performance, because of the potential threat of reprisals by interest groups who are allied with the agency and benefit from its programs. It is not hard then to comprehend why oversight may be neglected.

Congressional powers of authorization enable the standing committees to exercise greater scrutiny of executive programs than would otherwise be possible. Prior to the Second World War, it was not uncommon for Congress to approve the authorization of new programs without limit on time or money. "Such funds as are necessary are hereby authorized to be appropriated" was the phrase generally used in legislation. Since 1946, however, Congress has insisted on annual authorizations before appropriations. Today, therefore, over one-third of the funds in the president's budget cannot be appropriated until a number of authorization bills, which go into effect for one year only, are enacted. Annual authorizations are now required in program areas such as space, foreign aid, atomic energy, and defense weapons systems.

Consider the space program, by way of illustration. Since its establishment, congressional committees have gradually become more active —exercising control by means of special investigations and provisions for committee and legislative vetoes of agency proposals, and particularly by using annual review of space programs to probe carefully into agency performance. In the case of foreign aid, the agency for International Development and its predecessors have always been allowed broad authority in the use of funds; nevertheless Congress has required yearly authorizations. The process has allowed Congress to exercise both substantive and procedural restraints on agency activity. In the period from 1955 through 1967, it included approximately fifty limitations in authorization acts. Most recently the number and character of AID limitations have been expanded. Provisions have been included in authorizing legislation to improve the quality of foreign aid administration, enhance the quality of administrative decisions, and ensure compliance with legislative standards. The trend might have been reversed, but it is noteworthy that it was not. In 1965, for example, Senator Fulbright supported multi-year authorizations for development loans and the Alliance for Progress. The House failed to go along. The following year the House agreed to five-year authorizations. This time the Senate refused to go along. Because of dissatisfaction over American foreign policy, at a time when there is a trend toward increased congressional control, it is unlikely that the legislature will soon relinquish any of its authorizing powers.

The power of the purse may be the most potent congressional power of all. Authorizations set the upper-most limits of funds that can be given to agencies and their programs. Appropriations specify the amounts, although the executive branch may spend less. But even the power of the purse is somewhat limited. The makeup of the federal budget does not permit total congressional control. Given about a 200 billion dollar budget, approximately one-quarter is relatively uncontrollable, since these funds are to fulfill long-range commitments or are for mandatory programs whose expenses must be met. Another half or more of the budget is devoted to national defense or space activities, and in the past these funds have proven difficult for Congress to cut. The remaining proportion— a little over one-fifth—is more easily increased or decreased, but even in these budgetary areas entrenched political and administrative interests make certain levels of funding practically inevitable.

As a rule, therefore, Congress and its appropriations committees have comparatively little impact on the federal budget and levels of federal spending. But they do make some difference in the conduct of administration and the effectiveness of program performance. The difference may be limited because the congressional approach—especially that of the principal congressional agency, the House Appropriations Committee—is incremental. This means that budgets are almost never actively reviewed as a whole, in terms of estimating the value of all existing programs as compared to all possible alternatives. One year's budget is simply based on the previous year's with special attention given to a narrow range of requested expansions and increases. The greatest part of any budget and of any congressional appropriations action is always the product of previous decisions.[8]

Despite the incremental approach, the sheer bulk of congressional work on appropriations provides considerable opportunity for oversight and control of the executive. The House Appropriations Committee's review is intensive, repetitive, and constant. Its decisions are made annually, its hearings number about four hundred each year, and its power over the purse appears threatening to executive agencies.

Therefore, if only because of the scope and variety of oversight activities, congressional review has important effects. Administrators, who may have to justify a policy or procedure, are kept alert. Agencies, which face criticism or a reduction in funds, are kept more honest than they might otherwise be. Spending is carried out with greater efficiency; administration improves; and despite frequent ambiguities the intent of Congress is generally followed. There are signs, too, that congressional activity with regard to oversight has become more intense during the last few years. Seldom today is agency compliance taken for granted, as was often the case in the past.

Nevertheless, much remains to be done. Criticisms of congressional review and evaluation and recommendations for improvement are numerous. In its 1965 hearings the Joint Committee on the Organization of Congress received more suggestions on the subject of fiscal controls than on any other matter. Proposals for improved oversight were also many and varied. Most congressmen favored an increase in the investigative and supervisory powers of the General Accounting Office. Among a number of its recommendations, the Joint Committee proposed that each standing committee issue an annual report on its review activities, which should include ". . . an evaluation of programs under the jurisdiction of the committee, an assessment of the quality of administration of agencies investigated during the year, and recommendations as to organi-

---

8. The budgetary role of Congress is explained in fascinating detail by Richard F. Fenno, Jr., *The Power of the Purse: Appropriations Politics in Congress* (Little, Brown, 1966). See also Stephen Horn, *Unused Power: The Work of the Senate Committee on Appropriations* (The Brookings Institution, 1970).

zational and program changes and/or the elimination of unnecessary activities under the committee's jurisdiction." The committee's proposal is right on target.

As a result of the committee's work the Legislative Reorganization Act of 1970 provided in Title II for a number of potentially important changes in the way Congress performs its review and evaluation task. The act directed that the executive establish a standardized data processing system for federal budgetary and fiscal data and that it furnish congressional committees with information on the nature of available data on federal programs, activities, receipts, and expenditures. It also directed the president to submit to Congress five-year forecasts of the fiscal impact of every existing or new federal program. And it required that the reports of standing committees, with the notable exceptions of House and Senate Appropriations, include five-year cost estimates for the programs under consideration.

Other progress has also been made. During the last few years, Congress amended some of the basic legislation of the Johnson administration—including the Elementary and Secondary Education Act, the Economic Opportunity Act, and the Demonstration Cities and Metropolitan Development Act—to provide for program evaluation. The legislature is beginning to insist that the executive evaluate the extent to which programs are achieving intended results and delivering intended services to intended beneficiaries. Congress has also strengthened the role of the General Accounting Office, and is beginning to demand audits of program performance, which include examination of program effectiveness as well as administrative compliance and management efficiency. New types of data and analytical frameworks are being developed, and different information is beginning to be channeled to congressmen.[9]

Traditionally, review by Congress has concentrated on administrative competence and administrative compliance. The results have been useful, but not sufficient, mainly because committee and congressional evaluation of existing programs have been largely ignored. This is not to say that evaluation has been totally lacking. Practically every aspect of activity in Congress contains evaluative elements. And practically every aspect involves a concentration on specifics and details. Congress must continue to focus on specifics and details, since they serve as indispensable handles that congressmen use to work inductively to broader kind of program judgments. Yet evaluation based exclusively on bits and pieces is no longer satisfactory. In order to make good public policy for the future, Congress

9. For a perceptive and detailed discussion of Congress and the information revolution, see John S. Saloma III, *Congress and the New Politics* (Little, Brown, 1969), pp. 199-254.

must have more systematic knowledge of the effects of policy it made in the past. It must find out what works and what does not work: whether a program's objectives are being achieved and at what costs; whether one program is more or less effective than some other program with similar objectives; and what factors make for success or failure of a program in accomplishing its objectives.

New techniques, new procedures will not revolutionize decision making in Congress. Review and evaluation will continue to depend on the incremental method, with today's judgments based heavily on yesterday's. But the systematic and comprehensive components of congressional assessments and decisions can be increased as a result of new types of information. Congress has not abdicated to the executive; it is now making a serious effort to improve its own capacity to review and evaluate national policies and programs. It must do much more.

Public Education

As part of their representational tasks, congressmen and their staffs devote substantial energies to providing their constituents with information. Perhaps one-fourth of the average representative's day, and an even larger proportion of the time of his office staff, is spent communicating with the people back home. Somehow congressmen and Congress, in communicating and furnishing information, must also advance the education of the public. This is no easy task, but it is immensely important in a democracy, particularly one where citizen participation is broadening in extent and deepening in intensity. The task of education does not call for Congress to indoctrinate, if indeed it could; but it does require Congress to clarify problems and policies so that people can make better judgments from the staindpoint of their own preferences and interests.

Politicians in Congress, as well as elsewhere, seldom forego the opportunity to communicate to their constituents. Senators normally employ at least one press aide to specialize in the area of public relations and communications. Representatives and their staffs work hard at the job also. More than half the members of the House regularly report to people in their districts through the mass media. The average member makes about eight radio and four television appearances each month. On occasion the enthusiasm of congressmen for their responsibilities in communicating becomes rather curious indeed. One representatives's personal explanation, which appeared in the *Congressional Record* (December 27, 1969), merits attention:

Mr. Speaker, I take this time to indicate that I just missed the vote on the tax reform measure, because I was in the television gallery making a tape on how I voted on the tax reform measure. I would like to state that had I been present and not making the tape, I would have voted in favor of the tax reform measure.

Virtually every member of Congress inserts his remarks into the *Record*, makes speeches, introduces bills, writes letters, sends out mailings, and distributes periodic newsletters—all with an eye toward informing his constituents of what he is doing on their behalf.

But the individual congressman, however frequent his communications, rarely devotes much attention to education. Public education may result, but for the most part what the congressman does is for his own electoral ends—ordinarily to promote himself and occasionally to promote his party. Promotion is the rule; explanation—particularly when an issue is complex or constituents are unconcerned or hostile—is the exception. Most members, overwhelmed by myriad duties, naturally interested in reelection, and dependent on voters for their survival, cannot be expected to tell it exactly like it is. Fortunately, however, a few do; and this enables Congress to achieve some measure of success in educating at least a small portion of the electorate.

The real success of its public education function is contingent on what Congress does at its other tasks. As its performance in making policy and reviewing and evaluating administration and programs improves, so does its performance in educating citizens. Some years ago congressional performance was considerably inferior to what it is today. Nevertheless, there were times even then—such as during the Army–McCarthy hearings and the Senate's consideration of the nuclear test-ban treaty—when the public was afforded rich information about issues, options, and the governmental process. Until recently Congress paid only cursory attention to military policy and defense spending, and the result was little public information or instruction. Today, however, these issues are extremely salient in Congress, and the result is greater public knowledge and involvement regarding policies and priorities. Opposition to the American presence in Vietnam provides an example of the congressional role in public education. Among numerous Senate activities, hearings by the Foreign Relations Committee, which were televised and widely reported in the press, encouraged the public to become as concerned about the war as many senators. Arthur M. Schlesinger, Jr., a historian of the presidency and adviser to President Kennedy, described the congressional impact: "I don't think there can be any question," he said, "that the Senate Foreign Relations Committee opened up a national debate where one had really not existed before." And he continued: "The educational job performed by the senators on Vietnam has been quite extraordinary." [10]

In areas of domestic policy as well, Congress is fulfilling its educational tasks as seldom before. A Senate committee held hearings on birth control pills in 1970. A few years earlier, there was relatively little public concern about "the pill." A Gallup poll of women found that 45 percent believed it safe, and only 30 percent thought it unsafe. But people did not really know. At the Senate hearings, doctors and experts testified that the pill might be a factor in causing blood clotting, breast cancer, diabetes, sterility, and birth of malformed children. This testimony might give anyone concern, and evidently did. Thereafter, a Gallup poll found that only 22 percent of the women surveyed thought "the pill" safe, while as many as 46 percent considered it unsafe. Yet two out of three women continued as previously to believe that oral contraceptives were effective. Relevant information was communicated and it did make a difference, largely because of the forum offered by Congress. More recently congressional hearings on environmental problems helped alert Americans to the dangers to our air, land, and water, and citizens have mobilized as a result. Ralph Nader has probably done as much—and done it more successfully—as any other force in American life to stimulate the protection of consumers and to require responsibility by large corporations. To some degree at least, as his repeated appearances before congressional committees attest, Nader has depended on Congress as a forum abetting his efforts to arouse public concern.

Debate in Congress on major domestic problems continues, and the consequence must surely be better information for the American public. Intense activity, persistent investigation, and thorough probing by Congress mean more adequate education. This is especially true in an age dominated by the mass media (which ought to assume some of the responsibility for selecting and reporting congressional happenings to American citizens). But Congress has gone even further, although rather cautiously. By virtue of the Legislative Reorganization Act of 1970, the House and Senate have begun to make more information available to the public. The House also agreed to have committee hearings broadcast or televised, provided a majority of committee members approve. Previously, unlike the Senate, it had always refused this permission. It is too early to comment on the effects of these changes, but it is indicative that at the start of the 92nd Congress, the chairman of the powerful House Appropriations Committee, which always conducted its business behind closed doors, announced that his committee would hold some open hear-

10. Arthur M. Schlesinger, Jr. and Alfred deGrazia, *Congress and the Presidency: Their Role in Modern Times* (American Enterprise Institute for Public Policy Research, 1967), p. 106.

ings in 1971. And within two weeks the committee opened a hearing to public, press, and television, with the chairman remarking that the committee had been in existence for 105 years "and we thought a little experimentation would not be out of order."

A number of congressmen, especially Senator Fulbright, are demanding that the first branch of government be given television time to respond to the president. The new Speaker of the House is holding periodic press conferences. The problem, of course, is: who can speak for the legislature, since there are almost as many viewpoints in Congress as there are members? Clearly, no one can speak for the legislature as the president does for the executive. It is unlikely in the years ahead that Congress will develop an institutional voice; but individual members will speak and be heard more than before. In contrast to a well-orchestrated corporate executive, congressmen may produce a measure of dissonance. The results, however, should be beneficial. It will not be programmed instruction; but it will mean alternative perspectives, more information, and additional opportunities for citizens to choose intelligently as to whether and how they affiliate, vote, and expend their public energies.

THE DIFFERENCE CONGRESS MAKES

Congressional performance in policy making, review and evaluation, and public education has improved markedly. But what difference does an improved contemporary performance of these tasks by Congress make?

The way one answers this question depends upon which functions of Congress are judged to be most important or of greatest concern. The functions that Congress performs, or ideally should perform, in the American political system, as identified by political scientists,[11] normally include the following: the building of consensus, the management of conflict, the legitimation of governmental policy, and the provision of access to the decision-making process. In this essay we suggest that our major concern should be that Congress *make a difference both to governmental power and governmental response*. To fulfill its role, Congress must ensure that power does not become overly concentrated and it must provide that response accords with popular preferences, public demands, and the nation's needs. A congress that accomplishes these things might be said truly to "make a difference," and a big one.

11. See, for example, Saloma, pp. 3-27, and Roger H. Davidson et al., *Congress in Crisis: Politics and Congressional Reform* (Wadsworth, 1966), pp. 7-37.

Governmental power should be dispersed, so that all political interests have an opportunity, so that new and dissenting ideas get a chance to emerge, and so that conflict in society is reflected, channeled, and resolved by government. Congress is a political institution that encourages at least some dispersion of public power.

The setup of checks and balances, which is historically associated with our nation's legislature, is based on distrust and fear of centralized power. Perhaps tyranny by a president is no great danger, but there are still compelling reasons for Congress to check him. The president can make mistakes and do wrong. He may be weak, unwilling, or unable to act. Congress must be there to remedy errors, right wrongs, and provide national leadership whenever necessary. Lewis A. Dexter wrote most appropriately only a few years ago: ". . . suppose—which is by no means impossible—a couple of fire-eating chief executive men . . . or suppose just stupid and unimaginative Presidents, then many of those who now deplore check and balance would thank God for the Congress." [12]

The executive and legislative branches have similar responsibilities for promoting the public welfare. But the two institutions exist in different political environments, have dissimilar perspectives, and tend to respond in contrasting fashions.

In Congress the views of all people—small groups as well as large, minorities as well as majorities—are represented, and the demands of practically every relevant segment of the public are articulated. Not every interest has an equal chance to prevail, but virtually none is denied some spokesman, some access in the "multiple cracks" of the legislature. Nearly every idea has a chance to pick up authoritative support in a Congress that encourages their development, their testing, and their right to advance.

There are many ways to keep things alive in Congress, where members, representing different viewpoints, debate with one another. Debate in Congress arouses attention, forces disputants to explain their positions, stimulates invention, and often results in the best of all practical solutions. In the executive branch an idea or dissenting position is much easier to kill. Disagreement among departments, between an agency and the White House staff, or between the president and a cabinet member can quickly stifle the development of an idea before a consensus can be

---

12. " 'Check and Balance' Today: What Does it Mean for Congress and Congressmen?" in Alfred deGrazia, ed., *Congress: The First Branch of Government* (The American Enterprise Institute for Public Policy Research, 1966), p. 113.

reached. Dissent in Congress is the rule, but within the executive it is seldom tolerated and rarely encouraged. As the executive branch becomes increasingly centralized—a trend in part accelerated by new information technologies, and one reflected in the practices of recent presidents, and particularly Richard M. Nixon—internal bargaining diminishes and internal conflict becomes even less visible. Under such circumstances the role of Congress in providing an arena for the expression of conflicting ideas is even more important.

Not only does Congress balance the president by offering a rallying ground for criticism and dissent. It also checks the technicians and specialists in the administrative agencies of government, better perhaps than does the president himself. These people, as much as elected politicians in the two branches, have a tremendous impact on policies, programs, and the lives of citizens. Like all of us—governors and governed—administrators make mistakes. Some stem from faulty reasoning. Some occur because the values and assumptions of administrators are not always shared by people who are affected by their actions. Some are attributable to bureaucracy's total acceptance of the *status quo* in any issue-area, due to its investments of ideology, intellect, and energy in what presently exists. Congress brings to bear different insights and sensitivities. It can come up with ideas that are not likely to occur to professional administrators. Congress also corrects mistakes and can inform specialists and technicians as to whether their programs are working as they should.

For Congress to provide real rather than illusory access for new and dissenting ideas, and also to contest the president and administrators in the executive departments and agencies, it must have substantial power of its own. Indeed it does. No other country has a legislature with so great a capacity for acting independently. After two years in the White House, John F. Kennedy described the legislature controlled by his own party as follows:

> . . . the Congress looks more powerful sitting here than it did when I was there in Congress. But that is because when you are in Congress you are one of a hundred in the Senate or 435 in the House, so that power is divided. But from here I look at a Congress, and I look at the collective power of the Congress . . . and it is a substantial power.

Congress has been organized on the thesis that the party of the president supported him and the other party opposed him. This principle has facilitated executive leadership. But today party ties are weakening throughout the nation, and the distinction between parties has little meaning in the Senate and less meaning in the House than has been the case previously. Presidents will not be able to rely on their congressional parties for major support in the future as they have in the past. Congress is now taking its checks-and-balances role most seriously.

This seems all to the good. The executive-force model of government, with its stress on presidential ascendancy, was for a long time the dominant framework for those who observed and studied American politics. Since Franklin D. Roosevelt the fashion has been to encourage an aggrandized executive and a diminished legislature. Now things are different. Democrats and Republicans, liberals and conservatives, and people inside and outside of Congress are joining together in the belief that executive power must be limited. Congress must remain strong to ensure the emergence of ideas and the expression of dissent, and to take a leadership role when it becomes necessary. Arthur Schlesinger, Jr., put it well when he stated: "The struggle among the branches of government is part of the health of the American polity, and its continuation makes democracy possible by enabling the electorate to shift the weight of decision in one direction or another according to the results desired." [13] We cannot afford either branch of government becoming completely dominant.

Events and the responses to them by Presidents Johnson and Nixon have been responsible for the shift in the balance of American thought. Meanwhile Congress, in diligently pursuing its tasks of policy making, review and evaluation, and public education, has been responsible for remedying the imbalance of power. The legislature today checks and balances the executive. It surely exercises substantial power. But for what purposes does Congress exercise its power? Does it check and balance with little other end in view? Has its strength in government been purchased at the price of its responsiveness to the people whom it represents? These questions demand our attention.

Governmental Response

Implicit in the idea of checks and balances is the notion that if one branch of government is not responsive to national needs another branch will be. Yet for government and society to prosper, Congress must respond adequately, no matter what the behavior of the executive and judiciary. An unresponsive legislature, however powerful, would not be of much benefit. But just what does responsiveness actually mean? How can it be evaluated?

In evaluating congressional responsiveness we need to recognize that individual senators and representatives, elected by people in their states and districts, must present the views of and act on behalf of their various constituencies. At the same time, they have an equal responsibility to

13. Schlesinger and deGrazia, *Congress and the Presidency*, p. 18.

respond to national needs with effective policies. Few would argue that a congressman should overlook the national interest. But it is also important, from a constituent's point of view, that the district or state not be sacrificed in the name of the nation. The reconciliation of local representation and national responsiveness is no simple matter. Congressmen must manage it somehow. The determination of the national interest in a democracy is not a simple task. Each congressman encounters problems in following people's preferences, satisfying their demands, and acting on behalf of their needs. Often what people desire, what they organize to promote, and what they really need or is good for them are almost identical. But this is not always the case. If the national interest is defined by people's wishes, it is necessary only to identify the distribution of popular preferences and then follow the principle of majority rule. If the national interest is defined by the weight of demands, pressure must also be taken into account. Then not only the distribution of preferences, but their translation into organized behavior plays a role. If, however, the national interest is dependent on what the nation *really* needs, individual congressmen and the Congress may have to be able to perceive potential as well as present needs, and then act either before, in accord with, or in opposition to majority preferences and the weight of demands.

As a matter of fact, congressmen do respond to what people want, to what groups demand, and to what they themselves think the nation needs. For Congress the national interest is usually determined in terms of some combination of all three. The mix will vary from issue to issue, but more often than not the preferences of individuals will be of major relevance. And this is as it should be, for a representative institution cannot properly overlook each person's preferences and definition of his own good. Elected politicians in a democracy are obligated to represent the will of the people; thus what the nation needs is generally what its citizens think it needs.

The principle that the national interest can be identified by discovery of the public will, while of continuing and general utility, must be qualified in day-to-day practice. This is true for a number of reasons. First, it cannot be assumed that on many issues a public will actually exists. People have opinions on relatively few issues, and certainly not on all of those before Congress. Second, it is by no means sure that even when people hold opinions a public will can accurately be identified. On many matters it is virtually impossible. People are often sharply divided, one half supporting a proposal and the other half opposing it; opinions often lack stability, with people favoring one thing one week and quite another the next; not all opinions are equal, since some are only weakly held, while others are rather intense. Third, there is no reason to expect that the public will—if it exists and is clearly discernible—can furnish Congress specific guidelines. Opinions are usually general; legislative choices are usually discrete. By 1971, for example, polls showed that the public overwhelmingly favored some form of national health insurance. So did most senators and representatives. The question, however, was which of several specific plans and numerous technical provisions would win majority support among congressmen. The public may hold opinions that are mutually contradictory; Congress is less able to afford such a luxury. Lewis A. Dexter puts it this way: "In general, voters want to eat their cake and have it too; but always, Congressmen must realize that an improvement here is likely to involve cost and trouble there, and must try to balance the two against each other." [14]

The formula is complex, but the public will generally governs, although it may be tempered and shaped by Congress's own behavior. Over the longer haul, the public will and legislative action correspond rather closely. This is because Congress adopts policies that the public wants or can accept, and also because Congress can persuade, by means of its activities and their educational consequences, that its policies are tolerable or make sense. Over the shorter haul, correspondence may be less and differences may be greater. There are times when Congress acts with no evidence of a public will at all, or none in advance of its formation. Sometimes it moves more rapidly than a public will would appear to dictate; sometimes it is right in step; and sometimes it moves with more restraint. Occasionally it acts in a contradictory way. Each of these patterns of responsiveness deserves consideration.

On many issues there is no public mandate in existence when Congress takes, or begins to take, significant action. However quiescent the public, Congress still must make decisions, either in response to what particular individuals or groups demand or to what it believes best, or more likely a combination of the two. Much legislation—some of it directly important to many people and some directly important to only a few—is passed on this basis. Urban programs are an example. During the early 1960s, in the absence of widespread opinion or even a fully operative community of urban interests, Congress enacted a number of measures which benefitted the cities. Although not specifically designed to help urban areas, these measures succeeded in helping the cities nonetheless.

More recently and without prior sanction by public opinion, action by Congress has substantially eroded the power of significant private interest groups. At an earlier time interest groups, together with their congressional and administrative allies, dominated a number of policy areas. Largely as a result of congressional determination to respond to national

14. *The Sociology and Politics of Congress* (Rand McNally, 1969), p. 6.

needs, this is no longer the case. The defense industry is now being challenged. Food and drugs have come under stricter governmental controls.
Cigarette advertising has been banned from radio and television. Governmental subsidies for wealthy farmers have been reduced. Consumer
bills, designed to ensure the safety of children, have been passed. A
stringent health and safety measure to protect coal miners and another
to protect industrial workers have been enacted. Protection of the
environment has become a national issue, as much because of congressional debate and action as anything else. Far-reaching measures to curb
or reduce pollution are now law. Although both the administration and
the automotive industry opposed deadlines for a 90 percent reduction of
pollutants from new automobiles, Congress persisted and prevailed.

The list of accomplishments, and particularly those of most recent
Congresses, could be extended. But the point is that Congress is making
critical decisions today without the benefit of public mandates. Congress
is not acting contrary to the public; instead, it is helping to fashion
opinion to recognize national needs as Congress recognizes them.

Congressional activity promotes public concern. And public concern
stimulates congressional activity. When the mass media succeed in
dramatizing issues, when the attentive citizenry expands, and when the
rank and file begins to stir, Congress does not fail to take note. It may
not respond immediately, because it may wait for opinion to crystallize
and become stable. When it does respond, however, it may outdistance
the public will that first stimulated it.

Civil rights legislation provides a good example of how Congress can
come from behind and rather quickly move out in front. Civil rights
bills had been passed earlier, yet major legislation was not enacted until
the mid-1960s. It was then that events and their portrayal by the mass
media made significant action possible. Congress moved when it had the
opportunity—in response to events, pressures, and its own perception of
national needs. The mass public appeared willing to accept some measure
of social change, but surely there was no mandate for decisive action,
even at the time that Congress acted decisively. During the 1960s Gallup
polls repeatedly showed that most people thought the pace of governmental action on behalf of Negroes was about right. There were never
majorities who wanted government to move much faster; in fact, depending on the specific time, anywhere from twice to six times as many
people felt that racial integration was being pushed too fast as felt it was
not being pushed fast enough. Still, throughout this period Congress
took significant steps to advance the rights of Negroes, enacting major
legislation in 1964, 1965, and 1966.

Thereafter the public became resistant to the pace of change with
regard to race. Dissatisfaction was evidenced by a disturbing polarization

in voting in both national and local elections. In the presidential election of 1968 some 97 percent of Black voters cast their ballots for Hubert Humphrey, but less than 35 percent of the White voters did so. Two elections in Cleveland, one in Newark, one in Los Angeles, and others throughout the nation, showed similar patterns of racial voting. Dissatisfaction was also evidenced by distributions of opinion reported in the national polls. As far as further integration was concerned, during 1967–69 public opinion was relatively stable. About 45 percent believed the pace of change too fast; another 45 percent were equally divided betwen those who thought it about right and those who believed it too slow. By 1970 only 17 percent felt racial integration was not moving fast enough, another 21 percent thought the pace about right, and nearly half considered that things were going too fast.

Today if there is any mandate in existence it is to halt the slow progress taking place, and not to accelerate it. Congress still passed an open-housing law in 1968. Two years later, despite the Nixon administration's opposition, it extended the voting rights law it had enacted in 1965 for another five years. In conformity with public sentiment and in view of the uncertainty of legislative remedies, however, the pace is certainly slowing down. Integration is extremely difficult to achieve, and it is doubtful now whether the cause commands even substantial minority support. In many communities in both the North and South, for example, integration in public education is virtually impossible without busing children betwen racially segregated neighborhoods and schools some distance away. But busing is anathema to the public, with almost nine out of ten people opposed. The legislature, composed of representatives, cannot help being sensitive to such sentiment.

All in all, the record of congressional responsiveness with regard to civil rights during the last decade has not been a bad one. Congress has moved faster and further than majorities outside would have preferred. It has by no means solved the nation's racial problems nor fully answered the nation's needs, largely because it has been unwilling to go "too fast" or "too far", or to move beyond the limits of public tolerance.

On other issues Congress, or articulate elements therein, take a position in advance of, or even contrary to, public sentiment and still manage to prevail. This is illustrated by the congressional role on issues of national power. In this domain congressmen have traditionally been free of constituency pressures and have more often led than responded to public opinion. The war in Vietnam provides a good example. Scattered protests in Congress began earlier, but serious opposition to America's involvement started to mount in 1967. Significant dissatisfaction, especially in the Senate, occurred well in advance of widespread dissatisfaction in the country. In early 1968 the public still took a hard line. Twice as many people identified themselves as "Hawks" as identified themselves as "Doves." Despite immediate, popular interpretations, the success of Senator Eugene McCarthy in the presidential primaries that year was not attributable to a "peace vote" or a widespread desire for withdrawal from Vietnam. In the New Hampshire primary, as a matter of fact, McCarthy voters who were unhappy with the Johnson administration for not pursuing a harder line against Hanoi outnumbered by three to two those who advocated withdrawal.

Within a few years public opinion shifted considerably. By 1970 twice as many people thought of themselves as "Doves" as thought of themselves as "Hawks." Polls showed the public divided on America's intervention in Cambodia, but mail received by Democratic senators was ten-to-one against the venture and mail received by Republican senators was four-to-one in opposition. Polls showed the public divided on America's intervention in Laos, with most people concerned that it would tend to prolong the Indochina war. By 1971 practically everyone —the administration, the Congress, and the public—favored withdrawal from Vietnam, although there was disagreement as to the timetable and the conditions.

There has been a progressive disillusionment with the United States commitment in Southeast Asia, and with the amount of money spent for military purposes rather than for domestic needs. This change in the national mood is attributable to a variety of factors. Events themselves bred disenchantment. The activities of dissenters and groups demonstrating for peace had an impact. So did the attitudes of members of the newspaper and television press and the coverage by the mass media. But the election to Congress in 1968 of a number of committed opponents to the war, the increasing number and outspokenness of senators and even representatives who challenged American foreign policy, and the forum for legitimate opposition that the national legislature provided—all these factors had significance in promoting the transformation of public opinion.

There are times and issues that find Congress quite responsive to the public will, particularly when that will has assumed unmistakable shape. One time was during the 91st Congress, and the issue was crime. Throughout 1968, 1969, and 1970 crime and lawlessness were perceived by the public, according to Gallup polls, as among the most important problems facing the nation. There could be little doubt in the minds of most politicians that most people wanted more police protection, stricter law enforcement, more convictions, and tougher sentences for those who were convicted of criminal offenses. The Republican party was conscious not only of the problem, but also of the public mood. Its 1968 platform, criticizing the Democrats for ignoring rising crime rates, declared that "lawlessness is crumbling the foundations of American society." A few years later, during the 1970 congressional elections, President Nixon proclaimed at a campaign rally: "All over the country today we see a rising tide of crime . . . If a candidate has condoned violence, lawlessness, and permissiveness, then you know what to do."

By 1970 the frequent incidence of crime was undeniable. The direction of public opinion was unambiguous. The threat of having their responsiveness tested in the elections was impending. Therefore congressmen moved almost in unison in the direction in which the winds were blowing. Congress balked on some and modified other administration measures, but under considerable pressure it adopted a number of crime bills. One major bill, which was denounced as unconstitutional and bearing the seeds of repression, passed the House by a vote of 341–26 and the Senate by 73–1. Given the public disposition and an atmosphere marked by fear, congressmen had to get themselves on record against crime. Many believed that elements of the presidents' anti-crime program were poor. Yet, faced with a choice of a bill with some bad sections or no bill at all, and with elections forthcoming, congressmen felt obliged to vote "yea" and let the Supreme Court and another Congress sort things out later. Public opinion, presidential demands, and objective need were all there; Congress responded, though perhaps not precisely in accord with the national interest.

Frequently Congress proceeds cautiously, even though the American people are inclined to quick action. Congress may resist or outlast the force of public opinion. The case of contemporary dissent and protest is illustrative in this respect. The electorate has been extremely dissatisfied with the manner of dissent and protest during the past few years. In 1968, for instance, even the majority of people opposed to the war in Vietnam were hostile to the behavior of protesters. By contrast, those who were sympathetic to their methods constituted only 3 percent of the electorate. Since then roughly nine out of ten persons have expressed the opinion that government should crack down. Citizens are overwhelming in their belief that college administrations should take a stronger stand against campus disorders, and that student strikes are not a proper way to protest the way things are being run in the country. Even after Cambodia, which divided opinion in the United States, relatively few people voiced any sympathy for the protests being conducted by college students and others.

Things thereafter took a quieter turn, but the prevailing public mood at the time might well have impelled Congress to enact legislation prohibiting certain forms of protest and imposing sanctions against certain types of protesters. Individual congressmen did speak out vociforously on the issue of campus unrest. But their bark has been louder than their bite. Congress acted with considerable restraint. It did insert provisions restricting the spending of funds in a number of bills, thus prohibiting aid to students who had threatened force or seized property to interfere with school activities. It did not, however, enact any major repressive legislation or respond to what the public clearly seemed to desire.

Most recently Congress has also proceeded cautiously in considering President Nixon's revenue-sharing proposal, whereby the federal government would provide some of its tax revenues to state and local governments. Since early 1967 the concept has had the overwhelming support of the public. By early 1971 as many as 77 percent of those polled by Gallup supported revenue sharing, while only 14 percent opposed it. Governors, state legislators, and many mayors have rallied around the president in order to secure funds for their hard-pressed jurisdictions. Uncertain as to who would benefit by the administration's scheme and skeptical that state or local governments would be more effective than the federal government in solving social and economic problems, Congress has withstood public preferences and organized pressures. Instead it has insisted on thorough consideration of possible alternatives—such as the federal assumption of welfare costs or a tax-credit plan for distributing revenues—and a major national debate. Unresponsive or slow to respond to the national mood, Congress may indeed be safeguarding the national interests.

Still another pattern of congressional responsiveness must be noted. Not frequently, but on occasion, Congress takes action in the face of public desires to the contrary. The enactment of legislation to lower the voting age to 18 illustrates the point, once a contradiction is cleared away. Some might say that the public was long in favor of the vote for 18-year-olds; since 1953 repeated Gallup surveys have shown majorities in support of the proposition. Following the outbreak of student disorders, the percentage favoring dipped but a majority continued to favor the change. Did a mandate for change exist? No, quite the contrary was the case. Whatever people said positively when interviewed, the active public behaved negatively when acting on a specific voting-age proposition. Since 1966, and before Congress enacted legislation in 1970, nine states held referendums on proposals to lower the voting age to either 19 or 18. In not one of these states—Michigan (1966); Hawaii, Maryland, Nebraska, North Dakota, and Tennessee (1968); New Jersey and Ohio (1969); and Oregon (1970)—did such a proposal pass. In five of them, proposals were rejected by more than 55 percent of the voters.

Despite some contradictory signs, the most potent indicators of the public's disposition—votes—were quite clear. In the face of what might reasonably be interpreted as a mandate to remain with the status quo and despite some constitutional doubts, the 91st Congress enacted a bill to reduce the voting age to 18 in national, state, and local elections. In the Senate, four out of five members who voted favored the measure. Considering the senators of the nine states whose electorates had declared their opposition in referendum, 13 voted in favor, only two voted against and three did not vote on the proposal.[15] Even after the act giving the vote to ten million Americans between the ages of 18 and 21 was signed, the public remained unconvinced. At the November elections in 1970, voters in 10 of 14 states with referendums to lower the voting age in state elections refused to do so. Several states in fact, questioned the constitutionality of Congress's action and the Supreme Court, upholding the 18-year old vote in federal elections, ruled that Congress had acted unconstitutionally in changing the voting age for state and local elections. The 92nd Congress, to remedy the problem, approved a constitutional amendment lowering the voting age to 18 in all elections. The Senate approved the amendment by the astounding vote of 94 to 0 and the House by 400 to 19. The amendment was ratified by the states in mid-1971.

Why did Congress defy repeated expressions of public sentiment? Perhaps congressmen were more concerned that youngsters, on coming of age, would remember their negative votes and oppose their re-election than they were about immediate opposition from those people who were against lowering the voting age. More likely, congressmen stood to gain or lose little politically as a result of their actions. What is unmistakable, however, is that in a period marked by popular dissatisfaction with vast numbers of young people and consistent decisions of state electorates, Congress pursued its own idea of the national interest.

These patterns of response indicate no simple one-to-one relationship between the preferences of the public and action by Congress. What people want and what Congress does are not terribly far apart, especially over the long run. Take issues involving social welfare. For the past decade majorities have expressed their support for policies designed to provide increased benefits and to raise the living standards of citizens. Congress in turn has responded with a wide variety of programs, including aid to education, job training for the unemployed, the expansion of social security, medicaid, the funding of health services and hospital facilities, and so forth. Congressional response has not been steady, but rather by fits and starts, depending on public dispositions and political opportunities at particular points in time.

In the short run Congress may not respond quickly enough to meet national needs with effective policies. Part of the fault lies with Congress,

15. The roll call vote in the House cannot be interpreted, since it was on a measure that included not only the lowering of the voting age but the extension of the Voting Rights Act as well.

but only part of it. A major problem is that citizens do not always agree on what the nation needs. And Congress cannot get out too far ahead of the people on whom it depends. If the gap is great, individual members will risk repudiation; more importantly, congressional determinations will be unacceptable and as a result ineffective. The policy decisions of a representative body customarily are looked upon as *legitimate* and the consequences are accepted as *authoritative* by those who are represented. But there are no guarantees. To paraphrase President Kennedy, great innovations cannot be forced on dissenting majorities or even imposed on large minorities. As well as being suited to meet national needs, congressional decisions therefore must be tolerable to a good many people affected by them.

Policies are *authoritative* when they are accepted and adhered to by the vast majority of citizens. If proposals withstand legislative probing, testing, and bargaining, and if Congress does not ride against the tide of public opinion, the odds are that its policies will command broad support. Medicare for the aged, for example, was the product of more than a decade's work from its conception to its enactment. The process need not have taken so long, but time did have an effect. Major changes were made to meet objections, particularly those of congressional Republicans. Once passed, the bill, which embodied ideas many people and groups could claim as their own, became part of the national consensus. The debate now is no longer over governmental responsibility in this domain, but rather on the methods by which medical insurance will be extended to the entire population.

The outcome can be substantially different when Congress abdicates its responsibility for reaching authoritative decisions. The Economic Opportunity Act serves as an illustration. James L. Sundquist describes its enactment.[16] The president declared war on poverty, a task force prepared the battle plan, and committee chairmen and prospective sponsors were notified of the administration program. Congress, however, was given no real opportunity to study the program or render advice. Its consideration of this undertaking was almost cursory; it "rubber stamped" the measure within five months of the time it was announced. The outcome was a legislative achievement of historic scale, attained in record time. But it was the president's program—not that of Congress or the country. Throughout the nation important aspects of the antipoverty program came under quick fire. In Congress a sense of paternity was lacking; Republicans made it a partisan issue, and Democrats felt little responsibility to defend it. In passing the legislation, Congress had responded rapidly to a national need, but, as it turned out, not authorita-

16. Sundquist, *Politics and Policy*, pp. 493-494.

tively. Its action, in Sundquist's words, ". . . left the program without the base of reliable and continuing congressional and public support accorded those measures that were the product of the legislative branch's own initiative and tedious processes of refinement."

For an important policy to be effective, there must be widespread support within Congress and across the country. The policy must be workable as well. Can it be implemented to achieve what is intended? Achieving results that make a difference is a difficult challenge. But policies really work only when they accomplish what they are intended to accomplish, solve problems they are designed to solve, and meet society's real needs. If they do not fulfill these requirements, they may actually be more of a liability than a help.

Social security and medicare are examples of congressional policies that have worked fairly well. More recently congressional response to the problem of automobile safety provides an apt illustration. Since Congress legislated in 1966, cars have been equipped with numerous safety features, and largely as a result the death toll from traffic accidents in 1970 showed the first significant decrease in more than a decade and the lowest rate in many years. A more typical illustration, perhaps, is the truth-in-lending act, which went into effect in 1969 and required true interest rates on loans and credit purchases to be made known to consumers. There has been a high level of compliance with the acts's disclosure requirements and a significant increase in consumer knowledge. Nevertheless, many borrowers still do not know what interest rates they are being charged, because they do not read the notices supplied by lenders or do not remember the figures. Few are motivated to look for the best credit possibilities, which was one of the acts underlying purposes. Moving down the scale of "workability," other congressional measures, such as mass transit and occupational training, have probably been even less effective.

Congress itself is aware that it must not only respond with gestures and symbols; it must also produce authoritative, tolerable, workable policies. It is aware that it is not always healthy to raise expectations without furnishing some means of satisfying them as well. The job is hard, and this is one reason why the legislative process is often slow. Yet, because of its political competence, its independence, and its perceptiveness, Congress has been able to guarantee that most of its policies are authoritative and tolerable. It has not been nearly so successful in guaranteeing that they are workable. This may be mainly the responsibility of administration. Still, it is up to Congress to fashion policies that are *likely to work*, and then to take note and see that they do. It is here that congressional performance—and governmental performance generally—surely needs improvement.

THE CONGRESSIONAL INSTITUTION
AND CONGRESSIONAL PERFORMANCE

The way Congress performs its tasks and the difference it makes in the American political system depend primarily on the environment in which the congressional institution operates. Most importantly, as we have seen, Congress is a representative body, one that seldom ignores its constituents —their preferences, their demands, their needs. It reflects, although by no means perfectly, the values of the society it serves. When people want change, Congress moves more quickly, but perhaps more slowly than the public would desire. When people want stability, Congress moves more slowly, but perhaps more quickly than desired. Politics and the public in short, affect Congress' exercise of power in government, and have even more to do with influencing the patterns of congressional response.

But the congressional institution also plays a role. Congress is more than an instrument performing tasks and fulfilling functions. It is a human institution, with a life of its own somewhat apart from the society it serves. Its internal life influences the manner in which it undertakes tasks and the kinds of differences it makes. If we are to understand why Congress behaves as it does, we must look at its internal life, and particularly the ways it maintains itself and adopts to new conditions and new problems.[17]

Institutional Maintenance

Any institution—whether a university, a corporation, or a private association—devotes much attention to its own survival and well-being. Regardless of the goals it is supposed to achieve, and often at the expense of satisfying demands from outside, an institution will concentrate resources on itself. Congress is no exception. It provides for itself. If it did not, it could hardly provide for the nation. What it provides for itself, however, affects what it accomplishes for the nation.

The maintenance of Congress is linked to four fundamental institutional characteristics: autonomy, complexity, coherence, and dispersed power.[18] These characteristics have important consequences for the effectiveness of Congress. Some of these consequences are strongly positive, others less so.

17. The discussion below is supplemented by more detailed consideration in the following section, "The Congressional Institution."
18. My thinking along these lines has benefited from exploration of the concept "institutionalization" by Nelson W. Polsby, "The Institutionalization of the U.S. House of Representatives," *American Political Science Review*, 62 (March, 1968), pp. 144-168, and Samuel P. Huntington, *Political Order in Changing Societies* (Yale University Press, 1968), pp. 12-24.

Congress is a relatively autonomous institution. It is well-bounded or differentiated from its environment; despite its representative nature and the linkages between congressmen and constituents, the organization and procedures of Congress are not simply reflections of demands from outside. They are independent, with an integrity of their own. Furthermore the congressional career is unique. It is a particularly attractive one: both the Senate and the House are highly desirable locations for those aspiring to political office. The work is probably like no other. There is much for each member to do; the work-days are long, the sessions practically year-round, and the pace increasingly hectic. Congressmen regard themselves as professionals. They enjoy ample emoluments, including salaries of $42,500, expense allowances, fringe benefits, state or district offices, and various kinds of staff assistance. Congressmen value their institution for its own sake; they share feelings of identification with the legislature and loyalty to it. Regardless of their allegiances to parties, ties to constituencies, or affiliations with groups, members have a strong commitment to Congress. Both the Senate and the House attract able people and manage to hold them. Few incumbents voluntarily leave, and not many are defeated in primary and general elections. Entry is difficult and turnover is low.

Congress is a relatively *complex* institution. Within it are specialized agencies of party leadership, such as steering committees, policy committees, campaign committees, and whip organizations. There are specialized agencies to engage in substantive tasks and do legislative work, such as the standing, special, and select committees, and numerous subcommittees. The labor of members is divided. In both the Senate and the House, a significant part of institutional life revolves around the standing committee and subject-matter specialization. Committees and subcommittees, served by approximately one thousand staff members and holding over four thousand meetings each year, are the focal points in the legislative process. Specialization, by means of a division of labor among committees, is especially conspicuous in the House, which has over four times as many members as the Senate, but only a few more committees. Representatives can concentrate on one committee assignment, while senators by comparison are spread thin.

Congress is a relatively *coherent* institution. It attempts to maintain consensus, cohesion, and integration in order to prevent external forces from totally disrupting its internal life. It manages to do this, despite its being organized by two opposition parties, despite its dealing with contentious substantive issues, and despite its reflecting and resolving societal conflict. Many of the norms or expectations within Congress serve to promote the coherence of the institution. First are the norms of negotiating, bargaining, and compromise, which govern at every point where conflict is likely to intrude on the welfare of the institution. No solution is ideal from everyone's point of view; no one should expect an unequivocal or personal victory. Second is the norm of impersonality. Conflict must be confined to issues and not involve personalities, for the friends a member has on today's issue may be his enemies on tomorrow's. Automatic and objective criteria for the conduct of business and individual advancement are important. Precedents and rules should be followed because they decrease areas of discretion and increase predictability. The recruitment of leadership is based on apprenticeship within the system. Seniority, as a means of allocating chairmanships and committee rank, is useful because it minimizes contention and reduces personal dispute. The third of these norms is reciprocity. Members must be tolerant and accord others the same rights they desire for themselves. The code is to deal fairly and frankly with one another, and to keep one's commitments. Without mutual helpfulness, cooperation, and reciprocity in an institution in which members depend on each other, the system could easily break down.

Congress is an institution in which power is relatively *dispersed*. This derives in large part from specialization and from division of labor. The distribution of power in the Senate is today essentially "individualistic." Each individual member is influential as a result of a committee or subcommittee chairmanship, the formidability of the constituency he represents, the informality of procedures, the lack of hierarchy, and the equality of opportunities on the floor. Every senator has some institutional base which accords him influence and allows him to exercise leadership from time to time. Power in the House is also dispersed, but in a "decentralized" rather than "individualistic" manner. Committees and committee chairmen are the principal loci of influence. Because of the size of the House, organization is more hierarchical, leadership is more oligarchical, the rules of procedure are more rigid, and opportunities on the floor are fewer. For the most part, individual members must exercise whatever influence they can within the committees on which they serve.

Characteristics, such as autonomy, complexity, coherence, and dispersed power, have positive consequences for the performance of Congress. Beyond doubt they strengthen Congress as an institution, promoting its ability to participate in policy making, review and evaluation, and public education, and buttressing its capacity to check and balance the executive.

Institutional autonomy furnishes great incentives for individual members, results in stability of personnel, allows for the accumulation of experience, and enhances congressional competence in undertaking its tasks. *Institutional complexity*, marked by a division of labor and specialization through committees, makes it possible for most congressmen to have interesting jobs, to acquire knowledge, and to exercise influence on policy and administration. It also makes it possible for Congress to generate the information it needs to perform its tasks, to afford points of access for people who want to influence government, and to provide seedbeds for the initiation and development of different ideas. *Institutional coherence* permits members to derive greater satisfaction and security, to reduce personal risks, and to focus their energies on substantive jobs. This in turn enables Congress to make, review, and evaluate policy, as well as devise authoritative and workable solutions. *Dispersed institutional power*, whether individualistic or decentralized, means greater incentives for individual members. It also permits Congress to check and balance the executive. If, by contrast, power within Congress were highly centralized, there might well be an imbalance in governmental power. It is possible, although not very likely now, that Congress would dominate the executive. It is more probable, especially when the president's party and the majority party in the legislature coincided, that the executive would dominate Congress.

By increasing the capacity and power of Congress, all these effects appear essentially *positive*. But the same institutional characteristics also have effects that seem essentially *negative*. They engender a distinctive —although hardly immutable—emphasis on stability within Congress. In the past devotion to institutional stability has helped promote the principle of incrementalism and advance the values of minorities within the institution. This has limited, at least to some extent, Congress' ability to respond as rapidly as may be necessary to the nation's most pressing needs.

Incrementalism does not necessarily mean that congressional products and policies have any dominant ideological hue. It does mean that change is likely to be gradual and piecemeal, rather than radical and comprehensive. In part it is fostered by the continuity of congressional personnel. There is little alternation from one session to the next in the membership of the Senate and House. Committee membership is similarly stable, since the seniority system and emphasis on specialization discourage individuals from switching committee assignments once they have made initial investments. As a result, most members of Congress and most members of committees deal with like issues session after session. On the one hand this facilitates the development of expertness; on the other, it discourages new perspectives from being brought to bear. Even if problems change, issues may be perceived for some time as quite similar to those of the past. Previous policy discussions and decisions are emphasized; the legislative process is cumulative; and whatever change is made is apt to be marginal, incremental. To some extent, of course, today's issues are like yesterday's; but to some extent also the characteristics that shape institutional life make them appear even more so than they are in fact.

Incrementalism is fostered in part by the very processes of the legislature. These processes are cumbersome and sometimes tediously slow. The likelihood of radical policy change—either forward or backward—is minimal. Several factors play a role, not the least of which is the manner in which legislation is considered by Congress. There are multiple points at which consideration occurs and decisions are made. Subcommittees and committees of each house, debate and voting on the floor of each chamber, often an interhouse conference and subsequent agreement by majorities in each chamber—all mean staged consideration. The decision making is serial, requiring a number of different approvals; a single negative action along this line may be enough to defeat a proposal. Proponents have to prevail at every stage. Agreements reached must be cumulative, able to survive successive onslaughts; victory must be won and rewon. Opponents, however, have a disproportionate opportunity to prevail. They can bring a measure down to defeat at any one point, and they can modify it at any of several stages as a precondition for its eventual adoption. Rapid congressional response requires majorities at virtually every step along the way.

Majorities are difficult to summon at the right time and the right place. Minorities desirous of stopping a measure or action do not always win, but intense and organized minorities can badly delay or even defeat measures supported by apathetic and disorganized majorities. And if a minority includes the chairman of the committee which exercises jurisdiction, it is in an especially favorable strategic position. Thus the congressional system is designed to placate minorities, weighing each demand with utmost political deliberation before action is taken. The filibuster in the Senate still serves as a graphic illustration of minority negative power. If a minority of one-third plus one is opposed to a bill or resolution, the Senate majority may be unable to act. At the very least it will usually have to grant concessions in order to win over enough votes to end a filibuster. One can easily see that the job of proponents, who have to build majority coalitions at a number of points, is increased enormously by having to build a two-thirds coalition on the Senate floor.

Autonomy, complexity, coherence, and dispersed power, by fostering incrementalism and advantaging minorities, produce negative effects. It is doubtful that these can be completely avoided, unless we are willing to throw the baby out with the bath water. The positive effects of these same characteristics are critical to congressional performance and congressional power. The characteristics cannot be dismissed, not unless we dismiss Congress as an effective political institution. On the other hand, it is possible for improvement to be made—for Congress to alter its internal life for the purpose of increasing responsiveness to external needs, without diminishing either its performance or its power.

Institutional Adaptability

Every institution must change and adapt itself to changing conditions and times. The family, for example, cannot withstand the pressure of industrialized society or the more rapid maturation of youth without some form of adaptation. The university, for instance, cannot serve as the same citadel of learning in the 1970s as it did in the 1950s; it must adapt to technocracy, larger enrollments, and new demands by its clientele. Similarly Congress must change to keep abreast of new times and new problems. Can Congress change? Is it adaptable? If survival is the test, then there is little doubt about the answer. If meeting challenges from outside is the test, then there is room for dispute. Some years ago the adaptability of the congressional institution was more doubtful than it is today. Since the mid-1960s, while major transformation was taking place in American society, Congress too was transformed. One observer, with no more than slight exaggeration, has referred to change within Congress during this period as being so profound as to merit the term "revolution." [19] Partly due to influences from outside and partly of its own making, Congress has undergone important alteration in its personnel, its norms, its organization, and its procedures. As a result, the bonds of incrementalism and the advantages of internal minorities have been somewhat eroded, and the opportunities for individual members have become somewhat expanded. The system is more flexible now than at any time in the recent past.

The men—and consequently the institution in which they serve—are quite different today. About a decade ago, the Senate man was accurately depicted as one who went through a long apprenticeship before trying to assert himself and who specialized in a few policy areas. He was an "insider," distinguished by his regard for and conformity to institutional norms. But there were also "outsiders," men who were less concerned about the esteem of their colleagues and more intent on speaking out on behalf of ideological allies across the nation.[20] The Senate then tolerated both roles, and now it tolerates them even more comfortably. A freshman need no longer wait, not only to speak out, but also to take the initiative and to exercise influence in committee or on the floor.

19. Stephen K. Bailey, *Congress in the Seventies* (St. Martin's Press, 1970), p. vii.
20. For the contrast between "insiders" and "outsiders" see: William S. White, *Citadel* (Harper & Brothers, 1956); Donald R. Matthews, *U.S. Senators and Their World* (University of North Carolina Press, 1960); and Ralph K. Huitt, "The Outsider in the Senate: An Alternative Role," in Huitt and Robert L. Peabody, *Congress: Two Decades of Analysis* (Harper & Row, 1969), pp. 159-178.

Primarily because of its large size, the House has not changed quite so much. The "insider" role still predominates, but more and more younger members are participating in important ways and deriving satisfaction because they are getting something done.

Gradual turnover of personnel has helped erode traditional folkways and make the system looser. It has also resulted in the erosion of Southern dominance. Between 1946 and 1970, for instance, the number of Democratic representatives elected from non-Southern states (in midterm elections, when the presidency was not in contest) has steadily increased—85, 132, 133, 184, 163, 165, and 176. Northern Democrats suffered from the Republican sweep in the elections of 1946, but recovered and made great gains in 1958. Now they are becoming the most senior members of Congress. Southern over-representation on the most important party committees and standing committees and as chairmen of subcommittees is waning; and in the 1970s Northerners, not Southerners, are rising to the top and reaping the fruits of seniority. Congress is no longer a Southern institution.

Whether Northerners or Southerners benefit, the stability of individual tenure in Congress is still a problem. This is because senators and representatives are, to some extent at least, prisoners of their initial "mandates"—partially reflective of popular sentiment and partially self-defined at the time of their first election. Such mandates tend to exert influence on congressmen's perceptions and behavior years after they were received. So despite changing problems and needs, congressmen who are reelected time after time may continue to see things in approximately the same old way.

How can a change in membership be encouraged, so that new "mandates" are more likely to be represented? One method would be to decrease the attractiveness of the congressional career for incumbents. This, however, is neither desirable nor workable. Another would be to limit the number of terms a senator or representative might serve. This method may have merit, but understandably it commands almost no support within Congress and is not likely to be adopted. Yet there is reasonable hope that turnover will increase in the future. First, able and skilled individuals are seeking congressional office in greater numbers than before. Second, modern technologies and the services of expert campaign consultants may reduce the advantages of incumbents. Third, new bases of campaign support are being developed, and the ability of traditional party organizations to impose their will may be diminishing. Fourth, the reform of campaign financing, with provisions for public disclosure and a limitation on expenditures, may give a number of challengers a better chance of unseating incumbents. Fifth, with a major change in the composition of the electorate due to the Eighteen-Year-

Old-Vote Amendment, it may turn out that few incumbents are as safe in the future as they have been in the past.

The advantages of incumbency still exist, but things already appear to be changing. A portent is found in the primary elections for the House in 1970. In seven previous elections, from 1956 through 1968, only 33 House incumbents who ran in primaries were defeated by non-incumbent challengers.[21] Of these, 21 were from the South or border states, where primaries in effect substituted for general elections. Only five northern Democrats and seven Republicans lost primary races during this period. In 1970 one Republican and nine northern Democratic House incumbents lost primaries. This is hardly a monumental shift, but in comparison to the past it is notable indeed.

With change in personnel over the past decade there has also been a change in the opportunity structure in Congress. Standing committees maintain much of their strength, especially in the House, but alternative opportunities for participation and leadership are arising. Some are provided by the recent invigoration of the party organization in Congress. In the Senate, for instance, the Democratic Policy Committee and the caucus have taken on new life under Majority Leader Mike Mansfield. Both agencies are now committing the Senate Democratic party to positions on national policy. In the House the power of the Democratic caucus has also developed in past years, with the majority taking party stands on more and more issues. There is an effort by leaders in both chambers to encourage the rank and file to play a greater role through the mechanism of the legislative party. Other opportunities are provided by the establishment of relatively new party groupings. Formed in 1959, the Democratic Study Group in the House has a membership of about half the majority party and a whip system of its own. It has prodded the Democratic leadership, pushed a number of procedural reforms, and exerted considerable influence on many policy outcomes. Still other opportunities come about because of the salience of new issues. In 1967 a bipartisan, bicameral group—called Members of Congress for Peace through Law—was formed to focus on foreign and military policy. By 1970 it included 28 senators and 70 representatives, and gave its members a chance to develop knowledge and proposals outside the regular standing-committee structure. More and more, younger congressmen are holding informal rump hearings on controversial issues in order to bypass regular committees.

The autonomy of committees and the power of minorities on them have recently been challenged more vigorously than before. Many

21. A few more were defeated by other incumbents, after district lines were changed by reapportionments.

standing committees in both the Senate and House have adopted rules for more democratic conduct, designed to enable a majority of members to work its will. Revolts against arbitrary chairmen have occurred with increasing frequency. Most important, the seniority system, whereby the majority party members with the longest consecutive service on the committee automatically became chairman, has come under attack. House Democrats, for example, have overriden seniority in several recent instances. In 1965 they denied the seniority rights of two southerners who had publicly supported Goldwater for president. Two years later they stripped Representative Adam Clayton Powell of his seniority and his committee chairmanship. In 1969 they deprived a southern congressman, who had supported George Wallace for president, of his seniority on a standing committee.

At the beginning of the 92nd Congress the seniority system underwent substantial modification. In the House both parties decided that seniority should not be the sole basis for the selection of committee chairmen and ranking minority members. Now, if ten or more members desire, the Democratic caucus will vote on the recommendations of the party's committee on committees regarding the chairmanship and membership of each standing committee. Now the Republican conference can vote on nominations for ranking minority members (or chairmen, when Republicans become a majority in the House) of the committees. In the Senate, Democrats agreed that their caucus would approve all chairmen and members of standing committees, and Republicans also took steps to modify their seniority system. Although seniority will continue as the principal criterion, the new party rules make it much easier for members to challenge irresponsible or arbitrary chairmen (and ranking minority members). The caucuses now can warn—and may even depose—erring chairmen, and party leaders have greater leverage to back their demands for more responsible, cooperative chairmanship behavior.

Some other changes that affect committees also deserve mention. The Senate Republican party decided that no member could have the ranking minority position on more than one standing committee; the House Democratic party decided that no member could be chairman of more than one legislative subcommittee, freeing about thirty subcommittee chairmanships for younger members of the majority. Now, power is more dispersed, because more than one-quarter of the members of the House are chairmen of subcommittees. The Legislative Reorganization Act of 1970 made a variety of revisions that pertain to committees. In the future, senators can serve on only two major committees and one minor, select, or joint committee; they can be members of the Armed Services, Appropriations, Finance, or Foreign Relations Committees, but not more than one; and they can hold the chairmanship of only one full committee and one subcommittee of a major committee. In addition, there are provisions requiring that votes cast in a committee be made public, that a committee report a bill shortly after a majority so requests, that hearings be announced in advance, and that the use of proxy votes in committee be limited. All of these changes, if effectively implemented, should serve to reduce control by chairmen and to increase opportunities for individual congressmen.

One reform of the 1970 Act merits special note. Previously many important amendments have been decided in the Committee of the Whole of the House of Representatives, without any possibility of a record vote identifying each member's position on the issue. Only from one-quarter to one-half of all the representatives participated in non-record votes, even on important amendments. Now, upon the request of twenty members a teller vote will be recorded, identifying by name members voting for, against, and not voting on the question. Recorded votes in the Committee of the Whole promise to increase rank-and-file participation. On the first such vote ever taken, a historical occasion early in 1971, as many as 391 members passed by the tellers to be counted. On the second such vote, shortly thereafter, 419 members took positions on the question of funding further development of the supersonic transport plane (SST). During the first 6 months of the 92nd Congress, an average of 383 members voted on each of the 41 recorded teller votes on key amendments. This was twice the average vote on non-recorded votes. Recorded votes also promise to decrease committee influence. Ordinarily the members of a committee reporting a bill have dominated on the floor. Their attendance has been good and they have tended to vote as a bloc against non-committee sponsored amendments. With more representatives participating, and with the possibility of *ad hoc* coalitions on particular issues, challenges to committees should be stiffer and the chances of their being overruled should be greater.[22]

Whether exerted through committees or otherwise, the power of internal minorities is being contested in Congress. The House Rules Committee had long been a key point for minority opposition. It was

22. This is certainly indicated by the vote on appropriations for the SST. The Appropriations Committee supported funding, with almost two-thirds of its members —particularly the Democrats—in favor. Yet a majority of members of the House voted against the Committee's recommendation, and against the position of the leadership of both parties. Recorded votes may well reduce the influence of party leadership, which tends to support committee proposals and to vary inversely with the visibility of action taken by the House. They may also reduce the influence of organized lobbying and facilitate bipartisan coalitions. On SST, for example, many Republicans resisted pressures by the White House, and many Democrats resisted pressures by labor. A coalition composed of 53 percent of the Democrats and 48 percent of the Republicans voted in opposition to continued funding.

enlarged after major battle in 1961, thus enabling the Democratic leadership to have greater control. It was subjected to a 21-day rule in 1965, thus enabling the Democratic leadership to bring six measures out of the committee to the House floor. Though this rule was revoked two years later, a new chairman, as condition for accession, agreed to the adoption of committee rules that allowed a majority to work its will. Again in 1971 an effort was made by the Democratic caucus to enact a rule which facilitated the bypassing of the committee; but the attempt was beaten by a coalition of Republicans and Southern Democrats. The Rules Committee maintained a measure of authority, but over the course of a decade strenuous challenge had made it more of an irksome gatekeeper than a bastion of negative power in the House. Now, it may slow bills up, but it rarely keeps legislation from coming to the floor.

The Senate filibuster has traditionally been an obstacle to majority rule. For many years the filibuster was used to defeat civil rights legislation. Since 1964, however, cloture has been invoked three times to end debate and allow civil rights bills to come to a vote and be passed. Lately, repeated attempts have been made to liberalize the cloture rule by allowing less than two-thirds of the senators present and voting to bring a measure to a vote. Through the opening of the 92nd Congress, none was successful. Nevertheless, the filibuster is no longer the obstacle to majority rule that it once was, and recently it has been used as much by liberals and by moderates trying to establish new priorities as it has been used by conservatives trying to prevent change.

Much has happened of late, but much still remains to be done. Given incrementalism and checks inherent in the legislative process, there is little justification for not making cloture easier to obtain and permitting a majority to work its will in the Senate. Even more important is the matter of reforming conference committees. Occasionally members of these committees, which finally resolve disagreements on legislation between the Senate and the House, do not represent the views of majorities in their chambers. Perhaps conferees should be actually appointed by party leaders, who are more accountable to their followers, instead of by committee chieftains. In addition, provisions of the Legislative Reorganization Act need to be made to work; the rank and file should demand that new committee rules be faithfully observed; and the majority of members in each party grouping should insist on exercising some control over the organization and operations of their house.

Whatever remains to be achieved, there is little doubt that Congress has been undergoing major adaptation. It has changed, and yet without sacrifice of the positive aspects of its institutional life, without reduction of its capacity to perform its tasks, and without diminution of its collective power. Change in the contemporary Congress is notable, although not revolutionary. The institution is now more responsive to majorities of its members. It is also more responsive to the problems and needs of the nation.

CONCLUSIONS

Congress is by no means perfect. But it has been getting better, not worse. Its performance in policy making, review and evaluation, and public education has improved considerably. Internally the institution is probably healthier than ever before.

Congress is a positive and an effective force in our political system. If we desire access for grievances, discontents, and new ideas, Congress can and does provide it. If we wish to assure that no political interest lacks a spokesman or is deprived of a chance to achieve its goals, Congress can and does offer an adequate arena. If we want dissonance, opposition, and alternatives to have some base for expression, Congress can and does furnish such a base. If we are opposed to the accumulation of governmental power, Congress can and does prevent excessive concentration.

If we insist on quick solutions to all our ills, Congress cannot and does not meet our demand. It is a human institution and represents the strengths and weaknesses of the humanity it serves. Its solutions are never entirely satisfactory to one side or the other, or to one group or the next, nor do they even solve all of the problems that impend. Congress responds in different ways—to the preferences of people, the pressures of groups, and to what most of its members believe to be the needs of the nation. Congressional response is generally not too far from what the public wants or is willing to accept. Any divergence between Congress and the people is not attributable to the former's intransigence. Rather it is attributable to the fact that Congress is more informed, more tolerant of different views, more susceptible to new ideas, more resistant to momentary passions, more concerned with workable results, and more farsighted than most of the people it represents.

In view of the magnitude of problems and threats in the world and in America today, the effectiveness of the contemporary Congress may not be great enough. Overwhelming challenges show no signs of diminishing in the foreseeable future. Even the simple matters, where there is fundamental consensus, are complex. Their solutions require new technologies, greater cooperation among governments and private institutions, and the expenditure of vast sums of money. Then there are other matters—where disagreement prevails. Conflict among nations, tension between races, and economic and social inequality among people exist. Cleavages are sharp and deep-rooted, and there is little agreement as to how these problems can be solved or whether they can be solved at all.

The United States is in difficulty. But Congress should not be held responsible. It has done well in the recent past; it is doing better now. Paradoxically, the greater its efforts and the more substantial its accomplishments, the more Congress is condemned for its failure. Congress has not failed; it promotes change, but it also ensures continuity. We need Congress, and not terribly different from the way it is now. Particularly during a period of cleavage and tension, we need it to foster cooperation and accommodation. Particularly during a period of social and cultural upheaval, we need it to show concern with order and stability. Particularly during a period of temper and impatience, we need it to encourage tolerance. And should life ever again be calm, we need it to question conventional values and stir things up. All this we can and should expect of an effective Congress. But we should recognize that it is incapable of magic.

THE CONGRESSIONAL

INSTITUTION

To understand and evaluate Congress, it is necessary to examine the behavior of congressmen, the organization of Congress, and finally the legislative process in Congress, from the introduction of bills to their enactment into law.

THE BEHAVIOR OF CONGRESSMEN

The behavior of congressmen is, of course, shaped by a variety of forces. The constitutional and electoral systems of the United States are of obvious importance. The Senate is composed of 100 members—two senators elected by the citizens of each state for 6-year terms. The House is composed of 435 members, apportioned according to the relative populations of the states, and elected for 2-year terms. About one-third of the Senate seats and all House seats are up for contest in each even-numbered year.

Once recruited, nominated, and elected to Congress, members naturally do their jobs and fulfill their obligations in differing ways. Their personal and social background characteristics and the experiences of their previous careers all influence their behavior. But probably what affects their behavior as congressmen most are the interest groups with which they deal, the constituencies which they represent, and the parties to which they belong.

The Role of Interest Groups

Sometimes of great influence on congressmen, and usually of some influence, are the many organized interest groups—representing business, labor, professions, and others—that operate on the national, state, or local scene.

(1) *The Nature of Groups.* Strong groups are obviously in a better position to influence congressmen than are weak groups.

A group's strength is related to the resources it has available. Wealth is important, for it permits a group to employ skillful lobbyists and clever public relations experts. Economic power also counts, since it is difficult if not impossible to ignore the welfare of giant corporations in a capitalist society. Numbers and size matter: the larger the membership, the greater a group's potential electoral muscle. The wider a group's geographical base, the larger the number of senators and representatives to whom the group can make a constituency-related appeal. A history demonstrating endurance promotes strength, for permanence on the scene enables Congress to deal with the same interests, the same organizations, and often the same lobbyists over a continuing period of time. Legitimacy also is of great value: if a group and its aims are confidently recognized to be legitimate, both can be assured a sympathetic hearing on Capitol Hill.

Significant as such resources are, they alone are not sufficient. What is needed is a group motivated to use them. Without motivated use, the advantages of numbers, wealth, legitimacy, and so forth may never be realized. Indeed, the dedication and militancy of a group may often be critical, especially on the kinds of issues that directly affect a group's self-interest.[1] Provided there is incentive to shape legislative outcomes, then group skills and techniques come into play. Lobbyists serve as channels of communication. These professionals provide congressmen with information, both on the technical aspects of legislation and on how group demands relate politically to the congressman's career, his concerns, and his constituents. Credibility is a prime asset of interest-group lobbyists, who will therefore rarely risk distorting the information or exaggerating the claims they present to wary politicians. Lobbyists use persuasion, not so much on congressmen as on their constituents, who are urged by mail or phone to write or talk to senators and representatives and to testify at committee hearings. Pressure, by means of promising rewards or threatening punishments, is rarely used as a tactic; since congressmen resent pressure, there are doubts that it is effective, and it backfires easily.

(2) *Interaction With Groups.* Few congressmen question the legitimacy

1. But sometimes the self-interest of a group is not self-evident, and therefore an important objective of a group is to define and specify the interests of its members. See Raymond A. Bauer, Ithiel de Sola Pool, and Lewis Anthony Dexter, *American Business and Public Policy* (Atherton, 1963), part 4.

of organized groups.[2] But beyond the orientations of congressmen are the actual relationships between congressmen and interest groups. Groups usually interact with legislators who are on their side. Labor lobbyists are more likely to maintain continuing relationships with members who favor labor, and business lobbyists are more inclined to keep in close touch with those who sympathize with business. Often interest group representatives and congressmen work together when specific legislation, such as medical care, mass tranit, and civil rights, is of mutual concern.

(3) *The Situational Context.* If legislation is specialized, affecting directly only a small segment of the public, the groups concerned will have a greater say. If a group is a single-purpose one—concentrating on one type of issue—its interest will be given the most serious attention. The sugar lobby, for instance, is a group that has much to say about sugar quotas, mainly because this subject is practically its exclusive interest. When legislation requires a complicated bill or when implementation requires the cooperation of an interest group, that group will be consulted on—and perhaps indulged in—many of the details of legislation. When an issue is not significant to a member's constituents, when his personal philosophy or convictions offer little guidance, and when he and his closest colleagues possess little knowledge, then the information and assistance provided by groups may be extremely influential.

On issues that are general and arouse considerable public attention, any single group will play a less decisive role, because ". . . nearly every vigorous push in one direction stimulates an opponent or coalition of opponents to push in the opposite direction." Such countervailing power tends to reduce the effectiveness of particular groups, since "when groups push on both sides of an issue, officials can more freely exercise their judgment than when the groups push on only one side." [3] When the interested groups push on the same side of an issue, and the unorganized public is quiescent, the coalition naturally will carry the day.

Defensive groups ordinarily have a short-run advantage over offensive ones, since it is easier to preserve the status quo than to change it. Defeating a bill at one of the decision points in the legislative process is less of a challenge than steering it successfully by the many obstacles on Capitol Hill. In the long run, however, a persevering group that commands resources and can stir people will prevail despite the defensive nature of the congressional terrain.

The Role of Constituencies

A lobbyist will try to demonstrate to a congressman that a course of action is in the interest not only of a particular group but of his state or

2. Roger H. Davidson, *The Role of the Congressman* (Pegasus, 1969), pp. 162-174.
3. Lester W. Milbrath, *The Washington Lobbyists* (Rand McNally, 1963), p. 345.

district as well. A congressman must represent his constituents. Ignored or dissatisfied constituents can invoke the most severe type of sanction —withholding their votes and ending the congressman's career.

Representing a constituency means many things. It means answering mail, running errands, and doing "case work" for people back home. It means being aware of local interests and doing something to advance them by means of legislation. Finally, it means responsiveness to—but not always acceptance of—constituency mandates, if and when such mandates exist.

(1) *Linkages.* Although many studies have demonstrated relationships between congressmen and their constituencies, none has done so as persuasively as one that surveyed samples of constituents, interviewed incumbents and challengers, and analyzed the roll-call votes of representatives of 116 congressional districts.[4] An examination of three policy domains—social welfare, foreign involvement, and civil rights—shows varying degrees of congruence between the voting behavior of legislators and the attitudes of people in their districts. On social welfare issues there is substantial agreement; on matters pertaining to foreign involvement there is no agreement whatsoever; and on issues relating to civil rights there is the greatest agreement between congressmen and their constituents.

Generally, there are two ways in which a constituency may control the actions of its representatives. It can choose as representative a person who shares its views, or it can choose a person who will follow his perception of district opinion, primarily to get reelected. These two paths of constituency control are shown in Fig. 3.1. Given Paths A and B, as depicted in the figure, two principal conditions must be met if constituency influence is actually to be exercised.

First, a legislator's roll-call voting behavior must agree with either his own attitude or with his perception of his constituency's attitude. In each of the three policy domains, this condition is met. The voting behavior of congressmen is strongly related to a combination of their

4. The following discussion is based on Warren E. Miller and Donald E. Stokes, "Constituency Influence in Congress," in Robert L. Peabody and Nelson W. Polsby, eds., *New Perspectives on the House of Representatives,* 2nd ed. (Rand McNally, 1969), pp. 31-53. It should be noted that a recent survey of public opinion in ten congressional districts, sponsored by the American Business Committee on National Priorities, found that voting on roll calls by ten House leaders had not reflected the views of majorities of their constituents on a number of key issues. Nonetheless, when asked, constituents could rarely recall how their representatives had voted on these issues, but nonetheless rated their performance high. One congressman, who reflected his district's views on key issues more than any other leader, however, ranked second from the bottom among the ten—with only 54 percent registering approval—on his job rating. *New York Times,* August 23, 1971.

Figure 3.1. Channels of Constituency Control

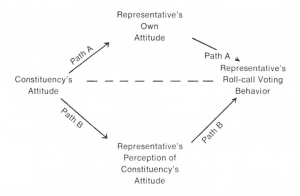

Source: Adapted from Warren E. Miller and Donald E. Stokes, "Constituency Influence in Congress," in Robert L. Peabody and Nelson W. Polsby (eds.), *New Perspectives on the House of Representatives,* 2nd ed. (Rand McNally, 1969), p. 41.

own views on policy and their perceptions of their district's views. Second, a representative's own attitude or his perception of his constituency's attitude must correspond, to some extent, with the constituency's attitude. In each of the three policy domains the linkage is weaker. But it varies considerably. On civil rights, representatives perceive constituency opinions quite accurately, and their own attitudes correspond somewhat with those that prevail in the district. On social welfare, perception is inaccurate, and the correspondence between the representatives' own attitudes and constituency views is slight. On foreign involvement, perception is also inaccurate, and there is little relationship at all between representative and constituency attitudes.

One more condition must be satisfied for constituency control to exist. Constituents must take the policy views of candidates into account in choosing their congressman. This seldom happens, since only about half of the people in a district have even read or heard something about the incumbent (and fewer have read or heard about the challenger), and hardly any have knowledge of the candidates' views on legislative issues. Strangely, however, this condition is met, although imperfectly, because congressmen believe that their constituents are watching them and fear that they may become aroused and repudiate them. Politicians want to win. Thy think in terms of increments and margins. They recognize that a few voters who do consider issues, and numbers of others who may be mobilized by these few, can make the difference between victory and defeat. Lightning does not strike incumbents often, but every congressman is aware that it may strike him.

(2) *Impact.* That "congressmen from different kinds of constituencies are likely to vote differently on matters of public policy, and those from

similar constituencies are likely to vote in similar ways"[5] has been recognized by many students of congressional voting behavior. Senators from different types of states occasionally differ, because of the effects of issues on constituency interests. Representatives who come from more homogeneous constituencies than senators are even more likely to differ on issues that directly affect their constituents. Congressmen from urban, suburban, and rural districts do vote differently, at least some of the time. The types of people who are represented certainly count, although less than the party affiliations of the persons who represent them.

The Role of Parties

Whether a congressman is a Democrat or Republican has a greater bearing on how he votes than whether he comes from one type of state or district or another. Two senators from the same state but belonging to different parties disagree frequently, despite the fact that their constituencies are identical. Successive members of the House of different parties but representing the same districts—a Republican succeeded by a Democrat, for example—will vote quite dissimilarly in successive Congresses.

(1) *Constituency and Party Congruence.* Usually constituency and party are not in conflict. Certain types of constituencies are more likely to elect Democrats, and other types are more likely to elect Republicans. The lower the socio-economic status of voters, the larger the number of non-whites, and the higher the percentage of urban population in a district, the greater the chance that it will be represented in the House by a Democrat. By contrast, the higher the socio-economic status, the fewer non-whites, and the smaller the urban population, the more likely the election of a Republican representative becomes.[6]

The pattern of partisan representation has been fairly stable. During the period from 1954 to the elections of 1970, as many as 255 of the 435 House seats (58.6 percent) have been controlled by the same party. At any specific election about three out of four congressional districts are considered "safe" for one party or the other. In the 1970 elections only 27 House seats changed hands, with the Democrats winning a net of nine from the Republicans. In the Senate 56 seats have remained under the control of the same party from 1954 until the election of 1970. In the latter year only six Senate seats changed hands, with the Republicans making a net gain of two.

(2) *Differences Between the Parties.* When party and constituency

5. Lewis A. Froman, Jr., *Congressmen and Their Constituencies* (Rand McNally, 1963), p. 11.
6. Ibid., ch. 7.

factors coincide, congressmen find it easy to vote with their party. On most occasions, as a matter of fact, congressmen will go along with their party rather than go against it. The partisan identification of members of Congress is usually strong. Congressmen are normally raised in one party or the other; they pursue political careers in the context of party; they form friendships within Congress along party lines; and they are appealed to most by leaders of their party and the interest groups allied with it.

The views of rank-and-file citizens differ, depending upon the party with which they identify. The views of congressmen from the two parties diverge even more.

Differences between the parties is persuasively demonstrated by the opinions on thirteen current issues of 437 candidates for the House—both incumbents and non-incumbents and Democrats and Republicans—in the 1970 elections.[7] On nearly every issue the opinions of Democrats and Republicans diverge. Table 3.2 shows that consistently higher percentages of Democrats take what might be termed the "liberal" or "activist" position. On the Supreme Court, Vietnam, inflation, defense spending, health insurance, minimum income, and abortion laws the differences are extremely sharp. Democrats, moreover, appear to be becoming more liberal, as is indicated by a higher percentage of Democratic non-incumbents than incumbents taking the liberal position on each issue. No such pattern appears for the Republicans, which suggests that differences among Democrats are not attributable only to the fact that incumbents have modified their views as a result of the practicalities of congressional service. As the bottom row of the table shows, an average of 63 percent of Democratic incumbents and 80 percent of Democratic non-incumbents take liberal or activist positions, while an average of only 38 percent of Republican incumbents and 40 percent of Republican non-incumbents take similar positions.

Such sharp differences are not reflected in voting in Congress, mainly because issues that reach a roll call are more specific and usually have been compromised in order to ensure majority support before a vote takes place on the floor. Nevertheless, "party differences tend to be more persistent than any other pattern of division in both the House and

7. A mail questionnaire was sent to 874 candidates by *Congressional Quarterly.* A total of 437 House candidates and 36 Senate candidates responded. Included in my discussion are only the opinions of House candidates, since too few incumbent senators responded. *Congressional Quarterly Weekly Report,* 28 (October 16, 1970), pp. 2542-2569. Because the issue is of a different type, excluded from consideration are responses pertaining to the seniority system in Congress, which was the fourteenth subject in the poll.

Table 3.2.   Opinion Differences between Democratic and Republican
House Candidates, 1970

| | Percentages Taking "Liberal" or "Activist" Position | | | |
| | Democratic Candidates | | Republican Candidates | |
Issue	Incumbents	Non-Incumbents	Incumbents	Non-Incumbents
Campus disorders	73	79	56	55
Marijuana laws	83	87	79	65
Supreme Court	59	77	24	28
Vietnam war	55	86	18	14
Industrial pollution	78	92	58	63
Automotive pollution	65	82	50	55
Inflation	70	77	29	33
Civil rights	48	63	15	21
Defense spending	55	87	17	24
Military draft	56	72	81	72
Health insurance	69	83	19	23
Minimum income	54	86	15	35
Abortion laws	59	63	34	29
13-Issue average	63	80	38	40

Source: Adapted from *Congressional Quarterly Weekly Report*, 28 (October 16, 1970), pp. 2562-2569.

Senate. . . ." [8] The pressure of party is more important than any single other type of pressure. An examination of House votes in 12 selected sessions since 1921 reveals that on virtually all non-unanimous roll-call votes the behavior of Democratic and Republican representatives differed significantly. This does not mean that all members of one party vote in opposition to all members of the other or even that 90 percent of the members of one oppose 90 percent of the other. Such divisions rarely occur. But frequently a majority of Democrats votes on one side of an issue, while a majority of Republicans votes the opposite way. Since 1921 these "party votes" have occurred anywhere from about 36 to about 61 percent of the time in the House, depending on the particular Congress. Since the 1920s and 1930s the proportion of "party votes" has declined. But they still occur on a significant number of issues.

(3) *Party Groupings.* Constituency attitudes, electoral competition, and personal beliefs all help to explain why some senators and representatives are less inclined to vote with their parties than others. For Democrats, deviation from party can most easily be explained by sectionalism. Southern Democrats have less loyalty to the "national party" than

8. Julius Turner, rev. ed. by Edward V. Schneier, Jr., *Party and Constituency: Pressures on Congress* (Johns Hopkins Press, 1970), p. 15. The historical discussion of differences in party voting is based largely on this work. Also see essay on the parties, pp. 46 ff.

Northern Democrats. They are less likely to vote with the majority of their party colleagues and more likely to side with the Republican opposition.

An analysis of voting in the House during the 86th and 87th Congresses (1959-1962) shows how deep the cleavage is in the Democratic party. Data on voting in ten issue-domains by Northern Democrats, Southern Democrats, and Republicans is shown in Table 3.3, where "liberalism" scores can vary from +1.00, the most liberal voting by all members . of the group, to −1.00, the least liberal (or most conservative) voting by all members of the group.[9] With the exception of civil rights, Northern Democrats score higher on "liberalism" than either Southern Democrats or Republicans; and on civil rights there is little difference between Northern Democrats and Republicans. On area redevelopment, aid to education, minimum wage, housing, and welfare nearly all Northern Democrats vote in the liberal direction. By contrast, Republicans vote in the conservative direction. As for Southern Democrats, their behavior resembles that of Republicans more than that of their Northern colleagues. Only on welfare is there a distinct resemblance between them and Northern Democrats.

Table 3.3. *Voting by Party Groupings in the House, 1959-1962*

	"Liberalism" Scores *		
Issue Domain	*Northern Democrats*	*Southern Democrats*	*Republicans*
Labor	+.23	−.86	−.87
Area redevelopment	+.94	+.06	−.59
Aid to education	+.92	−.17	−.20
Minimum wage	+.90	−.21	−.07
Housing	+.88	+.03	−.84
Welfare	+.98	+.81	−.31
Foreign aid	+.71	−.35	−.02
Trade expansion	+.80	+.38	−.23
Civil liberties	+.63	−.99	−.67
Civil rights	+.71	−.96	+.74

* Scores may vary from +1.00, the most liberal, to −1.00, the least liberal or most conservative.

Source: Adapted from W. Wayne Shannon, *Party, Constituency and Congressional Voting* (Louisiana State University Press, 1968), tables 18 through 34.

9. These data are based on the analysis by W. Wayne Shannon, in *Party, Constituency and Congressional Voting* (Louisiana State University Press, 1968), ch. 4. Shannon's roll call voting scales are for 17 issues in ten domains. My "liberalism" scores for groups are derived by assigning a value of +1 for all members with the lowest (most liberal) scale score, a value of −1 for all members with the highest (least liberal) scale score, and a value of 0 for all scores in between. The sum of all values divided by the total number of members in the group results then in a group "liberalism" score.

THE ORGANIZATION OF CONGRESS

In addition to such institutional characteristics as autonomy, complexity, coherence, and dispersed power, two areas of congressional organization demand attention. Of major importance in Congress are party leadership and standing committees.

Party Leadership

The principal functions of party leaders and leadership agencies are the following: (1) helping to organize the parties and distribute party members among standing committees; (2) scheduling legislative business, including the reference of bills to committees and the determination of when bills will be considered on the floor; (3) promoting attendance for floor votes, so that bills reported by committees and backed by party majorities can be passed; (4) collecting and distributing information about the substance and scheduling of legislation and about the intentions and strategies of various participants in the legislative process; (5) attempting to persuade party members to follow their lead on the relatively infrequent occasions when they take a strong party position; and (6) expressing from time to time the view of the congressional party, and maintaining institutional liaison with the White House.[10]

(1) *Leadership Structure.* There are several different agencies of party organization in the Senate and the House.

The Republican and Democratic conferences in the Senate and the Republican conference and Democratic caucus in the House include the members of each party contingent. The major purpose of these bodies is the selection of party leaders at the start of each new Congress. Occasionally the conferences supply members with information concerning legislative activities, and from time to time during a session they meet to discuss major issues.

There are also party policy or steering committees. The House Republican policy committee has lately been an integral part of the leadership, stating policy positions and giving advice to the minority leader. In the Senate the Democratic policy committee served as a sounding board for Lyndon Johnson when he was floor leader; but the current leader, Mike Mansfield, relies to some extent on the advice of a broadened policy committee, and in the 92nd Congress the committee did propose a general Democratic program, which was then adopted by the party caucus.

The party campaign committees in each house have as their job getting

10. See Randall B. Ripley, *Majority Party Leadership in Congress* (Little, Brown, 1969), and Charles O. Jones, *The Minority Party in Congress* (Little, Brown, 1970).

party members, and particularly incumbents, elected to Congress. They provide research and information, furnish some staff assistance, and raise funds which they distribute to party candidates.

Party committees on committees are responsible for the appointment of party members to standing committees. They determine the assignments of newly elected members as well as of senior members who want to switch from one committee to another. The Republican committee on committees in the House, which operates by means of a subcommittee chaired by the minority leader, consists of one member from each state with Republican representatives. House Democratic committee assignments are in the hands of Democratic members of the Committee on Ways and Means, who represent the different regions of the nation. In the Senate the Republican committee on committees and the Democratic steering committee make assignments.

There are assistant leaders, whips, and whip organizations. The Democrats, as the party in control of the House, have in addition to their principal leader, the Speaker of the House, a majority or floor leader, a majority whip, and a whip organization of about twenty members. The minority Republicans in the House have, in addition to the minority or floor leader, a minority whip and a whip organization of about fifteen members. The majority leader assists the speaker. The whips and their organizations communicate information from leaders to rank and file, and vice versa, polling members to ascertain their positions on issues crucial to the party, and helping to assure the maximum floor attendance of members who support the party position. In the Senate there is a majority whip and a minority whip, who assist the majority and minority floor leaders. Senate whip organizations are smaller and less formal than those in the House.

The Speaker of the House, the Senate majority leader, and the two minority leaders are the most important figures in Congress. But party leadership is essentially collegial, with a few individuals consulting, reaching agreements, and sharing the tasks and power. Democratic and Republican leaderships differ somewhat, partly because of their long status as majority and minority parties respectively. In both the House and the Senate, Democratic leadership is slightly more centralized than Republican leadership, but it is also more willing to tolerate dissent.

(2) *Leadership Resources.* Top leaders—the Speaker of the House, the majority leader in the Senate, and the minority leaders in the two chambers—can draw on various resources in order to exercise influence. A leader cannot command, mainly because he has no authority to fire members of Congress; he can only try to persuade. As far as persuasion is concerned, he is in an advantageous position because of the resources available to him.

The leader can evoke feelings of party loyalty. Most members would prefer to be with the party on an issue rather than against it. The same people cannot be approached all the time, but there are always some whose support, or at least neutrality, on one matter or another, can be won by a leader's partisan appeals. The leader can also appeal on personal grounds. Since members have elected him to a leadership position, they feel obligated on occasions to help him out. Moreover, how the leader feels about members is of concern to them. Being out of favor with the leader hurts, while being recognized with "a smile or nod of the head" by the leader "can bolster a member's ego and lead him to seek further evidence of favor." [11]

The leader is not only able to confer psychological benefits, by offering or withdrawing personal esteem, but he can also influence the allocation of many tangible rewards. He can provide extra office space, minor patronage, and better access to executive agencies for members who need projects back home. He has much to say about who is appointed to select committees, commissions, public boards, and special delegations. Most important, a leader can have an effect on a member's initial appointment to a standing committee or his later request for a change in assignment. Former Speaker Sam Rayburn, for example, played a considerable role in appointments to major committees, as is illustrated by the following House verse:

> *I love Speaker Rayburn, his heart is so warm,*
> *And if I love him he'll do me no harm*
> *So I shan't sass the Speaker one little bitty,*
> *And then I'll wind up on a major committee.*

The leader also exercises the greatest control over the conduct of legislative business. Although restricted by established committee jurisdictions and precedents, the speaker and the Senate majority leader have some discretion in referring bills to standing committees, especially when bills propose new programs or cover several subject areas. In consultation with the minority leaders, the speaker and his majority leader in the House and the majority leader in the Senate control the scheduling of bills on the floor. The Senate majority leader is accorded the privilege of recognition by the presiding officer whenever he wants to speak, and he introduces unanimous consent agreements, which govern what items are considered and for how long. The House Speaker has even greater managerial authority: he can delay the appearance of bills on the floor, in order to heighten prospects for victory; he can effectively decide

11. Randall B. Ripley, *Party Leaders in the House of Representatives* (The Brookings Institution, 1967), p. 23.

whether to bring bills to the floor under suspension of the rules, and particularly at the end of the session can speed through the pet bills of House members; and he also has the power of recognition when he is presiding, and if he refuses to recognize a congressman his ruling cannot be contested.

Finally, the leader dominates internal communications, and thereby commands substantive, strategic, and tactical information that gives him an edge. Aided by skillful staff and by whip organizations, party leaders more than anyone else know what is going on in the labyrinthian processes of Congress. They know what congressmen want and need, and what they are willing to give in return.

(3) *The Conditions of Leadership Influence.* Party organization and resources help the leader, but the situations in which he has to operate may limit his opportunities to exercise influence.

A congressional leader's influence depends in part on whether his own party controls the White House. In the case of a popular and legislatively aggressive president of the same party, a speaker or majority leader may have great leverage. His influence really derives from the president. A president of his own party who is legislatively aggressive but unable to muster much support for presidential programs, is a problem for either of these leaders of a majority. With a passive president who demands little, the leadership position is favorable. It is relatively favorable when the president is of the opposition party; then either the majority or the minority leadership can rally its troops against the executive. The leader of a congressional minority, who has to advance the programs of his own president, probably faces the most difficult situation.[12]

The leader has no control over the size of his congressional party's membership. The larger the membership, generally speaking, the easier it is for the leader to influence legislative results. The nature of the opposition party's leadership counts as well. A cooperative opposition is helpful. Lyndon Johnson benefited from his close relationship with Everett M. Dirksen, the Republican minority leader in the Senate. Sam Rayburn encountered fewer difficulties when Joseph Martin led the Republican minority than after Charles Halleck was elected to replace him.

Other factors also may restrict a leaders' influence. The issues before Congress and the methods used in dealing with them are important, as a study of House Democratic leadership indicates.[13] First, the influence

12. Ralph K. Huitt, "Democratic Party Leadership in the Senate," in Huitt and Robert L. Peabody, eds., *Congress: Two Decades of Analysis* (Harper & Row, 1969), pp. 142-143.
13. My discussion here is based on Lewis A. Froman, Jr. and Randall B. Ripley, "Conditions for Party Leadership: The Case of House Democrats," *American Political Science Review*, 59 (March, 1965), pp. 52-63.

of leaders hinges initially on the extent to which they commit themselves and their resources. House leaders do not make major commitments on many issues during any one session, but when they do they can probably change the votes of at least ten members. Second, the more the issue relates to substance (i.e., specific amendments to legislation) rather than to procedure (i.e., the adoption of House rules), the tougher it is for leaders to affect outcomes. Third, as the issue itself becomes more visible to the public—either because the president or the press dramatizes it or because it is relatively simple and easy to understand—the chances of leadership influence diminish. Fourth, as actions on an issue become more visible, proceeding for instance from unrecorded to roll-call votes, the opportunity for leadership influence declines. Fifth, when there is counter pressure from constituencies, leaders are less likely to prevail.

In both houses leadership is highly personal. The leader's own perception of his role, his skill, and his techniques—in other words, his leadership style—help determine the quality of his performance and the level of his success. Still, the role of leaders in structuring the options and choices of individual members is limited. This is especially true in the Senate today, where members fear that "greater power in the hands of the leaders might mean diminished power in the hands of individual senators." [14] In the House, leadership is more centralized and more organized, and has a greater impact on the rank and file. Still, House leaders operate under restraints. If they go much beyond the limits implicitly set by their members, they face defeat on substantive issues, restriction of their powers, and ouster from their positions.

Standing Committees

If the influence of leaders is circumscribed, one reason—looming larger in the House than in the Senate—is the strength of standing committees. The substantive work of Congress is primarily the business of committees.

(1) *Committee Structure.* At the opening of the 92nd Congress in 1971, there were 17 standing committees in the Senate and 21 in the House, as well as several select, special, and joint committees. A number of the standing committees—such as those dealing with agriculture, armed services, foreign relations, and interior—were organized along functional lines, roughly paralleling organizational and jurisdictional patterns within the executive branch. Other standing committees, however, were not oriented toward specific functions. For example, the two appropriations committees were concerned with allocations of governmental funds, and the Senate Finance and House Ways and Means Committees were concerned with measures raising federal revenues.

14. Randall B. Ripley, *Power in the Senate* (St. Martin's Press, 1969), p. 106.

Committees vary in their composition. Their size, which is generally worked out by the majority leadership in consultation with the minority, changes from time to time. The particular size of a committee often depends on the political and policy advantages that additional members may confer on the majority party. All committees are bipartisan, and the ratio of majority to minority members is important. These ratios, which are decided by the majority leadership after negotiation with the minority, reflect the distribution of party strengths in the chamber as a whole. The principal exceptions are the Rules, Appropriations, and Ways and Means Committees of the House, for which ratios are fixed to give the majority a distinct advantage, however close its margin in the chamber.

House committees tend to have about twice as many members as Senate committees. Representatives serve on one or sometimes two committees, but senators usually serve on three and sometimes more. If subcommittees are also considered, representatives average about four assignments, whereas senators average as many as ten.

Who gets appointed to which committee is of critical concern to individual congressmen and to the two parties in each house. Once appointed to a committee, a member holds his assignment as long as he is reelected and so desires, except when there is a change in party control or a reduction in committee size, which may cause him to be displaced if he is a junior member. Most members will try to remain on committees to which they are initially assigned or to which they have been switched at their own request during the first few years of congressional service. This is because the right to move up the committee ladder is seldom questioned, with seniority—the longest continued membership on the same committee—and majority party status being the criteria for appointment to a committee chairmanship.

In the process of assigning members to committees the importance of the committee counts most heavily. Because of the nature of their subject matter, their prestige, or their power, certain committees are more attractive than are others. In the House, the Rules, Appropriations, and Ways and Means Committees are the ones that have been most preferred by congressmen. In the Senate, Foreign Relations, Finance, Appropriations, and Armed Services rank at the top. Both chambers have institutionalized the ranking of committees. For some time the House has designated the three committees mentioned above as exclusive committees, and has permitted members to serve on only one of them. Recently the Senate decided, by means of the Legislative Reorganization Act of 1970, that no future senator might serve on more than one of its four most desirable committees.

In the House, assignments to the exclusive or choice committees tend to go to members who have some seniority, represent relatively safe districts, and have demonstrated "legislative responsibility" (i.e. the ability to get along with their leaders and colleagues). If there is a vacancy on a top committee, preference is ordinarily given to a representative from the state, or at least the same region, as that of the member who previously held the position. Party leaders play a critical role in these appointments, endeavoring to have a majority of members loyal to them on the key committees.

Criteria for assignments to other committees of the House are less strict. The main considerations are whether an assignment to a particular committee is desired by the congressman and whether it will help him in his district. Thus, representatives of farm districts are given preference in filling vacancies on Agriculture, those from port districts have an advantage in getting assigned to Merchant Marine and Fisheries, and those from districts with large areas of public land have the inside track to Interior and Insular Affairs. In addition, the wishes of committee chairmen count, if the chairmen are in favor with party leaders. Occasionally, too, leaders will intervene to shift the orientation of the party's membership on a particular committee or to reduce a certain chairman's control. In the Senate the same kinds of considerations shape the appointment process. Personal preferences, seniority, geography, and the ideologies of applicants all matter.

(2) *Committee Operations.* As political instrumentalities designed to facilitate the bargains and compromises necessary for the building of majority coalitions on substantive issues, committees act as surrogates for their respective chambers. Just how—and how well—they do this is related to (1) the distribution of power within committees and (2) the ability of committees to maintain themselves as integrated units.

Nearly always the major figure in the life of a committee is the chairman. The chairmanship position is critical in both bodies, but especially in the House. A chairman's powers, while by no means unlimited, are substantial. The chairman controls the agenda of the committee, and can decide what business is scheduled and what bills receive hearings. He can dispense, or withhold, rewards to committee members. Such rewards range widely: recognition and praise; designation for special trips; protection from issues that may be controversial in a member's constituency; having an individual's ideas incorporated in a committee bill, or permitting him to receive major credit for a committee measure; and the opportunity to speak for the committee on the floor, or to represent the committee in a conference. The chairman also has the most to say about the committee's professional staff, determining the number who serve, who they are, and what they do. By limiting the number or supervising what staff there is, he can control the information available to members and thereby limit the activity in which they can engage.

Chairmen can also control the division of labor within their committees, deciding whether subcommittees will be created or not and determining their jurisdictions. In recent Congresses only a few committees have resisted some sort of subcommittee organization. These include Aeronautical and Space Sciences and Finance in the Senate and Rules and Ways and Means in the House. Others, such as Senate Foreign Relations and House Armed Services, maintain subcommittees, but either provide for very vague subcommittee jurisdictions or allow the full committee to do most of the work and make the most important decisions. Still other committees—such as Appropriations, Judiciary, and Labor and Public Welfare in the Senate and Appropriations, Interior and Insular Affairs, and Education and Labor in the House—operate mainly through their subcommittees.

Even with the work divided among subcommittees, chairmen of full committees retain considerable authority. They can determine the size of subcommittees, establish party ratios, appoint members, and designate subcommittee chairmen. Their discretion is somewhat limited. The ranking minority member of the full committee usually makes subcommittee appointments for his own party. Often, too, the most senior members —in terms of committee service—of the majority party are considered to be entitled to subcommittee chairmanships. Full committee chairmen allocate staff and budget to subcommittees, although there are some exceptions. Chairmen can keep a bill in full committee, rather than referring it to a subcommittee; they can also establish an ad hoc or a new standing subcommittee to handle a particular problem.

The very existence of subcommittees, as it works out, is a restraint on the power of the committee chairman. Subcommittees, adhering to the norm of reciprocity, tend to defer to one another, at the very least respecting each other's work. Often subcommittee consideration is tantamount to full committee consideration, the latter perfunctorily reviewing the work of the former. This is best illustrated by the case of the House Appropriations Committee. Each of its dozen subcommittees deals with a segment of the budget, and each segment becomes a separate appropriation bill. Virtually all appropriations tasks are accomplished by subcommittees, while the full committee "meets only to organize itself at the beginning of each Congress and to give a majority vote of approval to the recommendations of its subcommittees.[15] In the case of other committees, review may be more thorough. Subcommittee conflicts may

15. Richard F. Fenno, Jr., *The Power of the Purse: Appropriations Politics in Congress* (Little, Brown, 1966), p. 134.

be reargued in full committee, and the balance for and against a measure might change as a result.

Even with subcommittees, the committee chairman makes a difference. He may exercise a decentralized and permissive style of leadership, giving subcommittees free rein and support. Or, where there are no subcommittees, he may exercise centralized but democratic leadership, as does Wilbur Mills of Ways and Means, encouraging a collegial process, searching for consensus, gaining respect, and cautiously directing members along the lines he favors.[16] A chairman may also restrain his committee, not unfairly or abusively, but subtly—dragging his feet and giving scant help to a committee majority. On matters that are not of major import or where determined majorities do not exist, the chairman can wield decisive power. On major matters, he can use his resources skillfully to keep potential opponents from coalescing and undertaking the effort necessary to defeat him.

The dictatorial chairman, however, is the exception in Congress today. Members expect their chairman to be fair, responsive to majority party demands, and considerate of minority party wishes. To be successful a chairman must retain the support of his committee. Although he may prevail in the short run, no chairman can withstand determined opposition very long. When a majority feels he has behaved outrageously, or when the party leadership decides he is obstructionist, his wings will surely be clipped.

Examples of revolts against chairmen, adoption of committee rules of procedure, provisions of the Legislative Reorganization Act of 1970, and modification of the seniority system by the congressional parties combine to ensure that chairmen act in a responsible way. Chairmen will continue to possess important power. But in view of recent changes, responsiveness to the congressional party and committee majority will be encouraged and extreme nonresponsiveness virtually prohibited. Not even a few chairmen will be able to rule despotically in the face of determined opposition by committee members and party majorities.

The attitudes and behavior of the chairman affect the committee's ability to maintain itself as an integrated unit. Some chairmen keep a committee together, others tend to blow it apart. Committee integration —that is, the maintenance of the power and prestige of the group, regardless of internal differences—depends on other factors as well.[17]

16. John F. Manley, *The Politics of Finance: The House Committee on Ways and Means* (Little, Brown, 1970), ch. 4.

17. This discussion is based on the conceptualization of Richard F. Fenno, Jr., "The Appropriations Committee as a Political System," in Peabody and Polsby, *New Perspective on the House of Representatives*, pp. 125-154.

First, the strength of members' identification with a committee, which is related to a committee's attractiveness, affects integration. In the case of the House Appropriations Committee, members agree on the committee's general goal—guarding the Federal Treasury—and its instrumental purpose—cutting executive budget requests. They agree on hard work as a way of committee life and share a strong sense of group identification and solidarity; morale is high. On Ways and Means also consensus is high. This is not because members take the same position on policy, but rather because they value their membership on the top committee in the House. By contrast, on the Education and Labor Committee consensus is low, since service on it is not prestigious, and no unifying norms hold members together.

Second, the nature of a committee's subject matter affects its integration. Largely because of the type of issues they handle, some committes can operate with a minimum of internal conflict and effectively resolve any conflict that develops, while others are rent by partisan or ideological disputes. The House Appropriations Committee makes money decisions, and money decisions provoke less controversy than program decisions. Members do not make prior commitments on precise dollar amounts; funding levels can readily be compromised; and partisanship on the committee hardly exists.[18] House Education and Labor provides a contrast. It handles controversial subjects that have long been divisive, and is often split along partisan and ideological lines. Still, even with controversial issues a committee may successfully manage conflict. In the Ways and Means Committee party disagreement occurs frequently, but conflict does not dominate the committee's internal processes because of the presence of restrained partisanship.[19]

Third, the orientations and the stability of committee members affect integration. The recruitment of congressmen judged to be "responsible" and "pragmatic," predisposed toward legislative give-and-take, to Appropriations and Ways and Means promotes their integration. The recruitment of ideological congressmen, predisposed toward legislative combat, to Education and Labor promotes disintegration. Membership stability also matters. When many members continue to serve on the committee from one Congress to the next, it is easier to break in the few newcomers to the established patterns of behavior and operation. The most attractive committees have the most stable memberships.

18. In the period from 1947 to 1962 more than nine out of ten of the appropriation bills reported to the House floor were without dissent from any committee member. In only five of 197 cases were there differences between the two party contingents on the committee. Fenno, *The Power of the Purse*, p. 203.
19. Manley, *The Politics of Finance*, pp. 63-97.

Integration of committee members is an important concept, but it is less significant to committees in the Senate than to those in the House. As in the lower body, there are differences in the attractiveness among the Senate committees, the stability of their memberships, and their levels of partisanship, as well as the obvious differences of subject matter. But committees are less important to individual members in the Senate than in the House. The expectations and satisfactions of senators revolve around personal influence, not committee influence. Hence participation in committee work is less important to the average senator than participation in the decision-making processes of the entire body.

(3) *The Conditions of Committee Influence.* Once a committee reports a bill favorably, its position is extremely advantageous. The committee generally controls most of the pertinent information and has the most to say about a bill's timing. It can usually gain support from the party leaders. This is particularly true in the House, where the standing committees are so significant.[20] Unless there is a good reason to the contrary, the tendency in Congress is to go along with a committee's recommendation.

Admitting its normative and procedural advantages, a committee's success on the floor is not assured. A committee has a better chance to prevail when the issues involved are technical and complicated than when they are ideological and general. In the former instance members of the committee are presumed to be expert. It also has a better chance when large numbers of congressmen do not feel that they or their constituencies are directly affected as they would be when widespread controversy exists.

Perhaps no single factor is quite as crucial as that of the committee's unity in favor of its recommendation. The greater the cohesion of the committee, the more likely it is that its views will be accepted on the floor.[21] Partisan division in a committee militates against committee cohesion, and the degree of partisan division in committee is an indicator of the degree of partisan conflict that will occur on the floor. But even a committee that is sharply divided can prevail, if its chairman is sensitive to the distribution of preferences in the Senate or House.

20. During the period from 1955 through 1964, committees were successful on bills they reported out on nearly 90 percent of House roll calls. See James W. Dyson and John W. Soule, "Congressional Behavior on Roll Call Votes: The U.S. House of Representatives, 1955-1964," *Midwest Journal of Political Science,* 14 (November, 1970), p. 632.

21. Ibid., pp. 641-645; Fenno, *The Power of the Purse,* pp. 460-469, 597-598; and Donald R. Matthews, *U.S. Senators and Their World* (University of North Carolina Press, 1960), pp. 168-170.

THE LEGISLATIVE PROCESS IN CONGRESS

Although the enactment of legislation is not the only task that Congress must perform, it is a central one. Today the typical two-year Congress enacts over one thousand bills into law.

Each chamber shares in the power to enact bills, since legislative proposals must pass both the Senate and the House in order to become law. According to the Constitution, the Senate alone can confirm presidential appointments and ratify treaties, but the House originates all bills raising revenues—including tax, tariff, and social security bills. According to tradition and practice, appropriation bills are also passed first by the House. With these exceptions, bills may originate in either or both bodies, and may be passed by either one first.

The stages of the process by which bills become law range from introduction to presidential approval, as depicted in Figure 3.2. The rules and procedures of the Senate and the House at each stage, although quite comparable, differ in several important respects, as we shall see below.[22]

Figure 3.2. The Stages of the Legislative Process in Congress

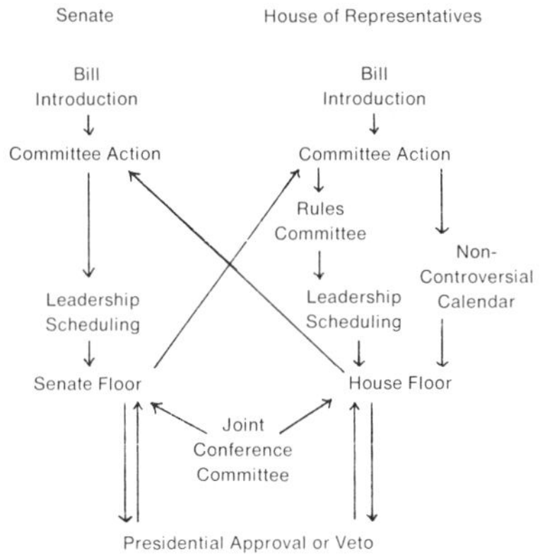

The Introduction and Referral of Bills

In the House a member may introduce a bill by dropping it into the hopper at the clerk's desk on the floor at any time the House is in session. In the Senate a member must gain recognition from the presiding officer

22. The description of the legislative process closely follows Lewis A. Froman, Jr., *The Congressional Process* (Little, Brown, 1967), chs. 3-9, and Donald G. Tacheron and Morris K. Udall, *The Job of the Congressman* (Bobbs-Merrill, 1966), chs. 7, 9.

to introduce his bill. Often a senator will get co-sponsors before he introduces a bill, or at the time of introduction will ask that the bill lie
on the presiding officer's desk for several days before referral so that
additional members may sign as co-sponsors. Before 1967 House rules
did not permit joint sponsorship, so individuals with the same proposal
had to introduce separate but identical bills. Since 1967 co-sponsorship
has been permitted, with a limit of twenty-five co-sponsors on any one
bill.

Once a bill is introduced, the presiding officers—the President of the
Senate (the Vice-President of the United States), the President Pro Tempore, or the senator in the chair at the time, and the Speaker of the House
—are responsible for its referral. Committee jurisdiction, as specified in
Senate and House rules, and the way a sponsor drafts his bill largely
determine the committee to which it is referred. Ordinarily the reference
is made by the chamber's professional parliamentarian. After reference,
a bill is given a number, printed, sent to the committee, and made available for distribution.[23]

Committee Action

Every referred bill is placed on a committee's calendar. The first
action a committee ordinarily takes is to request comment on a bill by
interested agencies in the executive branch. Many bills do not go
further.

Major bills, especially if they are introduced on behalf of the administration, are given thorough consideration, either in subcommittee, full
committee, or both. Subcommittee and committee hearings consume the
bulk of meeting time. At these hearings members of Congress, witnesses
from executive agencies, representatives of interest groups, experts and
other citizens are allowed to testify on the particular bills under consideration. Hearings serve a number of purposes. They provide members with technical information and also make them aware of what interests and what groups are for and against bills, and how strongly ad-

23. A bill that originates in the House is designated by the letters "HR" (for
House of Representatives) and a number. One that originates in the Senate is designated by the letter "S", followed by the bill number. Bills are the most frequent
means of initiating legislative action, but there are also other types of measures. A
joint resolution (designated either "HJ Res" or "SJ Res") is not very different from
a bill and must be passed by both houses and signed by the president, except for
those proposing an amendment to the Constitution, which must be approved by
two-thirds of both houses before submission to the states for ratification. A concurrent resolution (designated either "H Con Res" or "S Con Res") is used to
express the sense of Congress on a particular matter or to apply to problems affecting
the operations of both houses. A simple resolution (designated either "H Res" or
"S Res") is used for a matter that affects only one house, and needs only to be
passed by the body in which it is introduced.

versaries are committed to their positions. They serve as a propaganda channel, by means of which public support or opposition can be solidified and enlarged.

It is exceptional for hearings to be completely one-sided affairs, with witnesses all agreed on an issue. But to ensure equal opportunity for different points of view, Congress adopted as part of the Legislative Reorganization Act of 1970 a provision requiring that a majority of the minority party members of a committee be entitled to call witnesses during at least one day of hearings on a matter. It is not exceptional, however, for committees to bar the public from their meetings. In order to remedy this situation, the 1970 Act provides generally that committee business meetings and hearings be open to the public unless a committee by majority vote specifically decides otherwise.

Even more important than hearings is the process that takes place when the subcommittee or full committee discusses the bill, marks it up or redrafts it, decides on the various provisions it will recommend, votes on the bill as a whole, and has a committee report drafted. Because committee members want the opportunity for frank discussion without representatives of interest groups looking over their shoulders, "mark up" sessions are almost always closed to the public. The 1970 Act, however, makes a few modifications in the process by which committees decide on legislation and their reports. One provision generally requires that all roll-call votes taken in committee be made public and/or be stated in the committee report. Other provisions require that, with certain exceptions, committee reports on bills be available several days in advance of floor consideration, so that other legislators may have information on which to base their own decisions.

Scheduling for Floor Consideration

The overwhelming majority of bills that are referred to committee are never reported out. But once a bill is reported, it must be scheduled for consideration on the floor of the House or Senate.

After being reported by a House committee, a bill is placed on one of three calendars. All bills of a private nature—such as those permitting the immigration of specific individuals or allowing claims by specific individuals against the government—are placed on the Private Calendar. This calendar is called only on the first and third Tuesdays of each month, and most of the private bills are passed quickly and without debate. The Union Calendar is for public bills that raise or appropriate revenues; the House Calendar is for public bills that do not affect revenues. Bills on either of these two calendars may be transferred, at the request of their sponsors, to the Consent Calendar. These bills, which are noncontroversial and backed unanimously by committees, are taken up only on the first and third Mondays of each month. If one member objects to consideration of a Consent Calendar bill on one day, it carries over to the next day the calendar is in order. If three or more members object the second day, the bill is striken from the Consent Calendar. A fifth calendar in the House—the Discharge Calendar—contains only bills that have not been reported by committees, and is called only on the second and fourth Mondays of each month. When 218 signatures are obtained on a discharge petition, a bill blocked by a committee can be brought to the floor.

Bills of some consequence that are listed on either the Union or House Calendar have to pass another hurdle before debate on the floor. They must be granted a rule by the Rules Committee. This committee exercises a leadership function in deciding which of the bills reported by other standing committees should receive consideration and which should not. The committee in granting a rule determines the number of hours of general debate in the Committee of the Whole of the House, decides whether amendments will be allowed, and specifies when possible points of order against the bill's provisions will not be allowed.

The Appropriations and Ways and Means Committees are privileged to report general appropriation and revenue bills directly to the floor. Nonetheless, these committees generally appeal to the Rules Committee for a rule. Ways and Means customarily obtains a "closed" (as opposed to an "open") rule, which prohibits the offering of amendments other than committee amendments, and thus ensures that the bill be either accepted or rejected on the floor as reported. Appropriations occasionally obtains a rule which waives points of order on the floor and thus permits the committee to include legislative "riders" in its proposals, although legislating in appropriation bills is contrary to House rules.

Once a bill has been granted a rule, it is up to the majority leadership to decide when to schedule it on the floor. If a bill is not granted a rule, there are currently a few methods—such as the discharge petition and Calendar Wednesday—by which a bill can be pried loose from the Rules Committee. But these are seldom successful.

In the Senate the procedure for bringing a bill to the floor is much simpler. There are two major calendars. A Calendar of Business, or General Orders, is for all legislation, and an Executive Calendar is for treaties and nominations. No mechanism of the Senate is comparable to the Rules Committee of the House. When bills are reported from Senate committee they are rarely held up for floor action. They are quickly scheduled by the majority leadership in cooperation with the minority, and virtually every senator has some say.

There is less likelihood in the Senate than in the House that a committee can kill a bill desired by a majority or even by a minority. There are formal devices, such as a motion to discharge or suspension of the rules, that can be used to bypass a Senate committee. But these devices rarely have to be used, because in the Senate, unlike in the House, there is no way to prevent consideration of a subject on the floor. The House has a "germaneness" rule, which limits floor amendments specifically to the subject of the bill under deliberation. The Senate's "germaneness" rule, however, applies only to general appropriation bills. Thus, any matter—whether previously introduced, referred to a committee, reported by a committee, or germane to the pending measure— can be proposed as an amendment to practically any bill in the Senate.

Floor Consideration and Voting

Major legislation in the House is debated in the Committee of the Whole. Generally, a rule reported by the Rules Committee is considered by the House, debated for an hour or less, and adopted. Then the House resolves itself into the Committee of the Whole. This device enables the House to avoid some of the problems that its regular procedures would raise. A quorum for the Committee of the Whole is only 100 members, instead of the majority of 218. A specified time for general debate—usually running one or a few hours and occasionally ten hours or more—is set by the adopted rule. This time is divided between the majority and minority. It is controlled by floor managers, who customarily are the chairman and the ranking minority member of the committee reporting the bill. Preference to speak is accorded members of the reporting committee.

When the time for general debate expires, amendments are in order. The Reading Clerk reads the bill paragraph by paragraph, section by section, or if the rule permits, by title only. Any member may offer an amendment after the reading of each section. Debate on each amendment is theoretically limited to ten minutes, five for the amendment's proponent and five for an opponent, under the "five-minute" rule. Debate on each amendment, however, can last substantially longer, since any member may gain time to speak by offering a pro forma amendment "to strike the last word.[24]

At the conclusion of debate under the "five-minute" rule, three kinds of votes (but not roll-call votes) may take place. Voice votes come first, and the chairman of the Committee of the Whole, who has been designated by the Speaker, determines whether the "ayes" or the "noes"

24. Several types of amendments may be introduced and be pending at the same time: (1) an original amendment; (2) an amendment to the original amendment (but never an amendment to an amendment to an amendment); (3) a substitute amendment to replace the original; and (4) an amendment to the substitute. Amendments are voted on in the following order: (2); (4); (3); and (1).

predominate. A member may then demand a division, or standing vote. First the "ayes" rise, then the "noes" rise, and the chair counts and announces the result. At this point, a teller vote may be ordered, if one-fifth of the members present support such a request. To take this tally, a teller for each side (usually the sponsor of the amendment and its chief opponent) counts first the members for and then those against, who file up the center aisle.

Voting in the Committee of the Whole generally affords an advantage to the committee reporting the bill and the leadership supporting the committee version. More often than not the committee majority can defeat either strengthening or, more likely, weakening amendments. This is extremely important, because amendments that lose in the Committee of the Whole may not be put to a roll-call vote when the Committee concludes its business and the full House reconvenes to take final action. When the Committee of the Whole has finished with a bill, the Speaker returns to the chair, and all amendments that passed—but not the ones that failed—are reported back to the House. The amendments are voted on, usually as a bloc and in pro forma fashion. The next major step is the motion offered by opponents to recommit the bill to the committee from which it was reported. Passage of a simple motion to recommit effectively defeats the bill, since the committee is unlikely to report it out again. Passage of a motion to recommit with instructions to report back the bill with amendments leads the committee to change the bill substantially before reporting it back to the House.[25] If the recommittal motion fails to carry, the House proceeds immediately to vote on final passage. Recommittal and final passage decisions on important bills are made by roll-call votes.

In the Senate, floor procedures are simpler, more informal, and more flexible than in the House. Whereas the latter body uses the Committee of the Whole to expedite business, principal reliance in the Senate is on unanimous consent agreements. The purpose of such agreements is to limit debate so that a vote on an amendment or bill can be scheduled for a particular time. The majority leader, after consultation with the minority leader and all concerned senators, makes the request for unanimous consent. A single objection can defeat the request, but objection is infrequent and rarely persists. Thus debate on nearly all controversial legislation is ended by unanimous consent.

The procedure breaks down when a few senators intensely oppose

25. The Legislative Reorganization Act of 1970 provides that there be ten minutes of debate on a motion to recommit with instructions, the time to be divided equally between the mover of the motion (who opposes the bill) and a supporter of the bill. Previously, the rules reported by the Rules Committee had usually specified that there would be no debate on a motion to recommit.

some measure. Then a filibuster may be threatened or take place. This tactic is designed to focus public attention on an issue, to solicit modifications of the measure, or to talk a proposal to death. There is a rule that a senator can speak only twice on the same subject on the same "legislative day," and the possibility exists of stretching the same legislative day into weeks or months by recessing instead of adjourning; but this tactic is of little use in limiting debate, for any senator can offer as many germane or nongermane amendments as he desires, and each amendment is considered to be a different subject under the two-speech rule.

Opponents of a bill may have two opportunities to filibuster. A motion is required to take a bill off the calendar and make it the pending business of the Senate. This motion can be filibustered. Once a bill becomes pending business, it can be filibustered to prevent it from coming to a vote.

The only way to break a filibuster is by means of cloture. When sixteen senators sign a cloture petition, the motion to close debate is voted on two calendar days later. If the cloture motion is supported by two-thirds of those present and voting, cloture is instituted and no senator may speak more than one hour more on the pending measure. If one-third plus one of those present and voting vote no, debate continues.

When agreement to end debate is reached, whether through cloture or unanimous consent, a bill or amendment will come to vote.[26] Unlike the House, an amendment or bill in the Senate can be decided only once, by one type of vote—either voice, division, or roll-call. Most bills are noncontroversial, so most votes are by voice. On important matters one-fifth of the senators present request a roll call, and then a record vote is taken.[27]

Before being sent to the president for his signature, bills passed by the Senate and the House must be in identical form.

Many noncontroversial bills passed by one house are routinely accepted by the second chamber with no change at all. Many other noncontroversial bills may differ somewhat after being passed by the two

26. A motion to table an amendment can also be made. Since a tabling motion is not debatable, a vote will follow immediately after the introduction of the motion. Normally, tabling motions are seldom made, because they infringe on norms of comity in the Senate.

27. In both chambers voting procedures include "pairing." A "live pair" occurs when a senator or representative who is present withholds his vote and pairs with an absent member who is on the opposite side. A "simple pair" applies to two absent members, who would vote on opposite sides of the measure. A "general pair" is when two absent members pair, but do not specify on which side they would vote had they been present.

bodies, and it becomes necessary for one house to agree to changes made by the other. If the Senate, acting second, passes a version that differs from the House version, it can return the bill to the House with its amendments. The House may then agree to the Senate version. If the House, acting second, passes a bill differing from the Senate's, it can return the bill to the Senate with its amendments. The Senate may then agree to the House version.

On approximately one-tenth of all bills passed, there is substantial disagreement between the two chambers, and differences must be resolved by means of a conference committee. Either body may insist on its own version of a bill. When one house insists and the other refuses to accede, a conference committee is appointed.

The Speaker of the House and the President of the Senate have the authority to name members of the conference committee. As a rule, the floor managers of the bill make the appointments. Those named as conferees—like the floor managers themselves—are usually members of the committees that have reported the bill. They are usually veteran congressmen, and often include the committee and/or subcommittee chairmen and ranking minority members. Both parties are represented, with the majority having the majority of conferees in both the Senate and House delegations. The two delegations may be of unequal size (each one usually ranging between three and nine mmbers), but this does not really matter, since a conference report must be approved by a majority within each delegation.

Reconciling differences in a conference committee is one of the most critical stages of the legislative process in Congress. Conferees have considerable power. Frequently the process takes day and even weeks. Sometimes conferees are instructed by their respective bodies to insist on certain provisions; more often they are free to compromise on differences between the Senate and House versions of a bill. Conferees are expected to back their own chamber's version, but it has been known for conferees who have unsuccessfully opposed specific provisions on the floor to readily abandon them in conference. Although conferees may delete things, they are theoretically prohibited from adding new language or provisions to a bill, but sometimes they do so to reach a compromise acceptable to both delegations.

On occasion agreement simply cannot be reached, and a bill that has passed both bodies dies in conference, or the impasse leads to the appointment of a new conference committee. Most times, however, differences are reconciled. Then a conference report, explaining why conferees did or did not retain some features of the bill and delete others, is drafted and submitted to the Senate and the House. Such a report is privileged and is brought to the floor immediately. It cannot be amended, but must be accepted or rejected in toto by each house. If a conference report is not acceptable to one chamber, the bill can be recommitted to the old conference committee or a new committee can be formed. If the report is accepted by both houses, the bill is ready for the president's approval.

Recently a number of changes have been adopted with respect to conference committees. Before 1965 the House Rules Committee had the power to grant or refuse rules to send House-passed bills to a joint conference. In the 89th Congress the House adopted a rule which made it possible for the speaker and a majority in the chamber to send a bill that had been altered by the Senate to a conference, without interference by the Rules Committee. A few years later the Legislative Reorganization Act provided for other changes. The act required that Senate and House conferees jointly prepare an explanatory statement for every conference report. (Previously this had been done only by the House delegation.) It required that debate on a conference report be divided equally between the majority and minority. (Previously debate had been controlled by the chairmen of the two conference delegations.) It prohibited House conferees from including new items or unduly modifying old ones in compromising differences with the Senate. Finally, since conference reports had often been brought to the floor for a vote with little or no notice, it prohibited the House, except during the last six days of a session, from voting on a conference report unless it had been available to members and had been printed in the *Congressional Record* three calendar days (excluding Saturdays, Sundays, and legal holidays) prior to consideration.

Presidential Approval or Veto

A bill that has been passed in identical form by the Senate and the House is then sent to the White House for presidential action. The White House requests the views of concerned executive agencies on the enrolled bill. If it receives clearance, and does not conflict with the administration's program, the president signs it. The president also may veto a bill, refusing to sign it and returning it to Congress with a message stating his reasons. He cannot approve one part of a bill and reject another, but must either approve or disapprove the bill in its entirety.

Once a bill is vetoed, the bill is close to being dead. There are only two options left to Congress if it wishes to push further on the bill's behalf. Congress may proceed to enact another bill, omitting those provisions to which the president objected in his veto message. Or it may attempt to override the president's veto and have the bill become law despite his disapproval. To overcome the president's veto two-thirds of those members present in both the Senate and House must vote by roll call to override. Few such attempts are made, and even fewer are successful.

When a bill is passed and signed, or passed over a veto, enactment is complete. One bill has become law. But the legislative process in Congress continues.

4

PRESIDENTIAL POWER:

A SPLENDID IRONY

by Charles E. Jacob

Fifteen years ago, in the opening lines of a book that was to become the most widely read commentary on the presidency, Clinton Rossiter quoted with approval and adopted as his thesis the apotheosizing judgment of John Bright, that the world had been offered no finer institutional spectacle than the American presidency. Rossiter went on to describe the office as "one of the few truly successful institutions created by men in their endless quest for the blessings of free government." [1] Today, probably few observers would credit so sanguine an observation. Indeed the presidency is subjected to a wide variety of criticisms from different influential sources. For some the office has become too powerful; they view the potential peril from the decision of one misguided man to be truly frightening. Paradoxically, it is also argued that the presidency is too weak, in the sense of being unable to persuade either the Congress or the president's party to pursue policies in the national interest.

Yet it must be remembered that at least in some degree these qualms have been expressed throughout our history. A number of factors must therefore be noted to keep the criticisms in perspective. First the elements of time and circumstance play a role. Institutional behavior which is taken to be a norm in relatively stable and quiescent times becomes controversial and arouses alarm in times of general crisis. Moreover the target of criticism is sometimes unclear, even in the minds of the critics, since the office of the presidency is such a complex amalgam of man and institution. In some instances, distaste for the man (whether out of partisanship, ideology, or style preferences) provokes apocalyptic judgments about the health and future of the institution.

1. Clinton Rossiter, *The American Presidency*, 2nd ed. (New York: Harcourt, Brace & Co., 1956), p. 15.

In order to achieve a balanced evaluation of the presidency today, it is essential to ask how well the institution serves the needs of society within its range of competence. The standard to be applied is the response offered to demands made upon the institution. At once the idea of "demands" creates problems. There is surely an infinite number of specific demands that might be cited—as many as the personal wants and imagination of men could conjure. The citations themselves would constitute an endless inventory. It seems more profitable for analytical purposes to group demands into broad functional categories based upon historical observation. It is to this necessary exercise that we now turn.

FUNCTIONS OF THE PRESIDENCY

Moral Leadership: A Philosopher King

The office of the presidency, like other institutions (governmental and non-governmental) is a multi-purpose agency. But first a distinction should be drawn between institutions and mere organizations. We may say that the former perform a variety of functions, whereas the latter are more narrowly circumscribed in their activities. The institution tends to uphold and foster a number of values, whereas the organization tends to be motivated more narrowly toward the achievement of a single goal or value such as efficiency in production.[2] To use an example, the functions and mode of operations of a bicycle factory, oriented toward the efficient and profitable production of bicycles, typify the organization. In contrast, the United States Congress, Harvard University, and the *New York Times* are organizations which have gone through the process of institutionalization. To be sure, Congress passes laws, Harvard educates, and the *New York Times* sells newspapers. But each does many other things as well. These institutions promote and serve additional values such as representation, the creation of national leadership, service to the state, and so on.

Preeminently the American presidency is an institutional vessel for interpreting, upholding and re-interpreting social and political values important to the polity. Another way of describing this function of the presidency is to think of it as the popular expectation of moral leadership. This is part of the symbolism of the presidency, but it would be a mistake to think of it as mere symbol devoid of substance. To be sure, Fourth of July speeches and other patriotic utterances are a dime a dozen. Yet any incumbent of the presidential office must give concrete meaning to principles upheld verbally, in order to function as a real leader.

2. These distinctions are analyzed in Philip Selznick, *Leadership in Administration* (Row Peterson, 1957), especially chapters 1 and 5.

Presidents, of course, draw upon the whole corpus of American political philosophy in interpreting to the nation the fundamental justifications for their actions and their bases for innovative proposals. Many of the traditional values come to mind: liberty, equality, justice, constitutionalism, to note a few. The real demand finds its response, however, in the interpretation of these and other core values at any moment in history. The nature of the response will vary somewhat with the personal history, philosophy, and character of the president. One kind of response—seemingly least demanding—is the pragmatic one by which the president faithfully echoes what appears to be majority sentiment (or the sentiments of an electoral majority). Real leadership, nonetheless, involves exhortation and persuasion on the part of the president in identifying new areas of public need. In short, the institution offers the opportunity to the man to be a national educator or even preacher, suffusing proposals with value, programs with legitimacy.

Chief Interest Broker

The characterization of our society as a pluralistic one in which competing interests vie for a favorable allocation of values is one which has long been accepted. This image usually assumes that most of the competition is carried on by and among groups and, following David Truman's analysis, that groups are collectivities of individuals sharing some characteristic in common. When the groups behave or interact on the basis of such shared characteristics, they are thus asserting an "interest." The values sought (or demands made) by groups are infinite—and perhaps, to borrow from economic thought, insatiable. Although the values sought are commonly thought of as economic ones, in reality many others are at issue. Over the years we have come to recognize the depth of the quest for values beyond crude income, such as status, prestige, deference, freedom, justice and security.

One of the major functions of governmental authority, of course, is to provide a framework within which the group struggle can be carried on and values allocated peaceably. It should also be noted that this job is carried on by non-governmental groups as well; but if sovereignty has any modern meaning, it is that ultimate allocative authority *can* be exercised by governments. Each of the formal institutions of American government participates in the process of representing interests and allocating scarce values among them. It is simply contended here that the presidency has come to be seen as the most comprehensive agent to be served with this demand. The reason is that the office is taken to represent all the people rather than a particular region, class or even party. Legitimacy and responsibility are grounded upon popular, general election. While congressmen are assumed to represent districts or states, and administrative agencies to represent functional categories of demands (welfare, conservation, defense), the demand on the president is that he somehow represent all these interests—or what is commonly and vaguely called the "public interest." Indeed, this is what most people mean by statesmanship. And while any public figure *may* rise to the statesman level by putting aside partial and short-term interests in favor of long-term general interests, the presidency-as-institution is endowed with a legitimacy which promotes and sanctifies this role and a range of authority which facilitates it.

The means by which competing interests and demands are brought to the attention of the president are manifold. First, of course, there is his own personal, pre-formed appreciation of the importance of various interests which he brings with him to the office. In office, he is the immediate target for the articulation of special interests from organized pressure groups, members of Congress, bureaucrats, his political party, and private, influential opinion leaders including the press and other media. Sometimes these sources of interest-articulation work in concert to persuade the president of a widely felt need; at other times the sources form a babble of conflicting demands. In all cases the president must seek to manage the conflict and promote social consensus. How this is done—and how well it is done—depends upon the resources available to the president and his own operating style, aspects which will come under scrutiny in succeeding pages.

Policy Leadership

At this simplest but most fundamental level, the policy process is that activity involving the search for and application of means to serve a desired end or goal. As such it is a complex and necessarily cooperative endeavor. And while no single actor or set of actors in the political process can lay claim exclusively to the function of national policy making, the presidency is clearly the focus of leadership in modern America. This leadership consists, among other things, in identifying national needs, assessing the availability and utility of various means, calculating the impact of one policy on other policies, determining the appropriate timing for the inauguration of a policy, and most crucially, persuading other individuals and institutions sharing in the policy-making function to cooperate. Finally, a particular function of executive leadership consists in assuring that policies initiated are, in fact, implemented. Of all the demands on the institution of the presidency, this is surely the most time-consuming, the most important, and the most difficult.

The institution has, over the past two centuries, drawn to itself a greater and greater supply of political resources necessary for policy leadership. Numerous statutes have been enacted which delegate to the executive the formal responsibility for policy in many areas of American life. A vast bureaucracy has evolved which functions in part to offer to (or press upon) the president the advice and expertise necessary for policy evaluation. Moreover, the president has at his command unlimited sources of information and advice from outside the executive establishment.

Among the people from whom presidents must elicit cooperation and support for policies, the Congress as a collectivity presents the greatest challenge. In addition, however, support is often needed from private, organized interest groups, opinion leaders of national repute, governors, political parties, the press, and in some instances involving foreign policy, even leadership and opinion sources outside the United States.

The means for eliciting cooperation vary with the individual policy, but often (and unsurprisingly in a political universe) the ancient device of the *quid pro quo* gets frequent use. Domestically, the president has many favors to offer the ambivalent or negative congressman, ranging from electoral support to support for a pet project, or federal fund support for the congressman's constituency. State governors on occasion are amenable to similar importunities. Patronage plays some role in garnering partisan support. Appointments and project budgetary support are resources for gaining cooperation from national notables. For press support, the president is dependent in large measure on his own personal relations with the fourth estate and his own ability to cultivate the image of the sincere and determined leader. Similar qualities are important to win support abroad for foreign policy, along with the suggested availability of good future relations, often involving foreign aid or similar diplomatic or economic concessions. An astute selective application of these executive resources will usually augment the president's role in providing leadership in the policy process.

Executive Management

For the performance of the policy-making function, and all others, the president must rely on the executive establishment, and it is in attempting to insure that the bureaucracy is reliable that the president responds to another demand—that of executive management. The federal bureaucracy is an indispensable part of the American governmental machinery for two major reasons. First, it has extensive operating or administrative functions, and second, it serves as the primary source of information and intelligence available as an input to the presidential decision-making process.

In excess of 2.5 million public servants perform their tasks in several different kinds of settings: the federal departments and subordinate agencies: the Executive Office of the President; the independent regulatory commissions, and the public corporations. For each of these varied forms of bureaucracy the president has some degree of managerial responsibility. In all cases, he appoints (usually with senatorial approval) the supervisory personnel (department heads, regulatory commissioners, and corporate board members). Even this lever of authority is limited, however, in that many of the commissioners have statutorily fixed terms of service or special requirements such as partisan or regional representation. Moreover, the president's discretionary power of removal is limited legally and informally.

While, as chief administrator the president does have certain organization and reorganization powers, these are severely limited by basic congressional acts which provide for a veto of his reorganization plans by either house. Perhaps the most potent device a president possesses for exercising control over the bureaucracy is central control over the allocation of funds (and thus support for his programs) exercised by the Office of Management and the Budget under his direction. Still, an agency favored by Congress can usually make effective "end runs" around the executive since it is Congress which ultimately disposes in this area. The sum of these authorities and relationships suggests that, even though the president is expected to manage the American bureaucracy, the legal means at his disposal for accomplishing the job are not unqualified.

Political Party Leadership

One means of affording political representation to interests is the party system that has developed in the United States over the past two centuries. Since nominally the system is characterized by an oligopoly of two parties, the definition of differences between them is a broad one which states general tendencies rather than precise, programmatic distinctions. Hence most groups attempt to find *some* support in both parties, and the general tendencies are determined by that combination of interests which predominates in one or another of the parties at any time. In any case, the major function of American parties is to serve as organizational vehicles for gaining political power, ideological underpinnings being rather fluid and highly negotiable over time. Beyond the hard fact of a severely limited choice between two parties is the equally significant phenomenon of each national political party being the expression of differences among its constituent state party organizations. The federal structure remains relevant in the 1970s.

The only effective source of central leadership over the coalition of interests and state party organizations is the president. Even this potential for central control normally is fulfilled only sporadically at times of elections. Ultimately presidential leadership over party rests upon the confidence of a majority of party leaders, and this, in turn, depends upon their assessment of the president's (or presidential candidate's) general support among the people. If this latter support is clearly lost, then presidential leverage with the party barons is severely diminished if not totally destroyed. While he is in office and his popular support is at least ambiguous, if not clearly supportive, he can exercise considerable influence over party tendencies. Flowing from his own crucial, national constituency support, the president has a strong arguing point in persuading his party's congressional leadership to follow the administration line. Moreover his personal status can be lent selectively in supporting candidacies for congress and occasionally state offices at election time. His constitutional appointment power gives him still additional resources of influence through the dispensation of patronage. Another form of patronage available to the administration is the allocation of funds for federal programs and projects to favored states and congressional districts. Finally, the president has the traditional tool of party management growing out of his appointment of the national party chairman.

Since the *raison d'etre* of the political party is the attainment of political power, the ultimate criterion of the success of presidential leadership in meeting this demand is the degree to which he contributes to the effectiveness of his party as the dominant political personnel agency of the nation. If the popular image of the party is tarnished, if the linkages among the various levels of organization in the party are weakened, or if the monetary resources of the party are depleted, then the president has failed in some measure to meet the specialized demand for party leadership.

PERFORMANCE OF THE PRESIDENCY

We have now defined five broad functions of the presidency. An examination of the office and the men who have filled it allows us to assess their performance. It also allows us to discover the many and increasing restraints on the president's power that make his office a splendid irony.

Presidential Moral Leadership

The demand for national moral leadership on the part of the president is present at all times in some measure. However, it is in times of crisis that response to this demand is most crucial—times characterized by a sense of threat to the existing social order, by a seeming uncertainty about the direction in which the nation should go, and finally by the overwhelming need for action on the part of leadership. The French statesman and student of politics, Pierre Mendes France, has said that: "To govern is to choose." As a general proposition, it may seem little more than a truism, but in times of crisis, the full impact of the injunction is more keenly felt.

Throughout our history it has been times of crisis which have thrown into relief the necessity for moral leadership on the part of presidents as they were required not only to make hard choices, but to explain, communicate, and even plead the principled bases for these choices. When the choices are critical, the need for a philosophical basis of legitimization is compelling. To inquire into the nature of presidential response historically it is useful to survey briefly certain periods of crisis with a view to appreciating how presidents have interpreted values in the name of choice.

(1) *The Civil War.* The Lincoln presidency was marked by two major confrontations with crisis, each of which today reveals an historic response to the demand for moral leadership. The first issue was Union, and the second slavery itself. When Lincoln was called to office the dimensions of the first crisis were already clear. A month before the inauguration of March 1861, seven southern states had seceded from the Union and formed the Confederate States of America. Indeed it was feared by many that the inauguration would never take place, that the president-elect would be assassinated. It was in these circumstances that Lincoln laid down the challenge at his first inaugural in terms that rested upon his interpretation of the principle and value of nationhood.

> I hold that in contemplation of universal law and of the Constitution the Union of these States is perpetual. Perpetuity is implied, if not expressed, in the fundamental law of all national governments. . . . Continue to execute all the express provisions of our National Constitution, and the Union will endure forever, it being impossible to destroy it except by some action not provided for in the instrument itself.[3]

And further, addressing himself directly to the secessionists, he said: "*You* have no oath registered in heaven to destroy the Government, while *I* have the most solemn one to 'preserve, protect, and defend it.' "[4]

Lincoln adhered so resolutely to the value of Union as a first principle, that he justified a series of unconstitutional acts in the weeks following his inaugural. ("Are all the laws *but one* to go unexecuted, and the Government itself go to pieces lest that one be violated?") Thus in those spring weeks of 1861 the president, by proclamation, summoned the militia, blockaded the South, enlarged the army beyond legal limits, paid out unauthorized public funds, negotiated a public loan, censored the

3. First Inaugural Address, March 4, 1861, in Richard B. Morris, ed., *Great Political Decisions* (Fawcett Publications, 1961), p. 238.
4. Ibid.

mails, authorized the arrest of potential traitors, and suspended the writ of habeas corpus in certain parts of the country.

The question of slavery was to Lincoln clearly subordinate to the principle of Union. Indeed, though he opposed the institution as anti-humane and morally reprehensible, he was no abolitionist and, as historians unfailingly point out, when he did issue the Emancipation Proclamation in September 1862, not one slave was freed. Still, the Proclamation would have revolutionary consequences and converted the war into a great moral crusade. That the timing of the act itself was motivated by strategic considerations does not demean the fact that the way was prepared for the Thirteenth Amendment and probably made that sanctifying document inevitable.

(2) *The Progressive Era of Reform.* Not all crises are as stark and immediate as that encountered in the Civil War period. A more slowly evolving and less perceptible form of crisis is the alteration of widely accepted understandings about social relations. Another way of describing such events looks to the questioning of the very legitimacy of existing distributions of social, economic, and political power and privilege. In such times of challenge the presidency is institutionally fitted to respond to the call for leadership in reinterpreting social values.

During the first decade of this century such a state of flux was evident. From the time of the end of the Civil War the reigning dogma explaining and justifying social relations was the principle of laissez-faire. Social philosophers, presidents, jurists and legislators were usually united in the belief that the role of government in the social and economic affairs of the citizen should be a benign one. A popular corollary to laissez-faire was the tenet of social Darwinism that men differ in intelligence, skill, ambition, and virtue, and that those who are superior (or "fittest") should survive socially and economically, the less fit falling by the wayside. Indeed it would be unintelligent and even immoral for society or government to intervene in what was seen as a process of natural selection.

Government—and particularly the courts—reinforced this belief-system by a rigid adherence to certain parts of the Constitution. Thus the due process clauses of the Fifth and Fourteenth Amendments were interpreted as prohibiting economic regulatory intervention by government and the contract clause was strictly read as a bar to labor organization, or collective bargaining, or even the rights of states to regulate child labor or conditions of work. The challenge to laissez-faire orthodoxy was produced by the results of adherence to it. That is, it came to be recognized that the ideology was being employed to justify economic monopoly, social oligarchy and political corruption.

In the course of his presidency, Theodore Roosevelt grew to appreciate more, year by year, that social change must overcome an outworn and pernicious social principle. As president he moved from the van of the Progressive movement to its national leadership.

Theodore Roosevelt accomplished this move at both an oratorical level and an active level. The major target of President Roosevelt's attacks were the giant economic trusts which he brought under legal prosecution. Northern Securities, the Beef Trust, and Standard Oil are only among the better known victims of legal challenge by the federal government. What is perhaps even more important than the prosecutions, however, is the moral basis for initiating the action which the president laid. In what one historian of the period has called Roosevelt's "endless sermonizing," the president repeatedly assaulted the industrial plutocracy of the country as malefactors of great wealth which had to be brought under government control. His first annual message, while hardly incendiary, served notice of his crusade against the doctrine of "let alone":

> Artificial bodies, such as corporations and joint stock or other associations, depending upon any statutory law for their existence or privileges, should be subject to proper governmental supervision. . . ." [5]

Moreover, the lesson he preached was that times were changing and the country was changing, and that legally enshrined dogmas supporting privilege had to give way to a new era:

> When the Constitution was adopted, at the end of the eighteenth century, no human wisdom could fortell the sweeping changes, alike in industrial and political conditions which were to take place by the beginning of the twentieth century. [6]

The impact of Roosevelt's leadership in bringing advocacy of progressive reform to the "bloody pulpit," as T. R. characterized the presidency, consisted in legitimating a force that had theretofore been denounced as alien socialism. And the enthusiasm and vigor of his advocacy was self-consciously labeled as his stewardship of the popular will, thus underlining a moral measure of the exercise of presidential power.

(3) *The Great Depression.* If institutional leadership depends upon the interpretation and reformulation of social and political values, then the role demands the qualities of a teacher, skills of communication, and even powers of exhortation. In the dark days of the 1930s, Franklin Delano Roosevelt was unsurpassed in fulfilling this role. The ideas themselves were not usually profound or recondite. Roosevelt's skill consisted in framing very basic propositions in often eloquent but never scholastic or arcane language. Eschewing grandiose ideology, he delivered what he

5. Ibid., p. 334.
6. Ibid.

regarded as home truths. And yet these "truths" (read: political value propositions) confronted squarely the problems of the day.

Perhaps the root crisis of the 1930s was a crisis in confidence, the uncertainty that political man could indeed surmount or even effectively attack general economic malaise. Indeed, the political opposition argued in effect that such was the case, that things would have to work themselves out naturally over time. To this posture Roosevelt retorted with conviction that institutions *could* respond if leadership expressed the will:

> So first let me assert my firm belief that the only thing we have to fear is fear itself—nameless, unreasoning, unjustified terror which paralyzes needed efforts to convert retreat into advance.[7]

The road to recovery, the president counselled, consisted in collective actions by the citizenry under the leadership of bold statesmen, unafraid of the use of power. Confronting the remaining heritage of laissez-faire and the corollary of extreme individualism, the president asserted: "We now realize, as we have never realized before, our interdependence on each other. . .".[8]

At the same time that F.D.R. admitted a variety of forms of experimentation with institutions, jurisdictions, and habitual practices, he repeatedly argued that fundamental institutions (the Constitution, a capitalistic economy, the basic structure of civil liberties) were sound and serviceable and merely called for modifications here and there to meet the emergency. He saw no contradiction between these institutions and the need for governmental intervention in the economy and public regulation, nor in the quest for social welfare reforms or public assistance measures entailing budgetary deficits.

Aside from the content of his exhortations to the people, Roosevelt is perhaps more renowned for the skillful method of his appeals of which the "fireside chat" was the most innovative. Seizing upon the new electronic technology as none of his predecessors had done, he transported himself into the living rooms of the nation by radio in a supremely effective way. There is ample testimony to the effectiveness of the fireside chats. People came to think of the president as a member of the family —and usually the father. More significantly, the institution of the presidency itself came to be one directly experienced by the citizen, thus augmenting the impact of moral persuasion. It is not surprising that the president himself regarded the institution as "preeminently a place of moral leadership."

The three foregoing examples illustrate historic instances in which

7. Ibid., p. 410.
8. Ibid., p. 413.

presidents provided leadership of a special kind by responding to circumstances which called for statements of principle about fundamental social directions. Employing the status and the symbolism of the office, the incumbent in each instance exhorted the people in favor a some manner of departure from traditional ways. A number of observations should be made about this evidence. First, it would not be argued here that any of these men was more virtuous or morally pure or inspired than their predecessors or successors. Rather, in meeting some of the crises of the times, they were notably effective in utilizing the institution of the presidency for persuasion. Second, the general demand for this type of leadership is not a constant requirement of the office. Instead only occasionally—and usually in times of some form of general crisis— is this kind of leadership called for. Indeed, over-exercise of the preaching role open to presidents would probably be counterproductive. It is sometimes argued that Woodrow Wilson, especially during his second term, was less effective because he tended dogmatically to identify non-crisis issues as tests of great moral principle. His unbending stance on the League of Nations question may be cited in evidence.

Finally something should be said about the implied criterion of "successful" response. That criterion is essentially one of results. Thus, to put it very simply: to the extent that presidential leadership played an important role in each of the crises noted, it is deemed effective in that (1) the Union was preserved in the 1860s; (2) the power and privileges of economic oligarchy justified by reference to the dogma of laissez-faire, were eroded significantly during the years of the first Roosevelt's administration; and (3) a much more active government committed to social welfare concerns did result from the New Deal era and has become a moral and legitimated part of national expectations in the years that have followed.

THE CONTEMPORARY PRESIDENCY

Historical analysis gives perspective but it does not explain contemporary relationships. Looking at the present capacity of the presidency to respond to demands for moral leadership, it seems probable that a combination of factors makes such leadership much more difficult to exercise effectively than in the past. One of the factors which has become crushingly apparent in the decades of the 1960s is a widespread decline in automatic respect for symbols of institutional authority of all kinds. This could not help but undermine the moral authority of the presidency. The reasons for this skepticism are too complicated to be analyzed here, but it can be noted that all the major institutions of social control have been subjected to harsh questions concerning their legitimacy and authority.

The contemporary American family hardly resembles the close-knit primary group governed by the judgment of parents and elders of past generations. The school, from primary grades through the advanced graduate levels of higher education, once considered a prime agent of socialization, is challenged on its first principles. Both the methods of teaching and the substance of what is putatively taught are widely criticized in terms of their relevance to the needs of society. Religious institutions, military institutions, economic and political institutions have been subject to the contagion of anti-authority. The presidency as historic symbol of the political system and its acknowledged legitimacy is thus no longer rendered the relatively automatic respect given familiar institutions in the past.

One suspects that another reason the president is not automatically regarded a modern day philosopher-king is that the technology of the mass media has brought the institution very much down to earth. For generations the presidency has been subject to adulation by those who have professionally interpreted the office to the people—in a sense, oversold. This is a point of fundamental importance, since educated perceptions of the presidency have long been formed out of the lessons of textbook mythology which often implied greater majesty, grandeur, if not omnipotence, than was justified by experience. It has been taken as an article of faith that the office almost always enobles the mere mortal who fills it.

And what of direct experience? Particularly through the constant exploitation of the medium of television, citizens have come to appreciate the fallibility of their presidents in a clearer light. They have been taught that presidents are sometimes confused, that performance often falls far short of promise, and that presidents are not above misleading the people in their appeals. Whether the lesson took the form of the initial denial of knowledge of a U-2 flight by an Eisenhower, the secret preparations for a Bay of Pigs operations by a Kennedy, or numerous publicized denials of plans for actions that would be taken a few days later by a Johnson, the cumulative result is a greater popular skepticism about the authority of presidential pronouncements.

A further element in the erosion of presidential authority is the increased frequency and tenor of demands for presidential crusades in the name of some social value shared by a significant group in society. Moreover, the demand usually carries with it the implied expectation that it will receive an immediate response. This is understandable on a number of grounds. Among them is that part of the American ethos which assumes that all problems are soluble in short order if given proper attention in the right places. Proud of our technology and expertise, we tend to think that great social change can be brought about at a rapid pace. Moreover, experience in some areas can be called upon to reinforce this assumption. In the short period of a human lifetime, as a nation we have achieved preeminent status as a world leader, have built an industrial machine capable of providing material luxuries and relative affluence to a great majority of our people, have made education nearly universal—and the list could be lengthened considerably. At the same time, success in some areas breeds greater demands for perfection in others. A simplistic assessment of the scope of our national capacities encourages even our leaders to proclaim exaggerated goals. And when the goals are not met, a society made at least superficially more aware by our technology is frustrated and the confidence in leadership's authority diminished.

For example, poverty. Sometime in the early 1960s poverty was rediscovered in America. The demand that it be coped with was entirely legitimate. But the response to the demand was perhaps oratorically exaggerated. President Johnson declared a "war on poverty" and staffed up the program with an Office of Economic Opportunity and whole range of poverty-alleviating instrumentalities including Neighborhood Youth Corps, Community Action Programs, and so on. There is surely nothing challengeable about these acts in principle. The difficulty, however, rests more with the expectations encouraged. Wars *are* won, especially when concerted attacks are mounted. Although the number of those citizens falling within the poverty income range *has* been reduced significantly, five years later no one would contend that this particular "war" has been won. In fact we are discovering that the problem of poverty is more complex than we once thought. Yet two results of the failure to abolish poverty, the ghetto, and human misery in our country are first, a degree of frustration at government's inability, and secondly, downgrading of what has been accomplished.

A similar and even more agonizing instance of performance lagging behind promise is the cause of racial justice in the United States. Fifteen years after *Brown v. Board of Education* and a succession of presidential pronouncements (not to mention legislation) in favor of a racially integrated society and equal justice for all, the President's Commission on Civil Disorders has reminded us that we are still a cruelly divided society racially. In the area of foreign policy presidents since Kennedy have been telling us, for example, that we are engaged in a war to stop aggression and preserve democracy in South Vietnam. Our power and technology should easily bring us to the solution of this problem. Yet the war goes on and democracy fails to flower in Indo-China. This observation is made not as a facile explanation of a tortuously complex series of historic events, but rather to suggest a still further source of popular disenchantment with presidential leadership.

The effectiveness of presidential response to the demand for moral leadership is impinged upon by the president's response to other demands.

That is, the demands identified at the outset of this essay need not be mutually reinforcing, and indeed often one demand is inconsistent with or even contradictory to another. Such is often the case with the demand that the presidency be a brokerage office, representing a broad spectrum of interests. The argument is simply that presidents may be prevented from taking a firm, principled position on great issues because of their assessment of duties owed to conflicting parties-at-interest. We proceed to explore this and other aspects of the representative function below.

The Representative Function

The struggle among competing interests at the presidential level manifests itself in many different ways. At a very broad level, interests compete over issue-areas which are really collections of more specific interests. Thus domestic interests may compete with foreign policy interests; defense interests with welfare interests; national security interests with conservation interests, and so on. At a more confined level, conflict and competition arise *within* issue areas. Within the welfare issue area there may be competition among advocates of tax and fiscal approaches to the problems and advocates of public works approaches. Within the foreign affairs area, regions of the world may compete for the attention of the president, one against the other; or diplomatic interests may seek precedence over military interests, or the reverse.

Finally, within a relatively confined policy or issue-area differing interests may compete over the strategies appropriate to the furtherance of the general policy interest. For example, there are several differing representatives of what each regards as the interests of agriculture. In actuality one of these may seek a preference for cotton producers, another for meat producers, still another for wheat producers. All of which simply suggests that the identification of "interests," their promotion, and the reception given them is a highly complex and shifting phenomenon. In the pages which follow an attempt is made to illustrate this proposition by focusing upon the means which presidents have used to deal with interests asserted at differing levels. Two strategic environments are suggested: First, presidents are called upon to negotiate among existing interests at all times. Second, in some cases presidents may take a hand in the fostering of new interests seeking governmental attention by giving recognition to the claims made by unorganized or less well-organized groups.

(1) *Juggling Interests.* Let us begin with a consideration of some of the means presidents have used to deal with conflicts among existing interests. Our first example is a recent one drawn from a domestic interest area, that of education. In one way or another, government has

responded to the claims for public educational support from the earliest years of our history, beginning with the Northwest Ordinance of 1787. In the middle of the nineteenth century, the Morrill Act gave recognition and support to the land-grant college development. As education at the college and university level became more widely available in the twentieth century, demands increased for greater and greater federal support for such things as building construction, teachers' salaries, fellowships and scholarships, and other monetary grants. In 1958, in large part because of scientific and technical needs perceived as a result of the Soviet launching of its sputnik, a National Defense Education Act was proposed by the administration and passed overwhelmingly in Congress. This was a clear case of the interest of educational support linked to that of national security and profiting thereby.

Throughout the late 1950s and early 1960s, the interest in and the case for federal aid for elementary and secondary education foundered on the rocks of opposition thrust up by other interests overlapping the education question. After a time, issues referred to as the "three Rs—Race, Religion and the Reds"—sometimes separately and sometimes in concert, caused the mobilization of sufficient opposition to scuttle a series of federal aid proposals made by both Presidents Eisenhower and Kennedy. Race entered the education issue domain as a competing claim for governmental recognition on its own. That is, following the desegregation decision of 1954 and further demands for a general recognition of the rights of Negroes, spokesmen for that interest succeeded in linking its fortunes with the quest for school aid. Thus to school-aid proposals Representative Adam Clayton Powell would regularly attach an amendment (which came to be known by his name) to the bill requiring that any funds appropriated for aid would be withheld from states engaging in discriminatory practices in public education. This was consequently sufficient to arouse the concerted opposition of the Southern bloc in Congress and prevent passage of the bill.

Religious considerations similarly predestined many proposals for defeat. On the one hand, increasingly, religious and private schools made claim to federal support on the ground that they were carrying a major burden of education in the nation and thus relieving the public school system. On the other hand, ideological opponents of aid to church-related educational institutions interpreted literally the separation of church and state principle traditionally revered in American society. Hence aid proposals were beseiged typically by the Roman Catholic hierarchy and its allies when they did not provide aid to religious institutions, and by a powerful anticlerical opposition when they did.

The third "R"—"the Reds"—signifies yet another basis of opposition in the middle years of this century. This epithet symbolized the ideological stance which found in aid programs still further and alien intervention of the national government into hitherto state and local spheres of responsibility. It carried with it the conviction that federal aid would only be a beginning from which federal control, indoctrination, and ultimate tyranny would follow. Combinations of these three interests, overlapping and sometimes transcending the fundamentally popular interest in public education, were successful in blocking a series of measures for many years until 1965.

When President Johnson returned to office in 1965 with an overwhelming electoral mandate, high on his domestic reform agenda was the issue of expanded educational support. His enthusiasm was, of course, chastened by the prospect of the competing and conflicting interests that would have to be dealt with in order to achieve a breakthrough in this area. And yet in the summer of 1965 a massive Elementary and Secondary Education Act was passed, fulfilling the hopes of a generation of educational aid supporters. How might this success be explained? From different perspectives, a number of answers might be offered. It could surely be noted that the new Congress carried in with the president was more supportive quantitatively (more Democrats) and qualitatively (more liberally-oriented Democrats). It might also be argued that this was, at long last, an idea whose time had come.

From the vantage point of presidential interest brokerage, however, still another explanation might be offered. In sum this could be described as a case of presidential melding of the educational support issue with another, transcendent issue: the plight of the poor in our society. For these were the years of the recognition of widespread poverty in a nation hitherto characterized as affluent. With the help of activist congressmen, social reformers, and publicists, the president succeeded in identifying one of the root causes of poverty as educational deprivation. The "preformed" bill which the administration sent to Congress was a bundle of provisions granting recognition to each of the overlapping interests noted above but withholding undue prominence from any of them.[9] Thus the measure provided aid based upon a federal formula which directed it proportionally to areas serving children of low-income families. (Hence it was a *poverty* bill.) Correspondingly, the formula had the impact of mandating aid to districts heavily populated by Negro children. In addition, Title II of the Act, though of modest proportions financially, did cross another Rubicon by authorizing federal aid for library resources, textbooks, and other published materials for use of children in both public *and private* elementary and secondary schools.

9. On the planning details, see Stephen K. Bailey and Edith K. Mosher, *ESEA, The Office of Education Administers a Law* (Syracuse University Press, 1968), chap. 2.

The Elementary and Secondary Education Act of 1965 emerges as the result of an act of shrewd brokerage of many affected interests, successful because the president made the education issue part of a larger issue of the times, a constituent part of his Great Society program. And in the process of doing so he subtly balanced advantages and disadvantages felt by involved interest groups.

In some circumstances the most careful advance planning will be insufficient to bring about what the president regards as a reasonable and just balancing of interests. In such instances a president may resort to a constellation of executive prerogatives in order to right the balance. Such a non-subtle recourse to action on many fronts is illustrated by President Kennedy's clash with the steel industry in 1962. In this case the primary interest felt by the president—indeed what he regarded as the "public interest" was the prevention of runaway inflation in part caused by a continued wage-price spiral. The strategy employed by the president to confront inflation was to support in every way possible the economic guideposts established by his Council of Economic Advisers. These directives (which are no more than recommendations) set up boundaries within which labor-management negotiations over wages and industrial price-setting decisions should be confined in order to prevent excessively rising costs and prices.

The steel industry was regarded as key in the economic sector. Hence the administration worked closely with both the steel industry and the steel workers in an effort to achieve a non-inflationary contract in the spring of 1962. It appeared in the early days of April that a non-inflationary agreement had been reached, due in large part to successful persuasion exerted over the steel workers to keep their wage demands in line. Such hopes, however, were cruelly, if temporarily, disappointed when unexpectedly the United States Steel Corporation announced publicly on April 11, without prior notice, that it would increase the price of steel by six dollars a ton. At this point presidential mediation and conciliation gave way to a broad range of pressures, the sum of which illustrates many of the resources available to a determined executive when milder forms of interest brokerage prove insufficient.

Immediately the president denounced the U.S. Steel move (and that of a number of the largest other steel companies as well) as an "unjustifiable and irresponsible defiance of the public interest." He personally persuaded by telephone the executives of two steel companies who had not immediately followed the U.S. Steel lead to hold back any price increases. He put the Antitrust Division of the Justice Department to work on the question of whether there had been violations of the Sherman and/or Clayton Acts in the simultaneous price increases by several steel producers. The Treasury Department was ordered to reappraise certain tax benefits intended for industry, the implication being that these might now be withheld. The Defense Department announced that it would transfer orders to companies which had *not* increased their prices. Seventy-two hours later the chairman of the board of U.S. Steel reported that his company had rescinded the price increase, and President Kennedy felt that he had adjusted the balance between the claims of workers for wage increases and industry for price increases. But more crucially, he felt that he had served a more general interest than either of these: the interest of the American consumer. [10]

(2) *Promoting New Interests.* We are so accustomed to emphasize the clash of organized interests as the basis of the pluralistic politics that sight is sometimes lost of the existence of shared wants or interests which have not achieved the level of functioning organized groups of perceptible consequence. This latter category has been characterized by David Truman as "potential interests," interests which have not at any point in time yet gained access to the political process.[11] An important part of the president's brokerage function consists in articulating such interests. One of the reasons that this is a natural presidential function is that the articulation of interests is heavily dependent on access to channels of communication, and the nature of the presidency is such that, given the desire to communicate—and to communicate widely, prominently and frequently—a president cannot be denied. Nor is a monopoly of the communications media the only resource at the disposal of a president. In the pages that follow we will explore how presidents have put their other prerogatives in the service of the articulation of interests.

A historic example can be drawn from the activity of President Theodore Roosevelt on behalf of conservation in the early years of this century[12]. Little thought had been given to the conservation of natural resources prior to the twentieth century, except for the setting aside of a few forest preserves and parks in the Harrison and Cleveland administrations. At the very outset of his administration, Theodore Roosevelt took up the cause of conservation in public messages. Previously the predominant, nearly exclusive interest in natural resources had been maintained by private entrepreneurs, particularly ranchers, lumbermen, and power companies in the western and southwestern parts of the nation. Needless to say, their opposition to public poaching on what was regarded as a private turf was powerful.

Aside from his own interest in the preservation of resources, the president extended his influence by including in the official family Gifford

10. Grant McConnell, *Steel and the Presidency,* 1962 (W. W. Norton, 1963).
11. David Truman, *The Governmental Process* (Alfred A. Knopf, 1951), pp. 510-24.
12. George E. Mowry, *The Era of Theodore Roosevelt* (Harper & Brothers, 1958).

Pinchot, a zealot among conservationists. A major reclamation program was initiated, and the Reclamation Service was established in the Agriculture Department under the supervision of Pinchot. In short time conservation extended to oil reserves, coal and mineral lands and power sites. During the Roosevelt administration government land reserve acreage was tripled, and regulations concerning grazing, mining and lumbering were promulgated, in addition to an unconventional degree of enforcement of existing laws. When Congress, primarily moved by the western land interests, struck back by a legislative rider to an appropriations bill prohibiting new forest reserves, the president finessed the issue by creating thirty-two new forest preserves four days before signing the legislation. In another exercise of delegated executive prerogative, Chief Forester Pinchot withdrew twenty-five power sites from the grasp of private developers by designating them ranger stations. When Congress retaliated by legislative action, the president exercised the veto twice. In this and in other ways did Theodore Roosevelt definitively articulate a new interest which would become a permanent claimant on public recognition in the decades which followed.

The prominence given in the 1960s to poverty as an issue and the interests of the poor as a group suggest yet another form in which presidents have responded to what seemed to be the needs of a potential interest. Though poverty is as old as man, in recent American history the poor have not been regarded as an interest group. Much public attention, particularly since the 1930s, has been given to various *aspects* of existence which contribute to poverty, but appreciation of the generic condition of poverty is a recent phenomenon. How this has come about provides an interesting observation on the function of presidential interest representation.

For a long time many of the causes of poverty were apparent and were treated by acts of public policy. In the depression years, unemployment was seen as the root cause, and a crude application of Keynesian economics (public works, pump priming, etc.) was the result. As it was recognized that inflation was particularly debilitating for those living on fixed incomes and savings, anti-inflationary policies were adopted. As it became apparent that a changing occupational structure was increasing the white-collar sector and the opportunities of professional and technical workers to the detriment of unskilled or semi-skilled workers, education and advanced training on a larger scale were seen as partial answers to the plight of those technologically left behind. The special disadvantages of older people were recognized, and a social security system, which by 1965 included a medical care provision, was established to treat the symptoms. In part because of each of these partial palliatives, the problem of poverty was widely assumed to have disappeared.

And then the recessionary years of the middle 1950s provoked fresh thinking about the problem. In 1958 the highly regarded and relatively popular economist, John Kenneth Galbraith, wrote *The Affluent Society*. Even those who read (and reviewed) the book paid scant attention to a chapter toward the end entitled "The New Position of Poverty." In this chapter Galbraith observed:

> . . . the concerns for inequality had vitality only so long as the many suffered privation while a few had much. It did not survive as a burning issue in a time when the many had much even though others had much more. It is our misfortune that when inequality declined as an issue, the slate was not left clean. A residual and in some ways rather more hopeless problem remained." [13]

But there were a few who took notice and who took the message to heart. One of these was Michael Harrington, a former social worker who in 1962 published what was to become a manifesto for the poor: *The Other America*. According to his biographer, President Kennedy read both Galbraith and Harrington.[14] By 1963 the President had charted a course which would lead to recognition of the poor as a class, whether the cause be poor education, unemployment, bad housing, broken families, or a combination of contributory factors. Assassination prevented President Kennedy's personal mobilization for a war on poverty, but Lyndon Johnson took up the cause in succession. The administration dispatched a comprehensive program to the Congress, which in 1964 was ready to rubber-stamp such a measure. Perhaps the most significant aspect of the Economic Opportunity Act, with its community action provisions and its apparent promise of "maximum feasible participation" of the poor in mounting programs, was the implicit recognition and presidential legitimation of the poor as a forceful interest group—indeed, one which would challenge established political organizations and welfare bureaucracies.[15]

BARRIERS TO EFFECTIVENESS

Presidents have historically employed these means in articulating the manifold interests of the polity. The ideal sought has been that chief executives represent and balance the interests of all significant groups in an equitable manner, both through the adjustment of existing interests

13. John Kenneth Galbraith, *The Affluent Society* (Houghton Mifflin, 1958), p. 329.
14. Arthur M. Schlesinger, Jr., *A Thousand Days* (Houghton Mifflin, 1965), p. 1010.
15. See John C. Donovan, *The Politics of Poverty* (Pegasus, 1967), chap. 2, and Daniel P. Moynihan, *Maximum Feasible Misunderstanding* (The Free Press, 1969).

and the supportive articulation of new or potential interests. We must now note a number of obstacles to the fulfillment of these demands by any president.

To begin, a truism must be repeated: Not all the interests involved in any policy arena are of equal power and influence. Moreover the bases of the power and influence of these interests are most often extra-presidential and, indeed, extra-governmental. In short, presidential judgment and presidential power are often *not controlling*. The independent sources of influence exercised by interest groups are many and include financial supports, regional supports, support in massive and/or well-organized numbers, and the support of prestige groups or symbols.

A combination of these sources of power may make of a particular interest aggregation an elite group with a discrete issue-domain. And the totality of presidential prestige and power may be insufficient to overcome the predominance of that elite. Examples abound. For generations presidents have attempted to chip away at the preferred position of the oil industry as benefactor of a special advantage known as the depletion allowance. They have been notably unsuccessful in bringing about any appreciable change in the name of equity, the consumer, and needed sources of public funds. The powerful regional-industrial interests reflected in key positions of leadership in Congress have been sufficient to rebuff presidential invasions of this policy satrapy.

The breakthrough in the area of educational aid chronicled above was used to illustrate one means by which one president was able to bring about an adjustment of interests in favor of a desirable end. More instructive at this point, however, is the persistence of other interests clustered about the education question that was sufficient to stave off the federal aid thrust for so long. Because of a concern about infringements of their narrower interests, professional educational groups, religious groups, and racial groups, alternately and sometimes in concert, blocked the passage of proposed general aid policies. (This illustration incidentally suggests the negative impact of the phenomenon of overlapping interests.)

Presidential attempts to articulate new interests are subject to even more threats to their effectiveness. One of these is the institutionalization and legitimation of the interest bargaining system itself. What Theodore Lowi has characterized as the ideology of interest-group liberalism proclaims that organized inteerst groups that are not a part of the formal governmental system have a right to exercise public power through a process of delegation. The institutional result of this process is normally the establishment of a bargaining situation in which issue-specialized administrators treat with private clientele groups over policy determinations in the specialized issue-domain. And since any new interest a president may choose to champion will inevitably overlap and compete with established interests, effective penetration is very difficult. Hence, even though the president possesses the ability to advocate and publicize, his maneuverability for effectiving substantive, as opposed to symbolic, change is severely limited. To quote Lowi's conclusion:

> Flexibility and legitimacy are likely to be further reduced by the oligopolistic character of the interest group liberal's mechanisms of representation, because (1) the number of competitors is deliberately reduced to the most interested and best organized; (2) this tends to eliminate rather than encourage political competition; and (3) this is bound to involve some exchange of legitimacy for the false comfort of stability and the false impression that the problem of power has been solved.[16]

Nor have attempts by presidents to promote interests explicitly within the institutionalized bargaining context been notably successful. The case of the poverty program discussed above illustrates precisely this tactic. The various community action programs (CAPs), designed to rest policy making activity in the hands of the concerned interests of the poor or their representatives, ran afoul of previously existing arrangements and modes of operation. In some instances the CAPs operated independently of existing local and federal agencies overlapping their interests; this resulted in deep antagonisms and ultimate self-destruction. In other instances the CAPs were largely absorbed and controlled by city administrations and thus were resentful and ineffective. In still other instances a combination of administrative inexperience and peculations led to the intervention of the Bureau of the Budget and the withholding of funds.[17]

The problems reviewed suggest obstacles lying in the path of a president once he has decided to give his support to an interest. A deeper source of failure in performing this function is a president's inability to assess, or unawareness of, important emerging interests. It is argued here that it has become more difficult for presidents to appreciate the extent and poignancy of emerging or potential interests because of developments in the executive institution itself. With the growth in the size of the institutional staff—Executive Office, White House Office, and the entire bureaucratic arm of the institution—presidents appear to have become more remote, more isolated from the outside world.[18] Information, attitudes and the ultimate bases of judgment are filtered through to the man by an encompassing network of aides. Moreover, these subordinates often tend to shape their recommendations to the American monarch

16. Theodore J. Lowi, *The End of Liberalism* (W. W. Norton, 1969), p. 96.
17. See Moyihan, *Maximum Feasible Misunderstanding*, chapters 6 and 7.
18. For the most recent and insightful explication of this thesis, see George E. Reedy, *The Twilight of the Presidency* (World Publishing Co., 1970).

in terms and tones which they anticipate will accord with his own predispositions; indeed, they tend to adopt those predispositions as their own. Murray Kempton has written:

> The best of servants must end up being very like his master. The view is the same; you are looking out upon the countryside from a window of the Court.[19]

Recent history offers some support for this view. Secretary Hickel's dismissal from the Cabinet by President Nixon in 1970 after the secretary had publicly called for greater presidential attentiveness to the aspirations and demands of the young, might be viewed as the sanction for not behaving in the manner expected of court advisers.

The consequences of failures of presidents to appreciate and then give reinforcement in every way to the less articulated interests in society can be momentous for the system as a whole. David Truman, a pioneer in the study of the role of interests in society, was prophetic when he suggested two decades ago:

> In a domestic crisis the continued latency of these unorganized interests may prevent the development of a viable compromise and encourage resort to less orderly means of adjustment.[20]

Presidential Policy Leadership

Representation of interests is inherent in the process of formulating and executing all policies. Yet the policy function is really the heart of the matter, since it is concerned with the mechanics of moving from aspiration to action. The conventional meaning of policy—and the one accepted in this essay—is plan, or course of action. In turn, two elements must be present in the consideration of any policy: ends or goals to be achieved, and means or methods deemed appropriate to the achievement of the ends. The policy process is essentially a process of decision making by which alternative sets of means are surveyed in order to find which is the most desirable to be employed in achieving the sought-after end. It should be noted, however, that the end is not always the determining factor. In some instances the costs of all perceived means may be too high to be borne, and the initially desired end must be reformulated or qualified.

A basic characteristic of the policy process must be understood at the outset: it is a shared process. That is, no one institution, level of government, or social grouping controls the process. It is always subject to a

19. Murray Kempton, "At King Lyndon's Court," *New York Review of Books*, 10 April 1969, p. 8.
20. Truman, *The Governmental Process*, p. 516.

multitude of influences from many different sources. It is usual to ascribe to the presidency the major function of leadership over policy making in the national arena. This assumption is based both upon a value judgment (that the president, as representative of all the people *should* govern the process by which decisions about their interests are made), and a factual observation (that he possesses, in the federal administration, the means to make rational decisions among prevailing alternatives). And yet close scrutiny reveals that the president is one of several sources of leadership in the process—and not always the dominating source. In this sense, presidential power has been oversold.

The fact remains that presidents are expected, and they themselves expect, to take the initiative in national policy making. *How* they have responded to this imperative is best seen by examining a number of tasks chief executives perform in the policy-making arena. Though the tasks could be refined and the list lengthened, there would seem to be four major jobs: the mobilization of ideas; the assessment of various means to a policy goal; the establishment of interrelationships and priorities among various desired policies; and the mobilization of support for the establishment and implementation of proposed policies. In each of these job assignments, it should be noted how *dependent* the president is.

(1) *Mobilizing Ideas.* It is assumed that somewhere in the complex equation leading to the promulgation of a national policy there is a personal unknown which represents the president's own values, predispositions and priorities. Yet it is the institutional sources of advice and influence coming to bear on the president's judgment that are of interest here. Indeed it is usually taken to be the great resource of the presidency that the office has at its disposal unlimited reservoirs of expert judgment and counsel. The departments and agencies of the federal establishment, functionally specialized and experienced, are expected to provide a distillation of the best thinking on any question of moment. The institution of the Cabinet is popularly looked upon as embodying the collective wisdom of political leadership. Yet this is only a small beginning of the probings of sources of advice.

In the early decades of this century it became obvious that the complex array of governmental responsibilities and the concomitant growth and diversification of bureaucratic institutions often produce inconsistency and confusion. Mechanisms of coordination were needed to harmonize overlapping jurisdictions and contending partial views focused upon any problem of significance. A landmark decision was made in 1939 when President Franklin Roosevelt established the Executive Office of the President. This body has continued to grow and function as an agency of problem amalgamation and advice close to the president. Within its ambit additional coordinating and advising agencies serve the chief executive. Thus the Department of State is regarded as an insufficient source of counsel for foreign policy making and is often eclipsed by the National Security Council, which was created to bring into consideration foreign, military, and domestic aspects of national security questions. Similarly in 1970 a Domestic Council was created in the Executive Office to formulate and coordinate domestic policy recommendations to the president. Another means sought to bring into focus the "big picture" of national policy implications is the employment of the mechanism of resource allocation. Thus the Office of Management and Budget (formerly Bureau of the Budget) is enjoined to act as an agency of clearance for departmental recommendations on policy, taking into account their costs to society. Other major areas given recognition at the Executive Office level are welfare, preparedness, science and technology, and space.

For a number of reasons the Executive Office has replaced the Cabinet as the president's chief advisory body. First, the very physical proximity of the Executive Office (and particularly the White House staff) eases immediate access to the president. Second, the basis of personnel selection often makes executive officers more functionally effective. That is, whereas Cabinet officers are frequently tokens of political, regional, ethnic, or interest group recognition, non-Cabinet executive officers are more often sought out for their expertise or long association with the problem areas governed by their agency. Finally, Cabinet officers wear two hats. Nominally presidential advisors, they have managerial responsibilities over vast operating departments. These responsibilities (in the time they consume and the functional parochialism they engender) often eclipse the advisory role. A telling contrast is the luxurious simplicity of the role definition of a presidential economic adviser.

With all the elaboration of bureaucratic mechanisms of advice available to the presidency from within the government, modern presidents have come more and more to look *outside* the permanent federal establishment for ideas. One institutionalized form this has taken has been the use of special, ad hoc advisory commissions and task forces. These commissions are usually established to study and make recommendations for policy in a particular issue-area such as health, world trade, or population growth. They are appointed by and are directly responsible to the president. Given this distinguished imprimatur, it is expected that responsible and recognized private sources of expert judgment will be attracted to the public service on a short-term basis. A recent study by the Twentieth Century Fund documents the increased use of this source of intelligence by contemporary presidents. Between 1945 and 1970 some forty-four presidential commissions were created, but two-thirds of them were called into existence since 1960 by Presidents Kennedy, Johnson and Nixon.[21] A variation on the presidential commission method is the use of task forces to investigate the ramifications of a policy problem, such as housing or education, and make recommendations to the president. To cite one example, in the year 1967 alone there were fifty task forces operating.[22]

The use of "outside" sources of advice is even greater than suggested by the preceding examples. Indirect use of extramural expertise in national policy making is found in the well-established practice of the various departments and agencies of government appointing advisory groups for purposes of germinating recommendations *within* the bureaucracy. Thus one study indicates that between 1962 and 1964 there were some nine hundred such advisory committees in existence. The Department of Health, Education, and Welfare alone received the recommendations of 229 ad hoc committees.[23] Finally, neither the advice of the permanent bureaucracy nor the additional resources of ad hoc groups appears to be sufficient for the needs of national policy making at the executive level, for another recent development carries the search for advice even further. Especially since the Second World War, the executive bureaucracy has engaged in the practice of buying advice from private sources under contractual arrangement. Thus studies are made, projects assessed, and recommendations offered by numerous private research organizations such as the Rand Corporation and the Hudson Institute.

(2) *Assessing Means.* In a sense it is artificial to view policy making as a process involving first, a choice of goals and, second, the calculation of means best suited to the achievement of the goals, since in reality the two kinds of calculations are always intermingled, either consciously or unconsciously. In some cases, ideal goals are soon forsaken since a brief inspection of the means necessary to their achievement reveals that the latter are simply too costly. And thus the goals are reformulated. Still, the two kinds of calculations are usually separated for analytical purposes. To decide how given policy ends may be achieved, presidents employ all the institutional mechanisms described above for mobilizing ideas. And very often broad policy goals are inherited "givens," and the real task is to employ appropriate methods for achieving them.

21. Frank Popper, *The President's Commissions* (Twentieth Century Fund, 1970), Appendix 1, pp. 66-67.
22. Norman C. Thomas and Harold L. Wolman, "The Presidency and Policy Formulation: The Task Force Device," *Public Administration Review*, 29 (Sept./Oct., 1969), p. 461.
23. Roscoe C. Martin, ed., *Public Administration and Democracy* (Syracuse University Press, 1965), p. 196.

Let us illustrate the process with a recent example. Early in the Kennedy Administration, economic recession was a readily identifiable domestic problem. The economic climate was marked by high unemployment, lagging expansion of productive capacity, and consequently increasing poverty and social hardship. Basic policy was to reverse recessionary forces. But how? One influential source of economic advice opted for the inauguration of an expansive program of public works, akin to projects of the New Deal era. The theory argued that by employing the unemployed in building projects of public utility, (1) general social value would be achieved in new hospitals, schools, and roads; (2) income accruing to workers would be purchasing power and thus be returned to the productive economy; and (3) unemployment would thereby be further decreased. An alternative route to the same end—and the one advocated by the Council of Economic Advisers—was to increase purchasing power by reducing taxes and thus placing spendable dollars in the pockets of American consumers. When spent, these dollars would then encourage greater expansion of productive capacity. The Economic Advisers judged that the public works route was likely to be more costly, take longer to have the hoped-for expansionary effect, and be much more difficult politically to get enacted. In the end the president opted for the tax reduction method and in 1964, his successor, President Johnson, pushed through an $11 billion income tax reduction. The tale of President Kennedy's gradual acceptance of this method is one which shows in the telling the crucial role played by the Council of Economic Advisers in educating and persuading the president of the wisdom of the principles of the "new economics." [24]

Every policy, foreign and domestic, depends upon a complex set of calculations of costs and benefits relating to alternative means. In the inflationary atmosphere of the early years of the Nixon administration, the hard choice of restricted domestic spending and tight credit was made, knowing that one of the social costs would be increased unemployment due to the slowing of productive investment. The alternative of wage and price controls appeared too costly (ideologically and politically) to the president, and for a long time he even eschewed persuasion in the form of the economic guideposts so popular with his predecessor in the 1960s.

(3) *The Interrelationship Among Policies.* The options available to presidents in the advocacy of policies are limited because government itself functions in a universe of limited resources. Hence, in addition

24. The tale is well told in Walter Heller, *New Dimensions of Political Economy*, (W. W. Norton, 1967), especially chap. 1, "Advice and Consensus in Economic Policy Making."

to calculating policy needs and formulating specific measures to satisfy those needs, presidents must also *choose* among a range of potentially ideal policies to determine the effect of one upon another and establish the appropriate timing for their advocacy. This is thus largely a matter of strategy. Two examples will illustrate the nature of these choices.

John Kennedy came to the presidency in 1961 dedicated to the cause of civil rights. In the election campaign he had been highly critical of his predecessor for lagging initiatives in this issue-area. Yet during the first two years of his administration, the president did next to nothing about the problem. Ambivalence or hypocrisy was the assessment made of the president's non-perfomance by many civil rights activists. The real reasons, however, seem to be based upon considerations of timing concerning the president's whole legislative progam.

High on the president's policy agenda were such items as aid to education, increase in the minimum wage, a liberalized trade act, and an area redevelopment poverty program. The president judged that if he immediately advocated civil rights legislation, he would alienate Southern legislative support and provoke a filibuster in the Senate which would delay most and destroy some of his other priority programs. He thus chose to pay the costs of overtly ignoring the civil rights issue in order to make gains in other policy areas. In this he was partially successful, for in the first session of Congress, a Trade Expansion Act was passed; the House Rules Committee (that historic barrier to liberal legislation) was reconstituted; and area redevelopment was inaugurated.[25]

An instance of cruel choice in the area of foreign policy is seen in the history of the Skybolt affair. Before retiring from office, President Eisenhower had agreed to an arrangement with the British by which the United States would furnish an independent ground-to-air missile, called the Skybolt, in return for which the British would make available Holy Loch in Scotland as a base for our nuclear submarines. When the Kennedy administration entered office, the Skybolt project was reassessed, and it became clear that the cost of the missiles would be much more than originally anticipated. Defense Secretary McNamara advocated the cancellation of the project and the president ultimately concurred. The cost involved was the embarrassment of the British Government at home and the implanting of seeds of suspicion about the durability of the historic Anglo-American foreign policy alliance. Yet 1961 was a hard year domestically for the new president and high priority was being given to public spending to ease the economic recession and bring about

25. See James L. Sundquist, *Politics and Policy: The Eisenhower, Kennedy, and Johnson Years* (The Brookings Institution, 1968), pp. 256-57.

needed domestic reforms. The prospect of the estimated $2.5 billion additional cost for the Skybolt operation was too costly a luxury, even if the result of cancellation led to a temporary impairment of good relations with our allies.[26]

(4) *Mobilization of Support.* Even the best calculated and most ingeniously timed policies of a president are seldom made operative by his own act. Enactment even more than formulation is dependent on the behavior of many other participants in the process. At base, as Richard Neustadt is entirely correct in pointing out, the major job of the presidency is one of persuasion. At the outset the president must persuade "his own" bureaucracy to follow through on his recommendations, often finding it necessary to nudge repeatedly a sometimes inpenetrable complex of involved officials. Often the spirit of the higher bureaucracy is one of proprietorship over issues touching upon its specialized domain. Confident of its own expertise and its own mode of operations, the bureaucracy sometimes tends to excessive deliberation even in the face of executive demands for support.

Even after a presidential policy has been enunciated, however, the concurrence of the Congress is usually necessary. Here the president confronts another, and often competitive institution, jealous of its own integrity, authority, and modes of operation. In order to influence the Congress, presidents often must appeal to still other groups to bring pressure on the legislators. Sometimes party leadership can be translated into supportive votes in Congress. Another path to support for presidential policies leads to groups outside the governmental structure, such as an interested clientele or other groups with acknowledged expertise in the issue-area under contention. Thus in 1963 President Kennedy's quest for support in the Senate for the Nuclear Test Ban Treaty he had negotiated led to presidential pressures levied on the Joint Chiefs of Staff as well as the mobilization of scientific support attesting to the technical safety of the verification procedures for limiting nuclear tests.

At other times presidents use whatever influence they can in persuading the nation's press and media to give sympathetic coverage of their proposals. Appeals to the press, of course, are also indirect appeals to the president's national constituency, i.e., the citizenry. In the area of foreign policy, the president sometimes finds it necessary to appeal to his world constituency. When President Harry Truman decided upon a policy of armed intervention following the aggression of North Korea against South Korea in 1950, he simultaneously sought to internationalize

26. For a perceptive analysis of this case, see Richard E. Neustadt, *Alliance Politics* (Columbia University Press, 1970), chapters 3 and 4.

American action by appealing to world opinion through the United Nations.

LIMITATIONS ON EFFECTIVE LEADERSHIP

That presidents can be only partially effective in meeting the demand for policy leadership is, of course, in some measure due to the capabilities and styles of the individual holding the office. Our concern here, however, is not to rate individuals—a preoccupation of much of the literature on the presidency—but to identify institutional features of the presidency which are potential barriers to the leadership of any incumbent. To this end we shall view obstacles arising at two stages: policy formulation and policy implementation.

Institutions which participate in an advisory capacity for the formulation of policy have been identified. At this point it is particularly relevant to examine these institutions in terms of common organizational behavior patterns. Any institution, soon after its establishment, develops a life of its own. A sense of loyalty to the mission of the organization grows among its personnel. Usually, after a time, that sense of loyalty is transferred from primary allegiance to substantive goals, to a preoccupation with the health, stability, and security of the organization itself.

While this development has benefits for stability of the organization, parochialism runs counter to the need for a broader perspective and a sense of interdependence in national problem solving. This is one of the reasons that the executive departments have lost much of their utility as a collectivity for advising presidents. The various department heads are often more concerned with the implications of a policy problem for their own budgetary well-being than with the broader nature of the problem. The best—but by no means unrepresentative—example of such organizational self-interest has been the rivalry among the separate military services. So critical did the problem become by the 1950s that the services were unified administratively in the Department of Defense. Even so, the competition between Defense and the Department of State, for example, persists.

Nor have institutional coordinating mechanisms solved the problem. The National Security Council was created to coordinate the interests and recommendations of domestic, diplomatic, and military agencies. Yet, if one considers the uses made of the council in those crisis policy decisions about which we have some information, it appears that the body constituted but one—and usually not the dominant one—input in the decision process. Decisions *not* to intervene in the Indo-China conflict in 1954; to send troops to Lebanon in 1958; to proceed with the Bay of Pigs adventure in 1961; and to employ a naval quarantine in the Cuban Missile Crisis of 1962, all appear to have involved the NSC, as such, minimally or not at all.[27]

If the permanent executive institutions designed for advice-giving and coordination have not been notably effective for the purpose, what has been the experience with outside sources such as presidential commissions and ad hoc advisory groups? These mechanisms were devised to avoid some of the internal, organizational inhibitions of the permanent bureaucracy. What is sought is a fresh look, unencumbered calculation. Yet such bodies disclose inherent disadvantages of their own. They are multi-membered and thus their deliberations often turn out to be exercises in consensus-building which result not in a cogent set of recommendations, but in a broad review of existing options. The members of these commissions are busy people. Usually holding positions of leadership and responsibility in private life, they serve on a part-time basis and in some instances serve only symbolically, the major work of investigation and analysis being accomplished by a staff. The very fact of their impermanence detracts from the effectiveness with which any proffered recommendations can be followed up with support by the members.

Finally, they reveal the same disjunction between manifest and latent functions as do other bodies. Manifestly they are employed to deal seriously and rationally with policy problems; often the latent function of symbolically addressing, and perhaps burying, a problem is served. The most recent study of presidential commissions concludes: "Commissions have, in the past, involved far more prestige and publicity than substance, and several commissions can only be described as extravaganzas." [28] A similar charge has been leveled at the executive task forces employed so extensively by contemporary presidents. A recent study suggests: "The task forces which had the greatest immediate impact on legislation recommended programs which could more appropriately be characterized as political rather than intellectual breakthroughs." [29]

Still other problems abide in all advisory mechanisms utilized to date. One of these is simple inertia. Especially in the permanent bureaucracy, there is a tendency to accept totally the existing framework of policy in any issue-area and to reserve for "new" policies a range of options which constitute only modifications or incremental adjustments of the status quo. In part, this common attitude is motivated by a regard for

27. See Paul Y. Hammond, "The National Security Council as a Device for Interdepartmental Coordination: An Interpretation and Appraisal," *American Political Science Review*, 54 (December, 1960), pp. 899-910; J. C. Heinlein, *Presidential Staff and National Security Policy* (University of Cincinnati, Center for the Study of Foreign Policy, 1963), p. 48; and Chalmers M. Roberts, "The Day We Didn't Go to War," *The Reporter*, 11 (14 September 1964), pp. 31-35.

28. Popper, *The President's Commissions*, p. 64.

29. Thomas and Wolman, "The Presidency and Policy Formulation," p. 469.

"sunk costs." That is, once a policy has been invested with intellectual, political, ideological, and monetary resources over a period of time, it is difficult for bureaucrats—and men—to envision the scrapping of a fixed asset for an uncertain substitute.

No better illustration of this principle can be offered than the development of American policy leading to full-scale war in Vietnam. The general principle of containing the penetration of Communism (particularly the Chinese variety) in Southeast Asia was accepted before 1960. It was in the evolving means selected to achieve this policy goal that the policy itself was changed. Beginning with American advisors, moving to troop support, and from troop support to still greater increments of fighting troops, and finally resulting in massive bombing attacks, American policy became a commitment to end the civil war in Vietnam, expel the North Vietnamese from the South, and uphold the Saigon regime. As the investment grew larger at each stage, turning back seemed more impossible. President Johnson and his top Vietnam advisors seemed incapable of reassessing the situation in terms of its larger implications and costs of American society.

The story is perhaps best recounted by Townsend Hoopes, a senior bureaucrat involved in the process at various stages. Two major factors stand out in the context of bureaucratic policy advice. First, even as serious questioning of the policy evolved into disaffection and disenchantment among high-level administrators in the State and Defense Departments and the National Security apparatus, these officials for many years saw no effective means of influencing those officials who sat at the very top. Second, dissenters were stymied because of a known ideological commitment on the part of the president and a small coterie of foreign policy advisors—a commitment which made effective opposition impossible for some time.

But what prevented dissent from percolating to the top for so long? The answer in part relates to the fundamental difficulties of institutionalized policy making. Presidents are subject to such vast quantities of advice from all sources noted in the preceding pages that they often find the only way to bring order to the cacophony of pleading voices is to rely primarily upon a small group of trusted advisers in given policy areas at the White House level. The price paid for this illusion of rationality is, of course, partial and biased intelligence. Indeed, Hoopes argues that President Johnson's reliance on Walt Rostow was the source of a tragic lopsidedness in developing policy:

> . . . Rostow had become the channel through which President Johnson received almost all written communications on foreign affairs; he had, moreover, a large hand in determining who, outside the closed circle of

advisers, the President would see or not see. He possessed great weight on Vietnam policy because he was both physically close and intellectually reassuring to the President.[30]

One solution to this problem is suggested by a later stage of the Vietnam policy case. It involved a change in the guard. When Defense Secretary McNamara retired and was replaced by Clark Clifford, a long-time intimate of the president, a policy shift ensued. Clifford was more sympathetic to the pleas of those frustrated bureaucrats down the line and eventually was convinced by them. Because of his close relationship to the president, he was instrumental in persuading Mr. Johnson to adopt a policy of deescalation of the war. Moreover, it is certain that growing political repercussions of the prolonged war in the form of widespread popular opposition strengthened the hand of Clifford and the bureaucratic dissenters.

Obstacles also arise in policy implementation, which necessarily involves cooperative behavior among extra-presidential institutions. The usual requirement of adoption of legislation by Congress is well known. It need only be observed that if half of the proposals of the president are enacted by Congress, he has compiled an estimable record. More important is the consideration which involves legislative reformulation of executive proposals that *do* achieve passage. Rarely does any policy emerge from the legislative battlefield in the precise form in which the president introduced it.

Most policies are long-term policies and, for their continuing implementation, require annual funding. Thus the legislative appropriations process is a crucial one. A policy designed to combat poverty is emasculated when funds for the various constituent programs are sharply reduced or deleted in succeeding years. Aside from the congressional barrier to implementation, the administrative arm is also capable of withholding the promise of policy. When prosecution in conformity with the law is delayed or avoided by the Department of Justice, the law at that point is of mere symbolic value. When field offices of federal agencies exercise wide discretion in the interpretation of policy and its execution, their activities are so numerous and so remote that accountability to fundamental policy intent is not assured in practice. In all these and in many other ways a magnificent range of obstacles exists, capable of frustrating the effective exercise of presidential leadership in the policy-making process.

30. Townsend Hoopes, *The Limits of Intervention* (David McKay Company, 1969), p. 59.

The structural outlines of the federal bureaucracy were drawn in the early pages of this essay. It remains to examine the modes available to the president in responding to the need to manage this gargantuan complex and to assess the effectiveness of the executive institution in doing so. A job description for executive management might suggest two major goals: to keep the machine running with maximum efficiency, and to assure that it runs in a way which is loyal and responsive to the public interest, whether this takes the form of adherence to the Constitution, the laws, or presidential directives.

Tools of Management. A cardinal example of management holds that the manager must be able to exercise ultimate control over the personnel of the organization. In an organization made up of some 2.5 million employees, the extent of control is obviously limited and often indirect. The president does have the constitutional authority to appoint all "high officers" of the federal government, and in practice these mean what have come to be known as the political executives (cabinet members, assistant secretaries, agency heads, and some bureau chiefs). The history of American personnel administration, however, has been one of progressive classification of the public service within a civil service system based upon merit.

To augment efficiency in the public service, the president has historically been granted the authority to reorganize the administrative branch. Corresponding to the rapid, exponential growth of the bureaucracy beginning in the 1930s, a series of advisory commissions investigated the administrative complex and recommended legislation providing executive reorganization authority. From the Brownlow Commission's Report of 1937, through two Hoover Commissions, and including a series of reports from Senator Henry Jackson's Subcommittee on National Policy Machinery, the study-recommendation-reorganization syndrome has become a tradition of the American personnel management. President Roosevelt's creation of the Executive Office of the President in 1939 is invariably cited as master-stroke of executive management. Most recently, as a result of a report of another study commission (the Ash Council), President Nixon was granted authority by Congress to reorganize the Executive Office, creating the new Office of Management and Budget, and a Domestic Council.

By the use of executive orders presidents have a capacity to rationalize administration in other ways. Note has already been made of the plethora of advisory committees employed by the federal bureaucracy, and the question might be raised as to whether the number of these bodies is

excessive and their existence prolonged beyond their utility. The same
question occurred to President Kennedy in 1962, and he thereupon
issued Executive Order #11007 which prescribed regulations for the
formation and use of advisory committees and placed a two-year limit
of the life of any of these bodies not formally established by statute.[31]

Another effective tool for presidential control of administration is
the budgetary authority resting in the executive office. All proposals
of all departments and agencies must be cleared by the Office of
Management and Budget, which works in close cooperation with the
president. This provides a constant check on the activities of the various
administrative units to assure that they are, in the jargon, "in accord
with the program of the president." A contemporary experiment
designed to permit still greater executive control over the activities of
the bureaucracy at the program level is the institution of a new Planning-
Programming-Budgeting System (PPBS). The system seeks to require
a more penetrating analysis and more meaningful justification for all
agency proposals and activities. Since the system is new, evaluation
is difficult, but it can be noted that its implementation by Secretary
McNamara in the Defense Department of the 1960s led to more effective
and centralized control over the activities of that disparate holding
company than had been possible in the past.

The Limits of Management. It is already apparent that the president's
span of control over the personnel of the far-flung bureaucracy is limited
and sporadic, even in terms of his legal authority. However, even in
that area of maximum formal control over political appointees the
president cannot always be master in his own house. In some instances
high federal officials have acquired a kind of extra-territorial immunity
from presidential influence. For example, though he is a controversial
figure, the director of the Federal Bureau of Investigation, J. Edgar
Hoover, has been historically untouchable. A recent example of the
director's independence of higher authority was his refusal to comply
with the attorney general's order that, henceforth, references would no
longer be made to such organizations connoting ethnic backgrounds,
as the "Mafia" or "Cosa Nostra."

The basis for such independence (and Mr. Hoover is not unique)
is the security offered by an independent constituency to whom the
official is more answerable than to the president. The constituency may
be Congress, an influential private group in society, or "public opinion"
in the nation. Nor is this a novel situation. As vigorous a manager as
President Franklin Roosevelt was unable to make a directive stick
favoring the Bureau of Reclamation over the Army Corps of Engineers

31. Martin, *Public Administration and Democracy*, pp. 194-95.

as sponsor of certain public works activities. The Corps had (and continues to have) such a close working relationship with crucial congressional committees that its officials could safely ignore not only the commands of the department of the Army, but of the president himself.[32]

A limitation of presidential and civil service discretion relating to the management of public servants is connected with broader developments in the technocratic age we live in. It is becoming ever more clear that the public service is characterized by a galloping professionalization. The needs of modern America, and thus the demand for federal bureaucrats, can be satisfied only by more civil engineers, geologists, public health specialists, sociologists, psychiatrists, systems analysts, and other such specialists. Rather suddenly we find ourselves informed by the Census Bureau that about one-third of all "professional, technical, and kindred" workers in the United States are employed by government at some level. Of special interest at this point is the mode of entry of these functionaries constituting a professional elite. It has developed that a large part of the process of recruitment and the setting and maintainance of standards is delegated, formally or informally, to *private professional organizations*. Frederick Mosher has commented recently on this phenomenon:

> The means whereby the professionals assert their control over personnel policies and actions are many and diverse. Some are specified and required by law and/or regulation; others grow out of gentlemen's agreements within—or in spite of—general civil service laws; some reflect a silent abdication by the general civil service agencies or a failure to assume an effective role; and some are unintended (or mayhap intended) consequences of others.[33]

The imperatives of professional specialization in government probably make this development rationally desirable, but it does place at a somewhat more distant remove the potential for presidential involvement.

The impact of presidential reorganizations of the administrative branch should likewise not be exaggerated. What must be made clear is that presidential authority in this area is relatively extensive for unimportant or uncontroversial managerial shifts. However, Congress controls the process by retaining a suspensive veto over presidential reorganizations, and experience shows that where a reorganization proposal touches upon an agency in which Congress is really interested, the lawmakers are not loath to exercise a veto. Thus when President John Kennedy at-

32. See Arthur Maass, *Muddy Waters: The Army Engineers and the Nation's Rivers* (Harvard University Press, 1951).
33. Frederick C. Mosher, *Democracy and the Public Service* (Oxford University Press, 1968), p. 125.

tempted to create a Department of Urban Affairs and Housing in 1962 by executive order he aroused the wrath of several members of Congress, and the House vetoed the proposal.

In conclusion, the verdict concerning the effectiveness of the executive in administrative management must explode any myths about presidential dictatorship over bureaucratic minions. Some powers he has, but for the most part the chief executive has relatively little maneuverability in appointing, removing, controlling or disciplining the "fourth, headless branch of government." The bureaucrats themselves have divided loyalties: partly allegiance to the incumbent president, but also partly to key congressional committees that control their destinies through legislation and appropriations, and often to clientele organizations which are capable of bringing pressures to bear on the hapless agency at various levels of government. Conversely, the congressional committees and clientele groups have many reasons for maintaining a close surveillance over the federal bureaucracy.

Party Leadership

Of all the demands on the presidency identified in this essay, the expectation that the office will function in part as one of political party leadership rests *least* on the capacity of the institution to respond to this demand. Party leadership as it is exercised at any given time depends far more upon the skills, personality, and style of the man than upon the endowments of the office.

The question of leadership itself is more ambiguous in this context than in others. That is, the president as party leader is much more dependent upon his followership than he is in other aspects of his leadership role. At the outset he comes to office owing a debt to those partisan followers who have worked for his election. In his relations with Congress (assuming his party controls the Congress), he is dependent on the loyalty of his party leadership and membership to support his policy programs. During his incumbency these dependencies will absorb some of his energy and time, both in policy negotiations and ceremonial support for the party as an institution. In short, a good part of presidential leadership involves performing chores for the faithful (and sometimes the not-so-faithful).

Yet presidents have been willing in the past to accept the grief as well as the rewards of party leadership not just out of a sense of obligation, but also because they were convinced that the ideological and programmatic directions of their party were at least marginally preferable to those of the opposition. Given parties that are coalitions of differing and even antagonistic interests, there is still some center of gravity in the Democratic Party which is perceptibly different from the center of gravity in the Republican Party. At least so it appears to anyone so politically conscious and ambitious as a potential presidential candidate.

In fulfilling the leadership function for their parties, presidents do not normally simply accept the elephant or donkey as is—complete with factions and contradictions. For while dedicated to party as to religion, they do have preferences. Part of the promise and part of the satisfaction of leadership historically has been the opportunity to shift the ideological center of gravity, if ever so slightly, in a direction more congenial to the president's own preferences. This is surely one criterion of effectiveness of party leadership. The more immediate test, however, is the extent to which presidential leadership strengthens the national status of his party. For both of these purposes any president can call upon certain resources, formal and informal, of the office. Limited as they are, they can be important.

At the formal level, as chief executive the president is expected to take the initiative in national policy formulation and execution. If he reads the national temper accurately and responds to the demands suggested by it, his reward will be his party's reward. If he can persuade his partisans in the legislature to support his programs, then together they can go to the country taking pride in and expecting electoral approval of their stewardship. Thus if a successful party is dependent on a successful president, an identity of interests and causes must be communicated to the electorate. In this sense Franklin Roosevelt was a supremely successful party leader. His personal attractiveness and that of the national Democratic Party were so intermingled that the coalition of interests formed around the New Deal persisted in the party long after the leader had passed from the scene.

One of the institutional means a president can call upon to reinforce his party's fortunes is his authority of appointment. Thus, typically, rewards go to the party faithful. But formal patronage in contemporary times is of less and less quantitative importance. Since the days of a national spoils system, the patronage available to a president has dwindled to a few thousand offices. Thus presidents attentive to the party leadership function tend to pay more attention to the informal mechanisms of influence at their disposal to shore up party fortunes (or the fortunes of that sector of the party they wish to become dominant).

Hence during his incumbency President Kennedy paid much more attention to the urban political organizations around the country which he saw as representing not only the future electoral promise of the Democrats, but also the interests which his party *should* promote. For example, he was actively supportive of the reform Democratic movement in New York City. In informal but important ways he sought to give the advantages of presidential status to "modern" Democrats. Thus he paid formal and highly publicized visits to such leaders as the late Herbert H. Lehman, while ignoring such overt practitioners of the old politics as Carmine De Sapio. To prove that electoral fortunes had first priority, however, he studiously paid court to such traditional "pols" as Boss Buckley of the Bronx, Mayor Daley of Chicago, and David Lawrence of Pennsylvania.

On the other hand, a president unattracted by the zest for party institution building, such as Dwight Eisenhower, would go through the motions of leadership—appearing at the Lincoln Day dinners, being photographed with candidates. and dispensing what little patronage was available to his partisan confrères. But he would not be extensively involved in the building of local and state party organizations or the grooming of future national leaders. For all his vaunted political instincts and energies, President Johnson, as president, seemed uninterested in building for a future Democratic Party, and perhaps incapable of it. At his retirement his party was a shambles, disorganized and indebted.[34]

Perhaps this suggests something about the inherent difficulties in meeting the demand for party leadership in America of the 1970s. There is a perservering tension between the obligations of party leadership and the call to *national* leadership which summons all presidents. Before entering the oval office, party often symbolizes the goals, aspirations, and commitments of presidential hopefuls. Once in office, however, the importance of the party institution tends to diminish in the scheme of values and system of priorities of the man who is perforce not only leader of all the people, but even proclaimed leader of the "free world." If George Reedy has it right, the contemporary president is so isolated from the more mundane concerns of partisan political life (except for occasional, ceremonial obeisances) that he is incapable of giving much energy for their apparently petty satisfactions. This trend seems to be borne out by the common practice of contemporary presidents to delegate much of the partisan campaigning to their vice-presidents, for the most part remaining loftily above the battle themselves.

At a time when the political parties seem even less able to get themselves together than in the past, when any sense of internal party cohesion is uncertain, when the electorate seems to display ever more independent tendencies, and when the real differences between the parties seem progressively more difficult to identify—at this time both the institutional resources of leadership and the temperamental proclivities of presidents to lead are also weaker. One must conclude that at this stage in our political history, the traditional demand for party leader-

34. See Theodore H. White, *The Making of the President* 1968 (Atheneum, 1969), pp. 104-06; 113-14.

ship made upon presidents is responded to only sporadically and largely ineffectively.[35]

Decades ago Professor Edward Corwin, placing the presidency in the context of American political institutions, concluded: "Taken by and large, the history of the presidency has been a history of aggrandizement." [36] Nothing that has occurred since that observation was originally made challenges its validity. A companion observation (suggesting a feature about which Professor Corwin was not unaware) might run something like this: The history of the contemporary presidency has been a history of progressive institutionalization. What is suggested is that the structure of the office itself has become so elaborated and routinized that the sum of quantitative changes (structural proliferation) has produced a qualitative change in the nature of the presidency. Seemingly the presidency is in fact less, and in capacity less, able to become again a personal office. Not only, then, is the presidency a complex amalgam of man and office, but today it is much more office and much less man.

The significance of this line of thinking is its relevance to the basic structure of the essay: an assessment of the presidency in terms of its response to demands from the polity. One conclusion is that many, if not all of the traditional functions performed by the presidency and discussed in the preceding pages, depend for their effective satisfaction on the response of a *person*. Each of these demands implies a quest for leadership, and leadership must in large part be that of an individual rather than a complex structure. Obviously structure has a major role, but that role is generically one of facilitating and reinforcing leadership, not providing it in the first instance.

Consider the demands reviewed in this light. With all the paraphernalia of modern communications, the pointing of moral directions must be a personal act. Even with a vast array of intelligence-garnering mechanisms, the assessment and representation of interests in society must be a personal act. Given a sophisticated, specialized, and highly organized policy-making apparatus, still the ultimate policy-making decision is a personal act. The same holds true for the mangement of the bureaucracy and the leadership of a political party—ultimately personal acts.

And yet the irony is that, with all the magnificent accoutrements available for the making of choices, rational personal choice seems

35. See essay on the parties, pp. 46 ff.
36. Edward S. Corwin, *The President: Office and Powers* (New York University Press, rev. ed. 1957), p. 307. First published in 1940.

that much more difficult. The very mechanisms created for the offering of options seem, in the end, to have appropriated the options and therefore the basis of choice. Phrased dramatically, organization has taken over.

Another way of describing this development is to note that personal presidential leadership is in large part dependent on the president's perception of the phenomena about which he is asked to make important choices. Bureaucracies, both public and quasi-public (and what is the contemporary distinction between public and private?), tend to set up interpretive screens through which presidential perceptions flow. Thus often the wants and aspirations, the anxieties and frustrations present in society reach the president's consciousness in a predigested—and necessarily biased—state.

In the light of this interpretation, most of the examples of ineffective leadership cited may be regarded as resulting from the partiality of the president's appreciation of the nature of the problems confronted. This review comes close to suggesting that modern presidents are dangerously subject to manipulation by elites in society, in and out of government. This need not be seen primarily as the result of a conspiracy of intention, but as a natural by-product of an age of organization and technology.

And what of the years to come? The organizational society is here to stay. Prescriptions for smashing the organization are chimeras of a Luddite mentality. In a technotronic age the material rewards of the large organization are too beguiling to be forsaken. Whether in big government, the big corporation, or the big university, size and specialization accommodate the spirit of the times.

Nonetheless, the prescription is not totally and bleakly for more of the same. Without succumbing entirely to a "great man" theory of history at the other extreme, we may hold that deviation from the norm is a norm itself, and the past reveals sufficient examples of unusually endowed or inspired individuals who were able, for a time, to break out of the conventional environment and accomplish unexpected achievements. This premise leads to a scenario which can only be imagined in terms of the personality and his idiosyncrasies. We might say that the need is of a prescription for one who consciously challenges the organization. Moreover, there is some historical experience upon which to base speculation about such a type. It seems that the strongest and most innovative of presidents have been those who have displayed a combination of traits, prominent among which have been ego strength, a keen sense of values, an enjoyment of power, and mental agility, if not intellectualism.[37]

37. Professor Erwin Hargrove discusses these qualities in the context of his two categories: "Presidents of Action" and "Presidents of Restraint." See his *Presidential Leadership-Personality and Political Style* (The Macmillan Company, 1966).

The necessity for a strong ego is crucial, given the weight of organizational persuasiveness. A man must be unusually self-reliant and confident of his own capacities. He must be willing to take chances, to withstand the tortures of self-doubt in face of dominant counsel in opposition to his personal position. The personal determination of a Theodore Roosevelt or the stubborness of a Wilson comes to mind. Such personal certainty is sometimes communicated in a near-charismatic nature by a Lincoln or a Franklin Roosevelt.

Firm values are indispensable and related to ego strength. While dogmatism is unattractive, a too easy willingness to see the merit in all philosophies and all positions will leave any man the victim of the inexorable organizational logic of the hour.

Ego and value strength often result in a characteristic thirst for power. By "thirst for power" we do not mean a neurotic fixation on undirected dominance for its own sake, but rather an appreciation of the pervasive need for leadership and a personal satisfaction in providing it. Indeed, such a congeniality to authority does involve manipulation and a willingness to impose sanctions; but this is, in some measure, the stuff of all leadership. And all of those whom historians have marked as strong presidents have shown such traits.

Lastly, a putative counterweight to the organizational machine must have a sophisticated intelligence. This is not the same as professional intellectualism—though Wilson and T.R. could surely be described as possessing that quality. Rather, this intelligence would be characterized by mental energy and quickness, the ability to see relationships, and even an element of shrewdness. Such intelligence is not necessarily marked by surface orderliness or even absolute consistency. It is often the kind of intellection which appears as insight and seizes the moment. Franklin Roosevelt provides a good example of this mental style and John Kennedy showed signs of it in his brief tenure.

Undoubtedly the foregoing prescription carries with it dangers. The combination of traits in excessive or exaggerated form summons up images of a Man on Horseback. Yet the external restraints of the system are so potent as to counterbalance fears of Caesarism. Our scenario rather looks more sanguinely on the emergence of an uncommon personality capturing the imagination of his fellow men. In representing the best instincts of humanity, he seizes upon the crucial issues of the time, communicates with society, infuses his party with programmatic values and his presidency with determined action. He subverts the organization.

In such a way personal leadership might reappear in the American presidency for a few moments in history.

THE PRESIDENTIAL

INSTITUTION

The preceding chapter analyzed the effectiveness of the presidency in responding to demands made upon it in various contexts. We now proceed to describe the nature of the modern presidency in its legal and institutional setting. Attention is directed to four major themes: the legal relationship between the man and the office; the formal, legal powers of the office; the informal prerogatives which have developed out of the legal framework; and the bureaucratic appendage which has its source, first, in a crude constitutional mandate, and secondly and more importantly, in an unanticipated response to social need.

THE MAN AND THE OFFICE

In framing institutions political architects must exercise their imaginations in such a way as to channel the functions intended along lines desired. This they do by establishing rules circumscribing the activities of the office and the roles of the men holding it. For the American presidency, these rules are set forth in the Constitution and the laws.

Election

The current of democracy was sufficiently strong in 1787 to assure that the presidency would be subject to some form of citizen selection. But the working out of that premise gave rise to considerable disagreement. A multitude of proposals at the Constitutional Convention tended to cluster about two attitudinal poles: proposals favoring a strong and independent chief executive, popularly elected, and proposals reflecting a fear of potential executive dictatorship and which therefore sought to incorporate some form of indirect election by another body such as Congress. The result was, typically, a compromise. Thus the electoral college was established as an independent institution to make the choice. Electors were to be chosen by the states in a manner decided by them and in number equal to the state's congressional representation. The system was intended to produce a president out of the deliberations of a body of elder statesmen or more often, by a contingent selection by the House of Representatives. With the almost immediate evolution of a political party system, however, the electoral college was transformed into a body which reflected popular, partisan majorities or pluralities.

This is the system as it remains today. Nevertheless the persistence of the system marks the dissatisfaction it has produced. There is the abiding concern about "minority" presidents, and indeed, in fifteen elections out of thirty-seven the winning candidate has had less than a majority of the popular vote, and in three of these cases the winner has had a lower popular vote total than his opponent.[1] There is also concern that custom and not constitutional law requires the presidential elector to vote for the popular winner in his state, and on occasion electors *have* exercised independent judgment in opposition to the popular mandate. Finally, the possibility of a contingent election whereby, in the absence of an electoral vote majority, the House of Representatives (voting by states) would elect a president and the Senate would elect a vice-president, is a chilling specter to modern believers in democracy.

Largely for these reasons, numerous reforms—ranging from the total abolition of the electoral system to minor modifications of it—have been advocated in recent years. The House of Representatives in 1969 passed a constitutional amendment proposal which would provide for direct, popular election with a forty percent minimum required for election. In cases where a presidential vice-presidential ticket did not draw forty percent of the vote, a runoff election would be held between the two leading tickets.[2]

Opposition to the proposed change is based upon many factors. One of major significance is that the existing system, under which the ticket winning a plurality of votes in a state receives all of that state's electoral votes, tends to give advantages to the large states with large urban populations. Those who see in this advantage a salutary effect in giving national recognition to the needs of an urban society feel that the direct election method would simply not be in the greater public interest at this juncture in history. Others oppose direct election out of a fear of possible unintended consequence for the system as a whole. Thus it is

1. Wallace S. Sayre and Judith H. Parris, *Voting for President* (The Brookings Institution, 1970), p. 58.
2. Ibid, p. 70.

suggested that such a change might encourage a multi-party system and further weaken the federal system. It is further hypothesized that such a system might spawn one-issue presidential candidacies which, if successful, could lead to presidents with extremely narrow and possibly distorted, ephemeral, and sporadic constituent bases. Ultimately, opponents of change argue, though the present system is not perfect, it has been functionally successful in producing results seen as legitimate. Even in the closest of recent elections (1960 and 1968) the victor was inaugurated without challenge.

Tenure

Like the mode of election of presidents, the question of the length and number of terms of office produced a compromise in Philadelphia in 1787. Two-year terms, six-year terms, and even twenty-year terms ("the medium life of princes") were suggested at various stages.[3] At length the presidential term was fixed at four years with no restrictions on reelection to successive terms. It was expected by many of the drafters that George Washington would serve as president for the rest of his life, and thus an important precedent was set when the first president chose to step down from office at the completion of a second term. The precedent was crucially reinforced when Thomas Jefferson pointedly retired after a second term on the ground that it would be dangerous to establish the practice of a long-term or lifetime presidency. From that time to 1940 the tradition of the two-term president was strictly adhered to. It was Franklin D. Roosevelt who defied precedent in accepting his party's nomination for a third term and went on to win reelection, not only to a third term, but in 1944 a fourth term.

In response to the Roosevelt precedent (and indeed to Roosevelt), the Republican 80th Congress produced a resolution which was to become the twenty-second Amendment to the Constitution that a president's tenure would be limited to two four-year terms of office. In the early postwar years the nation was ready for restrictions on the presidential office, and the congressional amendment resolution passed with the generous assistance of Democrats in Congress in 1947 and was declared to have been ratified by the requisite three-fourth of the states in 1951. Henceforth no presidents may serve more than two *full* terms, although if he succeeds to less than two years of another president's term, he is eligible to go on for an additional two terms. Thus President Lyndon B. Johnson could constitutionally have been reelected in 1968 to a full

3. Max Farrand, *The Records of the Federal Convention—1787* (3 vols.) (Yale University Press, 1911), Vol. 2, pp. 111-112, 145; and Jane Butzner, comp., *Constitutional Chaff—Rejected Suggestions at the Constitutional Convention of 1787*, (Columbia University Press, 1941), pp. 86-87.

four-year term, though he had served as president since November, 1963.

A president's tenure can be limited in other ways. In addition to death in office (which has occurred eight times), and resignation (which has never occurred), a president may be impeached for "treason, bribery, or other high crimes and misdemeanors." The House of Representatives must bring charges and vote impeachment, but only the Senate can act as a court (with the Chief Justice presiding), and conviction requires a two-thirds vote of those present. No president has even been convicted following impeachment, but Andrew Johnson won his trial by only one vote in the Senate in 1868.

Succession

The Founding Fathers chose not to deal with the question of presidential succession but instead left it up to Congress to provide for the appropriate order to be followed in the case of the deaths of both president and vice-president. In the early years of the Republic the legislators provided that the order of succession would be president pro-tempore of the Senate, followed by the Speaker of the House. Then in 1886 the Congress decided that succession should recognize the integrity of the executive branch and provided that the Secretary of State would be third in line, with other cabinet officers following in order of the creation of their departments.

This order prevailed until 1947, when the legislative branch once again injected its leaders into the executive succession line on the recommendation of President Harry S. Truman. Truman, himself a career legislator, and having succeeded to office on the death of President Roosevelt, felt strongly that a president should not be able (by cabinet appointment), in effect, to name his successor. The question was especially acute at this time since there was no vice-president. Congress agreed, and the 1947 act now provides that the succession order begins with the Speaker of the House followed by the Senate president pro-tem, and only then the cabinet.

The contention between the two varieties of succession we have experienced historically turns largely on one's views about the probable qualifications for the presidency found generally in legislative leaders as opposed to cabinet officers. In addition it has been argued that the legislative route is the more democratically legitimate, since a potential successor was *elected* to the office held before succession. In any case, the twenty-fifth Amendment speaks to the succession question in another way. Except in the event that both president and vice-president should perish simultaneously, the successor will almost surely be the choice of the president. This occurs because the amendment provides that whenever there is a vacancy in the office of vice-president, the president shall nominate a new vice-president who must be confirmed by a majority vote of both houses of Congress.

One of the most difficult contingencies bearing on presidential tenure is the problem of presidential inability to perform the functions of the office. So difficult was the problem of dealing with disability that the Framers once again left the details to legislative determination. The crux of the matter is what constitutes "inability," and who determines its existence? The question was left authoritatively unanswered for 180 years. In the course of that time presidents have been bed-ridden and hospitalized for considerable periods, and presidential business has been conducted in varying and uncertain ways. Most recently, the make-shift provision adopted by President Eisenhower during his extended illness from a heart attack provided that (a) the president would inform the vice-president of his own inability, and (b), if he were unable to do that, the vice-president would decide the question himself after appropriate consultation. This internal agreement was extended in the Kennedy Administration.

Concern about the vagueness and uncertainty of such informal arrangements had been expressed for generations. Proposals for meeting the problem were rife: the Supreme Court should decide. a disability commission should decide, a panel of doctors should decide, Congress should decide. Variations on each of these proposals were submitted by statesmen and scholars. Only in 1967 was a decision reached with the adoption of the twenty-fifth Amendment. Under its provisions a president may declare himself unable to perform his duties, in which case the Vice-president is acting president. Alternatively, the vice-president along with a majority of cabinet officers (or such other body as may be created) may declare to the Congress that the president is disabled. If and when the president notifies the Congress that he is able, he resumes his duties, unless the vice-president and an appropriate majority of officers disagree. If this latter happens, Congress must decide the issue with dispatch and by a two-thirds vote in both houses. Clearly, problems could arise even with this mechanism, but we are closer to procedural certainty now than during the first two centuries of the presidency.

RESOURCES OF LEADERSHIP—CONSTITUTIONAL AND LEGAL

If any one function sums up the complementary roles and powers of the presidency, it is leadership. As the highest elected officer in the nation, the president is enjoined to give direction to the course of national development. To accomplish this he has many resources, some formal and legally prescribed, others informal and growing out of the broader system of political relationships characterizing the polity. It is to the first of these that we direct attention at this point. It should be noted here that a consideration of available resources does not imply that they are not subject to limitations of various kinds. It is the president "in posse" rather than "in esse" that we encounter below.

Executive Powers

Article II of the Constitution commands the president to "take care that the laws be faithfully executed." For the modern presidency, the execution of the laws involves in reality the *making* of many other laws or, as they are often more humbly called, regulations. This is both the process and consequence of delegation. As our existence has become more complex and the role of government much more extensive, Congress routinely legislates in a way which prescribes rather broad mandates, the details of which must be filled in by the president and his subordinates, thus at once "executing" the will of Congress *and* making new rules and regulations. For example American foreign trade relations are established in the first instance by congressional tariff acts. However, the modern trend has been for Congress to legislate a basic act, in reality delegating to the executive authority to create specific trade regulations. A series of Reciprocal Trade Acts going back to the 1930s was followed by a 1962 Trade Expansion Act which permitted the president to cut tariffs by up to fifty percent on certain categories of goods and to eliminate tariff restrictions altogether on others. Much of the activity of each of the executive departments of the government involves the making of rules and regulations governing commerce, labor, public health, agriculture, housing construction, and so on, covering all aspects of modern existence.

Faithfully executing the laws means the execution of court orders as well. Thus when the governor of Arkansas sought to block the implementation of court desegregation orders in Little Rock High School in 1957, he was forcing the president's hand. When Governor Faubus removed the National Guard from Little Rock, he encouraged mob violence in response to integration. The president responded by ordering federal troops to Little Rock to disperse the mobs. The president called upon federal statutes dating back to 1792 authorizing such action when it proves impossible to enforce laws "by ordinary judicial proceedings." [4] In a similar situation, President Kennedy sent the National

4. Richard P. Longaker, *The President and Individual Liberties* (Cornell University Press, 1961), pp. 161.

Guard to Alabama in 1963, when the state persisted in preventing the integration of the state university.

The executive order is the usual presidential vehicle for carrying out his prerogatives. Thus the president may grant pardons, amnesties, and reprieves. In addition, and more significant, the president may implement sweeping social and economic changes by a stroke of the pen on an executive order. Thus in 1962 President Kennedy issued Executive Order 11063, by which he directed all departments and agencies of the executive branch to take all necessary action to prevent discrimination on the basis of race, color, creed, or national origin in the provision, rehabilitation, or operation of housing owned or regulated in any way by the government.[5]

Administrative Powers

Allied to the executive function is a range of administrative responsibilities a president must fulfill in seeing to it that the business of government goes on from day to day. The first resource of administrative power is the ability to appoint personnel. The president is given this power by the Constitution. But it is not a totally discretionary grant since in the case of all high officers (including cabinet members, ambassadors, judges and most administrative officials) the president appoints "by and with the advice and consent of the senate." Historically the Senate usually concurs, although on some occasions a high officer such as a cabinet member or Supreme Court appointment may be refused confirmation. In 1958 the Senate refused President Eisenhower's choice of Lewis Strauss as Secretary of Commerce and, more recently, the Senate blocked two of President Nixon's nominations to the Supreme Court.

Though the president normally has wide latitude in making appointments, his power to remove officials is more circumscribed. As the law stands at the present time, the president may remove at will members of his cabinet or other officers with essentially routine duties. However, a series of Supreme Court decisions proscribes removals of other kinds of officials. Thus the president may *not* remove officials whose jurisdictions transcend executive functions such as independent regulatory commissioners. The theory is that these officials were established to be independent of the president at the outset. Moreover, the most recent decision suggests that where there is a doubt about the intention of Congress in creating an agency, as to whether the president should enjoy

5. Executive Order 11063, "Equal Opportunity in Housing," 27 *Federal Register,* 11527 (November 24, 1962).

removal power, the courts will interpret this to *restrict* presidential power.[6]

Much of a president's administrative power comes by way of delegation by the Congress. Such is the source of his powers to reorganize the structure and functions of federal agencies and departments. The usual pattern followed is the establishment of a study commission on government organization which makes recommendations to the president. These recommendations may be handled in two ways. The president may follow the substantive recommendations and ask Congress for legislation implementing them. More commonly, he simply implements the recommendations on the basis of general reorganization authority which Congress has previously vested in him. Even in these instances, however, Congress has historically reserved to itself a veto power over presidential reorganizations. That is, in writing (and subsequently renewing) the reorganization statute, the legislators make provision that a president's reorganization order will take effect, if within a sixty-day period, either house of Congress has not objected to it. The exact nature of the veto provision has varied over the years (for example, at one point *both* houses of Congress had to disapprove a presidential reorganization in order to block it), but Congress has always reserved the power of negation in some form. Moreover, no Congress has been willing to pass a permanent reorganization statute; instead the legislators grant two- or three-year authorizations which must be renewed.[7] In instances where the intended reorganization proposal is of a sweeping nature (such as the creation of a new cabinet department), presidents tend to go directly to Congress and request special legislation, realizing that to act independently might serve instead to antagonize the Congress.

For the modern presidency, budgetary control has emerged as perhaps the most effective vehicle of administrative management. From the creation of the Bureau of the Budget in 1921, to its inclusion in the Executive Office of the President in 1939 (by reorganization order), to the most recent innovation, the creation of the Office of Management and the Budget, presidents have achieved structural and programmatic controls by having an important influence on the allocation of national resources. This route to administrative control was clearly laid out in President Nixon's message to Congress when he proposed the most recent reorganization:

6. *Myers v. U.S.*, 272 U.S. 52 (1926); *Humphrey's Executor (Rathbun) v. U.S.*, 295 U.S. 602 (1935); and *Wiener v. U.S.*, 357 U.S. 349 (1958).
7. See Ferrel Heady, "The Reorganization Act of 1949," *Public Administration Review*, 9 (1949), pp. 165-174.

The new Office of Management and Budget will place much greater
emphasis on the evaluation of program performance: on assessing the extent
to which programs are actually achieving their intended results and delivering the intended services to the intended recipients.[8]

Foreign Policy Powers

That the president has a special primacy in the area of foreign relations
has been recognized as long as the Republic has existed. In 1788, writing
Federalist Paper Number 64, John Jay stated the case definitively for
executive supremacy. The very nature of the executive office, said Jay,
is such as to make it the focus of foreign relations. The peculiar qualities
of unity, continuity, secrecy, dispatch, and the availability of superior
sources of information make the presidency *the* organ of international
relations. Indeed, in deliberating over a case in 1936, the Supreme Court
rested its decision in large part on that "naturalness" of executive prerogative in this area, citing the Federalist logic. Congress had authorized
the president to establish an embargo on the sale of arms and munitions
to South American countries when he considered it in the interests
of peace in the area. Subsequently President Roosevelt embargoed arms
sales to Bolivia which was at war with Paraguay. The Curtiss-Wright
Corporation, convicted of ignoring the embargo and selling arms, challenged the constitutionality of the embargo. The Court, in upholding
the congressional authorization and the presidential action, noted that
the president must often be accorded "a degree of discretion and freedom from statutory restriction which would not be admissible were
domestic affairs alone involved." [9]

The Constitution, of course, provides specific tools for presidential
use in the conduct of foreign policy. It is, for example, the right of the
president to extend American recognition to foreign states and governments. This is implemented by the simple act of receiving officially the
ambassador or minister of a foreign country. By the same token, the
president can withdraw American recognition. It is a matter of continuous debate whether recognition and non-recognition should be employed to reward friendly countries and punish unfriendly ones, on the
one hand, or used merely as impartial evidence of the existence of a
state or government on the other hand. In any case, the legal authority
is the president's—as President Roosevelt demonstrated in 1933 when
he recognized the Soviet government fifteen years after the Russian
Revolution, or as a succession of presidents to the present time have

8. Reorganization Plan No. 2 of 1970. See also, Executive Order 11541, "Prescribing the Duties of the Office of Management and Budget and the Domestic Council
in the Executive Office of the President." *Federal Register*, vol. 35, No. 128, Thurs-
day, July 2, 1970.
9. *U.S. v. Curtiss-Wright Export Corporation*, 299 U.S. 304 (1936).

shown by withholding recognition from the communist government of mainland China.

For the regular conduct of diplomacy, the president relies primarily upon his power of appointment to exercise control. Not only does he appoint all ambassadors and other diplomats, but he exercises as much supervision over his Department of State and the Foreign Service as he chooses. In some instances he may inject himself personally in diplomatic negotiations by attending conferences where he represents the nation, as President Eisenhower did in Geneva and President Kennedy in Paris. Indeed, such "summit diplomacy" has increasingly marked the evolution of American foreign policy in the twentieth century.

A qualified power of the president in foreign affairs is his right to negotiate treaties. The authority is qualified because, in order to bestow the legality of ratification on those treaties, the president must have the advice and consent of two-thirds of the members of the Senate. Such approval is not always automatic, as witnessed by the inability of President Wilson to gain United States membership in the League of Nations. However, there is still another means by which the president can bind the nation to a course of action with another nation without senatorial approval. The executive agreement has the full force and effect of a treaty without legislative consultation. By such agreements presidents have negotiated fishing rights, annexed territory, and reached international political settlements as in the case of the Yalta agreements of 1945. Generally, however, the use of the executive agreement is to implement broader national policy, as when presidents make "status of forces" agreements governing the rights and obligations of American military personnel abroad in conformity with a major treaty undertaking such as the North Atlantic Treaty Organization.

Military Powers

Allied to the president's powers in the area of foreign affairs is his constitutional designation as "Commander-in-Chief of the Army and Navy of the United States." Historically derived from the terse phrasing of Article II, section 2 is a broad mandate granted to the executive which adds military muscle to the diplomatic frame. In its most literal contemplation, the commander-in-chief role grants to the president control over the top military leadership of the nation. The power of appointment of all admirals and generals may seem, for the most part, a ceremonial distinction. Yet this power—and the related power of removal—has had practical historical significance. Indeed it is one of the factors which has reinforced the American tradition of civilian control over the military.

The significance of this power can be seen in the Truman-MacArthur controversy growing out of the conduct of the Korean War. It was the president's policy goal to fight a limited war and to avoid a direct confrontation between the United States and the Soviet Union or its apparent surrogate, communist China. As the agonizing conflict dragged on, the Supreme Commander, General Douglas MacArthur, publicly bristled at the limitations placed on his maneuverability. By spring 1951 MacArthur called for bombardment of China and ultimate invasion. In a letter to the Republican House Minority Leader, MacArthur pled for an expansion of the war on the ground that the issue was part of a global confrontation with Communism. President Truman, seeing a direct challenge to his foreign policy leadership, summarily removed General MacArthur from his command on April 11, 1951.[10] A national outcry ensued and the general returned home to a hero's welcome. Yet the president prevailed, and the war ultimately ended in a truce agreement two years later.

While the supervision of military leadership is important to a president's management of his own generalship, on many occasions presidents have injected themselves directly into the strategic planning of campaigns. Such decisions as President Roosevelt's emphasis on a Europe-first priority in the Second World War, or on a Normandy landing for the invasion of Western Europe in 1944, stand out. Nor will it be forgotten that in taking his stand during the Cuban missile crisis of 1962, President Kennedy ordered a military blockade which could have resulted in a nuclear confrontation with the Soviet Union having consequences beyond imagination. Just so, it was Commander-in-Chief Nixon who ordered American troops into Cambodia in 1970 and underwrote an American-protected invasion of Laos in 1971.

Wartime and the concomitant atmosphere of national emergency have resulted in egregious expansions of the commander-in-chief role. During the Second World War, in the bizarre case of the Nazi saboteurs, President Roosevelt by proclamation established a military commission which tried, convicted, and ordered the execution of six out of eight German nationals who landed in the United States by submarine with intent to commit acts of sabotage. On appeal to the Supreme Court the emergency provisions were upheld.[11] Of still greater consequence was the president's order to West Coast military commanders in 1942 which led to a discriminatory curfew imposed on those of Japanese origin, followed by his authorization for the relocation of Japanese-Americans. Thus were 112,000 Japanese-Americans (of which 70,000 were native-born Americans) interned in barbed-wire compounds called "War Re-

10. See Richard H. Rovere and Arthur M. Schlesinger, Jr., *The General and the President* (Farrar, Straus and Young, 1951), chapters 3 and 4.
11. *Ex Parte Quirin*, 317, U.S. 1 (1942).

location Centers." The Supreme Court upheld both infringements of basic liberties on grounds of emergency.[12]

During the Second World War broad emergency powers over domestic enterprises were justified as an extrapolation of the commander-in-chief clause. Numerous private industries were seized by the president including aircraft plants, shipyards, and a railroad. In one instance the president seized the Montgomery Ward mail-order house because of labor troubles. Probably the most extreme instance of the power of the commander-in-chief stretching to the individual citizen was in authority delegated to the War Manpower Commission by executive order in 1942. The Selective Service was literally transferred to the WMC and subsequently the chairman, Paul McNutt, issued a "work or fight" order which declared that workers in non-essentials jobs would either be transferred to high priority jobs or be inducted into the military service.[13]

Legislative Powers

The legal basis for a president's powers over the legislative process has roots in the Constitution and has been generally supplemented by congressional action. Article II states that he "shall from time to time give to the Congress Information of the State of the Union, and recommend to their Consideration such Measures as he shall judge necessary and expedient." This slim reed has become the support of the president's right of initiation of legislative projects. Modern presidents are indeed expected to present the Congress an entire legislative program, and this is accomplished on a continuous basis as presidential messages, including detailed provisions, are fed into the congressional hopper as bills. Moreover Congress has required specific messages of the president beyond the constitutionally enjoined State of the Union report. Thus in creating the Bureau of the Budget, Congress called upon the president to deliver an annual Budget Message—crucial because it constitutes legislative recommendations simply translated into dollars-and-cents terms. When congress passed the Employment Act of 1946 still another annual message was called for, the Economic Report. Once again, this report carries with it recommendations for legislative action concerning all aspects of the economy from employment to social welfare, from natural resources to international trade.

Aside from the message power as a vehicle of initiation, the congressionally sponsored Budget Bureau has come to symbolize the insti-

12. *Hirabayashi v. U.S.*, 320 U.S. 81 (1943) and *Korematsu v U.S.*, 323, U.S. 214 (1944).

13. Edward S. Corwin, *The President: Office and Powers* (New York University Press, 1957), p. 247.

tutionalization of the legislative function of the presidency. A complex system of legislative clearance has grown up around the budget function which requires that all legislative projects emanating from the various departments and agencies of government must be cleared through the (now) Office of Management and Budget to ascertain that they are "in accord with the program of the President." This has permitted modern presidents effectively to centralize and control the executive power of initiation.[14]

But the power to initiate does not guarantee acceptance of the President's proposals by Congress, nor, indeed, that they will even be given a serious hearing. Congress, while on the one hand feeling the need for executive recommendation and direction, is on the other, highly sensitive to its own independence and prerogatives. Thus opposition to White House proposals is as common as support. Indeed, if a president succeeds in persuading Congress to pass half of the legislation he supports he may be regarded as highly effective. "Boxscores" are regularly maintained showing the extent of presidential legislative success. The following table reports the proportion of presidential measures passed in Congress in the most recent years.[15]

Table 4.1. Presidential Boxscores, 1967-1970

1967 (Johnson)	- - 48	percent
1968 (Johnson)	- - 56	"
1969 (Nixon)	- - 32	"
1970 (Nixon)	- - 46	"

The other constitutionally authorized tool of legislative leadership is the power of negation. The president may veto a bill, returning it to the house of origin with his objections. If support for the bill in congress was extraordinary, it may then be passed over the president's veto by a two-thirds majority in both houses. The calendar can produce an alternative form of negation called the pocket veto. Thus, if the president takes no action on a bill within ten weekdays of its submission to him, and Congress has adjourned during that time, the bill is dead. The significance of this negative is in its frequent use. About forty percent of vetoes have been of the pocket veto variety. On the whole, the veto has been a very successful device historically, for only a little more than three percent of all presidential vetoes have been overridden between

14. See Richard E. Neustadt, "Presidency and Legislation: The Growth of Central Clearance," *American Political Science Review* 48 (September, 1954), pp. 654 ff., and Arthur Maass, "In Accord With the Program of the Presidency? An Essay on Staffing the Presidency," *Public Policy*, 4 (1953), pp. 77 ff.

15. *Congressional Quarterly Almanac*, 24 (1969), p. 1242 and *Congressional Quarterly Weekly Report*, 29, February 5, 1971, p. 307.

1789 and 1970 (75 out of 2252).[16] The effectiveness of the veto since World War II is seen in the following chart:

Table 4.2.   Presidential Vetoes, 1945-1970

President	Total Vetoes	Vetoes Overridden
Truman	250	12
Eisenhower	181	2
Kennedy	21	0
Johnson	30	0
Nixon	9	2

Three considerations should be taken into account in evaluating the veto power beyond the mere cataloguing of numerical successes. First, some of the vetoes overriden have been of great significance because of the importance of the measures thereby enacted. Thus the Taft-Hartley Labor Relations Act and the McCarran-Walter Immigration and Naturalization Act were passed in spite of President Truman's vetoes. More recently, vetoes by President Nixon of a hospital construction bill and Office of Economic Opportunity funding were overridden. Second, the *threat* of a veto can turn a negative power into a positive one. That is, foreknowledge that the president may veto a measure under consideration has often led to modifications of the measure designed to buy presidential approval. Finally, an interesting institutional relationship emerges from a survey of vetoes overridden. When the opposition party controls Congress, the chances are greater that a president's vetoes may be overridden. Thus Republicans in the 80th Congress succeeded in overturning some of President Truman's vetoes, just as Democratic congresses overrode some vetoes of Presidents Eisenhower and Nixon. Ultimately, however, the real potency of the veto power is essentially negative and thus of limited utility to a president who has strong legislative goals.

RESOURCES OF LEADERSHIP: INFORMAL

To speak of the informal resources available to presidents is to probe a much looser and less definable category, which contrasts with the neat constitutional and legal prerogatives associated with the office. One way

16. For the period 1789-1963, see Joseph E. Kallenbach, *The American Chief Executive* (New York: Harper & Row, 1966), p. 355; for the period 1963-1970, see *Congressional Quarterly Almanac*, vol. 20 (1964), p. 892; vol. 21 (1965), p. 1427; vol. 22 (1966), p. 1281; vol. 23 (1967), p. 1086; vol. 24 (1968), p. 23; and *Congressional Quarterly Weekly Report*, 28, December 18, 1970, p. 52. See essay on Congress, pp. 163 ff.

of describing this important element of presidential power is to summarize
it as the power to persuade, as Richard Neustadt has done so tellingly.[17]
Upon analyzing this "power" we find that it is in very large measure
a resultant of the formal, legal powers just surveyed. Yet it is more. It
stems from the personal, idiosyncratic element which the man brings
to the office and is colored by the personal choices of time and circumstances. But most of all, this power is an added dimension grounded in
the *combination* of the various formal powers employable by a president
in seeking a particular end.

The Private Personality

At least a part of a president's success depends upon the personal
qualities he manifests in dealing with others. Much of the most important
activity a president engages in is of a private nature. Formally, powerful
as the office is, any president must continually *convince* others to see
things his way, to cooperate with him, and to do his bidding. There is,
of course, no magical combination of traits which when mastered will
automatically assure this kind of authority. Nevertheless some qualities
stand out as crucial. Among them at the very least are energy, credibility,
and determination. The modern president simply must first be a hard
worker. He cannot be persuasive in his relations with others if he lacks
mastery of detailed information bearing on the problem, or betrays
an unawareness of the broader political implications of an issue.

Next, to be effective at a personal level, the president's words must be
believed. If doubts about his credibility are aroused, he heightens the
supreme risk of not being taken seriously and encourages a dangerous
game among his auditors of guessing about his "real meaning." Finally,
and allied to credibility, is the need for determination. Presidents are
surrounded by people who would like to push them around. Rightly
or wrongly, administrative officials, congressmen, political party leaders,
governors, influential private citizens, and foreign leaders are all convinced of the worthiness of their viewpoint and the importance of their
stake in the question. To have a hope to be effective as a leader, a president
must be secure in his own judgments and be able to say no, firmly,
to individuals and groups who would distract him from his course, for
whatever reason.

The Public Personality

Although much of the work of the presidency is carried on in private,
in a democratic system non-leaders do count. Thus—and again as Neustadt has pointed out—among the objects of presidential persuasion are

17. Richard E. Neustadt, *Presidential Power: The Politics of Leadership* (John
Wiley & Sons, 1960).

the nation, and indeed the world. At times the need is to persuade the "people" directly in initiating a course of action; often, however, this form of persuasion is instrumental, its purpose being to bring the weight of public pressure to bear on institutional leaders, thereby reinforcing the president's power of persuasion over them. Thus when the president speaks to the nation, his message may be primarily intended to influence a vote in the Senate, the position of the opposition party, or an important labor negotiation. For this purpose the qualities of the private personality—energy, credibility, and determination—are important, but something more must be added. The ability to communicate effectively with a mass audience is dependent upon that elusive quality of style which some men have and others do not. Granting that the aura of majesty surrounding presidential pronouncements creates a mighty advantage, the headstart afforded by institutional trappings can be dissipated if the personal style of the man does not come across.

A Superior Negotiating Position

A recurrent theme, echoed in the preceding essay on the presidency, posits bargaining as the routine method of exercising presidential leadership. For that process presidents call upon all of their resources, legal and informal, in different combinations under different circumstances. Thus let us assume a president wishes to bring about the enactment of a comprehensive environmental protection program. How might he attack the problem? Of course he could call upon his constitutional message power to introduce the program in Congress. But this step would be far from the beginning of the process. He would have established a study commission of prominent citizens to survey the problem, to present ideas, and to give the issue national salience. He would communicate to the nation the vital nature of the problem. He would have appointed domestic officials who could be expected to support his position in the departments and agencies and with their clienteles throughout the nation. Well before the introduction of legislation in Congress he would prepare the way by attempting to influence key legislators and committee and subcommittee chairmen. This approach could take many forms. The president might lend his personal status to the legislator by invitations to breakfast, outings on the golf course, or personal appearances in the man's district or state. He might promise support for a pet project of the legislator. He might direct a subordinate to negotiate a government contract bringing benefits to the legislator's state or district. He might promise future support for the legislator in the event of a political party primary contest at home.

Once the program proceeds along the obstacle-strewn course of the legislative process, the president will call upon the resources of party leadership to attempt a united front among his partisan supporters. At the same time he will articulate the issue nationally as a non-partisan crusade in the national interest. By executive order he will find it possible to make certain kinds of government subsidies, licensing procedures, insurance procedures, and the like, contingent upon compliance with existing conservation regulations or incremental executive adjustments to them. In these ways and others he will further demonstrate that he is determined to employ the full force of presidential power to achieve a policy goal. Finally, if the president is unsuccessful in the first round of a policy campaign—as he often is—he can again step into his role as party leader and attempt to make the issue one of major importance in ensuing congressional or presidential election campaigns. This catalogue of options for action is not exhaustive, but rather exemplary of ways presidents have orchestrated the formal and informal powers of the office in the exercise of leadership.

The Structuring of Options

A resultant of all the formal and informal powers available to a president is his ability to influence importantly the arrangement of alternatives available for any course of action. In its simplest form, this teaches the lesson that executive actions taken one day can have the consequence of closing off available alternatives the next day. For example, if a president is successful inaugurating a large, long-term, and high-priced federal highways program, the likelihood that significant national resources will subsequently be invested in supporting public transportation (such as an expanded rail passenger transportation system) is lessened.

Similarly, at the level of foreign policy, as long as presidents are publicly determined to maintain the existing Saigon regime in South Vietnam, or make the release of prisoners of war a *precondition* to negotiation with the North Vietnamese, the range of available policy options is restricted. These illustrations are not intended to suggest that courses of action cannot be reversed nor, indeed, that presidents are all-powerful determinig voices. Such is manifestly not the case, as the preceding essay illustrates. Yet in assessing the form which presidential power *can* assume, such considerations are revealing.

THE BUREAUCRATIC APPENDAGE

No consideration of presidential power would be complete without a recognition of the important role played by the American bureaucracy. While bureaucracy (or administration) is in many ways executive in nature—and thus commonly considered to be an off-shoot of the presidency—both in the terms of the diversity of its responsibilities and its tenuous relationship to the presidential office, it must be viewed as a fourth branch of government. The remaining pages of this essay will explore the nature of the beast.

The Sources of Bureaucracy

Why is bureaucracy so important in modern government? A reference to the most recent Civil Service Commission figures tells us that total federal employment in the United States stands at 2,928,186. Of that number the legislative branch employs 29,181 and the judiciary, 6,822. The remaining 2,892,183 public servants are listed in the executive branch.[18] This number represents a twelve-fold growth during the years of this century. This growth is sometimes loosely attributed to organic aggrandizing dynamics of bureaucracy similar to animal cell division and reproduction. And, to be sure, Parkinson's famous "Laws" (e.g., the multiplication of subordinates outpacing the multiplication of work) are not totally satirical. Yet the fundamental reason for the growth of bureaucracy is tied up with a growing social complexity which increasingly has demanded ever more sophisticated divisions of labor and exotic specializations of function.

One of the great thinkers at the turn of the twentieth century, Max Weber, foresaw the growth of modern bureaucracy and offered an essentially relevant rationale justifying it. Weber argued that a modern social order would inevitably be marked by a rational-legal structure of governance. The model for his regime envisages a host of highly specialized offices manned by experts whose claim to positions of responsibility rests upon certified competence in a technically narrow area of mental labor. To maintain the appropriate balance of functions and responsibilities among the bureaucrats, Weber relied upon an elaborate system of rules, regulations, and routines imposed formally and impersonally from above and flowing down in hierarchical order.[19] Like any model, Weber's ideal type does not precisely represent contemporary reality, but neither is it a bad description of *formal* organization.

At root, bureaucracy is the creation of necessity. A rapid development of technology in transportation, communication, industry, and commerce presents a host of problems and needs which can only be attended to by trained experts. Whole new responsibilities come to be exacted of government in the area of regulation, and these responsibili-

18. *The New York Times Encyclopedic Almanac*, 1971 (The New York Times Company, 1970), p. 149.
19. See H. H. Gerth and C. Wright Mills, transl., *From Max Weber* (Oxford University Press, 1958), pp. 196-244.

ties can only be undertaken by equivalent experts. To cite obvious truisms: There was no need for a Federal Communications Commission or an Atomic Energy Commission before the invention of radio and the development of atomic power. As society becomes increasingly urbanized a new set of problems involved with social interdependence and modern lifestyles must be met.

These then are outstanding sources of the bureaucratic phenomenon of modern government as well as modern life. We now proceed to sketch out the anatomy of bureaucracy in American government.

The Structure of Bureaucracy

There are really four structurally distinct manifestations of bureaucracy at the federal level in America. The oldest and most well known administrative form is the federal department. The first of these (State, Treasury, Justice) were establishd at the founding of the nation. In the years since, the president's cabinet has been expanded to include eleven such functionally specialized departments, including the most recently created departments of Housing and Urban Development and of Transportation. They are hierarchically organized, the political heads are appointed by the president, and the subordinate bureaus, agencies, offices, divisions, and services are staffed largely by career civil servants. In theory the departments are directly responsible to the president, but as their subfunctions have been elaborated so extensively, regular, formal accountability is difficult to enforce. Seven departments each employ over 100,000 public servants, which is some indication of the extent of their mission. Some, such as the Department of Defense and the former Post Office Department, have staffs larger than the largest corporations in the nation.

The most recent bureaucratic development has been the construction of a palace bureaucracy immediately surrounding the president. While the Executive Office of the President accounts for only about 4,000 federal employees, numbered among them are some of the most influential policy advisers and policy makers in the government. At the core of the inner circle in the White House staff are such personages as the assistants for National Security Affairs, Domestic Affairs, and a raft of counsellors to the president. Beyond the staff, the Executive Office includes the Office of Management and Budget, the Council of Economic Advisers, the National Security Council, the Domestic Council, and the Office of Economic Opportunity, as well as other agencies bespeaking the importance of contemporary foreign and domestic problem-areas.

Beginning in the 1880s, governmental experiment with a new form of administration was inaugurated. Emerging public problems in the area of commerce and transportation led to the creation of independent regulatory commissions. Beginning with the Interstate Commerce Commission and exemplified by the later Power, Trade, Communications, and Securities Exchange Commissions as well as the National Labor Relations Board, these multi-membered agencies were established to perform the job of regulation over the varied sectors of the private economy.

The crucial and controversial nature of the instrumentalities to be regulated motivated Congress to attempt to isolate these agencies from the influences of politics and the traditional branches of government. History has notably not fulfilled the promise of independence. While the president is prohibited from removing the commissioners, through the Office of Management and Budget he can influence their behavior. Even more can the Congress control their activities through legislation and *ex parte* involvement in specific regulatory acts such as licensing and adjudication. A further rationale for the independence of these agencies has been that they partake of more than strictly executive functions and thus should not be placed under the presidential umbrella. In practice, however, these agencies have been the target of importunities not only emanating from the other branches of government, but even more intensely from the private interests they were created to regulate.

A final institutional form of administration is revealed by the public corporations. These bodies, exemplified by the Tennessee Valley Authority, the new Postal Service, and the Federal National Mortgage Association, are chartered by government and patterned after the private corporations in their functions. The public corporation is governed by a board of directors, some or all of whose members are appointed by the president. The corporation has the right to acquire property, negotiate loans, bring suits (and be sued!), issue bonds, and in many other ways emulate the practices of the private corporation. Typically these corporations engage in the construction of power facilities, make loans to small business, make home-mortgage money available, and carry on a farm price-support subsidy system. The purpose of their creation was to encourage the efficiency associated with the private business model and to underwrite public innovation and experiment in ways not open to existing administrative bodies. Success in these aims has been limited because of the halfway house occupied by such corporations—not wholly governmental and not entirely autonomous.

The Bureaucrats

The American public service is in some ways a compromise. From the early days when a miniscule administrative branch was composed of an aristocracy of virtue and talents, to the middle period charcterized by a spoils system little affected by either virtue or talents, and into the

modern period of civil service reform, one finds overlays of the dominant charcteristics of each period. The dominant theme in the development of the American public service during the last century has been
the progressive institutionalization of a merit system. Under the direction of the Civil Service Commission an increasingly large proportion
of federal employment has been drawn into the classified career service.
Today nearly ninety percent of public servants enter the service via the
examination route.

The positions of these public servants are classified primarily according to level of responsibility along a General Service Schedule, with
rankings ranging from 1 to 18. Positions carry a high degree of tenure
security and are not controlled by partisan preferments. For the upper
reaches of the civil service schedule, position is gained through mobility
from below within the service, as well as by lateral entry, provided one
has special training and qualifications. In recent decades salary schedules
have improved and in most positions now approach equivalence to
salaries for comparable non-governmental positions. The security of
pensions and other "fringe benefits" add to the attractiveness of the
service.

The other, far less numerous sector of the federal service is occupied
by a class of high officials called political executives. They are appointive
posts ranging from the cabinet-level officials such as assistant secretaries
to some bureau chiefs and agency supervisors. While they are subject to
the same characteristics of short tenure and partisan preference which
marked the spoils system, on the whole their major claim to office rests
upon competence or even excellence in the performance of a specialized
function. In a society that has become generally more professionalized,
the higher public service has followed the same pattern. That is, a kind
of Weberian criterion of qualification—often attested by university-
level graduate and professional training—tends to be invoked informally
by the professional associations and guilds which are often called upon to
recommend personnel for high governmental service. Some very high
cabinet-level and ambassadorial positions are quite naturally still reserved
for those whose primary recommendation is a history of service to the
partisan cause or comraderie with notables already ensconced in positions
of power and influence.

The Job of the Bureaucrat

The most obvious role of the administrative arm is to implement the
policies set forth authoritatively by the appropriate organs of government. In this sense bureaucrats are the aides of the president in carrying
out the executive function. However, this tells us little about the nature

of the job to be done. Of the multitudinous variations on the executive theme, the following are some important categories.

At the outset it should be reiterated that the higher-level bureaucrats —by the advice they proffer and the discretion they exercise in implementation—participate in the policy-*making* process. Below them a substantial proportion of the professional bureaucracy is involved in internal housekeeping, the management and coordination of activities carried on by others in the service of a mandated policy goal. Further down the line tens of thousands of others perform routine staff functions ranging from the mangement of archives to implementing personnel systems and the maintenance of the agency payroll office.

In modern America a large part of the governmental function is concerned with the regulation of the property rights of citizens and groups. As was noted above, this development was responsible for the creation of special agencies charged exclusively with a particular task. Yet such regulatory functions are not the monopoly of the independent commissions alone. Most departments and agencies of government exercise some form of regulatory responsibility. This takes two general forms: rule-making and adjudication. Because of increased complexity, Congress has delegated to the administrative branch much of the responsibility for "filling in the details" of broad legislative mandates. Thus agencies daily make rules governing private behavior which have the full force and effect of an act of Congress. When the Civil Aeronautics Board makes rules governing air flight patterns, speeds, and altitudes it is making law. When the Federal Reserve Board raises the rediscount rate, thus affecting bank lending practices, it is manipulating behavior in the credit market authoritatively.

The adjudicatory function is less apparent. We are accustomed to *think* of judicial business conducted by black-robed judges in a solemn courtroom atmosphere. In reality, every time the faceless Internal Revenue Service challenges an income tax return by disallowing an exemption, it is reaching a judicial decision, tacitly adjudicating a controversy between the United States Government and a perhaps unaware citizen-defendant. Or when Mrs. Knight of the Passport Office denies a citizen's right to travel abroad, she has reached a judicial decision, if without benefit of mace and robes.

The job of the bureaucrat is then more variable and fulsome than often perceived. The moral offered is that it is one which far transcends presidential agency. But more important: it is one which—in its pervasiveness and its impact—can be dissonant as well as harmonious with presidential leadership.

5

JUDICIAL POWER

AND RESPONSIVENESS

by Jay A. Sigler

The extent of judicial responsiveness to societal needs and demands has perplexed legal philosophers for the past century. A great deal of legal speculation and theorizing has been produced, with some impact upon the legal education system and upon the outlook of the judges. Yet, most of this legal speculation has been lacking in hard data, so that legal writers have tended to concentrate upon what judges *ought* to do, rather than what they actually do.

Political scientists, on the other hand, have approached the judiciary from a highly political viewpoint. At first, most political scientists regarded the judicial policy-making function as virtually the same as legislative policy making. This attitude still permeates most political science analysis of the judicial process, and is exemplified by the kind of study which treats a judicial decision as a vote for or against a policy, just as legislators cast votes. Beyond this apparent similarity between the function of legislators and judge is a great deal of difference in the role, scope and policy impact of the parts of government which these actors serve. Judges cannot and do not behave like legislators, but neither can they be mere impartial purveyors of abstract justice, as the layman sometimes expects.

There are severe institutional limitations upon the role of the judiciary in the political system. Judges rarely treat questions of foreign affairs, taxation or appropriations, all of which the Congress or president regularly consider Judicial policies are usually narrow in scope and often retroactive in effect, unlike most legislative policies. Numerous other dissimilarities will be described later, but from the outset it should be understood that while all policymaking, governmental and private, bears some common characteristics, important distinctions exist among them.

To demonstrate the place of the judiciary in the social and political systems two approaches are adopted in this essay. The first emphasizes the functional roles of the judiciary in the social system. The second stresses the role of the judiciary as a political decision-making agency among other such agencies. These approaches are complementary, not contradictory, just as the political system is part of the larger social system and facilitates its operation.

THE JUDICIARY IN THE POLITICAL SYSTEM

The Functions of the Judiciary

Looking at any society from the perspective of a social scientist, several functions of social systems can be universally observed. First, social systems tend to maintain themselves by maintaining their own basic patterns, keeping basic features from one generation to another without drastic changes. However, the second function of a social system, somewhat counter to the first, is the adaptive function. This second function allows the system to alter in response to the physical environment and to the pressures brought about by contact with other systems. As a third function of a social system, integration of varying tasks and subfunctions must take place to keep the society moving in the same direction. Finally, each society must have goals which it seeks to attain, and goal attainment is a major function of any system. The political activity of society is devoted to goal attainment, and political action is the prime method of moving a society in a consciously designed direction. Politics also is concerned with problems of system maintenance, adaptation, and integration, and all of these functions can be observed in the workings of the political system.

The judicial part of the political system deals with the same basic functions of society, but in a special way. The first function, preservation of society, is performed through the adjudication of laws (usually created by legislatures) regarding treasonable, criminal or socially disruptive behavior. One aspect of this function, resolution of private conflicts, consumes a major part of the courts' time. More important for society, however, is the application of general law to particular individuals. The individuation of the preservative function can be exemplified in the efforts to control political dissenters through the judicial process. When Judge Julius Hoffman presided over the Chicago Conspiracy Trial in 1970, he gave, through his instructions to the jury, his rulings on objections and his sentences, specific application to the Anti-Riot Act passed by Congress in 1968. (In fact, Judge Hoffman exceeded the statute by sentencing several defendants and their attorneys for contempt of court, hoping to discourage future dissenters from excessive obstreperous behavior in courtrooms as well as from engaging in inflammatory talk.) Any judge in a criminal trial plays a similar role. The basic determination of the nature of criminal categories is made by the legislature, but the application of the categories to particular individuals is the task of the judiciary. Of course, many types of anti-social behavior are *not* regulated by the judicial process, either because the society has not officially proscribed that behavior, or because the administrative agencies related to the courts have not initiated judicial action.

Adaptation, the second function of a social system, is sometimes performed by courts. A leading illustration has been the role played by the Supreme Court under Chief Justice Warren in the area of desegregation of public facilities. The presidency and the Congress had been unable to tackle the problem of segregation in America. With some trepidation, the Supreme Court undertook the task, beginning in 1954, although the aid of other branches was needed to gain compliance with Court rulings. Judicial power has been used to retard change, and to slow adjustment. This has occurred at several times in the history of the Supreme Court, but most clearly in the early interpretation of the Sherman Anti-trust Act of 1890, when the Supreme Court succeeded for a time in constricting the application of the act by giving extremely narrow readings to various clauses of the act.

The integration function is especially important to political scientists because the courts are often employed for the purpose of providing surveillance of official action. The state legislatures, the national Congress, the federal and state administrators. the police, the prosecutors, the governors and even the president himself can be directly or indirectly checked by judicial actions. For the most part the judiciary supports or "legitimatizes" the decisions made by other branches of government, but the possibility of restraining improper actions by another branch of government is implicit in the American version of the "rule of law." The integration function is exemplified in suits against administrative agencies, in which the claim that the agency has exceeded the powers granted it by the legislature sometimes finds a forum. The possibility of excessive zeal on the part of administrators and police is a serious problem in America, and the judiciary can wield an influence upon the activities of these groups that keep them under a measure of control. The integration function is especially the province of the judiciary because of the gaps left in the law by the sweeping language of statutes and executive orders. By interpreting these measures the judiciary gives shape, substance, and some consistency to the law. Statutes, executive orders and administrative rulings emanate from various sources at various times. The courts ultimately apply most of these policies, fitting them into the existing body of law.

Goal attainment, the task of forging new policies in tune with societal aims, is a heavily political function. Courts in spite of the disclaimers to the contrary, do participate in politics, and make decisions having the effect of new policy. Judicial policy making is more widespread than most Americans are aware, but there are definite limits to judicial propensities to innovate and initiate policies. In the first place, courts are largely passive institutions. They cannot reach out and undertake policy making at will. Instead, they must await the arrival of a policy-making opportunity in the form of a case ripe for decision. Considerable judicial flexibility to taking or refusing cases exists, but courts cannot stage cases merely for the purpose of handling problems which interest them. In addition, judicial policymaking is likely to run afoul of other branches of government, and courts cannot stand alone against the more powerful legislatures and executives with whom they must deal.

How Judges Make Law

To say that judicial decisions are frequently flavored with the spice of politics does not mean that judges make law in the same way in which legislators, presidents, governors, administrators, and other members of the political system do. Judges are, under the ancient common law theory of Anglo-American law, merely discoverers or declarers of principles already inherent in the law. However, this transparent fiction has been punctured by legal philosophers during the twentieth century, who have demonstrated that judges do make policy. The dominant school of thought, called "sociological jurisprudence," now holds that judges should consider competing social advantages and disadvantages, and this is now a regularly accepted judicial obligation.

Roscoe Pound, the major American legal philosopher of the century, attempted to spell out the competing demands which judges must consider as a part of the judicial function. Pound discerned three types of interests: individual, public, and social. Individual interests include life, bodily integrity, personal liberty, reputation, privacy, belief, and opinions. Public interests, being more general, refer to claims made by the government as a property owner (TVA, for example) or as a guardian of social interests through the exercise of regulatory powers. This public interest sector has vastly increased in the twentieth century as more responsibilities have been placed in government hands. Social interests, the third category, is by far the largest. It includes the interest in general security (protection of acquisitions, of transactions and the maintenance of peace and order). The social interest in the security of certain established institutions, including the family, religious, political, and economic organizations, is a subcategory. General moral behavior is another type of social interest, and is exemplified in the laws concerning liquor, drugs, sex, blasphemy and obscenity. There are other social interests in conservation of natural and human resources, and a concern for what Pound called "general progress," including political, economic, and cultural progress through the protection of free opinion and free criticism. Finally, and most important, is the subcategory of social interest labelled "individual life." This social interest subsumes all general concerns with physical, mental, and economic development and opportunity.

Pound's division of interests allows for a clearer perception of the choices available to judges. Judges can rationally weigh competing interests in terms which allow for the total needs of society, not just the individual needs or claims of private persons. When individual interests are measured against other individual interests, as in the average civil suit, courts can deal with them without regard to social interests. However, when individual interests collide with social interests, the latter must prevail, because judges should act on behalf of the greater interest. Individual interests are often subsumed in larger categories, as in the claim to free speech, and in that way the individual claim can be compared fairly to a competing social interest. Consequently, the individual freedom to curse in public may be regarded as of less social significance than the individual freedom to engage in political discussion in public. The right to curse will be accorded less weight than the right to political debate.

Obviously, the theory of interests is little more than a rule of thumb. Interests cannot be quantified or tabulated with the aid of a bookkeeper. Interests must be defined and described for the judge, usually by the attorneys for the competing parties. Courts usually depend upon lawyers to demonstrate the ways in which their client's claim is part of some larger social interest. Judges must themselves detect the levels and degrees of social interests, and in this way they make policy.

The central peculiarity of judicial decision making can be perceived at this point. Determinations of social and public policy are made by judges in the very narrow framework of a case system. Two alternative views of social interest are presented by two contestants for judicial support. The bifold nature of presentation and the limitations of judicial resources in time, energy, and information usually force the judge to take a very narrow view of the problem at hand. The judge does not have an independent investigatory staff. He does not have the opportunity (with the occasional exception of *amicus curiae* briefs) to consult persons external to the immediate dispute. The judge receives demands in the immediate form of a dispute which was brought to him, and which he did not encourage or activate, but on which, in the end, he must make a policy decision. The process is quite different from that facing the legislator who, though subject to competing demands, can weigh them in terms of the political advantages and disadvantages which he discerns, as well as the "general public interest."

Judges are also subject to another constraint which concerns other policy makers much less. The judge must consider the cohesiveness, the consistency, and the continuity of the law itself. The law must correspond, to some extent, to current social practices and expectations. But it must also preserve the rules of the past for the sake of the future. Arbitrary or rapid changes in legal doctrines upset the stability of the social order. Predictability in law depends upon some attention to past precedents, a factor which the ancient doctrine of *stare decisis* takes into account.

The drive for continuity is probably rooted in a need for a feeling of social certainty, an emotional (and economic) need which law normally satisfies. As a consequence the judge confronted with a tough "problem case" may have to weigh in the scales the concern for social stability which simple adherence to previous rulings would provide. More frequently than most laymen know, the judge must choose whether the occasion is correct, the time is right, to depart from old precedent and to decide a case on the basis of considerations of current social needs. Judges, unlike legislators, must look to the past as much as to the future. The question frequently put to counsel in appellate courts is: "Why should this court reject past precedents in this case?"

To resolve these issues judges have relied upon quasilogical techniques, but judicial reasoning tends to be led by analogy rather than strict logic. Fact situations never repeat themselves exactly. Legal rules are usually broad generalizations. To apply rules to facts in a case context is the official obligation of courts, but in reality other social needs are introduced into the judicial process. Logic does not provide a sure guide to the determination of social need. Supposedly, judges use personal preferences less frequently than legislators, but at times the personal element must be the same, as in the settlement of the school desegregation controversy, in which judges have played a leading role.

Judges, then, do make law, but subject to definite limitations. Legislators set the boundaries for judicial policy making by drawing the basic statutes. Except for the ever-present possibility of judicial review to strike down legislation, the courts may not go outside or beyond the contours of policy set by statutes. When statutes are vague, indefinite or contradictory, courts move in to fill many of the vacuums established by statutes. In fact many state legislatures deliberately pass vague statutes, in anticipation of judicial action to formulate specific policy. In a sense those statutes are a demand for judicial legislation by delegation of the legislatures. But except in such instances, courts are not as free to innovate or concoct new legal principles as are most other political agencies.

Nor are courts equipped to evaluate and decide most large schemes of social reform. When they attempt to act in that fashion, as the Supreme Court has in school desegregation, reapportionment, and obscenity control, the process of policy formation is protracted, intermittent, and somewhat incomplete. Parties must return to the courts again and again to work out the details of the new policy. Courts rarely provide more of an answer to a social problem than the parties request of them. In that way social problems managed by courts are likely to brew and bubble for many years, until under the stress of events the courts either take a definitive position or retreat from previously held positions. Currently, in the 1970s, the Supreme Court has begun a period of retreat, so that large-scale social problems may not be handled to the same extent as during the years of Chief Justice Earl Warren.

The policy-making character of courts is most apparent in the interpretation of statutes. The common law, the judge-made law of ancient vintage, is still alive and growing, but in most matters of high political significance the common law has been replaced by statutes. The courts have, however, been responsible for the development of the meanings of most statutes. Administrative agencies do most of the daily work of statutory application, but judicial review of this task is usually available, making the courts the ultimate interpreters of statutory language. Consequently, to a degree not usually appreciated by laymen, judges help make law even after legislators have spoken.

Judicial consideration of statutes usually arises in a context of a legal dispute. The rendering of "advisory opinions," advance interpretations of statutes to test their constitutional validity prior to legislative passage, is available in a few states, but is a rare phenomenon. When pleaded as an issue in a case, the constitutional validity of a statute can be drawn into question. Obviously, to declare a legislatively enacted statute unconstitutional is an act of serious political consequence, and courts tend to avoid such a confrontation, preferring to exercise self-restraint, usually under a presumption that a duly enacted statute is probably valid unless clearly demonstrated to be beyond the boundaries set by the appropriate constitution. The making of social policy by the application of the judicial sword of judicial review is always a possibility whenever a court is faced with a statute and requested to interpret it, apply it or strike it down, but normally judges await a formal request by a party to test its constitutionality before unsheathing that sword.

Almost all the business of the United States Supreme Court involves statutory interpretation. For this reason, and for reasons of federalism to be discussed later, the Supreme Court is, of necessity, a highly political body. Its decisions and its non-decisions ramify throughout American society and politics. Even though the Court rarely exercises its power to declare statutes unconstitutional, it must, in the course of ordinary statutory interpretation, help direct and channel much of the work of the American system. To take an unfamiliar example, the law of labor relations in the United States is entirely statutory at the national level and almost so in the states as well. Yet the Supreme Court has played a large role in supplying the scope, direction, and limits of labor policy in America.

Thus, the First Amendment of the Constitution has been applied to picketing statutes, state and federal, in a fairly liberal way. State statutes on labor relations have been very narrowly construed and restricted by the Supreme Court to minor employment situations. The Court has served as a monitor or watchdog of the National Labor Relations Board, the federal agency charged with primary responsibility for federal labor policy. Then, too, the Supreme Court has invented "a whole new body of labor contract law" to fit in the spaces left by gaps in the basic legislation. There can be little doubt that the Supreme Court is a major source of labor law policy, in spite of its formal role as mere interpreter of statutes. It should also be recalled that the Supreme Court of the years 1900–1933 resisted and crippled most federal and state labor legislation through the use of its judicial review power.

To a lesser extent all American courts are political decision-making agencies. From the lowly police court which processes criminal cases in a rapid-fire assembly line procedure to the higher echelons of the state and federal judiciary, courts are called upon to play roles of allocating benefits and blame among individuals. When the stakes are high enough the case may reach sufficient visibility to be "political." The sifting out of political from non-political cases is beyond the scope of this essay. If the Marxists and the Black Panthers are correct, then all cases are ultimately traceable to class advantages or racist conceptions, and by those ideologies all cases become "political." But even from the vantage point of mere description of the status quo, a neutral observer must conclude that at every level a fairly sizeable component of judicial business involves the same considerations which could be weighed by other branches of government.

When a municipal tax ordinance is stricken down, when a zoning board is overruled, when the state highway agency is forced to change the placement of a highway, when the election laws are invoked, in all these matters which may reach a court, political choices are clearly to be made. A court may apply its own techniques, its own earlier rulings to a dispute (and judicial independence against political interference is usually honored), but the choice, when made, changes the course of a public event. That is political.

Judicial Power

The political character of the courts is further evident in the extent of their power. Judicial power in the political system varies from nation to nation. Although no quantitative measurement of relative judicial power is available for accurate comparisons, it is obvious that courts play a larger social and political role in some nations than in others. In Japan, for example, many disputes which would be settled by courts in America are handled extrajudicially. Go-betweens or mediators are used widely in Japan because of desire to avoid the formal confrontation among strangers which would take place in a lawsuit.[1] The use or avoidance of courts is related to the social habits and expectations of a people, and Americans have entrusted much more of their personal, social, economic, and political problems to courts than have most other peoples.

Judicial power is directly related to the demands and expectations made upon the judiciary by the public and by actors in the political system. If the courts are used more, they gain more influence and respect by the process of utilization. The English courts appear to have lost power to the Civil Service, which has taken on more and more administrative responsibilities to satisfy the demands of a public which wants swift and flexible decision making. Administrative tribunals have emerged to meet these demands and to manage new social and political issues generated by the energies of a welfare state. A narrow-minded legal profession and a traditional judiciary resisted the development of new types of law and "it therefore seemed in the mid-1960s that England's courts and lawyers were never likely to play as large a role as in some other countries." [2]

The Russian courts are closely linked to the system of political rule required by the dictatorship. Courts do not enjoy independent status, in spite of some provisions of the Soviet Constitution which seem to suggest so. In fact, as the Soviet legal expert Vyshinsky proclaimed in 1937, "the court is an instrument of the governing class; it assures the domination of this class and protects its interests." Since the ruling class in Russia is the proletariat through their ruling Communist Party, the Party sets the limits for judicial power, and judicial review over government

1. Takeyoshi Kawashima, "Dispute Resolution in Contemporary Japan," in Arthur Taylor von Mehren, ed., *Law in Japan: The Legal Order of a Changing Society* (Harvard University Press and Charles F. Tuttle Co., 1964), pp. 41-52.

2. Brian Abel-Smith and Robert Stevens, *Lawyers and the Courts: A Sociological Study of the English Legal System, 1750-1965* (Heineman, 1967), p. 463.

(Party) policies is unthinkable because courts are only expected to apply the enacted laws strictly. Laws can be declared unconstitutional only in the case of a contradiction between the law of one Soviet Social Republic and national laws.

American judicial power is considerably greater than Soviet or English. The reasons for this are rooted deep in American political and cultural history. The institution of judicial review has been carried to its furthest extent in America. As a result, American courts down to the bottom levels possess the potential power to strike down legislation, administrative rulings, and executive orders on grounds of unconstitutionality. Even a minor police court could declare a presidential order invalid with no fear of retribution. American courts do not use this power frequently, but there is considerable recognition of the potential power of courts.

Legislatures are not the final sources of American law, The United States Supreme Court has declared hundreds of state laws invalid, and more than eighty federal statutes. State courts have found thousands of state acts invalid because of violation of the state or federal constitutions. Legislatures have hit back at judges by restricting their jurisdiction or even by changing the constitutions, but the formation of an anti-judicial coalition in the legislature is usually so difficult that the courts can expect to have the final say on constitutionality. By contrast, in England, as in most nations, the word of the Parliament is final, there being no superior body nor superior principles to restrict parliamentary authority.

Executive and administrative actions are also subject to occasional exercises of judicial power. Governors, presidents, civil servants and bureau chiefs are subject to varying types of judicial constraint. No one may sue the president to enjoin him against the performance of his office, but a presidential order may run afoul of the court. Frustration of presidential orders is an almost unheard-of judicial activity, but surveillance of administrative activity is a routine function. Rulings regarding passports, use of the mails, patents, crop allotments, welfare payments, taxation, labor bargaining, railroad routes or licenses can all be brought to the attention of courts.

Judicial surveillance of administrative decisions is restricted by the statutes which establish the agency. Courts cannot intervene at will in the administrative process, but can only review administrative decisions in the manner defined by statutes. But regular American courts have not been kept out of the administrative process altogether, as in France, where specialized courts to review administrative tribunals have been established. In addition American courts can rule that administrative agencies have exceeded their statutory authority, and in that way bring the agency under close judicial scrutiny. Students should bear in mind that state colleges and universities are also partly administrative in nature, and their rulings can be the subject of litigation brought by students and others.

Courts rarely set aside findings of fact made by administrative agencies. That function is more appropriate to the expertise of specialized bodies. Judicial constraint usually takes the form of an insistence on "due process," which, in some cases, means that the parties affected by the administrative ruling are to be given some of the "rights" to a full and fair hearing which they might have received in a court trial. There are definite limits on the extent to which administrative hearings can be "judicialized," but judicial suspicion of the informality and flexibility of the administrative process is prevalent.

Judicial supervision of the police and the prosecutor is a special aspect of surveillance of the administrative process. The policeman is an arm of the criminal-administrative apparatus. He is the one "administrator" who has contact with every member of the public. The policeman's conduct also has impact upon the rights and privileges which are found in the federal and state constitutions. Of necessity, courts set rules for search and seizure, arrest, assembly, free speech, and in recent years the way in which suspects are interrogated. The policeman is on the front lines of crime control, but his conduct also sets the boundaries for individual rights. If suspects are hounded and browbeaten or arbitrarily incarcerated, then individual liberties are made a mockery. On the other hand, if courts set high standards of police conduct, the work of the policeman becomes more complex. Some policemen now regard judges as unsympathetic, but most recognize the obligation of courts to mediate between society and the individual.

In criminal trials, the admissibility of evidence is subject to rules of law largely set by judges, and these rules have become major safeguards against "improper" police conduct. Judges rule on evidence in order to protect juries from illegally obtained information as well as other varieties of questionable information. Thus evidence obtained by an improper police interrogation is clearly inadmissible. In fact, the issue of the legal adequacy of an arrest is based upon a judge-made formula. To a lesser extent, judge-made rules and practices restrain the public prosecutors.

The judiciary also has power to act as its own watchdog. Since the American judicial system is hierarchical, there is a need for uniformity. Trial judges, the workhorses of the legal system, are called upon to treat a wide range of questions, frequently without much time to prepare themselves for a novel or intricate issue. It is the task of the appellate courts to supervise the work of the trial courts and to weave their judgments into the fabric of the total legal system. Conflicting values, rules or ideologies at the trial level may create widely different readings of the law from one region to another. Intercourt conflicts do emerge, and complete surveillance is impossible, but the threat of appellate court reversal seems to play a unifying role within the legal system. In actuality, much less supervision of the lower courts by upper courts takes place than the traditional charts indicate. Avoidance, delay, and defiance are always possible at the lower judicial levels. But, of course, judicial control is even less intensive in the other functional zones of surveillance previously described. If appellate judges cannot completely regulate lower judges, how much influence can they exert upon extrajudicial officials?

As actors in the political system, judges and courts are subject to many influences, each of which may have significant bearing upon the reception and outcome of a case. Below the level of individual or group demands, which may at times reach significant proportions, are the daily run of trials and appeals in which an admixture of formal and informal inputs account for most of the judicial reactions and the legal results. Although judges may sometimes choose among various inputs, their choice is usually quite limited.

Formal Inputs

A good starting point for the discussion of inputs is the formal type, which lawyers emphasize. The federal and state constitutions are the most formal of all inputs. Technically, these are the "highest" form of legal input, but constitutional matters are minimal concerns in most cases. The "meaning" of the constitutional clause which may be at issue in a case is often dependent upon case precedents, since American courts have actively engaged in constitutional interpretation for over one hundred and fifty years. The literal text of these constitutions can also be a significant input on occasion, especially in the application of state provisions, which are often highly detailed and much more recent in enactment than the national constitution.

Another kind of formal input is prior case rulings. The common law rule of *stare decisis*, (Webster: to stand by decided matters) usually honored in the United States, requires all courts to abide by earlier and relevant case rulings wherever possible. The rule is ordinarily honored because of the important conserving function which it supports. The practice is for contending parties to refer to or "cite" prior cases as applicable precedents and for the court to choose among various versions of the precedents presented. Of course precedents can be overturned, ignored, or "distinguished" (explained away), but there is no doubt that case precedents are significant in American law.

The rule of *stare decisis* provides conservative and stabilizing benefits because it allows for self-steering and correction in the legal system. Earlier case decisions are outputs of the past. Some of these outputs are fed into later cases as significant inputs. In this fashion courts can veer between alternative policy choices, guided by the charts of earlier cases as reinterpreted on each new occasion. Obviously the rule strictly obeyed would cause the law to grow stale and out of touch with changing experience. This tendency is counteracted, to some extent, by the practice of overruling case precedents from time to time.

Lawyers are often able to point to competing precedents in support of their client's claims. This common procedure shows that it is the policy inherent in a precedent that really matters. As a result American judges can shop for precedents, selecting the rules which suit their value preferences to a greater degree than is usually appreciated.[3] There is a much greater fluidity of judicial choice in this country than in most common law jurisdictions. Even so, a policy choice must ordinarily be presented in the form of a case precedent, and overt judicial policy innovation is a rather rare phenomenon.

The common law preference for precedent is based upon a policy determination in favor of order which often is unarticulated. Even progressive legal thinkers feel ill at ease when *stare decisis* is threatened. The doctrine allows for more certainty in the law by permitting rules to become settled. It protects the stability of society by allowing people (especially lawyers) to predict how a court is likely to decide a dispute. It serves a conserving function in terms of societal demands.

Competing precedents, to be sure, appear in many instances, so the doctrine of *stare decisis* is not a sure guide to the law. Uncertainty is increased by the dependency of a precedent upon an analogous fact situation, which may present great difficulties in an actual case. There is also a logical flaw in reasoning on the basis of a precedent, an excessive reliance upon deductive reasoning. Ultimately the application of a precedent-rule to a present dispute resembles the logic of a classical syllogism, and like the syllogism such a deduction can be artificial and unreal. Reliance upon precedent is a feeble substitute for inductive, or empirically-grounded social policy making, but it is the primary tool applied by American judges in resolving cases.

Statutes now form the primary type of input into the judicial system. A statutory input must be examined both for its meaning and for its

---

3. J. Woodford Howard, Jr., "On the Fluidity of Judicial Choice," *American Political Science Review*, 62 (March, 1968), pp. 43-56 makes this point very well.

possible violation of a constitutional norm, such as "due process" or "equal protection of the laws." Because of the separation of powers principle, there is an assumption in American courts (which is ignored at times) that statutes duly passed are constitutional.[4]

Statutory interpretation is not an automatic process. A statute can "mean" any of the following:

1. Exactly what it says, when the language precisely covers the facts at hand.
2. Approximately what it says, when the language can be expanded slightly to cover the facts at hand.
3. What the legislature "intended" when the language is unclear, ambiguous, or contradictory.
4. What the legislature may have "intended" if it had forseen the facts which are now at hand.
5. What a judge thinks a legislature would have wanted it to mean if the legislature had forseen the policy impact of a particular application of a statute.

Language is often ambiguous, as the philosophers now tell us. If ambiguity is to be clarified, then judges must impute a meaning to a statute where no clear meaning appears from the words themselves. Poor draftsmanship, the passage of time, and the occurrence of unforeseen events may all afflict a particular statute. Judges cannot ignore a statutory input, since it is a central part of many cases, and they must uncover a meaning for every statute which is not unconstitutionally vague.

A practical question which arises in many cases is what kind of extrinsic aids may be used by judges in interpreting statutes. Judges frequently quote Justice Holmes when seeking to avoid excessive reliance upon extraneous materials. Holmes commented, "I don't care what their intention was. I only want to know what their words mean." [5] However, Holmes also said that "the meaning of a statute is to be felt rather than to be proved." [6] The latter statement shows that subjective judicial judgments must enter into the interpretative process. The quest for legislative intent may involve the use of transcriptions of committee hearings or other papers introduced as evidence, the dictionary, the stated intent of the drafters at the time of the statute's introduction, and historical and sociological data. Ultimately, many public policies rest upon judicial good will in statutory interpretation for, in spite of all aids, no

4. Stated as early as 1827 by Justice Bushrod Washington in *Ogden v. Saunders*, 12 Wheaton 213, but adhered to with inconsistency by later courts.

5. Quoted at p. 538 by Justice Felix Frankfurter in his very valuable article, "Some Reflections on the Reading of Statutes," *Columbia Law Review*, Vol, 47 (1947), pp. 528-540.

6. *United States v. Johnson*, 221 U.S. 488, 496 (1911).

science of interpretation has emerged to guide the choice of judges—only a few questionable rules of thumb.

Another variety of formal inputs are rules and orders of administrative agencies. Many of these do not reach the courts, but when they do, the same regard is given them as other formal inputs. Each federal and state agency generates its own rules and orders, and it is likely that each is regarded somewhat differently by the courts. Judicial review of administrative rules and orders is expanding as these agencies proliferate. Although the agencies are often shielded from judicial oversight, there is an increasing distrust of administrative discretion.[7] In addition to the orders of administrative agencies, the President of the United States issues executive orders, usually pursuant to his statutory responsibilities—another type of administrative rule or order, but given great respect by courts.

Informal inputs could include almost an infinite variety of factors which might affect the judicial process: the weather, the temperament of a judge, the physical appearance of a witness, the concern of a juror to see his family, for example. But there are several type of informal inputs that occur with great frequency, and these can be isolated and examined. The distinction between an informal and a formal input is, however, important to maintain, because informal inputs are outside the official stream of communication and do not emanate as outputs from other portions of the political system. For this reason informal inputs are unlikely to be given full credit or recognition by the judicial process.

Interest-group activity, to be discussed further below, is one of the best examples of informal inputs. Interest-group efforts are usually specially geared to suit the judicial process. Several types of activities are engaged in, including: "class actions" in place of individual litigants, test cases, participation in cases as *amicus curiae*, (friends of the court) providing advice, information, service, expert testimony, research assistance or financial aid for litigants. These tactics may also be employed for official purposes by government agencies, so that tactics alone do not identify interest-group conduct. Empirical study shows that interest groups play an important though relatively minor role in Supreme Court decision making,[8] and by inference the same may be true in lower courts. The official input channels are used to a considerable extent.

7. See Theodore J. Lowi's, *The End of Liberalism* (W. W. Norton, 1969), an attack upon certain "liberal" assumptions, especially upon the "decline of law" inherent in an increasing resort to the administrative process.

8. Nathan Hakman, "Lobbying the Supreme Court—An Appraisal of Political Science Folklore," *Fordham Law Review*, 35 (1966), pp. 15-50.

Media input is more troublesome for the judicial system to deal with. In trials juries are shielded from receiving information bearing upon a case. Prior to trial it is hoped that jurors will not have been influenced deeply by their reading of the newspapers or viewing of television. This insulation of the jury from impressions derived from the media is most difficult in notorious cases, and when notoriety becomes excessive it may produce a mistrial.[9] Undue publicity of a notorious trial may also have dire effects upon the judicial process, although the permission to allow television cameras, photographers, or reporters into the courtroom is still a matter for judicial control.[10]

Media commentaries on current cases and trials can have a disturbing impact upon the judicial process. On the other hand the media have helped stir long-needed judicial and legal reforms. For example, the *New York Times* has been a staunch champion of judicial reform for New York State, and the Philadelphia newspapers have helped spur reform of the local court system in that city.

Political party input is another important informal element, especially at the local level. Federal judges, once appointed, are relatively immune from partisan requests, but judges subject to periodic re-election are sometimes more approachable for partisan purposes. The dimensions of this factor are very difficult to estimate, but it is clear that in some cities local magistrates are heavily influenced by party suggestions and by political string-pulling.

The community itself supplies informal inputs in the guise of generally held, though rarely articulated, social values. Judges, jurors, lawyers and law professors are all susceptible to such influences. Indeed, as active members of society, it is desirable that judges be aware of community sentiments and values. Such notions as efficiency, honesty, morality, the sanctity of the family, freedom of expression, and privacy are commonly held as important personal values. However, the judicial system cannot be dependent upon the current state of community values, nor can it mediate value conflicts effectively. A judge may have to insert his own value preferences into a case, but it is difficult to be certain that the judge is then acting as a typical member of the community or as a representative of its highest values.[11]

Within the judicial system there is an internal network of communication which is technically unofficial, but often appears to weigh heavily in judicial decisions at the appellate level. This network is comprised of

9. As in *Sheppard v. Maxwell*, 384 U.S. 333 (1966).

10. Alfred Friendly and Ronald L. Goldfarb, *Crime and Publicity* (Random House, 1967).

11. See Benjamin Cardozo, *The Nature of the Judicial Process* (Yale University Press, 1921).

law professors, law reviews, law institutes and a few recognized non-legal "experts." The feedback response of law reviews to a notable appellate decision is a good example of this network in action. These legal periodicals provide detailed analyses of legal doctrines which frequently surpass, in quality, the briefs of lawyers in a case. Increasingly such articles or notes are cited in appellate decisions to support an argument. Probably the better-read judges are more affected by such literature and by the esteem of the profession than by many other factors.

Demands

Inputs are more than formal expressions of law or informal activities of interested parties. They are also demands by individuals and groups for substantive justice. When dealing with such inputs, courts most fully reveal their political character. While most cases do not arise out of societal demands, many important judicial decisions do begin in some long-brewing social problem which reaches the attention of the courts.

A demand may be narrow, specific, or simple. It may arise from a particular calamity, such as a flood or an earthquake. A generalized plea for clean government, for more attention for Blacks or for Indians may also be considered a "demand"; and even the vague action programs of an ideology are so regarded by David Easton.[12] Obviously, courts cannot, and are not asked, to manage all these types of demands. Most of them are more likely to be directed at the legislature or the executive branch.

Increasingly courts are being asked to manage more kinds of social problems. Issues of the military draft, abortion, malapportionment, welfare reform, discrimination, the prosecution of a war, the proper forms of political protest, the activities of political parties, and many other matters previously regarded as beyond the scope of judicial ken have been raised in courtrooms around the country. A more politicized view of the role of courts in the political system has become more popular. A modern brief list of the topics of cognizance might include the following areas:

(a) regulating, protecting and supporting private property
(b) protecting the consumer
(c) regulating and sustaining family and social relationships, excluding religion
(d) regulating morality to a very limited extent
(e) regulating anti-social behavior defined as criminal by legislation
(f) protecting infants, juveniles, insane people, and incompetents

12. See David Easton, *A Systems Analysis of Political Life* (Wiley, 1965), p. 38.

(g) controlling bureaucratic and governmental discretionary acts, including those of the police

(h) supporting and regulating the electoral process, including representation

(i) correcting social injustices, under statutes

(j) adjusting political and social institutions to achieve more "democratic" ends

This list is not exhaustive. It merely indicates the range of possible judicial activity. The actual use of judicial power is dependent upon other variables, including judicial attitudes regarding the proper scope of activity.

Examining the judicial response to societal demands reveals an extremely circumspect attitude on the part of most judges. To an overwhelming extent American courts support or legitimatize the actions of other branches of government. Failure to do so would indicate an undemocratic tendency on the part of judges to dictate policy to more popular branches of government. Legitimatizing is the central judicial function because the courts are essentially supportive, not subversive of the regime. Courts must translate the general policies of government into the context of everyday affairs. No other group, not even administrative agencies, is given so broad a responsibility to fit public policy to actual events. This activity may seem to be counter-legitimatizing, but in a sense it merely supplements policy made by others with the felt need of the time. Courts are admirably equipped to bend and shape statutes and rulings without breaking or subverting them.

Organizing Demands

Individuals may introduce important issues into the judicial system to gain redress of individual demands. However, many of the far-reaching decisions of the federal courts, especially the Supreme Court, are the product of organized efforts on the part of established groups which seek to achieve common policy ends through the judiciary. Most interest groups do not use the path of the judicial process as a regular matter, but for some groups this approach has been most fruitful.

The National Association for the Advancement of Colored People has been one of the most successful groups in obtaining judicial support for preferred policies. The NAACP was formed in 1910 to defend the American Negro against discrimination. One of its avowed purposes was that of seeing that Negroes "get in the courts the same justice that is given to their white neighbors."

The legal strategy of the NAACP has always absorbed a large part of that organization's energies, and the objective of ending discrimination is peculiarly subject to judicial correction. The NAACP at first hoped to end housing discrimination merely by pointing out evils, but housing segregation became very popular in the pre-World War I years, so that the NAACP was rebuffed by city councils around the country. To correct the tide of discriminatory legislation, the NAACP turned to the courts, until by 1929 the enforcement of racial segregation by ordinance was virtually ended, at very low cost to the NAACP, which funded most of the cases brought to the Supreme Court.[13]

Direct action against official discrimination was a relatively simple matter because officially enforced segregation was a clear violation of the Fifth and Fourteenth amendments, as courts grudgingly came to perceive. The indirect method of housing discrimination by means of restrictive covenants in title deeds was a thornier problem. Private discrimination in the sale of housing was thought by many experts to be beyond the reach of the Fifth and Fourteenth amendments, which had been applied, by earlier precedents, against governmental action only. The NAACP's problem was to convince the Supreme Court that restrictive convenants should not be legally binding, and to get courts throughout the country to negate these discriminatory clauses in private deeds. In essence the NAACP desired judicial intervention against discrimination.

The slow process by which the NAACP gradually obtained this goal has been detailed elsewhere.[14] To change this policy the NAACP had first to convince state courts to accept jurisdiction. This was accomplished in a few states shortly after World War II, and some convenants were broken in a handful of lower state courts. A test in the United States Supreme Court was then deemed vital as property owners continued to gain victories in the state courts.

The NAACP coordinated the efforts of civil rights lawyers all over the country. Conferences were held and papers prepared to present the strongest possible brief for the NAACP position. Eventually, the Justice Department itself was persuaded to side with the anti-restrictive convenant policy. When the Supreme Court finally heard the major cases, the NAACP was joined by allies including the A.F.L., the C.I.O., the American Civil Liberties Union, the Congregational Christian Church, the National Lawyers Guild, and the American Jewish Congress.

The victories of the NAACP cannot be attributed solely to effective organization of demand. Changes in the personnel of the Supreme Court also took place about the same time. In addition there was a growing nationwide concern for the rights of Negroes. Even so, the restrictive covenant cases represented a sharp departure from earlier Supreme

13. The key cases are *Buchanan v. Warley*, 245 U.S. 60 (1917), and *Harmon v. Tyler*, 273 U.S. 668 (1927).
14. Clement Vose, *Caucasians Only* (University of California Press, 1959).

Court interpretations of the nature of state action. The Supreme Court was persuaded that judicial enforcement of private discriminatory agreements was a form of state action barred by the Fourteenth Amendment, rendering restrictive covenants judicially unenforceable.[15] The success of the NAACP in 1948 is made more apparent by the realization that the Supreme Court had consistently refused to hear a racial restrictive covenant case as late as 1945.

The achievements of the NAACP reached an acme in the landmark desegregation cases,[16] which attacked the laws and social practices of most of the nation. The NAACP did not accomplish this feat alone, but it spearheaded the legal struggle against segregationist policies. Many southern state legislatures counterattacked against the NAACP by enacting new laws intended to weed out NAACP members and to expose them to their neighbors. One of these statutes was aimed at the litigation activity of the NAACP, requiring disclosure of membership lists of groups financing litigation to which they were not parties. When tested in the Supreme Court, the Court struck down the statute on the ground that litigation was a legitimate form of political activity, protected by the First Amendment freedom of expression.[17]

The Court majority accepted the view, without much examination, of an identity of interest between individual litigants and groups which supported them. The possibility of conflict between the desires of individual litigants and the aims of supporting interest groups was not raised by Justice Brennan for the Court majority. In effect, the Supreme Court has shown itself willing to recognize the common practice of groups expressing demands in the form of individualized litigation, ratifying a practice of growing significance. The form of litigation remains in the name of individual litigants, but interest groups are often sponsors of group actions.

As mentioned earlier in this essay, interest-group activity may take varied forms. Perhaps of greatest significance today are "class action" cases and the *amicus curiae* brief by which a group may insert its own policy views into an ongoing case, which the Court may, in its discretion, accept.[18]

Lobbying in the form of litigation is a relatively uncommon activity,

15. *Shelley v. Kraemer*, 334 U.S. 1 (1948) is the main case concerning the Fourteenth Amendment. *Hurd v. Hodge*, 334 U.S. 24 (1948), reached the same result for the District of Columbia through a similar reading of the Fifth Amendment and the Civil Rights Act of 1866.

16. *Brown v. Board of Education of Topeka*, 347 U.S. 483 (1954), and 349 U.S. 294 (1955).

17. *NAACP v. Button*, 371 U.S. 415 (1963).

18. See Samuel Krislov, "The Amicus Curiae Brief: From Friendship to Advocacy," *Yale Law Journal*, Vol. 72 (1963), pp. 694-721.

in spite of the dramatic work of the NAACP and other civil rights organizations. The parties in most Supreme Court litigation are usually concerned with private victories and vindication. Most Supreme Court cases represent individualized commercial or proprietary matters in which the real party-in-interest is usually the man or the company whose name appears in the pleading papers. This does not mean that important demands are not involved in many Supreme Court cases. The impact of Supreme Court cases usually extends far beyond the actual parties. Demands are typically organized by large groups only on highly visible issues. Private companies, labor unions, professional associations and business groups rarely engage in demand organization, while civil liberties groups are much more active.[19]

Group articulation of demand is probably even less prevalent at the lower echelons of the federal courts or in the state courts. Within those tribunals few cases of great significance arise on daily calendars.[20] Litigation management, in the form of selecting appropriate cases for appellate review, is a preferred and an economical tactic. Few groups are well-enough financed or staffed to engage in demand articulation at the lower levels of the judicial heirarchy, although the amount of such activity is not known.

It should be mentioned that the federal government and its various agencies is a major participant in the judicial process, in this way forming its own demands, or sponsoring the demands of others. The Justice Department and attorneys from other federal agencies present more than half the cases heard by the Supreme Court. Most of these cases involve technical administrative questions requiring statutory interpretation. State and local government agencies also are frequently before the Court, arguing for broader powers over taxation, labor relations, education, or for immunity against national or private action. Consequently, most cases heard before the Supreme Court are actually efforts by one branch or level of government to gain legitimacy for a policy position through the use of the courts. Demand articulation takes place by one decision-maker to be processed by another.

Amicus curiae activity by the federal government is unusual, but it has proven helpful to the NAACP and some other civil rights organiza-

19. This is apparent from *amicus curiae* activity. See Table 3 in Hakman, "Lobbying the Supreme Court," p. 44. This inference was supported by interviewing.

20. It is the author's impression that state and local ACLU chapters are most active in articulating claims of right at the trial court and state appellate levels. This group recognizes that individual rights are often sacrificed or curtailed if not defended in the courts as promptly as possible. There is also some evidence of other interest "group agitation for judicial review of state and municipal public policy" (Clement E. Vose, "Interest Groups, Judicial Review, and Local Government," *Western Political Quarterly*, 19 (March, 1966), pp. 85-100.

tions in gaining victories over state agencies and private parties. Many federal agencies suggest a statutory interpretation to the Supreme Court in the light of their administrative needs. State and local governments sometimes use litigation as a means of gaining partisan advantages,[21] but, more commonly they participate as principals in a case, joining together on a handful of issues such as the offshore oil lands which concerned many states, or more recently as *amicus curiae* in reapportionment and desegregation cases.

Demands in Criminal Justice

In the criminal justice system the impulse to make a major change in public policy is rarely evident. Most criminal cases seem to involve the fate of a handful of individuals, some of them obviously deviant. However, the prosecution of certain kinds of cases is highly political in impact, and large segments of the population can be affected by a governmental decision to institute legal action in the criminal courts. Those areas of the criminal law which verge most closely upon public policy issues include protection, antitrust, fraud, civil rights, pollution, labor and health. Different administrations may make the political choice of prosecuting offenses in one or more of these categories, or of over-looking violations. The decision to prosecute is subject to demands from the general public, from special publics, or from within the bureaucracy.

After a decade in which the rate of reported crime has increased by almost 148 percent, demands for more and better law enforcement have come from all quarters of society. White and Black, rich and poor, suburbanite and city-dweller have joined the outcry for better controls on crime. That the problem goes much deeper than the level of criminal prosecution is of course a truism, but unavoidably the demand for crime control has been read to mean a demand for stiffer prosecution and stiffer punishment of law violators (except, perhaps, of marijuana users).

In the criminal justice system the prosecuting attorney enjoys a central position. He "exercises the influence of leadership for all those . . . agencies that play a part in the system of criminal justice." [22] The grand jury, the coroner's office, parole boards and even, to an extent, the criminal courts are subject to his policy decisions. These decisions are made in an atmosphere of enormous legal discretion, which formally permits the prosecutor to pick and choose his cases.[23] The prosecutor is subject to few political checks upon his powers, since he is elected in the states

21. Kenneth M. Dolbeare, *Trial Courts in Urban Politics* (Wiley, 1967) pp. 45-51.
22. *The Administration of Criminal Justice in the United States* (American Bar Foundation, 1955), p. 83.
23. George F. Cole, "The Politics of Prosecution: The Decision to Prosecute," an unpublished Ph.D. dissertation, University of Washington, 1968, is the best source.

for lengthy terms, while federal attorneys are subject to the politics of appointment, following a turnover in national administrations.

The typical prosecuting attorney is subject to demands and pressures emanating from several sources within and outside the criminal justice system. For example, it is known that courts exercise a restraining influence on prosecutors in subtle ways. The tendency of a judge to give heavy or light sentences, or to dismiss weak cases, is a major determinant of the prosecutor's decision to prosecute or to bargain for a guilty plea. If the prosecutor feels that a particular judge is unsympathetic to his view of law enforcement, he may attempt to avoid him or simply settle for a lesser plea in order to obtain a guilty verdict. In this situation the uncooperative judicial attitude may express an inarticulate demand for less active or less harsh prosecution.

The demand for action against criminals today is generated from outside the criminal justice system. Politicians have articulated a public sense of increased anxiety about crime. For many citizens the courts are held responsible for the alleged "crime wave." Judges, though insulated from the direct impact of popular demand, do seem to be stiffening their punishment of offenders, and the federal Congress has conferred upon judges of the District of Columbia sweeping discretionary powers to detain offenders prior to trial. This grant of power may mean a mere surface response to public demand, but more suspects are certain to be jailed as a result.

There are many factors, social, political and personal, which influence the decision to prosecute. The impact of public demand, so strong if often unreasoned in recent years, is difficult to measure. From all appearances, public demand has not yet had a major effect upon the criminal justice system. If this is true, the explanation is to be found in the complexity of the system. Until judges, legislators, police, criminal lawyers, probation officers, and prosecutors can be brought to greater agreement about the proper treatment of offenders, the impact of public demands is likely to be minimized.

Processing Demands

The many political demands brought to the judiciary place it in a difficult situation. The failure of a system to fulfill demands, as Easton suggests, may lead to decline in support for the system. On the other hand, excessive demands placed upon a system may produce a "demand input overload," [24] making it difficult to continue operation. To regulate the flow of demands, "gatekeeping" devices are employed. This task

24. Easton, *Systems Analysis*, p. 58, note 102.

is performed for the judicial system by lawyers, by government agencies (especially the Justice Department), and by business corporations or interest groups which may sponsor suits. Judges, too, act as gatekeepers by encouraging out-of-court settlements or simply by denying or dismissing appeals.[25]

The main judicial rubrics for processing demands are "justiciability," "standing," "jurisdiction," "political question," and the concept of "judicial self-restraint." All of these devices provide the judiciary with the opoprtunity to reject an input, to avoid an issue, or to narrow the scope of judicial treatment of the problem. In the federal courts manipulation of the statutory rights of appeal and certiorari also permit great judicial flexibility in managing demands. Without these tools to avoid inputs the courts would be flooded with work and would be forced to deal with sensitive policy matters which they may not be prepared to confront.

In common law pleading, relief could not be given a plaintiff except in terms of the original writ. For each "cause of action" there was an appropriate writ. Failure to choose the correct writ would bar the court from acquiring jurisdiction of the case. Today most states have abandoned the strict pleading required by the common law, with the federal courts taking a very liberal view of pleading papers. However, the idea of jurisdiction remains important. It means that at least one party to the suit must be physically within the territory to which the power of the courts extend. In many cases, it means that the property in question must also be located within the boundaries of judicial power. Jurisdiction is often defined by statutes which confer the power to act upon a court.

The federal Constitution prescribes the essential jurisdictional boundaries for the federal courts. The Constitution speaks of "cases" and "controversies" in Article III, section 2. This has been interpreted by the Supreme Court to require adverse litigants, ones presenting an honest and antagonist assertion of legal claims. False disputes or concocted controversies are avoided by the federal courts, although many "test cases" carry with them a certain degree of artificiality.[26]

The Supreme Court is subject to many other statutory and constitutional limits upon its jurisdiction. However, the most important restrictions are those which the court has placed upon itself. Even the original jurisdiction of the Supreme Court, defined in the Constitution

25. Sheldon Goldman and Thomas Jahnige, "Systems Analysis and Judicial Systems: Potential and Limitations," an unpublished paper delivered at 1969 meetings of the American Political Science Association, p. 12.
26. Compare *Muskrat v. United States*, 262 U.S. 447 (1923) with the strained situation in *Griswold v. Connecticut*, 381 U.S. 479 (1965).

and under several statutes, is limited by the procedural rules prescribed by the Supreme Court.

As for Supreme Court review of state court decisions the basic statute permits appeal wherever a state statute is upheld as against its claimed invalidity because of its repugnancy to the federal Constitution or because a treaty or federal statute is denounced. To these provisions the judiciary has engrafted the requirement that the federal question presented must be a "substantial" one. Without this ingredient a case will be dismissed for "want of jurisdiction." [27] In addition the substantial federal question must be presented "distinctly and positively," or else Supreme Court review will be limited only to those questions properly raised.[28] These and other jurisdictional rules are subject to some judicial manipulation as the occasion warrants.

The Supreme Court has placed a number of self-imposed limitations upon its power of review. One of the most important, and sensitive, of these is the "political question" doctrine. This rule enables the Court to refuse to decide a question because it is a political one. The 1962 Reapportionment Case [29] revealed clearly that the political-question doctrine was a fuzzy rule of convenience, which could be invoked on delicate matters as long as the Court wished to avoid an issue. However, when demands are great enough, the Court may, and did in 1962, cast aside this self-restraining rule to plunge into a purported "political thicket." Apparently the Supreme Court was convinced by 1962 that the proper time had come to respond to numerous demands to correct the malapportionment which plagued state legislatures.

An arsenal of other convenient concepts is available to the Supreme Court if it wishes to avoid or sidetrack an input or a demand. Mootness, the ripeness doctrine, justiciability, standing to sue, collusion, and refusal to pass upon constitutionality except when "necessary" (or when alternative non-constitutional grounds are not available) may each be invoked. Each doctrine has its own body of law, but the Court need not abide by previous interpretations when invoking such a self-limiting rule. The grant of the writ of *certiorari*, created by statute, is clearly a matter of judicial discretion, but in the final analysis most jurisdictional questions are discretionary anyway. Furthermore, even if the Court takes a case, the issues may be sharply constricted by the opinion.

Every American appellate court has developed discretionary methods for avoiding issues. Only at the bottom echelons, in the trial courts, must issues (demands) be given some kind of hearing. Even there, judges, following the lead of the Supreme Court, may avoid the issues

27. See *Equitable Life Assurance Society v. Brown*, 187 U.S. 308 (1902).
28. E.g., *Steinbridge v. Georgia*, 343 U.S. 541 (1952).
29. *Baker v. Carr*, 369 U.S. 186.

in various ways. When this occurs, the demand or input is frustrated or deflected into some other outlet.

OUTPUTS OF THE JUDICIAL SYSTEM

For society, as for the individuals involved, the most important part of the judicial process is its results, or outputs. Legal outputs vary, however, in their relative importance and effect. Strictly speaking, the legal system recognizes the binding effect of a judicial decision only for the parties to be a particular dispute, and then only for the facts and issues which actually were in dispute between them. For lawyers this kind of output is entirely adequate because it permits them to close their files on a case and collect a fee from a client.

This undramatic ending is of no importance to society generally. Only those outcomes which indirectly become influential for other parts of the social and political system are worthy of general attention. These decisions of broader impact disclose whatever responsiveness the legal system has to the wider demands of the social or political system.

Not all judges are in the same position to render socially significant decisions. Responsiveness cannot, accordingly, be detected at every level of the judiciary. For example, in the federal district courts the cases in two crucial areas—civil rights and labor relations—have been managed disproportionately. Judge Skelly Wright of the eastern Louisiana district handled twice as many cases as any other judge in his area, while his colleague, Judge Christenberry of the same district, handled very few. Apparently Judge Wright's favorable treatment of plaintiffs in civil rights cases (especially race relations cases) has brought forth exceptional demands upon him so that "litigants unable to secure favorable decisions elsewhere in Louisiana regarded the district court in New Orleans as a haven to which they might turn for favorable judgments on civil liberties problems." [30]

No doubt other judges attract special demands as their reputations spread. The demands made upon a judge are fed by the expectations about his behavior which his past record stimulates. At the local level most lawyers know the political outlook of the local bench, and heavily political cases are likely to flow into that magnetic field. Perhaps it would be more accurate to speak of responsiveness in individual judges, rather than of whole court systems or levels; but aside from the Supreme Court little hard data has been as yet assembled.

Legal outputs are produced by political organizations as well as by

30. Richard C. Richardson and Kenneth N. Vines, *The Politics of Federal Courts* (Little, Brown, 1970), p. 101.

courts. In this sense a statute is an output of a legislative body, and an administrative rule is an output of a bureaucratic body. Typical outputs flowing from the judiciary include verdicts, court orders, and judgments. Criminal and civil verdict outputs differ a great deal because the structure of the output formation process favors the criminal defendant (the "beyond a reasonable doubt" rule). In spite of this formal barrier the prosecution often wins, but is barred in most states from appealing an acquittal, should the defendant win.

The most notable difference in legal outputs is the nature of the penality paid by the loser. A criminal risks fine or imprisonment. In civil suits damages, alimony, adjudication of bankruptcy, or a host of other outcomes is possible. Most of these matters are subpolitical, but some studies of verdict outcomes have political and social ramifications. For example, a New Jersey study of death sentences suggests that sex and race may be significant factors in handing down this grave penalty.[31] Assessing the sentencing behavior of judges is a risky business; it may come down to "the judge's own character, as influenced by legal controls and advice of others." [32] This area needs a great deal of attention if consistent sentencing results responsive to community needs and the welfare of the individuals concerned are to be obtained.

Outputs in the Supreme Court

Among the most dramatic outputs are the actions of the Supreme Court of the United States. Whether taking the form of the exercise of the formidable power of judicial review to strike down a statute, executive order or administrative decree, or merely interpreting a statute to give it a narrow construction, a Supreme Court opinion is read with great care and a fairly high proportion of them have sufficient impact to be marked down as political in effect. Given the scope of the Supreme Court's responsibilities, even a labor law decision or a government contract ruling is an output which touches many businesses and employers around the country.

The Supreme Court is, by force of the definition of politics, a political tribunal. Even when the Supreme Court declines to take jurisdiction of a case, the ripples of its decision—denial of certiorari—may be felt in many corners of the nation. Denial of certiorari is said by the Court to have no legal significance, but even if this is true (and lawyers dispute it), the effect may be to leave standing some dubious governmental

31. H. Bedau, "Death Sentences in New Jersey," *Rutgers Law Review,* 19 (1964), pp. 1-31.
32. John G. George, "Sentencing Methods and Techniques in the United States," *Federal Probation,* 26 (1962), p. 38.

practice. The Supreme Court, steeped in politics, is an obvious place at which to chart the ebb and flow of demand and response in American political life. Furthermore, some of the most vital political issues which have troubled the nation have been judicialized and ultimately managed by the Supreme Court. Kenneth Vines, writing about state supreme courts, has penned a passage which applies only to a lesser extent to the federal Supreme Court:

> Supreme Court decisions often occur at or near the end of the political process. . . . Thus a Court decision may end a long and troublesome argument that has developed in the political system or may point the way to a settlement of a serious grievance." [33]

Supreme Court cases do not always finish the struggle. Sometimes the issue is beyond judicial control, and the function of the Court in finalizing political disputes may be thwarted. Then, too, the Court may generate new political disputes, especially when it takes unpopular positions. Though insulated by traditional judicial independence from the political attitudes of the mass public, the Court cannot avoid for long the political backlash of popular discontent. The Supreme Court tends to trade upon an enormous store of esteem and popular awe, which preserves it from all but its most persistent critics. Indeed, the Supreme Court does not follow the election returns, as Mr. Dooley once claimed, but the mass public's dim awareness of the Supreme Court may be its greatest boon. Some empirical studies have shown that "critics are more likely to have paid attention to it than its supporters," [34] and the evidence suggests that the Court has its greatest effectiveness when the public is acquiescent and unaroused. [35]

Probably the major consequence of Supreme Court activity is to confer legitimacy upon the actions of other government agencies and upon the Constitution itself. The Court rarely runs counter to the dominant political values of the day, except in periods of unusual obstinacy. [36] Generally the Court has played the role of accommodating the Constitution to contemporary needs and, in recent times, of in-

33. Kenneth N. Vines, "Political Functions of a State Supreme Court," in Vines and Herbert Jacob, eds., *Studies in Judicial Politics* (Tulane University Press, 1963), p. 56.

34. John H. Kessell, "Public Perceptions of the Supreme Court," *Midwest Journal of Political Science*, 19 (1966), p. 188.

35. Kenneth M. Dolbeare, "The Public Views the Supreme Court," in Herbert Jacob, ed., *Law, Politics and the Federal Courts* (Little, Brown, 1967), p. 211.

36. This is the view of Robert Dahl, supported in "Decision-Making in a Democracy: The Role of the Supreme Court as a National Policy-Maker," *Journal of Public Law*, 6 (1957), pp. 280-296.

corporating the public policies of the dominant political alliance in the context of the Constitution. The Court has usually smoothed the path of change and has made the welfare state with its intrusive policies less offensive to the American public.

When the Supreme Court speaks out on behalf of political dissenters, minority group members, religious dissenters, criminal defendants, and other unpopular individuals, it risks public condemnation. The Warren Court was subjected to severe criticism in this regard, ultimately being drawn into the presidential election campaign of 1968. The "law and order" issue which helped elect Mr. Nixon also led to the appointment of less adventuresome justices to the high bench. But there is little doubt that most Americans regard the Supreme Court as a welcome defender of individual rights. So, if in the short run the Court has been "unresponsive" to the mood of the majority, there seems, in the long run to have been a grudging recognition on the part of most people that the Supreme Court was performing its task well, even its difficult task of defending and expanding the Bill of Rights.[37]

The Impact of the Judicial Opinion

The judicial opinion can carry diverse meanings and communicate multiple messages. Its impact, therefore, can extend considerably beyond the case at hand. An opinion may supply a definitive meaning for a statutory phrase, even though it technically is addressed only to the parties in the case before the court. The opinion resolves the legal issue in the case and at the same time supplies a message to the various audiences which the opinion is intended to reach. In essence, a judicial opinion is intended to communicate with several audiences at the same time, conveying doctrinal meanings to lawyers, other judges, administrative agencies, law professors, law reviews, and (to a much lesser extent) to political leaders and the general public. For this reason responsiveness in the usual sense of mass democratic accountability is neither the intention nor the result of judicial activities. The audience for judicial opinions is far too narrow and specialized for that.

In a less obvious way courts may use their opinions to send messages to interest groups. To take a notable example, the Supreme Court, over the years, has become able to determine the nature of its workload according to its own lights. The Court has broad discretion to take or to avoid cases. Although the Court is essentially passive in receiving cases brought to it, by subtle hints scattered in opinions a signal may be broadcast that the Court is ready to consider a case in a manner favorable

---

37. Considerable fluctuation in public attitudes took place from 1966 to 1968, as reflected in Gallup polls. The downward direction of public opinion in those difficult years now seems to have been reversed.

to a group. In school segregation the Supreme Court sent, and the NAACP received, certain case-opinion signals prior to the 1954 desegregation opinions. Less obvious signals have been conveyed through opinions respecting criminal procedures, labor law and reapportionment. These hints may be deliberately placed or unconsciously mixed in among other issues in an opinion; but regardless of the Court's open intention, its opinions are scanned avidly by lawyers for a possible clue to an impending change of attitude.

A judicial opinion is not intended to reach the mass public directly. Few laymen ever read judicial decisions. Few newspapers print their full text. Information about the opinions is usually sensationalized and oversimplified for a handful of cases, and simply not provided for the rest. Copies of particular opinions can be obtained by anyone from the Government Printing Office shortly after publication, but publication may occur as late as a year after the decision is handed down, and the correct name of the case may not be known to laymen, who also have no easy access to the professional law journals most apt to review the case.

The wire services, Associated Press and United Press International, are the principal sources of public knowledge of Supreme Court opinions. State and federal appellate court opinions are occasionally reported, but only when highly newsworthy. The wire services translate judicial opinions into more eye-catching news stories, a process which is likely to convey to the public false or distorted impressions of case opinions. Even the *New York Times*, which provides its own reporters to cover the Court, has been guilty of inaccurate news stories regarding judicial opinions. But it sometimes prints a decision in its entirety, and it is to the *Times* that public officials and highly interested private citizens usually turn for basic information.[38]

Judges of lower federal courts and state courts may be well read in recent cases, but usually lawyers must alert them to new case developments. Lawyers appear to be the major recipients, readers and translators of case opinions, but no lawyer can possibly keep abreast of all the decisions of all the courts in which he practices. He relies to a great extent on legal services, to which he subscribes, to keep himself posted, and on major law libraries where he will encounter cases indexed and briefed in the course of preparing a case for a client. In this fashion case opinions are typically absorbed by lawyers, digested and resubmitted to the courts. If lawyers are not efficient or competent, they may miss or misunderstand important opinions. Furthermore, "if counsel does not

---

38. David L. Grey, *The Supreme Court and the News Media* (Northwestern University Press, 1968), p. 74.

call such cases to the judge's attention, the latter might not know the relevant cases that exist." [39]

Ultimately judicial opinions become new inputs. Emphasis upon the self-regulating aspects of the judicial process has recently become more prevalent. The term "feedback" has been borrowed by social scientists to describe the activity. A portion of the output of a system becomes an input of the same system at some future point. This circular process helps keep the system in balance by correcting its errors or setting boundaries for its determinations. Courts receive a variety of inputs, including earlier case opinions, in the course of considering a current dispute. There are many kinds of inputs, some of which emanate from the mass public or from political officials, but on the whole case precedent is still important. The Supreme Court is less likely to follow case precedents than other courts, and consequently is more open to other inputs, including political and social factors.[40] The feedback analogy can be overdrawn, however, and considerable leeway, or "fluidity of judicial choice" is available to most judges at the higher levels.

THE FUTURE OF THE JUDICIAL SYSTEM

The inputs and demands upon the judicial system have increased so greatly that its future capacity is uncertain. There are many signs of strain and even of breakdown in the judicial system. In the civil courts of New York County a personal injury case takes slightly more than four years from the complaint stage until a jury trial is obtained. On the criminal side the problem is even worse because delay in trial or backlog may mean prolonged jail detention for some individuals or a continual fear of criminal punishment for others. In the federal courts in 1969, of 17,770 criminal cases pending in the district courts, 2,200 were more than two years old. In New York City in the same year the total backlog of nontraffic criminal cases was more than half a million cases for the several levels of criminal courts. Given a legislative propensity to create more and more criminal categories, a higher arrest rate, a complicated set of pre-trial protections for accused persons, and a growing crime rate, a sharp increase in the number of cases reaching the courts in recent years was inevitable and has taken place.

Statistics on court delay are very unreliable. Many cases, especially criminal suits, do not have a readily identifiable beginning, since arrest does not always result in prosecution. Furthermore, many cases are

39. Richard Johnson, *The Dynamics of Compliance* (Northwestern University Press, 1967), p. 62.

40. See Jay A. Sigler, "A Cybernetic Model of the Judicial System," *Temple Law Quarterly*, 41 (1968), pp. 398-428.

negotiated to resolution during the early phases of litigation. So when a case may be said to commence varies according to what is considered to be the actual inception of a case. Even the filing of a complaint is no sure clue to inception, since many complaints are filed and some placed upon court calendars with no expectation of actually going to trial. However, in spite of the paucity of reliable statistics, the problem of delay and congestion is evident and is rapidly growing. In an age of "law and order" the major safeguard of fair treatment, the court system, is being prodded to create assembly-line justice in order to clear court calendars or to "protect" the public against the risks of growing amounts of anti-social behavior. The pressure on the courts has become a socially and politically important influence, and one to which judges are responding. Hasty decisions may be made in such an atmosphere, and injustices may arise from such haste.

Chief Justice Burger has suggested that courts must get rid of the techniques of the "cracker-barrel corner grocery store" era, borrowing from the experience of modern management to streamline services. This would mean computerization of court calendaring and scheduling to cut down some currently wasteful practices and speed the processing of cases. There is no doubt that appointing more judges would be an even more useful reform to break the bottlenecks of justice, but there is little political support for either proposal, in spite of the relatively low costs involved. Furthermore, the leisurely pace of judicial work would have to be abandoned if greater efficiency within the system is to be obtained, a change which many judges would resist.

Another major cause of trial delays is hard to reach—dilatory tactics of lawyers. Many lawyers deliberately delay and postpone the day of trial in order to gain more time for bargaining. This practice is common on both the civil and the criminal side of law practice. In addition to a possible tactical advantage a lawyer may have in mind his law office maintenance problem—the work flow—which for many lawyers is crucial to an efficient and profitable law office. So naturally enough lawyers try to inventory their work ahead and to budget their time in the courtroom. The result is that courts are often adjusting their trial schedules to suit the convenience or the tactics of counsel. As Professor Alfred Conard has said:

> Even if it were possible to elect enough judges, build enough courtrooms, and draft enough jurors to cut down the trial backlog, a part of the problem would remain uncorrected. Lawyers would still threaten to hold out until trial as a bargaining device when they think the nerves or resources of the opponent are unequal to their own.[41]

41. "The Economic Treatment of Automobile Injuries," *Michigan Law Review*, 63 (1964), p. 315.

Many of the problems of judicial overload could be corrected without touching the major causes of court difficulties, which are created by public demands as reflected in legislative actions. The fact is that the courts are assigned many tasks by legislation for which they are ill-suited. The most numerous categories of cases in both the civil and criminal area are managed by the courts only as a matter of custom and public expectation. It would be possible to strip the courts of jurisdiction over many of these cases and to manage them administratively, but to do so would require a major adjustment in thinking by the public and by politicians.

A good place to start to lighten court loads would be with auto accidents and traffic offenses. Automobile accidents consume one-third of the time of all civil litigation. A growing body of legal opinion holds that these cases could be managed better in some administrative fashion. Traffic offenses are the largest category of "criminal offenses," even though the real purpose of traffic laws is to permit maximum safety, maximum flow and minimum inconvenience to the public. The application of criminal sanctions such as a fine, imprisonment or license suspension may be ineffectual and counterproductive to these ends. Certainly, much of the time of police departments and magistrates is expended on this essentially non-criminal matter.

The criminal characteristics of many kinds of behavior are created only by legislative designation, not by something inherent in the conduct. The tendency to manage social problems through the courts shows a certain social blindness, an unwillingness to treat problems in a flexible manner. Drunkenness, narcotics addiction, homosexuality, housing violations, and licensing violations are often turned over to the courts as a kind of social dumping ground, rather than as part of a rational social policy. The crisis in court management is, in part, the product of social indifference and insensitivity.

"Overload" is a technical term in cybernetics, engineering and communication theory. For our purposes, the idea that a system is receiving more input than it can bear can be applied to the judicial process. There are definite signs of overload leading to breakdown of parts of the judicial system. Too many social problems are being referred to the courts rather than being resolved on other political levels. The relegation of a pattern of behavior to a criminal category is an admission of social strain. The drug abuse problem, racial relations, housing, education and environmental pollution have all been judicialized, often without great success. The inability of courts to meet the growing demands of a burdened society is not just due to antiquated procedures or insufficient resources; it is a symptom of social unrest which could lead to social breakdown.

American courts have withstood almost two centuries of challenge, but they cannot resolve all the unsettled social issues which have been allowed to ferment over those years. The courts are not likely to collapse under the demands of recent years, but they cannot be expected to handle problems which other parts of the political system have avoided or postponed because of the difficulties they present.

THE JUDICIAL

INSTITUTION

Many influences affect the American judiciary. Here we shall first consider three important doctrinal factors: the common law, the concept of separation of powers, and the theory of judicial review, We shall then examine the formal structure of the courts and, finally, selected aspects of judicial behavior.

The Common Law Background

Common law was the predominant style of law in English-speaking nations until the twentieth century. Common law is a vast body of judge-made legal principles, found in the scattered opinions of numerous jurists. It is not a fixed body of definite rules, but rather a loose-knit grouping of concepts which is not found in any single location. In fact, it is more a method and a mood than a strict set of principles. Based upon precedents, the common law is built upon continuity between the past and the present by means of printed case opinions which provide guides for the present in rulings of the past. Common law expands by accretion of judicial opinions decade after decade, continually refining legal principles.

Common law emerged from English experience before legislation was developed as a means of setting public policies. As legislation has expanded, the common law areas have correspondingly shrunk. Common law has been supplanted by legislation to large degree in all American states. Nonetheless, the habits of common law thinking have been retained by judges and lawyers. Precedents still provide guidance to present and future actions of courts. Judicial rulings interpreting statutes have become significant sources of policy. The practical, flexible quality of the common law enables judges to fill gaps between statutes, to supply meaning to ambiguous phrases, and to give shape and coherence to the extremely complicated and numerous legal doctrines which a mass society has required. Those who seek to know what the law in America is must first read the Constitution, then the basic statutes, and conclude their research by examining judicial opinions interpreting all these texts.

The common law view of the proper scope of the judicial function has had great influence. In the works of Sir William Blackstone, one of the most famous jurists in legal history, one finds a most ambitious description of the scope of judicial authority. The judges "are the depositaries of the laws; the living oracles, who must decide in all cases of doubt." The wisdom and insight of judges stems from their experience and study. Their decisions "are the principal and the most authoritative evidence, that can be given, of the existence of such a custom as shall form a part of the common law." [1]

Few judges would claim such wide power today, but there is little doubt that the common law outlook has both broadened the claims of judicial power and narrowed the use of that power. When Blackstone wrote his *Commentaries* during the eighteenth century, the power of the Parliament was being developed, and the power of the common law courts contracted. However the idea of a judge as a source of law, as well as its interpreter has remained alive in the common law tradition. This view, which is essentially aristocratic, prevents courts from being completely responsive to popular demands. American judges particularly must never forget, as John Marshall once declared for his fellow justices: "that it is a constitution we are expounding," [2] and American courts sometimes do declare legislative acts unconstitutional.

The American legal system grew from the rich historic soil of the English common law. America did not suddenly or unconsciously adopt the English idea of common law. On the contrary, in colonial Massachusetts the Bible provided the first legal text.[3] Post-Revolutionary leaders drafted specific documents such as our Constitution and the Bill of Rights, but this was a brief flirtation with codification. There was a gradual reversion to the common law, an acceptance of the older English tradition, which assigned greater responsibility to judges and less to legislators.

Jeremy Bentham offered his services to President Madison in 1811 for

1. *Commentaries on the Laws of England* (American ed.; Callaghan & Cockroft, 1871), Vol. I, p. 69.
2. *McCulloch* v. *Maryland*, 4 Wheat. 316 (1819).
3. Roscoe Pound, *The Formative Era of American Law* (Little, Brown, 1938).

the purpose of providing America with a code. The territory of New Orleans, detached from French control, did adopt a Civil Code, modeled after the French, in 1808. In spite of the obvious appeal of a consciously designed package of laws, the national government rejected the idea of wholesale codification. A number of states did experiment with the practice, but, with the possible exception of Louisiana, no genuine written, systematic, comprehensive code of laws exists in the United States. The writings of prominent conservative jurists, such as Chancellor James Kent[4] and Justice Joseph Story in the 1820s and 1830s, supported this renewal of regard for the common law, and with it they encouraged a necessary growth in the power and influence of the judiciary in the United States.

There are, in fact, many differences between English and American versions of common law. The impossibility of applying many traditional English doctrines to American conditions was quickly recognized by most lawyers and judges. In addition, a great deal of legislative activity at the state and local level has displaced large segments of the common law with legislatively directed policies. Even so, the very willingness to admit that the United States is a common law nation strengthens the hand of the judiciary. The common law was "discovered" by English judges as part of the normal role assigned them by English legal tradition. In the American context judges could conceive of their role as akin to that of their English counterparts. Quite simply, the "common law presupposes the existence of a court," [5] and judges have regarded themselves as sources of law, or at least law interpreters.

Technically there is no federal common law. In spite of this fact, the habits of common law thinking continue to be instilled in judges and lawyers as a result of common law training in the law schools, reinforced by traditional thought in the legal profession. Many judges of the federal courts and the state courts agree that, in addition to the specific provisions of the Constitution there is a "law of the land" which aids jurists in ascertaining the meaning of the Constitution. At one time in American legal history, judges attempted to resolve difficult cases in terms of a "higher law" which may have been an amalgam of the common law and certain natural law beliefs.[6] Although judges have largely abandoned such metaphysical notions, the sense that there is an objective body of law which the judges find and declare still persists as a vestige of Blackstonian thinking.

4. James Kent, *Commentaries on American Law*, 12th ed. (Little, Brown, 1873).
5. Rene David and John E. C. Brierly, *Major Legal Systems in the World Today* (The Free Press, 1968), p. 351.
6. See Edward S. Corwin, *The "Higher Law" Background of American Constitutional Law* (Great Seal Books, 1957, originally written in 1938).

To those brought up in the formalistic setting of the American public schools, rigidly held ideas about the proper role of the courts would seem to come naturally. The simple formula of the separation of powers concept is usually committed to memory. Under this categorical view of American government, the proper role of the legislature is to enact the laws, the executive to enforce them, and the courts to interpret them. Very few students, and perhaps few of their teachers, perceive that this formula is purely linguistic. It does not correspond to reality, nor has it ever.

It is probable that most members of the public do not understand the concept of separation of powers, yet many judges and lawyers believe in a rigid approach to the scope of judicial power, partly in the belief that the public expects judges to avoid policy making. The few glimpses available concerning public attitudes toward the courts provide glaring evidence of a misunderstanding of the judicial role in a separation of powers system. In a 1966 survey the constitutional role of the Supreme Court was simply not known to sixty percent of the respondents.[7] The separation of powers concept is dimly perceived by most citizens in spite of public education, although awareness of the formal judicial role increases with education.

The mixing of the roles of legislation and adjudicating was commonplace in medieval England. As late as the fourteenth century, no distinction was made by judges between their decisions and acts of Parliament.[8] In the United States the separation between legislation and adjudication has been clearly maintained from the beginning. Legislation, the positive actions of an elected legislature, is seen as the primary source of public policy. Judicial activity has been largely confined to interpretation of legislation and to continuing the remaining judge-made areas of law which is found in the common law.

The doctrine of separation of powers, which is found in the writings of Locke and Montesquieu, among others, became very important in America especially after the Revolutionary War. Locke regarded the judiciary as part of the executive branch, lacking an independent status.

7. Walter F. Murphy and Joseph Tanenhaus, "Public Opinion and the United States Supreme Court" in Joel B. Grossman and Joseph Tanenhaus, *Frontiers of Judicial Research* (Wiley, 1969), pp. 280-283. The question asked was: Now I'd like to ask you what you think the Supreme Court's main job in the government is, as you understand it. I mean, what kind of thing do you think the Supreme Court in Washington is supposed to do? A vast range of responses was considered acceptable, but nonconstitutional categories, such as "to say what the law means" or "to maintain peace and order" were not accepted.

8. T. F. T. Plunknett, *Statutes and Their Interpretation in the First Half of the Fourteenth Century* (Cambridge University Press, 1922), pp. 22-25.

In America the judiciary was treated as a distinct and separate branch of government. Under a pure theory of separation of powers the judicial function would never be mingled with the legislative or executive functions. However, this extreme view of separation of powers is based upon a misconception of the methods by which policy is made. In fact, "the exclusive allocation of rule-making, rule application, or rule-adjudication to particular organs of government is not only inconvenient, it is probably quite impossible." [9] Even so, the view persists that judges must only adjudicate, and avoid policy making or policy enforcing activities. This mechanical view of separation of powers is not only unrealistic in its constraints upon the judicial role, but it is out of keeping with American political thought and practice.

A notable expression of this formalistic view of the judicial role was provided by Justice Owen J. Roberts in his 1936 majority opinion in *United States* v. *Butler*:[10]

> The constitution is the supreme law of the land ordained and established by the people. All legislation must conform to the principles it lays down. When an act of Congress is appropriately challenged in the courts as not conforming to the constitutional mandate the judicial branch has only one duty—to lay the article of the Constitution which is invoked beside the statute which is challenged and to decide whether the latter squares with the former. All the court does, or can do is to announce its considered judgment upon the question. The only power it has, if such it may be called, is the power of judgment.

This mechanical view has all but disappeared from the legal scene. Few judges today could be as näive as Justice Roberts regarding their role and function. But a neopositivist approach appeared in the early 1960s, following the writings of the eminent legal scholar, Herbert Wechsler, who claims to have attained a degree of objectivity and neutrality in the application of legal principles that Roberts might have approved. The "neutral principles" argument is a subtle reincarnation of the separation of powers doctrine of an earlier age. Professor Wechsler admits that judicial action necessarily involves value choices, but he calls upon judges to "function otherwise than as a naked power organ." Instead judicial decisions should be "entirely principled," which seems to mean that they should rest "on reasons with respect to all the issues in the case, reasons that in their generality and their neutrality transcend any immediate result that is involved." [11] For Wechsler, when no "suffi-

9. M. J. C. Vile, *Constitutionalism and the Separation of Powers* (Oxford University Press, 1967), p. 319.

10. 297 U.S. 1 (1936) at p. 62.

11. Herbert Wechsler, *Principles, Politics and Fundamental Law* (Harvard University Press, 1961), p. 27.

cient reasons" for overturning the value choices of other branches of government exist, than those choices must stand. He apparently believes that the Supreme Court should be guided by history, although not frozen by it, in its quest to interpret the Constitution. Obviously, the preference for history or tradition is itself a value preference—a highly conservative one, which may be untenable as a position in the fast-changing society which the courts must serve.

Judicial Review

Judicial review is the power of a court to declare the actions of a legislature of an executive or any other official unconstitutional. This doctrine, of major importance in the development of American law, has two very different aspects.

First, the Supreme Court of the United States has been called the "umpire" of the federal system. The allusion to baseball is appropriate because of the necessity to establish a final source of authority in the nation on the requirements of the Constitution and of federal statutes. Just as the teams in a baseball league must abide by the same rules if the sport is to survive, so some tribunal must declare the meaning of national rule. The possibility of conflict between state and national policies is always present in a federal system, and the power of judicial review by the Supreme Court provides a means of avoiding or lessening that conflict.

Article VI of the Constitution makes all federal statutes and treaties "The Supreme law of the land." It binds every state judge to the recognition of the supremacy of every federal law to any state law which may conflict with it. Any validity enacted federal statute, treaty, executive order, or administrative order is superior to any state law which covers the same subject matter. Since 1810 the Supreme Court has exercised its power of judicial review against hundreds of unconstitutional state statutes.

The power of judicial review is quite different in its second aspect, the oversight of Congress and the national executive. The delicate balance of federalism may require the intervention of the Supreme Court, while judicial intervention in the affairs of coordinate branches of government is less justifiable. As Justice Holmes once said:

> I do not think the United States would come to an end if we lost our power to declare an Act of Congress void. I do think the Union would be imperiled if we could not make that declaration as to the laws of the several states.[12]

12. "Law and the Court" in Mark DeWolfe Howe, ed., *The Occasional Speeches of Justice Oliver Wendell Holmes* (Harvard University Press, 1962), p. 172.

The theory of judicial review of coordinate branches of government is based on "higher law" concepts applied to the Constitution. Under this approach the Constitution is regarded as so superior to ordinary legislation that law-making bodies are subject to its ultimate rules. The judges, as the guardians of the Constitution, are expected to enforce its norms even in the face of strong pressures by the other branches of government, and by refusing to enforce any legislation or other governmental action which seems to the judges to be in conflict with the Constitution.

Unfortunately for its proponents, judicial review of federal policies is not specifically accorded to the Supreme Court by the Constitution. At the Constitutional Convention little mention of this question seems to have taken place. Alexander Hamilton, one of the most prominent framers, contended that judicial review definitely was intended to be conferred on the federal courts. James Madison, one of the leaders at the convention, regarded the judiciary as "truly the only defensive armor of the Federal Government, or rather for the Constitution and laws of the United States." [13] Prior to the Constitution, several state courts had experimented with judicial review, but the actual intent of the framers is shrouded in doubt and ambiguity.

In 1803 Chief Justice John Marshall saw an opportunity which the Court might not have had again for a few years, a chance to establish the power of judicial review of national actions. The intention of Marshall is evident below the subtle and well-polished surface of the opinion in *Marbury* v. *Madison*.[14] The legislation which Marshall chose to challenge, section 13 of the Judiciary Act of 1789, provided original jurisdiction for the Supreme Court to deal with disputed appointments. The law had been drafted by Oliver Ellsworth, who later became third Chief Justice, and it was passed by a Congress which contained many ex-members of the Constitutional Convention. In spite of the authority of the law's authors, Marshall declared the law void because it unconstitutionally enlarged the Supreme Court's original jurisdiction. Appearing to refuse power, the Court was actually increasing its power greatly.

Behind all the close-knit paragraphs of *Marbury* v. *Madison* is the hidden assumption that judges are more expert at reading and interpreting the Constitution than the president or the congress. Marshall also assumed, without much support, that the repugnance of a statute to the Constitution would be readily apparent to any fair-minded judge, but not so evident to others. The argument is essentially anti- or counter-majoritarian, since it creates a check upon the elected branches of gov-

13. As quoted by Charles Warren in *The Supreme Court in United States History* (Little, Brown, 1937), V. I. p. 740.
14. 1 Cranch 137 (1803).

ernment and places the checking power in the hands of a group of judges appointed virtually for a lifetime.

The Supreme Court of the United States has become the world's most powerful court, and even though the Court uses its power sparingly, the occasions for judicial review are chosen by the Court accordingly to its own lights, regardless of the public or of the politicians. Of course, the Court is aware of the contending forces which move the American society, and judicial review has, in fact, not been used to defy the wishes of the public or its elected politicians for any long period of time.

Many attempts have been made to curb the Supreme Court in the name of the people, but all have failed. The popular recall of judicial opinions was backed by Theodore Roosevelt and the 1912 Progressive Party platform. In 1921 a proposed constitutional amendment to require all but two judges to concur in an exercise of judicial review power failed to clear Congress. At the height of his popularity in 1936, President Franklin Roosevelt failed to rally Congress to his effort to challenge the Court by increasing its membership. In the 1950s and 60s numerous attempts to curb the Court or to reverse its judgments again foundered. Chief Justice Warren, an ardent champion of judicial review on behalf of civil rights claims, was threatened by political extremists with impeachment, but to no avail. From this catalogue of failure one can only conclude that the Supreme Court enjoys too much popular support to be effectively curbed or punished.

Under the leadership of Chief Justice Earl Warren, from 1953 to 1969, the Supreme Court entered a phase of great activism in which judicial review and other devices to expand judicial policy making were used with notable effect. The Supreme Court took great strides towards racial equality under the law by restricting most kinds of state activity of a discriminatory character. The state legislatures felt the impact of the Supreme Court at their most sensitive point, representativeness, when the Supreme Court declared many state apportionment schemes to be in violation of the Constitution. The apportionment of the Federal Congress also was subjected to judicial review. Criminal justice in America was drastically altered by Supreme Court rulings striking down many traditional practices of police and prosecutors. In free speech questions the Warren Court forged new constitutional doctrines, especially in the area of censorship. Mandatory Bible-reading in public school was declared unconstitutional. A freedom to travel and a right to privacy gradually emerged from Supreme Court opinions. All in all, the Warren years exemplify an impressive creative use of judicial review powers. The appointment of Chief Justice Warren Burger by President Richard Nixon signaled an end of a judicial era, and a subsequent withdrawal by the Supreme Court from energetic policy making. The vacancies created by the resignations of Justices Black and Harlan completed the process.

Judicial review is aristocratic in essence, but the public tolerates and accepts it as a fundamental part of our democratic system—a paradox perhaps. But democracy requires some attention to minority rights, and the Court has defended minorities many times in its history, including under its protective aegis corporate business, national banks, Negroes (in the twentieth century), Indians (sometimes), political dissenters, accused persons, children, suburbanites, laborers, aliens, minority religionists and others whose rights have come under majority attack. The Court is not always in the forefront, and it might misgauge the minority's best interests, but at least a counterbalance to majoritarianism is available.

THE COURT STRUCTURE

The structure of the judicial system is a matter of considerable importance. The choice of tribunal, the place, and the judge chosen are often important variables in judicial outcomes. The structure is more than a mere lifeless skeleton of judicial organization; it is a complex part of the machinery by which conflicts are resolved in this society.

Federalism and Court Structure

The American federal system, by implication, creates a dual body of laws and separate judicial structures to manage them. Although in a few areas state courts may handle suits arising from federal law, the normal condition is that each court system considers disputes arising only under its own laws. Trials conducted in state courts are considered separate from trials conducted in federal courts, even in criminal law. Double jeopardy, the constitutional limitation upon second trials for the same offense, does not act as a barrier to a state trial or a federal trial, since both are regarded as separate sovereigns, each with their own body of criminal law. So a man may be tried again for the commission of the same act for which he had earlier been tried in the courts of the other "sovereign." [15]

Intervention by one level of courts in the trial of another is possible, since Congress permits the issuing of injunctions by federal courts against state courts, and habeas corpus may also produce this result. It

15. *Bartkus* v. *Illinois*, 359 U.S. 221 (1959); *Ciucci* v. *Illinois*, 356 U.S. 571 (1958); *United States* v. *Lanza*, 269 U.S. 377 (1922).

is technically possible for federal district courts to issue injunctions against state courts in civil rights cases.[16] Habeas corpus might also be used against invalid state prosecutions which threaten irreparable injury to federally protected rights.[17] A state trial which could threaten federal rights could be removed from a state to a federal court. All of these drastic steps are exceptional and are narrowly construed by the Supreme Court, since they involve actions of the utmost sensitivity in federal-state relationships.

The basic structure of federalism in the judiciary is found in the existence of fifty-one judicial structures, one for each of the states and for the national government. This condition may permit a plaintiff a choice of forums. The defendant also may be able to obtain a transfer from a state to a federal court under certain circumstances. Subtle differences in procedure between state and federal courts, or even the obtaining of a different judge, may produce a different outcome for a plaintiff or a defendant.

The fifty state court systems are, in a constitutional sense, subordinate to the United States Supreme Court. Appeal to the Supreme Court from a state court is possible, but the litigant must have exhausted all the proper remedies available at the state level before the Supreme Court will accept his appeal. This means that the appeal normally follows an unfavorable judgment by the state's highest tribunal. The appellant must establish some suitable federal grounds for his appeal. If he has invoked a national statute or treaty and the state court of last resort has held it invalid, a ground for appeal is established. If he challenges a state law on the basis of incompatibility with a federal law, treaty, or the Constitution, or if a federal right has been improperly denied, appeal will be possible. Appeals can be rejected by the Supreme Court if no "substantial federal question" is presented, and the Court usually seeks to find some non-federal basis upon which the decision can rest, in order to avoid taking jurisdiction over the case and examining the merits.

The State Judiciary

Because of the wider scope of state law, the state courts handle a more varied number of cases than do federal courts. The federal system consigns most legal business to the states, and the workload of state courts is much greater than that of most federal courts within the same geographic region. Most legal matters in America do not reach the courts,

16. *Dombrowski* v. *Pfister*, 380 U.S. 479 (1965) permits this, but under limited conditions of great harassment, as indicated by *Cameron* v. *Johnson*, 390 U.S. 611 (1968).

17. *Rachel* v. *Georgia*, 345 F.2d 336 (5th Cir., 1965), affirmed, 384 U.S. 780 (1966).

and when they do it is usually the state courts or a local tribunal which the citizen utilizes. Approximately ninety percent of all judicial business is conducted by the states or their local courts.

Most of the business of the state courts concerns the adjusting of disputes between private parties. The civil courts which are established for this purpose apply the principles of non-criminal law which are to be found in the statutes of the state or in the common law of the jurisdiction. The largest class of state civil cases falls under the heading of "torts," a civil wrong somewhat resembling criminal law, but the dispute is between private parties, so that the result will usually be money damages for the plaintiff if he is successful in his suit. Automobile accidents, which glut the state courts, are the most common example.

Criminal law is defined by each state according to its own public policy. It is almost wholly statutory and defines activity which, in the judgment of the state, endangers the public interest. Since the risks to the defendant are so high the state must meet a higher standard of proof. Generally, the state must prove its case "beyond a reasonable doubt," and it must convince a larger proportion of the jury (usually a unanimous verdict is required). American criminal law is predominately state law, although a growing number of federal crimes have been created in recent years. Social problems of narcotics addiction, alcoholism, traffic control, obscenity, and environmental pollution are often treated as part of criminal law, although they might be treated some other way.

State courts play numerous other functions, ranging from keeping the executive and legislative branches of government within their constitutional boundaries, to providing for the adoption of children. Consequently a highly complex and specialized group of courts has grown up to adjudicate different kinds of cases.

At the lowest level, courts of a purely local character may be found. In rural areas there are often popularly elected justices of the peace whose jurisdiction usually includes minor civil and criminal matters, such as breaches of the peace or $100 civil suits. In municipalities magistrates or police courts are commonly found. In some large cities many different kinds of municipal courts can be found, a condition which sometimes breeds corruption because of the lack of clear responsibility. Some citizens are confused by the large number of courts, they cannot hold these many magistrates responsible.

The most important state trial court is held at the county level or may include several counties. Most important civil and criminal matters in the states begin at this level. Trial juries are employed extensively in these courts of general jurisdiction, and in most states the judges are chosen by popular election. A limited appellate jurisdiction also exists, to receive appeals from the magistrate or justice of the peace courts.

An appellate level of state courts is found in fewer than one-fourth of the states, but more are being created as the pressure of judicial work mounts. The highest courts in the states are usually called the "supreme court." In Kentucky, Maryland and New York this tribunal is known as the "Court of Appeals," while in Connecticut it is named the "Supreme Court of Errors." Most states have an elected supreme court of five or seven members who sit together to hear appeals. The state supreme courts are the final arbiters on questions of state law and of the state constitution. In a few states the supreme court is empowered to issue advisory opinions which recommend constitutional courses of action to the legislature or to the governor, a power which is lacking in the United States Supreme Court.

The Federal Courts

The federal courts comprise a simple tri-level system, with the United States District Courts at the bottom. The District Courts, the workhorses of the system, are the trial courts of general federal jurisdiction, the only national courts employing juries. There are eighty-eight district courts for the fifty states, one in the District of Columbia, and another for the Commonwealth of Puerto Rico. Each state has at least one district court, but some of the larger states have as many as four. Each district court has from one to twenty-four judges assigned to serve, depending on the quantity of work at hand. Normally only one judge is needed to try a case, although in special circumstances three judges may be called together to comprise a court.

The United States is divided into eleven judicial circuits, including the District of Columbia as a circuit. Each of the states is assigned to one of the circuits, as are the Territories of the United States. The terminology of "circuit courts," which accurately described the mixed judicial system of federal appellate courts prior to 1891, no longer applies to the current appellate organization, which is fixed and permanent. Supreme and District Court judges are not required to ride the circuit on horseback as they once did to get to an appellate hearing. Today a Supreme Court justice is still assigned to one or more circuits, but that authority is just a vestige of the past.

The United States Courts of Appeals, as they are called today, are intermediate appellate courts which relieve the Supreme Court of the burden of hearing a myriad of cases. These courts review appeals arising from the United States District Courts, except in those very few situations where direct appeal to the Supreme Court is provided. The Courts of Appeals also receive appeals from the decisions of the independent regulatory commissions, most frequently from the National Labor Relations Board. As such, these courts provide a valuable check upon the independent agencies. Each Court of Appeals usually hears cases in divisions of three judges.

Special courts have also been established by Congress to deal with particular types of cases. Appeals may be taken from these courts to the Supreme Court of the United States. The United States Court of Claims, established in 1855, has original jurisdiction to render judgment upon claims against the United States arising from acts of Congress, executive orders or implied contracts with the United States. Claims for the refund of income or excise taxes and for back pay are typical cases. The United States Court of Customs and Patent Appeals, created in 1909, deals with questions arising under the patent, trademark and customs laws and regulations. The United States Customs Court has exclusive jurisdiction over civil actions arising under the tariff laws, the reciprocal trade agreements, most customs and several internal revenue matters. Territorial Courts, with jurisdiction over local matters, have been established by Congress in Guam, the Virgin Islands, and the Canal Zone.

The United States Court of Military Appeals, commonly known as the G.I. Supreme Court, is the final appellate tribunal in cases arising out of military court-martial proceedings. This court, which hase come under the fire of several judicial reformers for its harsh views of military justice, must hear cases affecting generals or involving the death penalty, as well as cases certified to the Court by the Judge Advocates-General of the armed services. The court also considers petitions by individuals who have received a sentence of one year or longer or a punitive discharge. The Uniform Code of Military Justice provides the basic source of law applied by this court, and in several important respects the code does not extend the kind of justice available in civilian courts. Normally, the decisions of the Court of Military Justice are not reviewable.

The United States Supreme Court, consisting of a Chief Justice and eight Associate Justices, possesses both original and appellate jurisdiction. It may sit as a trial court in cases between two or more states, between a state and a citizen of another state, and between American citizens and foreign states. Exercise of trial (original) jurisdiction has taken place fewer than 130 times in the history of the Court. By far the greater number of cases come before the Supreme Court by virtue of its appellate jurisdiction, which is created by Congress, pursuant to its constitutional power under Article III.

The Supreme Court is normally in session thirty-six weeks a year, from the first Monday in October of each year until its business is completed, usually in the middle of June. On extraordinary occasions the Court will act when out of session, as in the school desegregation controversies in 1969 and 1970, when the Court had to make rulings prior to the opening of the school year in September. In spite of the apparently long "vacation," the members of the Court have enough homework to keep them constantly busy reading briefs or conducting legal research. Even Justice William O. Douglas used to take work along on his mountain climbing expeditions. Approximately three thousand cases are passed upon in a year, a formidable load for nine men.

The Court is housed in one of Washington's most beautiful buildings, a Greek-style white marble structure close by the halls of Congress. Business is conducted before the public in a small courtroom seating only three hundred persons. The Justices sit behind a raised bench, the Chief Justice sitting in the middle, the Associate Justices on either side of him in proximity according to seniority, the newest appointees at the farthest ends of the bench.

Oral argument is heard the first four days in two weeks of each month. Only 125–150 cases are argued openly before the Court. The oral argument is brief, usually an hour for each side, but oral argument can be a critical part of the work of the Court, since it allows the Justices to probe for the weaknesses in the briefs of the parties. Having heard the oral arguments, the Court spends the remaining two weeks behind closed doors considering cases and writing opinions.

Each week the Friday Conference is held. At these secret conferences the Justices, led by the Chief Justice, discuss and debate the merits of the cases heard at the oral arguments. At the same time consideration is given to all pending motions and applications. By custom the Chief Justice presents his view of the merits of a case followed by the other Justices in order of seniority. After this discussion a tentative vote is taken in reverse order. The writing of the opinions is assigned by the Chief Justice, or by the senior Associate Justice of the majority.

Unanimous opinions occur in fewer than one-third of the cases, so that dissenting or concurring opinions (a vote for the majority, but on different grounds) are quite common. Dissenting opinions, unless accompanied by some extensive explanation, are not useful to the public or the legal profession. However, a well-reasoned dissent may be the harbinger of the legal principles of the future.[18]

The Supreme Court is the nation's great appellate court. There are essentially three methods, or writs, by which the Court is able to con-

18. Perhaps the most famous single example of a prophetic dissenting opinion is that of Mr. Justice Marshall Harlan in *Plessy* v. *Ferguson*, 163 U.S. 537 (1896), the case which reinforced the segregationist "separate but equal" concept for Negroes. Harlan was the lone dissenter in that case in which he considered segregation as a "badge of servitude," contending that "our Constitution is color blind." Harlan declared that "there can be no doubt but that segregation has been enforced as a means of subordinating the Negro . . . [and] the thin disguise of "equal accommodation" . . . will not mislead anyone nor attone for the wrong this day done."

sider cases. Each of the writs is created by Congress and each is subject to expansion or contraction at the will of Congress, although no drastic change is likely at this time. *Appeal* is the primary route from state courts of last resort (usually state supreme courts). *Certiorari* is clearly a discretionary writ issued whenever four or more Supreme Court Justices have agreed to permit review. *Certification,* a rarely used writ is available whenever a lower federal court wishes to "inquire" about a question of law upon which it is not prepared to decide the issue.

More than ninety percent of all petitions for certiorari are denied, and approximately sixty percent of appeal petitions are thwarted by one procedural device or another. Approximately ten percent of all cases on the Court's docket are ultimately decided on the merits, half of these by a formal written opinion. The effect of a denial of certiorari or the rejection of an appeal is that the previous judgment of the tribunal below is left standing.

Selection of Judges

President Nixon recently experienced the unprecedented rebuke of having two of his Supreme Court nominees rejected by the Senate of the United States. This political setback came as a shock to the president who seemed to feel that the choice of Supreme Court nominees was virtually a presidential prerogative. To his dismay, the president discovered that the selection of judges is a politically sensitive issue, subject to the additional expectation of judicial competence and personal integrity.

Technically, the president can appoint anyone he chooses to the federal judiciary, regardless of previous experience. Even a non-lawyer or a child could be nominated, because no qualifications are set by federal statutes or by the Constitution. All presidential judicial appointments are subject to Senatorial disapproval. The Senate has rejected about twenty percent of all nominations, many of the rejections coming in the early part of the nation's history. Its power has given rise to the custom of "senatorial courtesy" by which the senator from the state where a judicial vacancy is present must be consulted in making appointments. Effectively, senators from the president's own party suggest nominees to the president, and he disregards their suggestions for the lower court appointments only at his own risk.

The negotiations with individual senators for judicial nominations are conducted by the attorney general or his deputy. The attorney general carries a heavy responsibility for protecting the president in the making of judicial appointments, especially Supreme Court nominations, which are not subject to senatorial courtesy. Attorney-General John Mitchell proposed two unsuccessful nominations of Clement Haynsworth and G.

Harold Carswell to President Nixon and bears some responsibility for not discovering the weaknesses in their personal careers and records. The American Bar Association makes a rating of judicial candidates, and the attorney-general cannot afford to ignore their negative rankings because of the respect in which the ABA is held in the Senate.

President Nixon, like most presidents, has tried to appoint justices to the Supreme Court who shared his outlook on social and legal matters. He has sought to appoint "strict constructionists," as he calls them, to the federal bench. By this he may mean political and economic conservatives who take a relatively narrow view of the scope of judicial power. His appointees have not been strict conservatives, but many, including Chief Justice Warren Burger, take a stiff view of criminal justice, one which tends to favor the police and prosecution in criminal cases more than most of the Roosevelt, Kennedy or Johnson appointees.

In contrast to the federal judiciary, in the states, judicial selection follows several different patterns, with partisan elections most common. Non-partisan elections are slightly less popular. In five states judges are elected by the legislature, while gubernatorial appointment is found in seven others. Six states employ the Missouri Plan which permits the governor to select judges from among a list recommended by a special commission, then requiring approval by the electorate in a public referendum. Whether a judge is elected or appointed, he is likely to be active in either the Democratic or the Republican party, and even be a major contributor to his party. Nominees are usually politically prominent people, and while competence and experience are significant factors, they are not usually enough to warrant the prestigious judicial appointments coveted by politically astute lawyers. There is no evidence that elected judges perform differently from appointed judges, although judges with deep political obligations can be sources of judicial coruption.

JUDICIAL BEHAVIOR

Mere description of legal structure does not give a lively sense of the actual behavior and attitudes of judges, of the personality of judges, their social backgrounds, their political affiliations, their interaction with other judges, or of their prejudices, and philosophies. Many influences beyond those of the black-letter provisions of law impinge on the behavior of judges when politically sensitive issues are at stake.

The Judges

The view that judges are merely impartial arbiters in black robes who simply discover the basic principles of law has been under attack throughout the twentieth century. Justice Holmes attacked his colleagues on the Supreme Court for basing their decisions on a particular political philosophy, asserting outright in a 1905 case (*Lochner* v. *New York*) that "The Fourteenth Amendment does not enact Mr. Herbert Spencer's *Social Statics*." Nonetheless, the judicial propensity to apply personal preferences to current cases is not entirely avoidable, simply because judges aren't angels.

Some legal philosophers suggested that judges not only could not be completely neutral, but they should not. Jerome Frank asserted that judges must become aware of the role that their prejudices and personal inclinations play in the making of judicial decisions by gaining a psychological insight into their own inner needs and desires. Others called upon the judge to develop his sense of the law as an active agent of society, reflecting not only the customs and traditions of an age, but also responding to the changing needs and interests of society. This view, loosely called "sociological jurisprudence," gained widespread acceptance in the law schools around the country, inspired by the writings of Roscoe Pound, Benjamin Cardozo, and Felix Frankfurter. Under this approach the judge had to turn away from his purely private estimates of social needs and measure competing social interests as carefully as his skill allowed. When asked how the judges know which interests outweigh another, Cardozo replied that "He must get his knowledge just as the legislator gets it, from experience and study and reflection." [19] This also might mean an increasing reliance upon social science data to aid in the judicial decision-making process by providing an external, "scientific," and relatively objective guide for the judge.

In social background judges are quite different from the average citizen. Detailed analysis of backgrounds of Supreme Court members discloses a definite upper-middle class bias, and a disproportion of white Anglo-Saxon Protestant representation on the Court.[20] Catholic and Protestant affiliation seems to have some bearing on judicial attitudes, but partisan affiliation is a much more significant variable.[21] Previous professional experience, especially for ex-prosecutors handling criminal cases as judges, seems significant in forming harsh attitudes toward defendants.[22]

Background factors are not clear determinants of judicial behavior.

19. Benjamin Cardozo, *The Nature of the Judicial Process* (Yale University Press, 1921), p. 113.
20. John Schmidhauser, "The Justices of the Supreme Court: A Collective Portrait," *Midwest Journal of Political Science*, Vol. 3 (1959), pp. 1-57.
21. See S. Sidney Ulmer, "The Political Party Variable in the Michigan Supreme Court," *Journal of Public Law*, Vol. 11 (1962), pp. 352-362.
22. Stuart Nagel, "Judicial Backgrounds and Criminal Cases," *Journal of Criminal Law, Criminology & Police Science*, Vol. 53 (1962), pp. 333-339.

Many judges arrive on the bench with half-formed attitudes on legal and social matters. Others are susceptible to influence from more experienced judges. Judges do try to influence each other, especially in the intimate setting of an appellate tribunal. It is clear that on the Supreme Court some Chief Justices are more skillful at persuading their colleagues than others have been. Many "social" and "task" strategies are available to a Chief Justice to influence the Supreme Court, and strong Chief Justices have made good use of these strategies.[23]

Many methods are being attempted by political scientists in an effort to measure, weigh and predict judicial decisions on the basis of objective evidence of judicial attitudes. Using appellate opinions from a particular court it is possible to quantify attitudes as expressed in judicial "votes" for one or the other outcome. Scaling according to various sociological techniques has been attempted by many political scientists. In fact many scales have been produced, but unfortunately no one can yet say for certain that the scales reflect genuine attitudes held by particular judges. More complicated predictive devices based upon factor and regression analysis, or even Boolean Algebra, have been produced, but again, with uncertain results. At best, the Supreme Court, as a court, has been shown to be a typical, small, decision-making body with attitudes discernible from voting patterns, but no fixed correlations are firmly established.[24]

Judicial Self-Restraint

Of all judicial attitudes, the most important is the doctrine of judicial self-restraint. Several federal judges including Holmes, Brandeis, Frankfurter, Stone, Learned Hand, and Justice Harlan of the present Court, have openly adopted an official attitude of narrowly reading the scope of judicial power, especially the power of judicial review. The basis for this outlook can be found in the constitutional doctrine of separation of powers and the majoritarian view of democracy. Separation of powers can be perceived as a limitation upon the authority of the Supreme Court to strike down the policies of coordinate branches of government, and majoritarian democracy a barrier to government by an essentially aristocratic judiciary.

The idea of judicial self-restraint can be found best formulated in a famous 1893 article by Professor James Bradley Thayer.[25] At the time

23. David Danielski, "The Influence of the Chief Justice in the Decisional Process," Walter Murphy & C. Herman Pritchett, eds., *Courts, Judges & Politics* (Random House, 1961), pp. 497-508.

24. For an excellent survey see Glendon Schubert, "Behavioral Research in Public Law," *American Political Science Review*, Vol. 57 (1963), pp. 433-445.

25. "The Origin and Scope of the American Doctrine of Constitutional Law," *Harvard Law Review*, Vol. 7 (1893), pp. 129-155.

he wrote this classic argument for judicial self-restraint, the Supreme Court was intervening actively in the formation of public policy by striking down numerous state and national statutes in the areas of social and economic legislation, often because of the conservative policy perspectives held by the judges. Thayer contended that statutes should be declared unconstitutional only when they are persuaded of their invalidity beyond a reasonable doubt. Legislative policy judgments should be honored if at all possible, and as long as there exists some basis for the legislature to believe the statutes constitutional, the courts should attribute sense and competence to them. Courts should not presume the legislatures to be ignorant of the requirements of the Constitution. Courts should realize that there might be several possible, and reasonable, interpretations of the meaning of the Constitution, and within that range of judgment "whatever choice is rational is constitutional."

Few judges have gone as far as Thayer desired in deferring to legislative policy determinations. The temptation to have a hand in coining public policy is irresistible for many judges. Furthermore, in sensitive areas of civil rights the judges may find the legislatures willfully blind to the requirements of the Constitution, and feel that unless judicial intervention took place democratic rights would be sacrificed.

The choice of attitudes toward the legislature and the executive is most difficult for a judge, but in a close case he must make a conscious choice. Judges must interpret statutes as well as apply constitutional limitations. In either process few clear guidelines to judicial practice are available. Ultimately there comes a time in the career of most judges when the issue of judicial activism or relative passivity must be faced. The very role of a judge in the United States requires it. To what extent can a judge innovate policy, or shape it, or reverse it, or create it in vacuums left by the other branches of government? There are no final answers to this important question. The judge must choose his stance for himself.

Compliance and Impact

When a court hands down a major decision, the policy process, a never-ending continuum, takes on other forms. The rulings of the Supreme Court, although a powerful source of policy, are by no means self-executing. "When a judge makes law, his action is no more final than that of any other lawmaker." Our political system is "marked by the constant communication, dissolution, and recombination of various political forces in the process of continuously adjusting the law to changing social needs and political demands." [26] Furthermore, a court decision

26. Martin Shapiro, *The Supreme Court and Administrative Agencies* (The Free Press, 1968), p. 58.

by its own force can have little effect upon the society unless it is supported, amplified, and implemented by other political and social groups. Speaking of a Supreme Court opinion Andrew Jackson may have once roared, "John Marshall has made his decision, now let him enforce it." A judicial order is not often flouted by the parties concerned, but it can be if other governmental agencies wink at violations.[27]

One of the classic examples of compliance occurred in the early history of the United States Supreme Court. In 1813 the Supreme Court reversed a decision of the highest court of Virginia regarding the land rights of British subjects, which had been protected by a national treaty (the Jay Treaty) terminating the Revolutionary War. The State of Virginia refused to respect the 1813 decision of *Fairfax's Devisee* v. *Hunter's Lessee* [28] because it felt that state court decisions were on a par with federal court decisions, since each was made by a distinctly separate sovereign authority—the state and the national government. Virginia conceded the superiority of federal statutes and treaties to state laws, but contended that state court interpretations of federal obligations were as valid as those of the Supreme Court itself. The Supreme Court order went unobeyed.

Three years later the Supreme Court reaffirmed its earlier claim of judicial supremacy in *Martin* v. *Hunter's Lessee*,[29] in which Justice Story answered the Virginia assertions by arguing that the Constitution extends appellate jurisdiction of the Supreme Court over the state courts because the Constitution was established by all the people of the United States, not by the states. Story pointed out that since the Supreme Court could reverse the determinations of state executive and legislative authorities, surely the state judiciaries could not be immune. To have accepted the claims of the Virginia judiciary would have shattered the federal nature of the American judiciary system.

In school desegregation questions the Supreme Court has had to turn to allies in the national government to obtain compliance with its mandates. President Eisenhower had to call upon federal troops to support desegregation orders in Little Rock, Arkansas, because a federal court order following Supreme Court doctrines was being flouted. President Kennedy used federal marshals in the South for the same purpose. Legislative support took the form of several national civil rights enactments. Administrative support has come through monetary threats by Health, Education and Welfare directed at non-complying school districts and

27. Stephen L. Wasby, *The Impact of the United States Supreme Court* (Dorsey Press, 1970), provides a careful examination of alternative meanings of "impact," "compliance," "evasion" and similar terms.

28. 7 Cr. 603 (1813).

29. 1 Wheat. 304 (1816).

from numerous Justice Department suits. The events set in motion by the 1954 desegregation cases were not concluded by the start of the 1970s, although substantial compliance in most districts had been obtained by the fall of 1970.

There is strong evidence that, even within the fold of the federal judiciary, judges sometimes resist the rulings of the Supreme Court in subtle ways. Segregationist attitudes have been detected among certain judges in spite of clear Supreme Court signals to the contrary. The social and political environment of the judges impinges upon their outlook, just as with other policy makers.[30] In the desegregation controversy, as in many others, the Supreme Court concocted ambiguous formulas for the new policy, placing the brunt of blame and recrimination upon the local federal courts, a pressure which most of them withstood. Less ambiguous orders might have made the task of desegregation easier and placed less of a strain upon the federal court in decoding and applying Supreme Court mandates for the local requirements.

The Supreme Court can still be resisted by state and even federal court judges in numerous ways. Trial court judges normally resent appellate judges who can reverse them and otherwise cause embarrassment. Federal court judges can express this attitude by narrowly applying a Supreme Court ruling, or render it ineffectual by "distinguishing" the case. When the Supreme Court has spoken, the federal courts must at least formally follow suit, but grudging compliance is a kind of resistance. Moreover, federal court judges at the trial level have extensive powers to find facts, and in doing so, may avoid reading the facts in a manner which would invoke a particular Supreme Court doctrine. State court judges have wider latitude than their federal counterparts. This is due partly to the extreme difficulty of overseeing the hundreds of thousands of state cases which might present federal questions.

State court judges may in fact be openly hostile to Supreme Court rulings. Judges can support other state political forces in resisting the Supreme Court. State laws contradicting federal standards have been upheld in many state courts. State court judges may even reverse Supreme Court rulings directly effecting the parties to the case as long as they can find a valid non-federal ground for their judgment. State court judges have balked at Supreme Court rulings in the areas of criminal procedure, reapportionment, religious freedom and desegregation. Usually their resistance merely delayed policy acceptance and did not thwart the Supreme Court mandate completely. Even so, state court noncompli-

30. Prior state political experience seems to have been a key factor in forming segregationist attitudes on the federal bench. See Kenneth Vines, "Federal District Judges and Race Relations Cases in the South," *Journal of Politics*, Vol. 26 (1964), pp. 337-357.

ance with Supreme Court rulings is probably very common, sometimes
due to a failure to perceive the requirements of the court, sometimes
due to different policy views.

The Supreme Court is certainly not powerless. Noncompliance in the
federal judiciary can be overcome by polite pressures brought to bear
within the judicial system. In addition, the Supreme Court can limit
evasionary techniques through its power to promulgate rules of procedure governing the lower courts. Rules for bankruptcy law, criminal
procedure and admiralty law are subject to Supreme Court controls.
The Supreme Court can deal with resisting state courts by directly
ordering a particular judgment to be rendered in a state court.[31] This
statutory power, very dangerous in a federal system, is rarely employed.
Instead, the Court depends upon the good will of state courts and upon
judicial integrity to produce eventual compliance. The Supreme Court
decides a case arising out of a state tribunal and remands it to the court
from which the case came for "proceedings not inconsistent with this
opinion." The wishful quality of the language indicates the weakness of
the process, but it usually works.

The Court affects society as well as lower tribunals. The Supreme
Court has had major impact on economic relationships. Most business transactions rest upon contracts, and the Supreme Court extended its protective arm to American business in the early nineteenth century by its interpretations of Article I, section 10, of the Constitution, which forbids
any state to "pass any . . . law impairing the obligation of contract."
John Marshall expanded the concept of contract obligations then prevailing by declaring in 1810 that public authorities were bound by
contracts in their dealings with private parties, even if the contracts were
procured by fraud.[32] Later, corporate charters issued by states were
also deemed contractual in nature, hence shielded from state legislative
alterations.[33] Judicial supervision of state regulation of business took other
forms at the end of the century. The "due process" clause of the
Fourteenth Amendment served the ends of business in the period from
1890 to 1935, as the Supreme Court resisted state efforts to regulate business.

The national government entered the field of economic regulation
through the Constitution's interstate commerce clause. Broad national
powers over the economy were implicit in the early decisions of the
Supreme Court, when partnership between business and the national
government was assumed. The impact of the Supreme Court on eco-

31. 28 U.S.C. Sec. 2106 (Supp. 1952). See *Stanley* v. *Schwalley*, 162 U.S. 255
(1896).
32. *Fletcher* v. *Peck*, 6 Cr. 87 (1810).
33. *Dartmouth College* v. *Woodward*, 4 Wheat. 518 (1819).

nomic regulation by national government was negative from the middle
of the nineteenth century to the New Deal era. The Court managed to
block most efforts at effective antitrust regulation and control of labor
conditions until political threats by President Franklin Roosevelt and a
consequent change of heart by the Supreme Court majority ended most
of the negative readings of national power. Today the Supreme Court
impact in the economic area is largely interstitial in questions of antitrust policy, taxation and administrative law where gaps have been left
by other branches of government.

Another influence of the Supreme Court has on the policies and
operations of other banches of national government and of state governments. In its role as ultimate regulator of the federal system, the Court has
a strategic role to play. Court interpretations of the Tenth Amendment
have prevailed over states' rights arguments. Since 1937 the Supreme
Court has held that the Tenth Amendment does not provide a basis for
state power independent of national government.[34] Instead, the amendment merely leaves to the states those areas which the national government has not occupied. The Supreme Court since 1927 has supported
most national claims of power vis-à-vis the states, upholding national
exercises of commerce clause, taxation, and civil rights power (through
the Fourteenth Amendment) against the states.

On the other hand, the Supreme Court rarely strikes down federal
statutes, and when it does, the grounds are usually very narrow. Deference to Congress has become the general Supreme Court stance. At
times the Supreme Court has intruded into the area of Congressional
investigations or salary payments to people deprived of benefits by
Congress, but these occasions are exceptional. One of the unusual instances of judicial intervention occurred in 1969 on behalf of a repesenta-
tive elected to Congress, but denied his seat by the Congress.[35] Judicial
intervention against the president is extremely rare, and is represented
largely by three decisions which do not go to the heart of executive
power.[36] The Supreme Court has avoided conflict with the president
because of its obvious difficulty in forcing an unwilling president to
accept its policy judgments.

The impact of state and local courts upon their local political systems
is a new but important subject. Issues which move the local political
system usually involve the courts eventually. Trial courts in urban areas

34. *United States* v. *Darby Lumber Co.*, 312 U.S. 100 (1941).
35. *Powell* v. *McCormack*, 395 U.S. 486 (1969).
36. *Ex parte Milligan*, 4 Wall. 2 (1866), respecting the limits of martial law
power; *Humphrey's Executor* v. *United States*, limiting presidential removal powers
and *Youngstown Sheet & Tube Co.* v. *Sawyer*, 343 U.S. 579 (1952), which *seems*
to limit presidential power to seize private property.

are frequently called upon to deal with pressing governmental problems. Subjects such as zoning, public works, tax policy, transportation, and education are often thrown into the courts, partly out of desperation and partly in the quest of a more neutral forum. But the evidence indicates, at least for local trial courts, that they are totally integrated with the local political system and are much more involved in the day-to-day activities of the political system than are the appellate courts.[37]

Finally, the impact of court opinions on public attitudes deserves mention. Most state courts are below the level of attention of the mass public. Their decisions don't usually reach the newspapers. The Supreme Court is the major judicial force in forming public opinion. Throughout the nation's history attitudes toward the Supreme Court and its policies has been an important part of the American political system. Usually most people support the Supreme Court, even when they are not really knowledgeable about its activities or powers. Many people do not know the number of Supreme Court Justices or their names (especially after the departure of Earl Warren), but they tend to support the work of the Court in legitimatizing the public policies of other governmental agencies. Regional, ethnic and temporal variations in support can be discerned, with Negroes recently admiring the Court, and white Southerners being most vocal in opposition to it. People with negative views of the Court often hold those views with greater intensity than the majority of the public. Awareness of Supreme Court policies is generally low, except for reapportionment, Bible-reading, criminal procedure, and desegregation issues or other high visibility matters.

In essence, the Supreme Court, an aristocratic agency within a democracy, serves as a source of symbolic and moral leadership for many Americans in and out of government. It is the capstone of the American judicial system and the envy of many judges in other nations. The failings of the Supreme Court have been forgiven over the long term of American history. Doubtless the Court will always have its enemies, but its reputation stands higher than other courts, and usually higher than other branches of government.

37. See Kenneth M. Dolbeare, *Trial Courts in Urban Politics* (Wiley, 1967).

6

GOVERNMENT

AND AFRO-AMERICANS

by Badi G. Foster

The United States is a "democracy." It is "the land of the free and the home of the brave." These phrases are not empty of meaning to the majority of American citizens. Rather they exemplify the pride and patriotism which most of us experience at one point or another, whether it is at the beginning of a football game or watching a parade on the Fourth of July. Much time is spent in the elementary and secondary schools in our country to explain and to give greater meaning to those traditions and values which have made this country what it is today. In short, the promise of America is often found in those words and phrases which we use during moments of reflection about our country and its future.

The backdrop of national pride and the record of technological success contrasts bewilderingly with pronouncements of scholars and opinion-makers on the impending collapse of our system of government. We are told of crisis after crisis which threatens to change the basic fabric of our society and in so doing fundamentally to alter the system of government that we have grown to know and to love. The issues of war, poverty, pollution, urban decay, and racism head the discussions of the impending crises of contemporary America. Our government today faces a loss of confidence among its people which can be traced to its inability to demonstrate its will or desire and its capacity successfully to meet the demands of its citizens. This inability explains in part the loss of authority of government which is evidenced by innumerable protests, some riots, barrages of verbal insults directed at government officials, and general disrespect for time-honored symbols of our country.

The purpose of this chapter is to examine the relationship of Afro-

Americans and government in the hope that such an examination will give us some idea as to whether government as we understand it, and as it has been discussed in the previous essay, has the will and capacity to meet the demand of its citizens of African heritage. The importance of this examination cannot be overemphasized: for millions of American citizens the issue of race has become the crucial problem of this century. The maintenance of our institutions and our values as a democratic society will largely be determined by the relationship between Afro-Americans and our government. What should the proper relationship be? Should we have two nations—one black, one white, separate and unequal? Or one nation based on total equality? Or several nations being separate but equal? The question of this relationship has plagued our society for hundreds of years; it is doubtful now that we shall have hundreds of years in the future to find an answer. Indeed the consequences of avoiding this question will be very great for those of us alive in 1980.

There are many who feel that the relationship between Afro-Americans and government does not represent a crisis. Blacks are said to occupy essentially the same position enjoyed by all Americans. The point is often made that much progress has been made in the past decade towards alleviating the problems facing citizens of African heritage, and that in fact government has demonstrated its will and its capacity to meet the just needs of Afro-Americans. Others add that the progress in race relations and particularly the improvement in the condition of Afro-Americans has been so rapid that it is misleading to continue to suggest that a crisis exists. Indeed some become indignant and frustrated when the issue of race is raised, because they feel that Afro-Americans have already received preferential treatment, in some cases at the expense of other groups. Therefore they argue that to continue to raise the question of the relationship of Afro-Americans to government and continually to pose new demands demonstrates an ingratitude on the part of Afro-Americans whose demands escalate after every success.

Often the question is posed, "What will satisfy Afro-Americans so that they will cease considering themselves a unique group requiring special privileges and attention?" The answer to such comments was best expressed by a writer of a letter to the editor of the *New York Times* Magazine when he used the following parable: "An innocent man was once condemned to life imprisonment. He took his case to the highest courts, wrote letters to the authorities, went on hunger strikes and finally became violent. He protested against everything, the prison conditions, the wardens and of course his life sentence. After years of disgraceful behavior, the prison authorities gradually and reluctantly made some concessions toward improving prison conditions. The prisoner's cell was heated when the outside temperature dropped below 40 degrees instead of 20 degrees, he was given two solid meals a day instead of one, he was also given a second blanket. You will notice that in each case there was one hundred percent improvement in living conditions. Surprisingly enough the prisoner continued his protest. The prison officials became indignant and threatened him with severe reprisals and finally, exasperated beyond endurance, they asked how many more improvements they would have to make and at which point would he desist from his extremist behavior. The answer of course is simply when his sentence is vacated and he is compensated for the time spent behind bars." [1]

A review of Negro history suggests that from the moment the first slave was forcedly taken from Africa and brought to the new world, that slave received a sentence of life in prison for a crime he did not commit. The numerous efforts on the part of both Black and White citizens to vacate that sentence continue to this very day. Afro-Americans will cease to be a special group with special demands when their punishment ceases, their sentence is vacated, and they are compensated for centuries of imprisonment through the achievement of full equality.

The importance of studying the relationship between Afro-Americans and government is twofold: (1) We will not be able to give full meaning to our values, our symbols, indeed the phrases "land of the free, home of the brave," until Afro-Americans receive just compensation for the grievous and slow-healing wounds they have suffered; (2) To avoid discussing the relationship of Afro-Americans and government would be misleading because one would describe the operation of political parties or the presidency or the Congress as if some 12 percent of the population did not exist.

In the remainder of the essay, we will first look at the relationship of Afro-Americans and government over a period of decades. It is important for us to gain a historical perspective on this question because the peculiar relationship that exists today is not the result of recent events but the result of a pattern of actions and attitudes which has existed for some 300 years. Second, we will move to a general discussion of the reality of the contemporary life of Afro-Americans. Third, we will make a closer examination of four case studies of government and Afro-Americans. Specifically, we will examine: income and employment, education, housing and urban renewal, and political participation. The essay concludes with a summary evaluation of the performance of American government in its relationship to Afro-Americans.

1. Richard Bardolph, *The Civil Rights Record: Black Americans and the Law,* 1849-1970 (T. Y. Crowell, 1970), p. 535.

We were not civilized through slavery and colonialism, rather our ancestors brought their civilization with them and kept it alive through epic
struggles. Today we are merely resurrecting their immortal dreams.

Jan Carew

Africa

An understanding of the historical relationship of government and
Afro-Americans must begin with the events, attitudes and values that
existed when Africans were first brought to the new world. The most
glaring set of assumptions during the early days of slavery, which continue to affect the relationship of government and Afro-Americans today, has to do with what some people call the myth of the Negro past.
This myth was composed of two components. The first component was
the belief that Africans were civilized through slavery. The second component was that Africans brought to the United States retained virtually
no Africanisms, i.e. particular peculiar patterns of behavior or beliefs
which originate in Africa.

Let us briefly trace the influence of the myth of the Negro past. What
is the impact of these assumptions? Essentially, this argument holds not
only that the African slave arrived physically naked when he was
marched off the gangplank onto the shores of America, but also that he
was mentally, spiritually, and culturally naked. The trauma of the passage
from Africa to America succeeded in erasing whatever qualities or beliefs, philosophies or religions Africans possessed prior to enslavement.
Furthermore, the psychological impact of the slave trade was considered
by many capable of erasing African heritage largely because there was
very little heritage to be erased.

The implications of accepting this analysis have been very serious.
For example, if it is true that Africans were civilized through slavery
and that they retained virtually no Africanisms, then one is at a loss to
explain differences that exist between Afro-Americans and other Americans. In the late eighteenth and early nineteenth century the popular
theory to explain differences was essentially a theory of genetic inferiority. Thus, Blacks spoke English differently because they were physi-
ologically unable to pronounce and replicate the intricate sounds of the
English language. Years of effort have been spent dispelling the theory
of genetic inferiority, although it should be noted that some contemporary scholars continue to place varying degrees of importance on
heredity as a determinant of racial behavior.

Once substantial doubt was raised against such a theory, scholars and leaders were forced to come up with another theory to explain continuing differences. The dominant theory of the latter part of the nineteenth century and for most of the twentieth century has been that Afro-Americans have not had the opportunity to learn those things which would make them similar to others. Furthermore, the traumatic experience of slavery has taken its toll in disrupting and distorting patterns of human behavior such as the family. For example, it has been argued, by Daniel P. Moynihan and others, that the reason Black families are matriarchal is the fact that slavery and the Reconstruction period forced the male to play a role which often led to his absence or subordination in the family.[2] This theory, however, fails to explain why cultural differences continue to manifest themselves among Afro-Americans who have had the opportunity to assimilate into the dominant American culture. Recent research, by contrast, suggests that there are some aspects of social and psychological behavior of Afro-Americans traceable directly to Africa, and that indeed certain survivals from Africa can be found in contemporary Afro-American life.

Such a theory of African survivalisms is not simply the product of romanticism but instead reflects a growing awareness of the history of man and of the nature of Africa before colonization and slavery.[3] New scholarship demonstrates that Africa, before the arrival of slavers, was a continent comprising several empires and high levels of civilization. The empires of Ghana, Mali, and Songhay are good examples of the civilizations that existed in Africa prior to slavery. The monetary systems, the complex religions, and the philosophies speak to a very sophisticated level of life. The development of agriculture suggests that Africa before slavery was indeed a continent that was not "dark." The work of Leo Weiner in the first quarter of this century indicates that indeed African traders may very well have visited the new world prior to the visit of Columbus.[4]

The level of crafts in Africa before slavery is another indication of the high level of culture on that continent. The ability to work with iron, the skills of weaving and woodcarving, the ability to work with bronze in art forms indicates a degree of skill and craftsmanship which can only result from a highly civilized community. Finally, the political and social institutions were complex and can be seen in the extended family structure in which two or more generations of adults descended from a common ancestor, as well as their spouses and children, all lived within

2. See the discussion in Lee Rainwater and William L. Yancey, *The Moynihan Report and the Politics of Controversy* (M.I.T. Press, 1967).
3. The leading account in Melville J. Herskovits, *The Myth of the Negro Past* (Beacon Press, 1941).
4. Leo Weiner, *Africa and the Discovery of America* (Innes, 1922).

a common living unit. The quality and style of family life, while different from the United States, nonetheless speaks to a degree of complexity and sophistication that belies the belief that Africa was an undeveloped continent.

As a result of our knowledge of the period before slavery, it is clear that Africans were not civilized through slavery. It is more correct to say that Africans had a different civilization and that when they were brought by force to America, survival required that they adopt another civilization, a western Christian civilization. To be sure, the civilization of Africa that was brought with the slaves did not die but rather was fused with western traditions to create a new and different type of civilization. It is for this reason that it is best to refer to Black Americans as Afro-Americans, because one immediately grasps the cultural fusion of Africa and America. Evidence for the maintenance of African civilization within America can be seen in the music that has been produced by Afro-Americans, in their language both in terms of their vocabulary and syntactical structure, in their dance and, most importantly, in their religion and in the history of Black churches.

Slavery

The institution of slavery has had a greater impact on contemporary relations between government and Afro-Americans than was originally envisaged. Patterns established hundreds of years ago persist to the present, and can be illuminated by examining some important events.

By the middle of the 1600's, the colonial courts in America reflected the existence of slavery by denying Negroes the right to be indentured servants, bound as an apprentice to an owner. In the early period of immigration, it was possible for Africans to come to the new world as such servants and, over a period of time, to purchase their freedom. This pattern was true for those European peasants who first came to America. But the courts later denied Blacks this right. By so doing they limited slavery—that is, perpetual slavery—to people of African heritage. It is true that several, although a small minority, succeeded in eventually purchasing their freedom largely on the basis of the individual compassion of masters. For the large number of Africans brought to this country, however, slavery for themselves and for their children was the dominant pattern.

The United States Congress enacted legislation in 1808 making slave trade illegal. However, the government action was undermined by two factors. First, the United States denied the right of search of ships flying the American flag. Therefore, while the British were actively attempting to stop the trade of slaves, their hands were tied when they approached a ship flying the American flag, which they could not stop and search.

Second, even after the passage of the law prohibiting the trade of slaves, those people who were apprehended for breaking the law received very light sentences from American courts, which were quite sympathetic to slavery and felt that only a minor penalty should be paid by those who broke the law. In many cases courts in the South did not even bother to prosecute slave traders when they were apprehended.

The use of law to reinforce the subordinate position of Afro-Americans increased during the first part of the nineteenth century. The fear of rebellion on the part of slaves against their masters led government to enact a series of slave codes to regulate the behavior of Africans. These codes applied to every imaginable aspect of life and controlled such things as marriage, freedom of movement, indeed the manner in which an individual could spend "his own free time." Permission to attend church services and to attend family gatherings were restricted because White masters were concerned that too much opportunity to mingle would lead the slaves to organize themselves and possibly attempt to overthrow the yoke of oppression. The slave codes clearly reflect a relationship between slave and government based upon the denial that the slave possessed an identity and will independent of his master. Rather, the slave was considered an extension of his master's personality, will, and power. The legacy of this relationship can be seen in contemporary America when government continues to treat Afro-Americans as lacking a separate will and power.[5]

Thomas Jefferson personifies the contradiction and hypocrisy of American government during the period of slavery. To be sure, Thomas Jefferson was a man of superior intellect and he possessed qualities of compassion and courage. His influence on the theory of government and the development of democracy was lasting. When we take a look at his attitudes and actions concerning Africans and slavery, however, we see that Thomas Jefferson occupies a position of hypocrisy on the question of slavery. Jefferson did not believe in slavery and felt that slaves should be freed, yet he owned slaves and refused to set them free until he died. It seems clear that Jefferson opposed slavery not for the impact that it had on the slaves but rather for the impact it had on the larger society. Slavery constituted a threat to the nation because it presented a possible source of conflict among Euro-Americans. We will see this pattern of concern for the nation and disregard for Afro-Americans as one which repeats itself throughout American history.

The personal contradictions of Thomas Jefferson can be seen in larger scale when one takes a close look at government policies and government debate over the issue of slavery. The formal legal structure can

5. See Bardolph, *The Civil Rights Record.*

be seen in the Constitution. When the Constitution was written, it was made very clear that on the issue of slavery, property rights were placed above human rights. For the purposes of direct taxes and for the purpose of apportioning representation in the House of Representatives, African slaves were considered three-fifths of a person. Further, Congress was not allowed to restrict the slave trade until 1808. The abolishment of slavery was directed at the larger economic and social interests of some Euro-Americans, not the welfare of the slaves. As a concession to slave-holders, the Constitution obliged the states to assist in returning fugitive slaves to their masters.

From another legal point of view, to consider slaves as property meant, in fact, that slaves had no rights. A slave could not be a party to a law suit except where a free person sued for a slave's freedom. A slave could not offer testimony in court except against other Negroes. A slave could not make contracts to buy or sell goods, which meant he could not marry. And often a slave could not own property.

Afro-Americans from slavery to the present have invoked the principles of the Declaration of Independence in requesting their freedom from "cruel and unjust punishment." They took the statement that "all men are created free and equal" to be a statement universal both in its meaning and its application. The refusal of America to honor the meaning of values such as freedom and equality represents the hypocrisy and lack of faith which characterize the government's side of the relationship between it and Afro-Americans. The costs of this inequality continue to this day, and the final bill for the exploitation of Afro-American slaves has yet to be submitted.

Civil War and Reconstruction

To many Americans the Civil War was fought to free the slaves, but a closer look invalidates this view. Government considered the issue of war not to be that of freeing the slaves but rather to preserve the Union. The reluctance of government under the direction of Abraham Lincoln to readily accept slaves as soldiers supports the view that slavery and the condition of Afro-Americans was a secondary, if not a tertiary, issue. In fact, it was not until after nearly two years of war that President Lincoln in his Emancipation Proclamation decided formally to legitimate a situation which he had very little choice but to accept. On the Southern side, the shortage of manpower in the Confederate army led to the introduction of Black soldiers. Many of these soldiers believed that their valor and sacrifice in the Confederate cause would be rewarded by emancipation. By suggesting that Blacks could obtain their freedom by deserting the Confederate cause and thereby depriving that army of important sources of manpower, Lincoln could increase the possibility of victory. Once again, the pattern of government viewing Africans as objects to be manipulated in the national interest is evidenced.

When we come to the period of Reconstruction, an important question was "What will be the future of Negroes in the United States"? The answer to many was essentially "the same as in the past." While such organizations as the National Equal Rights League fought hard for the abolition of slavery and for political equality, and though this league represented one of the first attempts of Afro-Americans to organize themselves, their efforts were somewhat in vain. Immediately after the conclusion of the Civil War, Afro-Americans through such institutions as the Freedmen's Bureau began to assert their rights to land and to equality. However, it was more expedient in many cases for the Union army, the army that "freed the slaves," to do business with those slave owners and owners of large plantations in an effort to reconstruct the South and in so doing to reestablish the Union of the states. Again, Afro-Americans suffered at the expense of remaking the Union, a Union in which they had little role to play.

The infamous Black Codes (1865–1866) represented the legal mechanisms that were used virtually to reestablish slavery, penalizing unemployed Negroes or Negroes who could not prove permanent residency, while aiding White plantation owners to recruit a labor force. An Afro-American arrested on charges of unemployment or lack of a permanent residence was often sentenced to several years of hard labor, in some cases on the plantation where he had previously been a slave. The difference between serving a sentence for violating the Black Code and outright slavery was very little to the African.

During the period of Reconstruction, some Afro-Americans were elected to high positions. It was often claimed by those Whites who wished to overthrow Reconstruction and to redeem the South, that Afro-Americans were corrupt and incompetent and therefore could not be allowed to have power. Negro domination and corruption were used as the excuses to strip slaves of their recently acquired rights and privileges. In fact, at no time can it be said that Negroes were in control of any state whether in the South or in the North. There was never a Negro governor, and only in one or two states did Blacks control or have a majority in the state legislatures. The state of Mississippi was the only state in the reconstructed South to send a Negro to the Senate. The truth of the matter is that even during the most glorious moments of Reconstruction, Afro-Americans had much less political power than is popularly believed.[6]

6. See W. E. B. DuBois, *Black Reconstruction in America: 1860-1880* (Meridian, 1964).

Although amendments to the Constitution were passed by 1868 which guaranteed freedom from discrimination, many Afro-Americans continued to experience segregation and oppression in a variety of forms. In the 1870's a supplementary civil rights bill was introduced (in Congress) which specifically prohibited segregation in transportation, schools, and public accommodations. Afro-Americans throughout the country rallied to support the passage of this bill because they believed it would provide them with the protection necessary fully to participate in American society. When the bill was finally passed in 1875, many Negroes tested the law both in the North and the South and found that the enforcement was negligible and relief far from certain. As a result, attempts to use this new statute were put aside. In 1883 the Supreme Court of the United States declared this law to be unconstitutional, thereby severely limiting the attempts of Afro-Americans to seek redress for their grievances in the law and the courts.[7]

The political compromise of 1877 represents another example of the relationship of government to Afro-Americans and the consistent attempts to deny or ignore the rights of Afro-Americans for reasons of political expediency. The limited political influence that Afro-Americans had acquired during Reconstruction was gradually stripped from them by Southern state governments controlled by White majorities. Through violence and such techniques as stuffing ballot boxes and complicating the registration of voters, the "threat" of Negro voting was eliminated. Other techniques that were used to deny Afro-American participation in government involved the rewriting of state constitutions to restrict the right to vote. These restrictions included the payment of a poll tax, literacy tests, property qualifications, and finally devices such as the "grandfather clause" which waived all other requirements if one's ancestors had voted in 1860. Since very few Negroes were voting in 1860, it meant that very few Afro-Americans could vote in the 1880's and 1890's. Again we see that Afro-Americans found that government was used as a mechanism to deny their freedom and to deny their equality.

By the beginning of the twentieth century, legal racial segregation was the law of the land in respect to Afro-Americans. The establishment of various "Jim Crow" laws made it impossible for many Afro-Americans to enjoy any form of equal treatment. Education offers a very good example of the way in which law was used to deny any form of quality education. Under the guise of separate but equal, as W. E. B. Dubois demonstrated, Negroes were denied the resources and opportunities to acquire a decent education. In most states the amount of money spent for Negroes was one-half if not one-fourth the amount spent for

7. The best history of the subject is V. Vann Woodward, *The Strange Career of Jim Crow* (Oxford University Press, 1957).

Whites and the consequences of this unequal treatment on attendance, length of school terms, the quality of equipment, the pay for teachers, and their qualifications were very great.[8]

In the famous case of *Plessy* v. *Ferguson* (1896) the Supreme Court upheld the doctrine of separate but equal. Again the relationship of Afro-Americans and their government was one of denial and oppression. In 1898 the Court went on to uphold literacy and poll tax qualifications for voting. The result was that within fifteen years the Supreme Court of the United States had succeeded in destroying the impact and importance of the Fourteenth and Fifteenth Amendments. In the process, it provided the legal cover for the discriminatory actions of White Americans.

North to the City

By the beginning of the twentieth century, a variety of conditions existed in the South which pushed and pulled large numbers of Afro-Americans to the North. For the most part these people left the rural South and came to the urban North. The causes for their movement are basically two, economic need and violence. Involved in both of these causes is the apparent inability of government to demonstrate its will and capacity to meet the just aspirations of Afro-Americans.

The significance of violence is easily demonstrated by the common incidence of lynching and physical assault in the South during slavery, during the Reconstruction period, during the first part of the twentieth century and indeed through the 1960's. Physical oppression led many to leave the communities they had learned to love because they could not bear the constant intimidation and the constant threat that one's life might be taken for some imaginary insult towards a White. Many discount the impact or role of violence in forcing Negroes to move to the North, yet a careful reading of the life histories of Afro-Americans will amply document the role of fear in the decision of families not only to move from the South but in some cases to select their profession and their life goals.[9] The performance of government in protecting the safety of Afro-Americans was negligible and Blacks knew that they could not look to government, whether at the federal, state or local level, for the guarantees of life, liberty and the pursuit of happiness.

Economic need also brought migration. The majority of Negroes after slavery became sharecroppers, renting a piece of land and in turn pay-

8. See Louis R. Harlan, *Separate and Unequal* (University of North Carolina Press, 1958) and W. E. B. DuBois, and A. G. Dill, *The Common School and the Negro American* (Atlanta University Press, 1911).

9. See Abram Kardiner and Lionel Oversey, *The Mark of Oppression* (Meridian, 1951). A major personal example is Malcolm X, *The Autobiography* (Grove Press, 1964).

ing the owner a share of the harvest. This system of sharecropping, while on the surface seemingly fair, in practice turned out to be a permutation of slavery. Often the person who rented the land had to buy his equipment and his food from a store owned by the landowner. Often the sharecropper had to purchase necessities on credit from the landowner's general store and would pay his bill at harvest time. Not surprisingly the sharecropper found himself, at the end of harvest, paying part of his harvest to the owner for renting the land and the remainder of his harvest to the owner of the company store.

This perpetual poverty and the increase of Black population in the South led many to the conclusion that they could no longer support themselves on the land. There were in addition various natural catastrophies such as floods and droughts which wiped out the livelihood of many rural Afro-Americans. The ravages of the boll weevil destroyed numerous cotton crops upon which numbers of Negroes depended. Finally, the demand for employment created by the First World War led many Afro-Americans to move to the North to work in war-related industries.

The conditions that Afro-Americans met when coming North were not those of the promised land which many Afro-Americans had expected from stories of success by bragging Northern relatives. Instead they found a situation of great hostility on the part of Whites in the cities who feared that Negroes would compete for their jobs. The latter part of the nineteenth century found numbers of Black craftsmen facing stiff opposition from European immigrants. As the decades advanced, under the guise of racial separation and unionization, Blacks were gradually blocked from entry into skilled jobs. In the area of unskilled labor the same pattern of exclusion existed.

The tension between new urban dwellers, primarily Afro-Americans and recent immigrants, sparked the race riots of 1919-1920 and set a pattern of racial and ethnic relations which in some part exists today. This pattern of conflict was reinforced by the official posture of government. The attitude of the Wilson administration left little doubt in the minds of Afro-Americans that government was not prepared to fulfill those rights guaranteeed to all citizens.

It is believed by some that the Great Depression (1929-39) had a leveling effect in American society. Many feel that Afro-Americans acquired considerable benefits from the Depression and the subsequent government initiatives of the New Deal. However, Afro-Americans failed to receive equal rewards or equal participation in the New Deal, as can be seen in the two illustrative areas of housing and agriculture.

Attempts of the federal government to meet the housing needs of its citizens was translated into the building of segregated housing, thereby reinforcing residential segregation. In many cases the patterns of residential segregation that exist today can be traced to the policies and actions taken by the federal government during the Depression. The federal government, in making agreements with banks and other lending institutions, refused to guarantee mortgages on homes purchased by Negroes in White communities. Its policy was to guarantee mortgages only for stable neighborhoods. Racially integrated neighborhoods were by definition transitional and unstable. The unstated assumption was that it would be unnatural for Whites to live in integrated neighborhoods for extended periods of time. In this way the Federal Housing Administration prevented significant numbers of Negroes from purchasing housing which they could afford, but which fell outside of defined Negro areas.

Agriculture also reflects the way in which Afro-Americans shared unequally in the benefits of the New Deal. The crisis in the cotton industry as a result of floods, diseases, and competition with synthetic fibers led the federal government to subsidize farmers for restricting the amount of acreage they planted. Ideally, the tenant farmers and sharecroppers were to receive a portion of the government subsidy for not planting. In practice however, these tenant farmers and sharecroppers, the majority of them Black, received little. Again we see where the policies of government were aimed at assisting the majority population and only incidentally aimed at assisting Afro-Americans. The result of these policies quite often were further alienation and distrust on the part of Afro-Americans concerning government.

The Second World War brought a number of changes in the conditions that Afro-Americans faced in the North. The war brought additional numbers of Afro-Americans from the South in search of employment. The initial reception in these industries was one of discrimination, in that Afro-Americans were either not hired or were given the most menial jobs. It was not until the early 1940's, when the famous Negro labor leader, A. Phillip Randolph, threatened a march on Washington, that President Roosevelt responded to the aspirations of Afro-Americans by issuing the famous Executive Order 8802 which established a Fair Employment Practice Committee. This committee was initially somewhat successful in opening up jobs for Afro-Americans. However, whenever the commission became controversial, its powers were restricted and its enforcement capability minimized.

The 1950's began a new era of civil rights struggle on the part of Afro-Americans. The Supreme Court decision, *Brown v. Board of Education*, which abolished separate but equal educational facilities, was a historic case. Although the meaning and the intent of that decision has yet to be implemented, a new spirit could be found in the efforts of Afro-Americans to find legal redress to their grievances. As a result the relationship between government and Afro-Americans changed slightly. In the Montgomery bus boycott led by the Rev. Dr. Martin Luther King, Negroes began to organize themselves openly to resist the intolerable conditions they faced in the South.

In summary, the relationship of government to Afro-Americans has not been one in which citizens of African heritage could anticipate, indeed expect, government to fulfill its role in terms of providing equal distribution of the rewards of society and equal participation in the decision making of government. In essence, the past 350 years have demonstrated that much remains to fulfill the dream of America as the land of the free and the home of the brave.

CONTEMPORARY URBAN LIFE FOR AFRO-AMERICANS

The demands of Afro-Americans on government stem directly from the conditions and quality of life they face. Our purpose in this part of the essay is to give the reader a general idea of the variety of issues and forces at work within urban communities of Afro-Americans. The American racial problem is concentrated in these cities. We therefore focus on the conditions of urban life for Afro-Americans in full awareness of the fact that not all Blacks live in urban areas and, within these urban areas, that not all Afro-Americans suffer from the same degree of deprivation and powerlessness.

What is particularly important to our understanding of Afro-Americans and government, especially when describing Black urban communities, are the social forces that have created them. These communities are the result, to a great extent, of racial discrimination and oppression. The quality of life and the opportunities available to Negroes are largely determined by White society. The powerlessness of Black communities is demonstrated by numerous statistics which reveal not only that Black people own little in their communities but, more so, that they have very little to say in determining the quality and quantity of their governmental services. This point cannot be overemphasized because there is a tendency in America today to assume that indeed Afro-Americans are the cause of the problems that exist.

Recent census statistics show that fifteen million Black people, out of a total population of twenty-three million, live in 163 urban areas. This distribution is the result of a rapid process of urbanization which began around the turn of the century and continues today. As thousands of Afro-Americans moved from the countryside to the city, spurred by racial discrimination and the inability of government to enforce civil rights laws, they were forced to live in what have become known as racial ghettos. As a result, seventy percent of the Black population in the land of the free and the home of the brave now lives in these ghettos. Census data further show that the Black population is increasing twice as quickly as the White population—that is to say, a annual growth rate of two percent for Blacks as opposed to one percent for Whites, and that close to ninety percent of this population increase occurs within racial ghettos. Projecting these figures, the present ghetto population will double by the end of this century. By 1980 about one in four babies will be Black and about one out of every four Americans will be born in the ghetto.[10]

Racial ghettos stem from two sources. First, it has been usual in American history for recent arrivals to urban areas to find housing in those areas where rents were cheap. These areas invariably were the slums of the city, and the pattern has been that as individuals rise in society, they escape their slum to move into a better neighborhood and are then replaced by more recent arrivals. This process worked for the Irish, Jews, and Italians, and the same pattern was adopted by Blacks.

Second, and unlike the experience of other ethnic groups, Afro-Americans are oppressed because of the dominant social group's emphasis on race or color. Because of one's color and racial origin, one is assigned a subordinate position within society, and this position is reaffirmed generation after generation so that *race* becomes similar to *caste* in its permanency. The fact that Black Americans faced racial discrimination has meant that they have been unable to escape urban slums by using the same route as those earlier ethnic groups.

There are five major characteristics of a racial ghetto: (1) a low level of income as a result of high unemployment; (2) high population growth with a large percentage of "illegitimate" births; (3) a very low percentage of local ownership of property and means of production and a high rate of absentee ownership; (4) high living costs; and (5) the limited number of cultural and social institutions and structures which provide a sense of security and stability within the community.

Taking these five factors in order, let us first look briefly at income and unemployment. In 1965 the Social Security Administration estimated that 9.3 million Blacks, approximately 41 percent of the Black population, lived on less than the poverty income of $3600 a year for a family of four. The incidence of poverty among Blacks is thus three and one-half times higher than that among Whites. Generally, the average Black family income is approximately one-half of the amount an average White family would earn in a year. Unemployment for Blacks in the nation is twice as high as that among Whites. In ghettos, these figures

10. *Report* of the National Advisory Commission on Civil Disorders (1968), pp. 390-392.

are still higher, averaging anywhere from 10 to 12 percent a year, and the incidence of unemployment among the young aged 16 to 19 can go as high as 40 to 50 percent. Underemployment, people holding only part-time jobs or full-time jobs paying less than $3600 a year, is two and one-half times greater than the unemployment rate. This means that for the Black population of the ghetto, the combined unemployment and underemployment rate is approximately 32 percent. Given this situation, it is not surprising to see some Black people move to illegal activities to earn a living. Dope peddling, pimping, prostitution, loan enforcement, gambling and racketeering are some of the illicit activities which Black people are under pressure to enter in order to maintain a living.

High population growth is another important characteristic of contemporary urban life for Afro-Americans. This growth is remarkable in the light of an infant mortality rate which is 60 percent higher than that of Whites, a life expectancy which is seven years shorter, and a maternal mortality rate which is four times higher. It is significant that this population growth is taking place in a situation where family stability is increasingly difficult. In some cities, as many as half of the children born may be "illegitimate." In Newark and Washington it is estimated that about one out of every four Black families does not have a "legitimate" father.

The forces of low income, unemployment, and of general social oppression have caused many Black men to either leave home or to deny paternity. Since most Black mothers must work in order to support the family, the opportunity for Black children in urban areas to have the benefit of a secure and rewarding childhood experience is severely limited. This condition leads one to have a dual sense of pity and admiration: pity, because no human being in a society as wealthy as the United States should have to struggle in such ways; admiration for those families who in spite of these handicaps provide their children with the best they can in order to face a hostile environment.

A third feature of the racial ghetto is absentee control over the wealth of the community. Not only are Afro-Americans restricted and denied opportunities in the economic and social system outside of their neighborhoods, but in fact they are prevented from controlling significant parts of their own communities. In Newark where more than 50 percent of the population is Black, only 10 percent of the licensed businesses are owned by Blacks. In Washington, D.C. which has a population which is 65 percent Negro, the figure is less than eight percent. In New York City with a Black population of 1.1 million, only 12 Negro-owned businesses in 1970 employed more than 12 people.[11]

11. Collin A. Moore, *The Concrete Plantation*, paper prepared for the Metropolitan Urban Service Training Institute, New York (1970).

The same pattern exists when one studies the ownership of real estate within these areas. It is not surprising therefore that in the urban riots in Newark, Detroit, and Los Angeles, the wrath of the participants was directed not at human life but at property—property not owned or controlled by people living in the community.

The dismal economic situation is further reflected in the fact that, because of racial discrimination and inability to find other housing, Black people are forced to pay a higher rent per square foot than people living outside of the ghetto. The cost of food, entertainment, and major appliances is also significantly higher because of a restricted and imprisoned market. Most residents of these communities have neither the transportation nor the credit facilities to shop in a selective fashion throughout the city. Therefore they are forced to purchase materials and goods of inferior quality and at exorbitant prices. For example, a normal consumer item is marked up 100 percent so that a ghetto resident pays $255 for a television set that is wholesaled at $109.

A normal business loan in the ghetto is pegged at 20 percent per month, or 240 percent a year. In some extraordinary situations and emergencies, the interest rate is known as "six for five"—that is to say, the borrowers receive five dollars on Monday and pay back six dollars on Friday—pay day. The annual interest rate on a "six for five" is 1000 percent plus. A system often used by those businesses in ghettos for collection of unpaid bills is the system of garnishment, under which the creditor can withhold the salary of his client through court action without trial or a hearing. It has been estimated that in New York City 20 percent of low-income families has been subjected to this type of action. Another study by the Federal Trade Commission shows that creditors used the method of garnishment to collect from one of every 11 ghetto customers. In contrast, department stores in non-ghetto areas used garnishment against one out of 14,500 customers. The disparity of these figures—for greater than the relative credit risks involved—explains to a large extent the strong feeling of exploitation that Afro-Americans feel in their own community.

The limited number of social institutions capable of providing an infrastructure for a viable community is the fifth of our characteristics of contemporary urban life for Afro-Americans. The lack of an adequate educational, health, and sanitation system, the inability to maintain social peace, and the resultant disorganization, all make the challenge of a decent life formidable.

The overcrowding of schools with high student-teacher ratios, lower teaching standards, low student performances, restricted budgets and little community control over school administration contribute to the high percentage of Black students who fail to complete high school. The most apparent characteristic of urban ghettos is the waste and filth which speaks primarily to the absence of an adequate sanitation service. Clean streets are a function of the political power a community can mobilize. As a result, those areas populated by White, higher income, professional people with greater political access and skills, receive better sanitation services. These conditions of deprivation, when contrasted to the world of luxury and fantasy of modern television, explain to a large degree the great sense of alienation on the part of the youth within these communities leading to the high rate of juvenile delinquency, narcotics addiction, and other forms of social disorganization. The inability of Black youths and in many instances Black adults to achieve status and power in legitimate areas of economic life forces them increasingly into fields which are illegal. As a result, the incidence of crime in these ghettos is much greater than in similar White working class areas.

In spite of the numerous programs sponsored by the federal government beginning in 1964 to abolish poverty, very little has been accomplished. Five years and 250 riots later, one sees that the situation has barely changed economically within urban Black communities. In general, Black ownership of land has decreased from 12 million acres in 1956 to 7 million acres in 1966, a decline of over 40 percent in a decade. Black business ownership is declining by 20 percent while business ownership as a whole in the United States is increasing. In Black communities, many restaurants, retail businesses, even funeral parlors and barbershops are failing, even though these businesses traditionally have been the strongest in the ghetto. The major explantion for their failure is that, with the breakdown of formal segregation, corporate competition from outside of the community has now moved in. Small businesses within the community have not been able to withstand the competitive force.

SOME CONTEMPORARY ISSUES

We now focus on a variety of issues within Black communities that clearly demonstrate the relationship and the pattern of encounter between government and Afro-Americans. In each, our concern will be to describe the issue, with attention to the possible origins of the problem and the dynamics within Black communities in meeting this issue. We will then be concerned with describing the form and content of demands made by Afro-Americans on government. Finally, we will be concerned with the response of government, distinguishing between the establishment of government policy through laws, executive orders, or court rulings, and the enforcement of that policy.

The struggle of Afro-Americans for adequate income and employment has paralleled their quest for freedom and equality. Daniel P. Moynihan has written: "The principal measure of progress toward equality will be that of employment. It is the primary source of individual or group identity. In America what you do is what you are: to do nothing is to be nothing; to do little is to be little. The equations are implacable and blunt and ruthlessly public.

"For the Negro American it is already and will continue to be the master problem. It is the measure of white bonafides, it is the measure of Negro competence and also of the competence of American society. Most importantly the linkage between problems of employment and the range of social pathology that afflicts the Negro community is unmistakable. Employment not only controls the present for the Negro American but in a most profound way it is creating the future as well."[12]

What are the problems involved in this issue of income and employment as it affects Afro-Americans? First let us take a look at the situation as it is today. The majority of Afro-Americans are concentrated in low-skilled, low-paid jobs, and they are the last hired and the first to be fired whenever technological changes are brought into industry or when the economy suffers a recession or depression. Afro-Americans tend to be out of work for longer periods of time than whites and in addition they suffer the ills of underemployment and part-time employment quite often at substandard pay.

In spite of the increased employment opportunities resulting from World War II and the Korean conflict, Afro-Americans have moved up only slightly in the economic structure. The jobs they held in the South as unskilled or service workers, farm laborers, and domestics, became in the North semi-skilled jobs in factories and construction. Afro-Americans have made very little progress in gaining skilled manual work, white collar positions, and jobs of professional status. Within the professional category, Afro-Americans have been concentrated in lower paying occupations such as clergymen, teachers, and nurses. Until recently Afro-Americans were virtually nonexistent in the professions of medicine, accounting and engineering. In 1960 Afro-Americans constituted less than half of one percent of all salaried managers and business officials.

These industries which once absorbed many Afro-Americans are now declining, and they find themselves with fewer job opportunities in new industries. The occupations in industries which attract most Blacks are industries subject to seasonal variations and, as a result, high unemploy-

12. National Advisory Commission on Civil Disorders, p. 252.

ment. A large proportion of Afro-Americans are not covered by minimum wage laws and they often do not have access to collective bargaining agreements or social security. Even those Afro-Americans who belong to unions tend to be recent members with less seniority and other forms of security. The general conclusion is that Blacks have occupied, do occupy, and most likely will continue to occupy the bottom levels of American economy.

Explanations of the economic condition of Afro-Americans include the belief that they live in a "culture of poverty" which prevents them from acquiring the values and work habits necessary for success in the American economy, e.g., punctuality, thrift, pride in work, etc. Another explanation argues that the instability and unpredictability of Negro families prevent children from acquiring personal values and norms that will provide guidelines for success in the economic world. A final explanation concerns the lack of opportunity for Afro-Americans to enter the various forms of economic activity. By denying Afro-American access to training, education, housing and jobs, American society insures that they will not be prepared for opportunities if and when they become available. Therefore the cause is not the condition of the Afro-American, but rather the condition of the larger society which chooses to restrict him because of his racial heritage. Of these three explanations, the evidence to be discussed below suggests that the restriction of opportunity by a larger society is the most significant factor in determining employment opportunities.

There are many barriers which act to prevent Afro-Americans from enjoying a better economic position. One of the most important is the pattern of residential segregation which locks Afro-Americans into communities lacking the educational and social facilities necessary to train and prepare people for a rewarding material life. The inferior education found within urban ghettos prevents Afro-Americans from acquiring the skills and outlook necessary for success in employment. Enforced residential segregation also makes it difficult for Afro-Americans to be aware of job opportunities in surrounding communities. In many cases, moreover, the transportation facilities that exist are inadequate to assist Afro-Americans to reach new jobs outside of their community. Lower car ownership among Afro-Americans removes the most suitable alternative to inadequate public transportation. The demands of modern industry for space in order to employ technological developments in production result in the movement of businesses and industry from the central cities to the suburbs, but this movement of business away from Black communities raises another barrier to greater economic advancement on the part of Afro-Americans. Furthermore, these technological developments often destroy those unskilled and semi-skilled jobs which traditionally have been the occupations in which Afro-Americans were concentrated.

Recent trends in the national labor force suggest additional problems faced by Afro-Americans. The demand for female workers in the clerical and service occupations has had a negative impact on increased participation of Afro-American men in the labor force. The demand for highly educated workers is another trend which works against Blacks with unequal opportunity to quality education. Finally, the impact of technology and the entrance of large numbers of youth into the labor force has forced a number of older Afro-American workers into early retirement even though the benefits and security of retirement are often not available to Afro-Americans.

Attitudes of White corporation mangement present another problem. The corporation decides what employment opportunities will be available for Afro-Americans, or whether compensatory training programs will be available to give Afro-Americans greater opportunity. Stereotypes of Negroes may be held by business decision-makers, such as a belief that Afro-Americans are ignorant, lazy, and unable to handle abstract thought. In addition, White corporation executives are often reluctant to place a Negro in a new position because they anticipate negative reactions from customers or from White workers.

The attitudes and prejudices of white co-workers are another important factor in determining Afro-American employment opportunity. The fact is that a worker, no matter who he is, must rely on the confidence and support of his co-workers if he is to learn a job quickly and to do it well. If white workers resent Afro-Americans being brought onto the job, then they will provide little of the support that is necessary; and this lack of support may result in the Afro-American not performing to capacity, or becoming discouraged to the point of resigning because of the hostile environment. Finally, it is in the relationship between a worker and his peers that information about new job opportunities becomes available. The refusal of white workers to accept Afro-Americans and include them in this information system has a limiting effect on economic opportunity.

Labor unions have a further effect. Historically many unions have discriminated against Afro-Americans because of the fear of White workers that Blacks would replace them in their jobs or would drive down the level of wages. The construction industry is a notorious example of how unions have been used to restrict Afro-Americans from occupying the better paying and more secure crafts. Those Afro-Americans that do belong to these unions are generally restricted to common laborer positions and barred from membership in the professional or crafts unions such as plumbers, electrical workers, and carpenters. These restrictions are maintained by setting conditions of membership which prevent Afro-Americans from qualifying or by establishing stringent apprenticeship programs which can be used to block their entrance to the better-paying jobs.

The demands of Afro-Americans on government for correction or improvement in their economic position have taken essentially two forms. The first is a demand for better training and preparation for new jobs, and the second is for greater access to existing jobs. The demand for greater access is closely tied to the demand that racial discrimination in employment be stopped by government antidiscrimination policies and the enforcement of those policies. The demand for better preparation is closely attached to the need for quality education at the primary and secondary level. In addition, demands are being made on government to provide larger and more sophisticated technical training programs for young workers as well as programs for retraining of Black workers who are displaced by technology. If government is not successful in providing adequate jobs in the economy, then it is felt that it should provide some minimum income support to enable families to survive and to prepare their children for greater success.

Afro-Americans have pressed these demands in a variety of ways. Legal action has been pressed by the Urban League and the National Association for the Advancement of Colored People's Legal Defense Fund. Other forms of these demands include legal suits, introduction of new bills in the various legislatures, lobbying for passage of such legislation, and finally a variety of confrontation tactics ranging from boycotting businesses and unions known to discriminate against Afro-Americans to picketing and harrassment.

The response of government to these demands includes the passage of numerous laws forbidding the refusal to hire, employ, or promote individuals because of race, creed, color or national origin. These laws have been followed by the creation of various fair employment practice commissions and equal opportunity agencies. In general the Federal government has used its budget as a way by which to force employers to comply with nondiscrimination policies. Any individual or organization receiving government support, whether directly or indirectly, must agree to abide by government policies barring racial discrimination. If it is found that an individual is discriminating, the government support may be withdrawn.

Another response of government has been the passage of numerous manpower training laws aimed at giving Afro-Americans greater skills to prepare them for full participation in the economy and to avoid the loss of employment due to increasing technological change. The government increasingly is becoming an employer of last resort, either by increasing the money for welfare assistance, thereby subsidizing unemployed Afro-Americans, or by hiring increasing numbers of Blacks within government. It should be noted that most of the job openings for Afro-Americans in government are at the lower levels of civil service and are generally of a semi-skilled nature.

The variety of manpower training programs are aimed at rehabilitating the person as opposed to correcting flaws within the larger economic system which perpetuates Afro-American economic disadvantage. These programs assume that retraining the individual will insure greater opportunity for employment. These actions ignore the fact that the significant factor in blocking increased employment among Afro-Americans is the racial prejudice found outside of Afro-American communities, particularly in business and unions. However, the government has attempted to use its influence and sanctions to convince unions to increase the number of Afro-Americans in their membership. The Philadelphia Plan, the Chicago Plan, and the New York Plan are programs designed by unions, government and Afro-Americans to insure rapid entry into all levels of construction work.

In spite of these laws, the economic situation facing Afro-Americans has not improved. The monumental Civil Rights Act of 1964 provides that government may cancel contracts with firms which practice racial discrimination. It is indicative of weak federal enforcement that no contract has ever been cancelled, and it was not until May 1968 that the first proceeding was started to ban a firm from future federal contracts under the provisions of the act. Every year since 1964 legislation has been introduced in the Congress to permit the national Equal Employment Opportunity Commission to issue cease-and-desist orders and require reinstatement or hiring of aggrieved workers in discrimination cases. It is disturbing that every year such a provision has been defeated. In 1968 the Justice Department filed 25 suits under the equal employment section of the 1964 Civil Rights Act, but only 10 suits were filed in the four previous years. In 1970, despite the Nixon administration's emphasis on black capitalism, Afro-Americans still operate less than one percent of the nation's private businesses.

There are two primary factors which explain the poor response of government to the demands of Afro-Americans for greater economic opportunity. The first is the failure to provide equal employment opportunity commissions and fair employment practice commissions with the necessary power to enforce government policy. These commissions operate on the basis of conciliation and education and have very little power to enforce compliance to the laws of the land. The second significant factor is directly associated with the political power of unions. Our political parties and candidates require votes and large sums of money for electoral campaigns. They risk losing these contributions and votes if they go against the wishes and practices of the large labor unions.

Education for Afro-Americans

The importance of education in American society cannot be over-emphasized. Education is considered to be the primary way by which an individual or a group advances. This issue has become important because Afro-Americans are blocked from advancement due to their lack of preparation for a modern and changing labor force. The skills required to cope with technological innovations and the realization that large numbers of people will change their profession two or three times during their working life explains why Afro-Americans are increasingly concerned about the quality and direction of the education they receive.

In general, the issue of education for Afro-Americans is quite similar to the issue of economic opportunity. The fact is that the quality of education available to most Afro-Americans is inferior. The past reluctance of government to provide education for slaves and for freedmen is paralleled in many cases by the reluctance of government to give high priority to the issue of contemporary education for Afro-Americans.

Specific indicators of inferior education are readily available, in unequal results. Only 58 percent of Black school children in grade school complete the eighth grade as against 73 percent of their White classmates. About 40 percent of Black teenagers finish high school compared with 62 percent of Whites. Black enrollment has almost doubled since 1964 in universities but the relative Black total has barely changed: only 6.4 percent of U. S. undergraduates are Black compared with 5 percent in 1964. Black undergraduates in 1969 numbered 434,000; almost half attend Black colleges, mainly in the South.[13] Afro-Americans account for an estimated one percent of doctoral candidates (most of them in education), less than three percent of law students and three percent of medical students. Although 10 percent of public school teachers are Black, few become administrators. In New York City, where 32 percent of students are Black, the school system has 24 black principals out of a total of 893. In 1968 Blacks constituted less than one percent of the faculties at 80 public universities.

The physical plant available for Afro-American education is similarly inferior. In Newark, 31 of the 75 school structures were built in the last century, and 44 buildings are more than 50 years old. The educational impact of such an obsolete physical plant is reflected in the following statistics. In September 1966, there were 49,240 pupil places in Newark. However, there were 55,292 pupils in the elementary

13. "Situation Report," *Time* (April 6, 1970).

schools; thus, the schools lacked 6,052 places. The superintendent of schools estimates that the shortage is growing, and as of 1969, there was a shortage of over 10,000 pupil places in the elementary schools.

Even where education has been available, it has not eliminated the disparity in life chances between Blacks and Whites. Afro-Americans with eight years or less of school have incomes only 75 percent of Whites with similar education. Black college graduates similarly have incomes 74 percent of that of their White counterparts. Black college graduates earn but $13 more per year at the median than White high school graduates.

The school experience has had unequal results. In the Northeastern metropolitan areas, Afro-American students start school with slightly lower scores than Whites on standard achievement tests. By the sixth grade they are 1.6 grades behind, and by the 12th grade, they are 3.3 grades behind. Moreover, many Afro-Americans have left school by this point. It is also significant that most city schools are segregated. Three-fourths of Negro elementary school students attend virtually all-Black schools, while five-sixths of White students attend schools that are 90 percent or more White.

The educational demands of Afro-Americans have been primarily the quest for (a) quality education and (b) an education which speaks to the social and psychological needs of Afro-American children. It is clear to Afro-Americans that quality education means providing students with the skills and knowledge necessary for economic success. The need for psychological reinforcement of Afro-American students in their education is the result of Blacks becoming increasingly aware of the fact that their survival in a racist society requires that their children receive compensatory measures to develop a positive self-image. The finest education without a positive self-image is deemed to be a handicap.

The concern for quality education has led Afro-Americans to focus on two strategies to achieve their goals. The first is for complete racial integration in the school systems. The assumption of Afro-Americans is that inferior education in Black communities is the result of their lack of power as well as indifference on the part of white society. Afro-Americans are convinced that white society would not allow its own children to receive as inferior an education. Therefore, the greatest guarantee of educational quality is to have racially integrated schools. In addition, it is felt that racial integration in school systems insures better citizenship and leads to new patterns of human encounter between the races which eventually will guarantee greater racial justice.

Numerous tactics and strategies have been used to bring government to meet this demand for racial integration in the schools. In 1954 the Supreme Court decision in *Brown vs. Board of Education* represented a major attempt by Afro-Americans directly to petition the government to meet the issue of quality education. At the national level, Afro-Americans also have lobbied to pass bills in Congress such as the 1965 Elementary and Secondary Education Act, which appropriated special funds to facilitate quality education for poor children of all races. At the local level groups of Afro-Americans have used the courts to enforce compliance with existing laws by ordering the school boards to adopt integration plans. In addition, groups of Afro-American parents have worked with local school boards in setting up various study commissions aimed at devising new ways by which the goal of quality education in a racially integrated setting could be a reality. These efforts have been coupled with numerous confrontations by angry parents who picket school systems, and in some cases have engaged in school boycotts whereby the parents keep their children at home to protest inadequate education. In many cases various forms of busing (recently supported by the Supreme Court) have been suggested to provide the racial balance necessary to quality education.

The drive for community control of education represents the other major educational strategy used by Afro-Americans. If parents living within the community can have a greater say concerning the quality of education being provided to their children, then there is a greater chance that the present inadequate situation would be corrected. Afro-Americans point to the long tradition of community control of education in the suburbs, where locally elected school boards determine to a large extent the personnel and curriculum of the school system. The argument is that if such a strategy works in White communities in the suburbs, then the same strategy should be applied in the Black ghettos of the cities.

What has been the response of government? On the demand for racial integration, the response can be characterized as: (a) a desire to overstudy the problem rather than to act on it; (b) procrastination; (c) a refusal to enforce existing policies at the local level; and (d) inadequate funding. While there have been laws passed, court rulings made, and monies made available, it is clear that governmet in most cases would prefer to study the problem of inferior education for Afro-Americans rather than allocate the money for direct intervention and experimentation. The initial response to demands made upon government commonly is to establish a commission to study the problem. An example is the famous New York City Commission on Integration, set up in 1955 to deal with the findings of the Supreme Court on the impact of racial segregation in education.

The Commission was divided into six subcommissions to study integration in New York schools. For three years the Board of Education held public hearings on the reports of each of the subcommissions and approved some of their recommendations and adopted further policy resolutions. The two most crucial and controversial reports on integration concerned teacher assignment and zoning. The first recommendation was that experienced teachers be assigned to ghetto schools. Because they had the greatest experience and skill, they should be placed where the greatest need was. The recommendation was defeated, because of the opposition of teachers who feared to work in Black communities, and that of the teachers' union which sought to increase its power within the city school system by meeting the threat of teachers being transferred against their will.

The second controversial proposal of the Commission was that a special unit be set up to locate new schools in areas where racial integration would be feasible. Although such a unit was eventually established, it was never given the authority to implement the recommendations of the zoning subcommission. The opposition of local real estate interests was sufficient to make this device harmless or ineffectual. The real estate industry is concerned with maintaining racially stable neighborhoods, so that the value of property remains constant. An integrated school system would, in its opinion, eventually lead to an integrated neighborhood which automatically means an unstable neighborhood with fluctuating land values.

The work of the Commission on Integration has been followed periodically by numerous other commissions charged with an analysis of the problem of quality education of New York City school children. The studies continue to document a situation which has changed very little, a situation of obvious educational disadvantage particularly for Afro-Americans. The difficulty in implementing the plans of these various commissions further convinces government that the best response to such demands is to appoint another study commission, with the knowledge that the amount of time and effort spent in studying the problem will provide government with the time necessary to defuse a potentially explosive situation. This strategy fails, however, when one sees the growing impatience on the part of Afro-Americans with the procrastination of government.

In other parts of the country, particularly the South, the major response of government to the issue of racial integration and quality education has been a refusal to enforce existing policies at the local level. The fear of alienating potential political support within White communities has led government to abdicate its responsibility to enforce the law of the land. When the Supreme Court in 1955 ruled that schools should be integrated "with all deliberate speed," it did not consider that deliberate speed would involve 16 years of "on again, off again" enforcement. In 1970, 38 percent of Black students in the South attended integrated schools, while only 27 percent of Black students in other regions attended such schools. The fact that the majority of Black students continue to attend segregated schools suggests that concerned Afro-Americans cannot be assured that the national government possesses the will and capacity to provide relief from the burden of inferior education.

Government at the local level is in many cases equally unresponsive on the problems of education, for two reasons. First, local government must contend with the increasing unionization of teachers. As these unions become stronger in organization and political power, they are more effective in deterring locally elected officials from innovating or enforcing policies aimed at providing quality education for Afro-Americans. Secondly, education in urban communities increasingly is coming under the control of large bureaucracies. The inability of local government to move the educational bureaucracies quickly and efficiently explains in part why there has been so little progress in education.

Finally, the refusal of government to place a high priority on education for Afro-Americans is reflected in the meager funds allocated for education. Title I of the Elementary and Secondary Education Act was funded at one billion dollars a year, to be expended for disadvantaged schools. This allocation came to roughly $100 per assisted pupil. This amount is not very much, considering that these monies go to schools that have been systematically underfunded, and whose children's needs are overwhelming. More important, much of the money was spent on those children and on those activities which did not really need high priority.

Frustration over the response of government to the demand for racial integration and quality education has led numerous Black parents and organizations to the alternative program—control of local schools by the community. Again New York City represents a case in point of the defeat of an educational program for Afro-Americans. The fight between community organizations and the teachers' union over the issue of community control resulted in the abdication of responsibility on the part of local government in the face of union opposition. Effective control over the local schools does not exist in Afro-American urban ghettos.

Housing and Urban Renewal

The issue of decent housing for all Americans is of recent origin. The proliferation of new housing over the past twenty years is the result of an increased awareness that, as the country became more urban, it was necessary to develop programs to revive decaying business districts and industrial areas, to design adequate transportation systems, and to protect the environment. Government activity in this important area

of human life first started in the early 1930s with creation of the Federal
Housing Administration, designed to raise the quality of residential
construction and to create new neighborhoods. The Public Housing
Administration, concerned with low-income housing, was an extension
of government efforts in this area. The Federal Housing Act of 1949
was another major step towards the goal of providing decent housing
for all Americans.

The concern for shelter has been one of the dominant issues in the
lives of Afro-Americans, particularly as the flood of southern rural
migrants crested during the last decades. The declaration of National
Housing Policy, which introduced the National Housing Act of 1949,
states very clearly the concern of government to meet the housing needs
of all citizens, particularly those who occupy racial ghettos:

> "The Congress hereby declares that the general welfare and the security of
> the nation and the health and living standards of its people require housing
> production and related community development sufficient to remedy the
> serious housing shortage, the elimination of substandard and other inade-
> quate housing through the clearance of slums and blighted areas, and the
> realization as soon as feasible of the goal of a decent home and suitable
> living environment for every American family, thus contributing to the
> advancement of the growth, wealth and security of the nation."

The specific purpose of the Housing Act of 1949 was "to provide
federal aid to assist slum clearance projects and low rent public housing
projects initiated by local agencies."

In light of this clear statement of purpose it is depressing to know
that, in spite of the great wealth of the United States, a large number
of American families today live in housing which is considered a serious
threat to health and safety. The 1960 census identifies one-eighth of the
nation's urban households as dwellings which are dilapidated or lacking
in sanitary facilities. An additional number of houses, while structurally
sound, are in violation of numerous local building codes. Fully six million
families, at least one-sixth of our urban population, reside in slum conditions. The majority of these families have incomes which are so low
that they are prevented from acquiring better housing. In addition,
for reasons of racial discrimination, those families now living in slum
conditions who might be eligible for better housing find that the market
is restricted. Slums include substantial numbers of the elderly, the racial
minorities, the unskilled, the handicapped, and the young. These are the
people whom our society ignores and oppresses.

Since the passage of the Housing Act, significant progress has been
made in meeting many of its goals of a decent house for every citizen.
Overcrowding has declined substantially for most Americans and the

number of substandard dwelling units has dropped by more than 40 percent. It should be underlined, however, that virtually none of the improvement resulted from programs initiated by the 1949 legislation. As of 1960, less than 100,000 substandard dwelling units had been demolished under the renewal provisions of the Act.[14] Progress seems to have been the consequence of rising incomes, full employment and liberal FHA (Federal Housing Authority) and VA (Veterans Administration) mortgage financing, all of which enabled families to obtain better housing.

While progress has been achieved for most Americans, Afro-Americans are again conspicuous by their unequal share in the wealth and progress of American society. Most communities with urban slums, faced with a loss of tax ratables and rising costs for municipal services, have used federal monies for other purposes than increasing available housing for low-income groups. As a result, 25 percent of the communities receiving aid under the Housing Act do not have a single residential low-income project. Instead, these communities demolish slums and ghettos in order to create sites for commerce and industry which will attract more tax money. Another 25 percent of the municipalities receiving assistance have reserved over 50 percent of their renewed acreage for nonresidential purposes. For all communities participating in the program, approximately 600 sites were residential before renewal, while only 350 will remain residential upon completion.

In those cases where local governments have made plans for residential units, the new structures are designed for higher income families. Upon examination it appears that a very small percentage of the three billion dollars allocated to local communities for federal renewal programs have been spent for projects intended to improve living accommodations for low-income families. In general, the attitude of government towards urban renewal and slum clearance has been one of Negro removal. What has been characteristic of most efforts has been a policy of destroying existing units, while making very little provision for providing new sources of housing. The result has been that many Afro-Americans living in urban areas have been forced to move from one slum to another with no provisions for suitable alternatives.

What is the housing situation for Afro-Americans today? Black Americans pay more than Whites for comparable housing and are four times more likely to live in substandard housing. In Black ghettos, housing density is almost double that of middle-class urban areas, and 100 times greater than in the suburbs. High density contributes to greater fire hazards, defeats garbage disposal, litters streets with junked cars, and

14. William Grigsby, *Housing Markets and Public Policy* (University of Pennsylvania Press, 1964), p. 229.

contributes to a generally unhealthy environment for family life. Over-crowding, leaky ceilings, rats, faulty plumbing, and cockroaches are the result of high density. High density is illustrated in Chicago, where the Black population is one-third of the total, yet Afro-Americans are confined to one-tenth of the land area of the city.

Poverty and racial discrimination condemn Afro-Americans to bad housing. Three other factors contribute to their inadequate housing: (1) Public housing, half of which is occupied by Afro-Americans, is very scarce. (2) Inadequate and distorted federal programs such as urban renewal and highway building have destroyed 800,000 city housing units between 1949 and 1967. (3) Until recently, federal programs such as FHA and VA were aimed almost exclusively at financing and insuring the construction of new housing in the suburbs or non-ghetto neigh-borhoods.

Given the income of Afro-American families, it is clear that many families cannot participate in the housing market. The median sales price for all new one-family houses in nonfarm areas in 1966 was more than $21,000. For conventionally financed houses, the median price was $25,000, and fewer than one in seven units sold for less than $15,000. Even at this comparatively low price, Afro-Americans are at a distinct competitive disadvantage. For example, the annual income necessary to afford a $15,000 home is estimated to be about $7,000 a year. Less than one-half of all Afro-American families have annual incomes at or above that level. Since 1966, the combined effects of inflation and a tight mortgage market have increased the obstacles to home ownership.

When measured against the estimate of housing need, past federal efforts of meeting this need appear almost trivial. The public housing program of 1937, for example, has provided fewer than 700,000 units in its more than thirty years of existence. The 221(d)(3) program of the Federal Housing Authority has provided fewer than 50,000 units since its enactment in 1961, and the Rent Supplement Program has been funded at so low a level that it has been unable to produce more than a handful of units. As a result, fewer than 800,000 low-income housing units have been produced through governmental programs, while the need exceeds six million.[15] In thirty years government has succeeded in producing fewer units for the nations poor than the home building industry provides in a *single* year for the affluent.

The lack of suitable housing is more serious when it is understood that patterns of racial discrimination force Afro-Americans to remain prisoners within a restricted area. In 1967, 55 of every 100 Negroes lived

15. Martin Sloane, "The 1968 Housing Act: Best Yet—But Is It Enough?," *Civil Rights Digest*, 1 (Fall, 1968), p. 2.

in central cities, as against only 27 of every Whites. The figures for suburbs indicate that 37 out of every 100 Whites lived in such areas, while only 13 of every 100 Blacks lived in outlying parts of the metropolis, including suburbs. While the federal government and 27 states have anti-discrimination housing laws on the books, they are notoriously unenforced. For example, the United States Justice Department has assigned but 13 lawyers to enforce the Fair Housing Act of 1968. These lawyers have brought 44 cases to court and have won 13.

Afro-Americans have pressed two housing demands: an effective program of urban renewal, and greater governmental efforts to abolish patterns of residential segregation. One form these demands have taken has been riot. One of the major causes of the Newark rebellion of 1967 was the fact that many Afro-Americans felt that the urban renewal plans of Newark were aimed at moving them out of the city while no provisions were made to provide alternate accommodations. More common forms of action have been legal battles in the courts, lobbying at all levels of government in the legislatures, and confrontation politics, such as blocking building construction in Black communities.

What has been the response of government? The urban renewal program and the Model Cities program have of course attempted to retard the following process: Negroes move slowly block after block, prices are inflated, space overutilized and undermaintained, the neighborhood deteriorates, and young couples who would prefer and could afford to own single-family homes are prevented from doing so because of patterns of racial discrimination. In addition, government is attempting to restructure the process by which urban renewal takes place and to broaden the range of people who participate in the decision making. In most cases slum clearance policy and urban development plans are the result of negotiations between the professional staff of local housing authorities and private developers. Attempts have been made to involve communities in the development of plans; however, the expertise available to community leaders is small and therefore the quality of their participation is deficient.

It should be noted at this point that the pattern of racial discrimination in employment again has a singular impact on the development of housing. Of 24,000 members of the American Institute of Architects, only 450 are Black. Of the 8,500 city planners in the United States, 80 are Black. Because there are so few Blacks expert in these fields, they cannot participate fully in the formulation of housing and urban renewal programs. The development of the inner city, the home of Afro-Americans, is thus necessarily planned by others. In general, therefore, despite initial good intentions, government is attempting to correct a situation which led Scott Greer to claim, "At a cost of more than three billion dollars the urban renewal agency has succeeded in materially reducing the supply of low-cost housing in American cities." [16]

To this point the governmental response has been inadequate. Federal funds have been limited. Restrictive union rules governing the method of construction and the availability of manpower have curtailed low-cost building. Furthermore, antique building codes are an effective deterrent to the development and use of innovative and cheap construction. Many techniques for prefabricated housing have been developed abroad, but local codes prevent the importation of these methods. In addition, unions which fear the impact of technology use these codes to retain traditional building techniques.

Government efforts to combat housing segregation vary from locality to locality. In general, the national government has adopted a policy of minimum enforcement of antidiscrimination laws which is similar to its policy on racial segregation in education. A vital barrier to action on behalf of racially "open housing" is the political influence and ideological verve of the various real estate associations. For example, the National Association of Real Estate Boards has 83,000 members. Opposing the federal laws banning housing discrimination by race, creed, color or national origin, it argued that such a law would be inherently evil and would sound the death knell of private property. Such legislation is viewed as an attempt to grant one group an alleged "right" by trampling on the rights of others.

Under the civil rights legislation an aggrieved party can sue in state or federal court for a restraining order against an owner, broker, or lending institution accused of housing discrimination. The court has authority to award the plaintiff punitive damages up to $500. In spite of the fact that the teeth of such a law are extremely weak, real estate spokesman continue to undermine and oppose government efforts openly to eliminate housing bias. The political power wielded by such a group and the sanctity of private property are the major sources of strength for the opposition to government initiative.

Political Participation

Afro-Americans are severely restricted in American politics in at least two ways. First, Afro-Americans have been restricted in the degree of participation in the various decision-making processes of government. These restrictions range from the initial act of voting to the holding of elected or appointed positions in local, state, and national government. Second, Afro-Americans receive unequal shares of goods, services, re-

16. Scott Greer, *Urban Renewal and American Cities* (Bobbs-Merrill, 1965), p. 3.

wards, and benefits of American government. Our analysis of the issue areas of income and employment, education, and housing clearly document the second form of limited participation. Therefore let us focus on the issue of restricted political participation in the decision-making processes of government.

Out of 203 million Americans, a reported 22.7 million or some 12% are Black. A recent survey by the Metropolitan Applied Research Center shows that there are now 1,469 Afro-American officials in the United States. Among these are 168 state legislators, 48 mayors, 575 other elected city officials, 362 school board members and 99 law enforcement officials. The rapid growth and expansion of officeholding has taken place in the South. However, the only state in which the proportion of Negro legislators is greater than the percentage of the Black population is the state of Ohio: it has 13 Negro lawmakers out of 132, although blacks constitute only eight percent of the population. By contrast Afro-Americans comprise 42 percent of Mississippi's population, but there is only one Black member in the legislature. Afro-Americans form a majority on the councils of only two major cities, Detroit and Gary. The only large Southern city in which Blacks come close to proportional representation is Jacksonville, Florida, where they hold four of nine city council seats.

On the federal level there are now 12 Black representatives and one senator. Ten years ago the figures were four and zero. At the policy-making level of the executive branch, Afro-Americans have little influence, although President Johnson appointed the first Black cabinet member and numerous other Afro-Americans to lower level positions, such as Carl Rowan as Director of the United States Information Agency. The exclusion of Afro-Americans in the Nixon administration indicates that this society views participation of Afro-Americans in decision making as more of a luxury than a necessity.

In terms of voting power, Afro-Americans have made dramatic gains in the South, where 52 percent of all Afro-Americans live. There are approximately 800,000 more black voters registered today than there were before the 1965 Voting Rights Act. In the nation as a whole, the increases in voting registration has been less than one million (from 6,345,000 in 1966 to 7,238,000 at the time of the 1968 presidential election). The relatively small increase in voter registration is due to the fact that there have been few sustained registration drives among Afro-Americans outside of the South, and it also speaks to the alienation, fear, and futility that many Afro-Americans experience concerning the act of voting.

An important indication of Afro-American participation in governmental decision making is the extent to which Afro-Americans participate in the various legal professions. The enactment and enforcement of laws is clearly a sphere of governmental activity, but more importantly the profession of law is quite often a prerequisite to an active political career. The number of political decision makers with a legal background indicates that movement from the profession of law to the holding of elected or appointive office is an established road to greater political participation. In general, Afro-Americans are under-represented in the profession of law and law enforcement and over-represented in crime and punishment as seen in Figures 6.1 and 6.2. Thurgood Marshall sits on the Supreme Court, but of 459 federal judges, only 22 are Black. Few Afro-Americans are lawyers, local judges, or even policemen. As for prison administration, California represents a typical case, in that 28 percent of the state's inmates are Black, but all 13 prison wardens are White.

A recent study by Harold Baron on Black powerlessness in Chicago provides additional data on political participation of Afro-Americans. Baron found that in 1965 some 20 percent of the people in Cook County

Figure 6.1.

RATIO 100:1

Proportion of Afro-American Lawyers in U.S.
300,000 Other vs. 3000 Black

Of 12,000 State & City Judges
178 Or .015% Are Black

OF 93 U.S. DIST. ATTORNEYS NONE
ARE BLACK

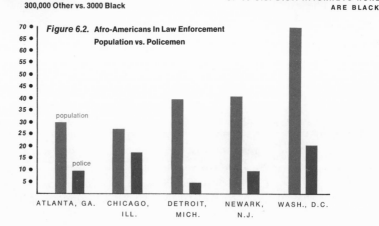

Figure 6.2. Afro-Americans In Law Enforcement
Population vs. Policemen

70
65
60
55
50
45
40
35
30
25
20
15
10
5

population

police

ATLANTA, GA.   CHICAGO, ILL.   DETROIT, MICH.   NEWARK, N.J.   WASH., D.C.

and 28 percent of the people in Chicago were Afro-American. Yet the representation of Negroes in policy-making positions was minimal. Of the top 10,997 policy-making positions in the major Cook County institutions, Afro-Americans occupied only 285 or 2.6 percent. In government, out of a total of 1,088 policy-making positions, Afro-Americans held 58. This five percent is about one-fourth of the racial percentage in the total county population. Of the 364 elective positions surveyed, Negroes occupied 29 or eight percent, which indicates that the franchise has helped Afro-Americans gain some representation. However, they held the highest proportion of positions on appointed supervisory boards such as the Board of Education and the Chicago Housing Authority. There they occupied 10 of the 77 policy-making positions or about 13 percent.

Afro-Americans were better represented in elected nonjudicial offices then they were in local administrative positions or in important federal jobs based in Chicago. Afro-Americans held 12 percent of the nonjudicial elected posts in Chicago's government, but only little over one percent of the appointive policy-making positions in the city administration. This same pattern appears at the federal level, where there are two Negroes out of 13 Congressmen from Cook County. In spite of the percentage of Negro population, Afro-Americans held only three percent of the presidential appointments for the Chicago area and two percent of the top federal civil service posts. In spite of this evidence of limited political participation, Afro-Americans held twice as many important posts in the public sector as they have in the private sector.

Baron concludes that the more powerful the post in public or private government, the fewer the Black policy makers. The actual power vested in Afro-American policy makers is calculated to be about one-third the amount of power held by Whites in policy-making posts. Notably, Afro-Americans rarely are appointed or elected to positions with a predominantly White constituency. As a result, Afro-American policy makers are limited to the existing predominantly Black constituencies. Edward Banfield and James Q. Wilson articulated the resulting dilemma of Afro-Americans in the political arena: "Not only are few Negroes elected to office but those who are elected generally find it necessary to be politicians first and Negro second. If they are to stay in office they must soft pedal the racial issues that are the most concern to Negroes as Negroes." [17] This suggests that even when important positions are held by Afro-Americans, there is no assurance that such policy-makers will deal forcefully with the issues that dominate the lives of the majority of their constituents.

"In short," as Baron ends, "not only are Negroes underrepresented in

17. Edward Banfield and James Q. Wilson, *City Politics* (Harvard University Press, 1965), p. 293.

the major policy-making positions in Cook County, but even where represented their actual power is restricted or their representatives fail to work for the long-term interest of their constituency. It is therefore safe to estimate that Negroes really hold less than one percent of the effective power in the Chicago metropolitan area. Realistically, the power structure of Chicago is hardly less white than that of Mississippi." [18]

What are some of the specific roadblocks to increased political participation by Afro-Americans? First there is the discrimination in voting registration and voting regulations. Historically this has taken the form of poll taxes and stringent requirements which can easily be used to disenfranchise Afro-Americans. Local and state governments which are hostile to increasing Afro-American political participation can easily find ways of interpreting vague laws to hamper and eventually block any real growth in registration.

Those break-throughs in voter registration that have occurred are often the result of intensive campaigns run by Afro-Americans and funded by private groups in White society, such as nonprofit foundations. The funds needed to support voter registration and voter education projects do not exist within Black communities, and the financial dependence on outside sources hinders the development of long-range efforts. Another roadblock is the availability of registration facilities. Since most Afro-Americans work during the day, it is difficult or an undue hardship for them to find the time to register at the local county courthouse or city hall. Sometimes an Afro-American is forced to take time off during the day, which means loss of pay, in order to register to vote in an election in which he has little faith that his participation would make much difference.

In some areas lack of political participation, particularly in office-holding, is the result of various forms of gerrymandering in which voting districts are drawn so as to limit the number of Afro-American constituencies and as a result limit the potential of their being elected to office. Another form of gerrymandering is the abolition of districts and the choice of officials in city-wide contests. This technique dilutes the Afro-American vote and thereby makes it difficult for an Afro-American to be elected. In addition, as some of the large urban areas become increasingly Black, there are new attempts being made to consolidate central city government with surrounding areas to form a new level of county government. The impact of this reform would be again to dilute the influence and power of Afro-Americans.

18. Harold Baron, "Black Powerlessness in Chicago," *Trans-action*, 6 (November, 1968), pp. 27-38.

Another reason for the limited number of Afro-Americans in local offices is the absence or inadequacy of financial compensation for the time spent on government business. In fact many officeholders find it necessary to support themselves in other professions, and their role as officeholder becomes a part-time affair. The absence of Afro-Americans in jobs which provide easy entree into elected politics is a corollary. It has been pointed out that there are few Afro-Americans in business, law, and other professions which traditionally have provided the individual with sufficient income and the social mobility necessary to run for public office.

Finally, there is a tendency to establish professional criteria which automatically exclude Afro-Americans from public jobs and offices because they lack the proper professional credentials. In some cases the criteria have little to do with the effective completion of the tasks. Rather, the criteria reflect the biases of the dominant culture and the refusal to entertain the possibility that professional competence may be achieved through the acquisition of different types of skills and competences. Examples can be found in civil service examinations which include test items on pronunciation. Mispronunciation of obscure words have been used, for example, as a basis for denying promotion of educators.[19]

Studies of the most active Afro-American communities in local and national political systems indicate that even where mobilization is total, the rewards rarely match the effort required to initiate action.[20] In some communities it takes a community boycott supported by over 80 percent of the population in order to force local government to train more Afro-Americans for positions as clerical staff. A similar request by Whites can often be accomplished through informal meetings and lunches with important civic leaders who can successfully put pressure on local government without the prohibitive cost of community mobilization.

Illustrative are the time, resources and human lives required to pass the Civil Rights Act of 1964. Afro-Americans and their allies maintained an expensive lobby in Congress to work day by day to convince individual members of Congress that the time was ripe for legislation to fulfill the rights guaranteed by the Constitution. It required the murder of several civil rights workers in the South for public opinion to be aroused in favor of new legislation in civil rights. The March on Washington of 1963, which involved over two hundred thousand persons, was necessary to demonstrate to both the president and Congress the concern of many

19. David Rogers, *110 Livingston Street* (Vintage, 1969), p. 228.
20. John H. Strange, "The Politics of Protest: The Case of Durham," in Virginia B. Ermer and John H. Strange, eds., *Blacks and Bureaucracy* (T. Y. Crowell, 1972, forthcoming).

Americans that government respond positively to the denial of civil rights to Afro-Americans. Although there can be no exact comparison, it is reasonable to assume that White Americans would not have to expend half as much time and resources to achieve the passage of legislation to deal with a similar and equally important issue affecting them.

THE PERFORMANCE OF AMERICAN GOVERNMENT

An evaluation of the performance of government in meeting the demands and aspirations of Afro-Americans must include answers to at least two questions: How democratic is the performance of government in its relationship to Afro-Americans? Does government possess both the will and capacity to respond successfully to issues raised by its citizens of African heritage? Finally, in light of the answers to those questions we will examine the political strategy presently being pursued by many Afro-Americans to secure those rights guaranteed by the Constitution but which have been denied them as a result of racial oppression.

The hallmarks of a democracy include respect for the inherent worth of the individual and equal participation by the citizens in the making of decisions that are binding for everyone matched by similar participation in the distribution of rewards of government. The first hallmark is based on the belief that human life is the most important value in a free and civilized society. An ever-increasing civilizaton requires that social, political and economic institutions be designed to assist each individual to reach his full potential. Each citizen then has a greater opportunity to make additional and positive contributions to society. Maximizing equal opportunity for all citizens guards against replacing the concern for human life and dignity with concerns for personal privilege based upon social class or material wealth.

The second hallmark of democracy concerns the extent and quality of citizen participation in deciding government policies. Our national rhetoric includes such phrases as "government of the people, for the people and by the people," "with the consent of the governed" and "no taxation without representation." These sentiments speak to the belief that government is endowed with certain powers only as long as the exercise of that power is responsible. Government must be responsible for its actions to the citizens who endow it with legitimacy. The most effective manner of insuring the responsible exercise of power by government involves the active participation of citizens, directly and indirectly, in the business of government. To limit citizen participation is to undermine the ability of free men to exercise considerable control over their lives.

To what extent do these hallmarks of democracy obtain in the relationship of government to Blacks?

Our review of Afro-Americans and government suggests that Blacks have not received treatment indicative of a great concern for the inherent worth of the individual. The vestiges of slavery and the continued condition of racial oppression are indications that government and American society consider Blacks to be of less worth than others. The response of government to the demands of Afro-Americans appears to be a continuation of the belief that a Black is three-fifths of a citizen. The limited participation of Afro-Americans in all levels of government, both in making decisions and sharing rewards, constitutes further evidence that Blacks have not been accepted as democratic citizens. We must conclude therefore that the performance of government in its relationship to Afro-Americans has not been very democratic.

The will and capacity of government to meet the demands of Afro-Americans can be measured by the enactment and enforcement of laws, and the design and maintenance of administrative machinery for the delivery of services. In the matter of enactment and enforcement of law, our essay suggests that government has a far better capacity to enact than to enforce. The enormous difficulties in passing the Civil Rights Act of 1964 indicates that the process of legislative initiative is difficult for Afro-Americans. The problems of getting enforcement of law are much greater. In the past sixteen years the Supreme Court has issued six major decisions instructing socially segregated school system to integrate. While the number of Black now attending integrated schools has indeed increased, well over half of all Black students continue to attend segregated schools. Afro-Americans must conclude that the will and capacity of government in law enforcement is sporadic and often inadequate.

In the design and maintenance of administrative machinery for the delivery of government services, our analysis suggests that government's capacity is limited in meeting the demands of Blacks. Large bureaucracies that deal with the issues of housing and urban development are examples. The development of program guidelines, preparation of proposals for funding, and complex methods of evaluation are steps in the administrative process which successively drain the initiative and potential impact of new housing programs. The end result is that, from the perspective of Afro-Americans demanding better housing, the response of government is to employ members of the salaried middle class to study the problem in order to create more jobs for the salaried middle class. The administrative machinery as a consequence functions to produce employment for professional administrators rather than housing for Afro-Americans.

The current debate on the correct relationship between Blacks, government, and American society comprehends alternatives from total separation to complete assimilation. It is important to note the diversity of opinion, particularly among Afro-Americans, in order to counter the tendency towards facile generalizations. For our purposes, however, we shall focus on one strategy which has been adopted by a significant number of Afro-Americans. This strategy is the election of increasing numbers of Afro-Americans to public office. Particular emphasis is placed on the election of mayors and members of city councils in those urban areas with a majority of Black citizens. The selection of candidates who will be "responsible" to the Black community and the organization of voter registration campaigns represent the key processes in implementing this strategy. The underlying assumption of this strategy is the belief that by capturing elected office, Afro-Americans will be able to direct the resources of government to meet their demands for equal rights and equal opportunities.

It remains to be seen whether such a strategy will bring more than hollow victories. The election of Black mayors in Cleveland, Gary, and Newark indicates that these offices were not so much captured by Blacks as abandoned by Whites who had fled to the suburbs. Urban decay, racial polarization, financial bankruptcy, and entrenched bureaucracies are some of the realities faced by newly elected Black officials. Finally, it seems that the locus of power is shifting from local to the state and federal governments. The pattern of Black powerlessness in Chicago discussed earlier seems to be repeating in the election of Afro-American officeholders.

Still, the election of Black officials can transform the present relationship of government and Afro-Americans from one of inequality and distrust to one characterized by freedom and justice. The success of such a transformation will depend to a large extent upon the commitment of the entire society to those principles embodied in the Declaration of Independence and the Constitution. In the final analysis, the performance of government is a reflection of the dominant values of our society. If the majority of citizens believe that the demands of Afro-Americans upon government are incorrect or immoral there can be little hope for a new and productive relationship.

SELECTED BIBLIOGRAPHY

The material in this essay is drawn from the sources below. Readers will find these works to be good references for further investigation.

Aptheker, Herbert, ed. *A Documentary History of the Negro People in the United States,* 2 vols. (Citadel Press, 1951).

Bardolph, Richard. *The Civil Rights Record: Black Americans and the Law, 1849-1970* (T. Y. Crowell, 1970).

Dixon, Vernon and Badi G. Foster. *Beyond Black or White: An Alternate America* (Little, Brown, 1971).

DuBois, W. E. B. *Black Reconstruction in America: 1860-1880* (Meridian, 1964).

Farley, Reynolds. *Growth of the Black Population* (Markham, 1970).

Gans, Herbert. *People and Plans* (Basic Books, 1968).

Greer, Scott. *Urban Renewal and American Cities* (Bobbs-Merrill, 1965).

Herskovitz, Melville J. *The Myth of the Negro Past* (Beacon, 1941).

Jordan, Winthrop. *White over Black: Attitudes Toward the Negro, 1550-1812* (Penguin, 1968).

Kardiner, Abram and Lionel Oversey. *The Mark of Oppression* (Meridian, 1951).

Malcolm X. *The Autobiography* (Grove Press, 1964).

Meier, August and Elliott Rudwick. *The Making of Black America,* 2 vols. (Atheneum, 1969).

Metropolitan Applied Research Center. *A Relevant War Against Poverty* (1968).

National Advisory Commission on Civil Disorders. *Report* (1968).

National Commission on Urban Problems. *Hearings,* 5 vols. (1968).

Rainwater, Lee and William L. Yancey. *The Moynihan Report and the Politics of Controversy* (M.I.T. Press, 1967).

Rogers, David, *110 Livingston Street* (Vintage, 1969).

Spear, Allan. *Black Chicago: The Making of a Negro Ghetto, 1890-1920* (University of Chicago Press, 1967).

Strange, John H. and Virginia B. Ermer, eds. *Blacks and Bureaucracy* (T. Y. Crowell, 1972).

Tabb, William. *The Political Economy of the Black Ghetto* (Norton, 1970).

Weiner, Leo. *Africa and the Discovery of America,* 3 vols. (Innes, 1922).

Woodward, C. Vann. *The Strange Career of Jim Crow* (Oxford University Press, 1957).

APPENDIX

The Constitution of the United States

We the People of the United States, in Order to form a more perfect Union, establish Justice, insure domestic Tranquility, provide for the common defence, promote the general Welfare, and secure the Blessings of Liberty to ourselves and our Posterity, do ordain and establish this Constitution for the United States of America.

Article I

Section 1. All legislative Powers herein granted shall be vested in a Congress of the United States, which shall consist of a Senate and House of Representatives.

Section 2. 1. The House of Representatives shall be composed of Members chosen every second Year by the People of the several States, and the Electors in each State shall have the Qualifications requisite for Electors of the most numerous Branch of the State Legislature.

2. No Person shall be a Representative who shall not have attained to the Age of twenty five Years, and been seven Years a Citizen of the United States, and who shall not, when elected, be an Inhabitant of that State in which he shall be chosen.

3. Representatives and direct Taxes shall be apportioned[1] among the several States which may be included within this Union, according to their respective Numbers, which shall be determined by adding to the whole Number of free Persons, including those bound to Service for a Term of Years, and excluding Indians not taxed, three fifths of all other Persons.[2] The actual Enumeration shall be made within three Years after the first Meeting of the Congress of the United States, and within every subsequent Term in ten Years, in such Manner as they shall by Law direct. The Number of Representatives shall not exceed one for every thirty Thousand, but each State shall have at Least one Representative; and until such enumeration

1. Changed by Sixteenth Amendment.
2. Provision for counting a slave as "three-fifths of a person" eliminated by Fourteenth Amendment.

shall be made, the State of New Hampshire shall be entitled to chuse three, Massachusetts eight, Rhode-Island and Providence Plantations one, Connecticut five, New-York six, New Jersey four, Pennsylvania eight, Delaware one, Maryland six, Virginia ten, North Carolina five, South Carolina five, and Georgia three.

4. When vacancies happen in the Representation from any State, the Executive Authority thereof shall issue Writs of Election to fill such Vacancies.

5. The House of Representatives shall chuse their Speaker and other Officers; and shall have the sole Power of Impeachment.

Section 3. 1. The Senate of the United States shall be composed of two Senators from each State, chosen by the Legislature thereof,[3] for six Years; and each Senator shall have one Vote.

2. Immediately after they shall be assembled in Consequence of the first Election, they shall be divided as equally as may be into three Classes. The Seats of the Senators of the first Class shall be vacated at the Expiration of the second Year, of the second Class at the Expiration of the fourth Year, and of the third Class at the Expiration of the sixth Year, so that one third may be chosen every second Year; and if Vacancies happen by Resignation, or otherwise, during the Recess of the Legislature of any State, the Executive thereof may make temporary Appointments until the next Meeting of the Legislature,[3] which shall then fill such Vacancies.

3. No Person shall be a Senator who shall not have attained to the Age of thirty Years, and been nine Years a Citizen of the United States, and who shall not, when elected, be an Inhabitant of that State for which he shall be chosen.

4. The Vice President of the United States shall be President of the Senate, but shall have no Vote, unless they be equally divided.

5. The Senate shall chuse their other officers, and also a President pro tempore, in the Absence of the Vice President, or when he shall exercise the Office of President of the United States.

6. The Senate shall have the sole Power to try all Impeachments. When sitting for that Purpose, they shall be on Oath or Affirmation. When the President of the United States is tried, the Chief Justice shall preside: And no Person shall be convicted without the Concurrence of two thirds of the Members present.

7. Judgment in Cases of Impeachment shall not extend further than to removal from Office, and disqualification to hold and enjoy any Office of honor, Trust or Profit under the United States: but the Party convicted shall nevertheless be liable and subject to Indictment, Trial, Judgment and Punishment, according to Law.

Section 4. 1. The Times, Places and Manner of holding Elections for Senators and Representatives, shall be prescribed in each State by the Legislature thereof; but the Congress may at any time by Law make or alter such Regulations, except as to the Places of chusing Senators.

2. The Congress shall assemble at least once in every Year, and such Meeting shall be on the first Monday in December, unless they shall by Law appoint a different day.[4]

3. Changed by Seventeenth Amendment.
4. Changed by Twentieth Amendment.

Section 5. 1. Each House shall be the Judge of the Elections, Returns and Qualifications of its own Members, and a Majority of each shall constitute a Quorum to do Business; but a smaller Number may adjourn from day to day, and may be authorized to compel the attendance of absent Members, in such Manner, and under such Penalties as each House may provide.

2. Each House may determine the Rules of its Proceedings, punish its Members for Disorderly Behaviour, and, with the Concurrence of two thirds, expel a Member.

3. Each House shall keep a Journal of its Proceedings, and from time to time publish the same, excepting such Parts as may in their Judgment require Secrecy; and the Yeas and Nays of the Members of either House on any question shall, at the Desire of one fifth of those Present, be entered on the Journal.

4. Neither House, during the Session of Congress, shall, without the Consent of the other, adjourn for more than three days, nor to any other Place than that in which the two Houses shall be sitting.

Section 6. 1. The Senators and Representatives shall receive a Compensation for their Services, to be ascertained by Law, and paid out of the Treasury of the United States. They shall in all Cases, except Treason, Felony and Breach of the Peace, be privileged from Arrest during their Attendance at the Session of their respective Houses, and in going to and returning from the same; and for any Speech or Debate in either House, they shall not be questioned in any other Place.

2. No Senator or Representative shall, during the Time for which he was elected, be appointed to any civil Office under the Authority of the United States, which shall have been created, or the Emoluments whereof shall have been encreased during such time; and no Person holding any Office under the United States, shall be a member of either House during his Continuance in Office.

Section 7. 1. All Bills for raising Revenue shall originate in the House of Representatives; but the Senate may propose or concur with Amendments as on other Bills.

2. Every Bill which shall have passed the House of Representatives and the Senate, shall, before it becomes a Law, be presented to the President of the United States; If he approve he shall sign it, but if not he shall return it, with his Objections to that House in which it shall have originated, who shall enter the Objections at large on their Journal, and proceed to reconsider it. If after such Reconsideration two thirds of that House shall agree to pass the Bill, it shall be sent, together with the Objections, to the other House, by which it shall likewise be reconsidered, and if approved by two thirds of that House, it shall become a Law. But in all such Cases the Votes of both Houses shall be determined by Yeas and Nays, and the Names of the Persons voting for and against the Bill shall be entered on the Journal of each House respectively. If any Bill shall not be returned by the President within ten Days (Sundays excepted) after it shall have been presented to him, the same shall be a Law, in like Manner as if he had signed it, unless the Congress by their Adjournment prevent its Return, in which Case it shall not be a Law.

3. Every Order, Resolution, or Vote to which the Concurrence of the Senate and House of Representatives may be necessary (except on a question of Adjournment) shall be presented to the President of the United States; and before the same shall take Effect, shall be approved by him, or being dis-

approved by him, shall be repassed by two thirds of the Senate and House of Representatives, according to the Rules and Limitations prescribed in the Case of a Bill.

Section 8. 1. The Congress shall have Power to lay and Collect Taxes, Duties, Imposts and Excises, to pay the Debts and provide for the common Defence and general Welfare of the United States; but all Duties, Imposts and Excises shall be uniform throughout the United States;

2. To borrow Money on the Credit of the United States;

3. To regulate Commerce with foreign Nations, and among the several States, and with the Indian Tribes;

4. To establish a uniform Rule of Naturalization, and uniform Laws on the subject of Bankruptices throughout the United States;

5. To coin Money, regulate the Value thereof, and of foreign Coin, and fix the Standard of Weights and Measures;

6. To provide for the Punishment of counterfeiting the Securities and Current Coin of the United States;

7. To establish Post Offices and post Roads;

8. To promote the Progress of Science and useful Arts, by securing for limited Times to Authors and Inventors the exclusive Right to their respective Writings and Discoveries;

9. To constitute Tribunals inferior to the supreme Court;

10. To define and punish Piracies and Felonies committed on the high Seas, and Offences against the Law of Nations;

11. To declare War, grant Letters of Marque and Reprisal, and make Rules concerning Captures on Land and Water;

12. To raise and support Armies, but no Appropriation of Money to that Use shall be for a longer Term than two Years;

13. To provide and maintain a Navy;

14. To make Rules for the Government and Regulation of the land and naval Forces;

15. To provide for calling forth the Militia to execute the Laws of the Union, suppress Insurrections and repel Invasions;

16. To provide for organizing, arming, and disciplining, the Militia, and for governing such Part of them as may be employed in the Service of the United States, reserving to the States respectively, the Appointment of the Officers, and the Authority of training the Militia according to the discipline prescribed by Congress;

17. To exercise exclusive Legislation in all Cases whatsoever, over such District (not exceeding ten Miles square) as may, by Cession of Particular States, and the Acceptance of Congress, become the Seat of the Government of the United States, and to exercise like Authority over all Places purchased by the Consent of the Legislature of the State in which the Same shall be, for the Erection of Forts, Magazines, Arsenals, dock-Yards, and other needful Buildings;–And

18. To make all Laws which shall be necessary and proper for carrying into Execution the foregoing Powers, and all other Powers vested by this Constitution in the Government of the United States, or in any Department or Office thereof.

Section 9. 1. The Migration or Importation of such Persons as any of the States now existing shall think proper to admit, shall not be prohibited by the Congress prior to the Year one thousand eight hundred and eight, but a

Tax or duty may be imposed on such Importation, not exceeding ten dollars for each Person.

2. The Privilege of the Writ of Habeas Corpus shall not be suspended, unless when in Cases of Rebellion or Invasion the public Safety may require it.

3. No Bill of Attainder or ex post facto Law shall be passed.

4. No Capitation, or other direct, Tax shall be laid, unless in Proportion to the Census or Enumeration herein before directed to be taken.[5]

5. No Tax or Duty shall be laid on Articles exported from any State.

6. No Preference shall be given by any Regulation of Commerce or Revenue to the Ports of one State over those of another; nor shall Vessels bound to, or from, one State, be obliged to enter, clear or pay Duties in another.

7. No Money shall be drawn from the Treasury, but in Consequence of Appropriations made by Law; and a regular Statement and Account of the Receipts and Expenditures of all public Money shall be published from time to time.

8. No Title of Nobility shall be granted by the United States: And no Person holding any Office of Profit or Trust under them, shall, without the Consent of the Congress, accept of any present, Emolument, Office, or Title, of any kind whatsoever, from any King, Prince, or foreign State.

Section 10. 1. No State shall enter into any Treaty, Alliance, or Confederation; grant Letters of Marque and Reprisal; coin Money; emit Bills of Credit; make any Thing but gold and silver Coin a Tender in Payment of Debts; pass any Bill of Attainder, ex post facto Law, or Law impairing the Obligation of Contracts; or grant any Title of Nobility.

2. No State shall, without the Consent of the Congress, lay any Imposts or duties on Imports or Exports, except what may be absolutely necessary for executing its inspection Laws: and the net Produce of all Duties and Imposts, laid by any State on Imports or Exports, shall be for the Use of the Treasury of the United States; and all such Laws shall be subject to the Revision and Controul of the Congress.

3. No state shall, without the Consent of Congress, lay any Duty of Tonnage, keep Troops, or Ships of War in time of Peace, enter into any Agreement or Compact with another State, or with a foreign Power, or engage in War, unless actually invaded, or in such imminent Danger as will not admit of delay.

Article II

Section 1. 1. The executive Power shall be vested in a President of the United States of America. He shall hold his Office during the Term of four Years, and, together with the Vice President, chosen for the same Term, be elected as follows

2. Each State shall appoint, in such Manner as the Legislature thereof may direct, a Number of Electors, equal to the whole Number of Senators and Representatives to which the State may be entitled in the Congress: but no Senator or Representative, or Person holding an Office of Trust or Profit under the United States, shall be appointed an Elector.

3. The Electors shall meet in their respective States, and vote by Ballot for two Persons, of whom one at least shall not be an Inhabitant of the same

5. Modified by the Sixteenth Amendment.

State with themselves. And they shall make a List of all the Persons voted for, and of the Number of Votes for each; which List they shall sign and certify, and transmit sealed to the Seat of the Government of the United States, directed to the President of the Senate. The President of the Senate shall, in the Presence of the Senate and House of Representatives, open all the Certificates, and the Votes shall then be counted. The Person having the greatest Number of Votes shall be the President, if such Number be a Majority of the whole Number of Electors appointed; and if there be more than one who have such Majority, and have an equal Number of Votes, then the House of Representatives shall immediately chuse by Ballot one of them for President; and if no Person have a Majority, then from the five highest on the List the said House shall in like Manner chuse the President. But in chusing the President, the Votes shall be taken by States, the Representation from each State having one Vote; A quorum for this Purpose shall consist of a Member or Members from two thirds of the States, and a Majority of all the States shall be necessary to a Choice. In every Case, after the Choice of the President, the Person having the greatest Number of Votes of the Electors shall be the Vice President. But if there should remain two or more who have equal Votes, the Senate shall chuse from them by Ballot the Vice President.[6]

4. The Congress may determine the Time of chusing the Electors, and the Day on which they shall give their Votes; which Day shall be the same throughout the United States.

5. No Person except a natural born Citizen, or a Citizen of the United States, at the time of the Adoption of this Constitution, shall be eligible to the Office of President; neither shall any Person be eligible to that Office who shall not have attained to the Age of thirty five Years, and been fourteen Years a Resident within the United States.

6. In Case of the Removal of the President from Office, or of his Death, Resignation, or Inability to discharge the Powers and Duties of the said Office, the Same shall devolve on the Vice President, and the Congress may by Law provide for the Case of Removal, Death, Resignation, or Inability, both of the President and Vice President, declaring what Officer shall then act as President, and such Officer shall act accordingly, until the Disability be removed, or a President shall be elected.

7. The President shall, at stated Times, receive for his Services, a Compensation, which shall neither be encreased nor diminished during the Period for which he shall have been elected, and he shall not receive within that Period any other Emolument from the United States, or any of them.

8. Before he enter on the Execution of his Office, he shall take the following Oath or Affirmation:—"I do solemnly swear (or affirm) that I will faithfully execute the Office of President of the United States, and will to the best of my Ability, preserve, protect and defend the Constitution of the United States."

Section 2. 1. The President shall be Commander in Chief of the Army and Navy of the United States, and of the Militia of the several States, when called into the actual Service of the United States; he may require the Opinion, in writing, of the principal Officer in each of the executive Departments, upon any Subject relating to the Duties of their respective Offices,

6. Modified by the Twelfth Amendment and, to some extent, by the Twentieth Amendment.

and he shall have Power to grant Reprieves and Pardons for Offences against the United States, except in Cases of Impeachment.

2. He shall have Power, by and with the Advice and Consent of the Senate, to make Treaties, provided two thirds of the Senators present concur; and he shall nominate, and by and with the Advice and Consent of the Senate, shall appoint Ambassadors, other public Ministers and Consuls, Judges of the supreme Court, and all other Officers of the United States, whose Appointments are not herein otherwise provided for, and which shall be established by Law: but the Congress may by Law vest the Appointment of such inferior Officers, as they think proper, in the President alone, in the Courts of Law, or in the Heads of Departments.

3. The President shall have Power to fill up all Vacancies that may happen during the Recess of the Senate, by granting Commissions which shall expire at the End of their next Session.

Section 3. He shall from time to time give to the Congress Information of the State of the Union, and recommend to their Consideration such Measures as he shall judge necessary and expedient; he may, on extraordinary Occasions, convene both Houses, or either of them, and in Case of Disagreement between them, with Respect to the Time of Adjournment, he may adjourn them to such Time as he shall think proper; he shall receive Ambassadors and other public Ministers; he shall take Care that the Laws be faithfully executed, and shall Commission all the Officers of the United States.

Section 4. The President, Vice President and all civil Officers of the United States, shall be removed from Office on Impeachment for, and Conviction of, Treason, Bribery, or other high Crimes and Misdemeanors.

Article III

Section 1. The judicial Power of the United States, shall be vested in one supreme Court, and in such inferior Courts as the Congress may from time to time ordain and establish. The Judges, both of the supreme and inferior Courts, shall hold their Offices during good Behaviour, and shall, at stated Times, receive for their Services, a Compensation, which shall not be diminished during their Continuance in Office.

Section 2. 1. The judicial Power shall extend to all Cases, in Law and Equity, arising under this Constitution, the Laws of the United States, and Treaties made, or which shall be made, under their Authority;—to all Cases affecting Ambassadors, other public Ministers and Consuls;—to all Cases of admiralty and maritime Jurisdiction;—to Controversies to which the United States shall be a Party;—to Controversies between two or more States;—between Citizens of different States,—between Citizens of the same State claiming Lands under Grants of different States, and between a State, or the Citizens thereof, and foreign States, Citizens or Subjects.[7]

2. In all Cases affecting Ambassadors, other public Ministers and Consuls, and those in which a State shall be Party, the Supreme Court shall have original Jurisdiction. In all the other Cases before mentioned, the supreme Court shall have appellate Jurisdiction, both as to Law and Fact, with such Exceptions, and under such Regulations as the Congress shall make.

3. The Trial of all Crimes, except in Cases of Impeachment, shall be by

7. Changed by the Eleventh Amendment, with respect to certain cases wherein a state is a party.

Jury; and such Trial shall be held in the State where the said Crimes shall have been committed; but when not committed within any State, the Trial shall be at such Place or Places as the Congress may by Law have directed.

Section 3. 1. Treason against the United States, shall consist only in levying War against them, or in adhering to their Enemies, giving them Aid and Comfort. No Person shall be convicted of Treason unless on the Testimony of two Witnesses to the same overt Act, or on Confession in open Court.

2. The Congress shall have Power to declare the Punishment of Treason, but no Attainder of Treason shall work Corruption of Blood, or Forfeiture except during the Life of the Person attainted.

Article IV

Section 1. Full Faith and Credit shall be given in each State to the public Acts, Records, and judicial Proceedings of every other State. And the Congress may by general Laws prescribe the Manner in which such Acts, Records and Proceedings shall be proved, and the Effect thereof.

Setion 2. 1. The Citizens of each State shall be entitled to all Privileges and Immunities of Citizens in the several States.

2. A Person charged in any State with Treason, Felony, or other Crime, who shall flee from Justice, and be found in another State, shall on Demand of the executive Authority of the State from which he fled, be delivered up, to be removed to the State having Jurisdiction of the Crime.

3. No Person held to Service or Labour in one State, under the Laws thereof, escaping into another, shall, in Consequence of any Law or Regulation therein, be discharged from such Service or Labour, but shall be delivered up on Claim of the Party to whom such Service or Labour may be due.[8]

Section 3. 1. New States may be admitted by the Congress into this Union; but no new State shall be formed or erected within the Jurisdiction of any other State; nor any State be formed by the Junction of two or more States, or Parts of States, without the Consent of the Legislatures of the States concerned as well as of the Congress.

2. The Congress shall have Power to dispose of and make all needful Rules and Regulations respecting the Territory or other Property belonging to the United States; and nothing in this Constitution shall be so construed as to Prejudice any Claims of the United States, or of any particular State.

Section 4. The United States shall guarantee to every State in this Union a Republican Form of Government, and shall protect each of them against Invasion; and on Application of the Legislature, or of the Executive (when the Legislature cannot be convened) against domestic Violence.

Article V

The Congress, whenever two thirds of both Houses shall deem it necessary, shall propose Amendments to this Constitution, or, on the Application of the Legislatures of two thirds of the several States, shall call a Convention for proposing Amendments, which, in either Case, shall be valid to all Intents and Purposes, as Part of this Constitution, when ratified by the Legislatures of three fourths of the several States, or by Conventions in three fourths thereof, as the one or the other Mode of Ratification may be proposed by

8. Made obsolete by the Thirteenth Amendment.

the Congress Provided that no Amendment which may be made prior to the Year One thousand eight hundred and eight shall in any Manner affect the first and fourth Clauses in the Ninth Section of the first Article; and that no State, without its Consent, shall be deprived of its equal Suffrage in the Senate.

Article VI

1. All Debts contracted and Engagements entered into, before the Adoption of this Constitution, shall be as valid against the United States under this Constitution, as under the Confederation.

2. This Constitution, and the Laws of the United States which shall be made in Pursuance thereof; and all Treaties made, or which shall be made, under the Authority of the United States, shall be the supreme Law of the Land; and the Judges in every State shall be bound thereby, any Thing in the Constitution or Laws of any State to the Contrary notwithstanding.

3. The Senators and Representatives before mentioned, and the Members of the several State Legislatures, and all executive and judicial Officers, both of the United States and of the several States, shall be bound by Oath or Affirmation, to support this Constitution; but no religious Test shall ever be required as a Qualification to any Office or public Trust under the United States.

Article VII

The Ratification of the Conventions of nine States, shall be sufficient for the Establishment of this Constitution between the States so ratifying the Same.

Done in Convention by the Unanimous Consent of the States present, the Seventeenth Day of September, in the Year of our Lord one thousand seven hundred and Eighty-seven, and of the Independence of the United States of America the Twelfth. In witness thereof We have hereunto subscribed our Names.

AMENDMENTS
Article I

Congress shall make no law respecting an establishment of religion, or prohibiting the free exercise thereof; or abridging the freedom of speech, or of the press; or the right of the people peaceably to assemble, and to petition the Government for a redress of grievances.

Article II

A well regulated Militia, being necessary to the security of a free State, the right of the people to keep and bear Arms, shall not be infringed.

Article III

No Soldier shall, in time of peace be quartered in any house, without the consent of the Owner, nor in time of war, but in a manner to be prescribed by law.

The right of the people to be secure in their persons, houses, papers, and effects, against unreasonable searches and seizures, shall not be violated, and no Warrants shall issue, but upon probable cause, supported by Oath or affirmation, and particularly describing the place to be searched, and the persons or things to be seized.

Article V

No person shall be held to answer for a capital, or otherwise infamous crime, unless on a presentment or indictment of a Grand Jury, except in cases arising in the land or naval forces, or in the Militia, when in actual service in time of War or public danger; nor shall any person be subject for the same offence to be twice put in jeopardy of life or limb; nor shall be compelled in any criminal case to be a witness against himself, nor be deprived of life, liberty, or property, without due process of law; nor shall private property be taken for public use, without just compensation.

Article VI

In all criminal prosecutions the accused shall enjoy the right to a speedy and public trial, by an impartial jury of the State and district wherein the crime shall have been committed, which district shall have been previously ascertained by law, and to be informed of the nature and cause of the accusation; to be confronted with the witnesses against him; to have compulsory process for obtaining witnesses in his favor, and to have the Assistance of Counsel for his defence.

Article VII

In suits at common law, where the value in controversy shall exceed twenty dollars, the right of trial by jury shall be preserved, and no fact tried by a jury shall be otherwise re-examined in any Court of the United States, than according to the rules of the common law.

Article VIII

Excessive bail shall not be required, nor excessive fines imposed, nor cruel and unusual punishments inflicted.

Article IX

The enumeration in the Constitution, of certain rights, shall not be construed to deny or disparage others retained by the people.

Article X

The powers not delegated to the United States by the Constitution, nor prohibited by it to the States, are reserved to the States respectively, or to the people.

[The first ten Amendments were adopted in 1791.]

Article XI

The Judicial power of the United States shall not be construed to extend to any suit in law or equity, commenced or prosecuted against one of the

United States by Citizens of another State, or by Citizens or Subjects of any Foreign State. [Adopted 1798.]

Article XII

The Electors shall meet in their respective states, and vote by ballot for President and Vice-President, one of whom, at least, shall not be an inhabitant of the same state with themselves; they shall name in their ballots the person voted for as President, and in distinct ballots the person voted for as Vice-President, and they shall make distinct lists of all persons voted for as President, and of all persons voted for as Vice-President, and of the number of votes for each, which lists they shall sign and certify, and transmit sealed to the seat of the government of the United States, directed to the President of the Senate;—The President of the Senate shall, in the presence of the Senate and House of Representatives, open all the certificates and the votes shall then be counted;—The person having the greatest number of votes for President, shall be the President, if such number be a majority of the whole number of Electors appointed; and if no person have such majority, then from the persons having the highest numbers not exceeding three on the list of those voted for as President, the House of Representatives shall choose immediately, by ballot, the President. But in choosing the President, the votes shall be taken by states, the representation from each state having one vote; a quorum for this purpose shall consist of a member or members from two-thirds of the states, and a majority of all the states shall be necessary to a choice. And if the House of Representatives shall not choose a President whenever the right of choice shall devolve upon them, before the fourth day of March next following, then the Vice-President shall act as President, as in the case of the death or other constitutional disability of the President.[9]—The person having the greatest number of votes as Vice-President, shall be the Vice-President, if such number be a majority of the whole number of Electors appointed, and if no person have a majority, then from the two highest numbers on the list, the Senate shall choose the Vice-President; a quorum for the purpose shall consist of two-thirds of the whole number of Senators, and a majority of the whole number shall be necessary to a choice. But no person constitutionally ineligible to the office of President shall be eligible to that of Vice-President of the United States. [Adopted 1804.]

Article XIII

Section 1. Neither slavery nor involuntary servitude, except as a punishment for crime whereof the party shall have been duly convicted, shall exist within the United States, or any place subject to their jurisdiction.

Section 2. Congress shall have power to enforce this article by appropriate legislation. [Adopted 1865.]

Article XIV

Section 1. All persons born or naturalized in the United States, and subject to the jurisdiction thereof, are citizens of the United States and of the State wherein they reside. No State shall make or enforce any law which shall abridge the privileges or immunities of citizens of the United States; nor shall any State deprive any person of life, liberty, or property, without due

9. Modified by the Twentieth Amendment.

process of law; nor deny to any person within its jurisdiction the equal protection of the laws.

Section 2. Representatives shall be apportioned among the several States according to their respective numbers, counting the whole number of persons in each State, excluding Indians not taxed. But when the right to vote at any election for the choice of electors for President and Vice President of the United States, Representatives in Congress, the Executive and Judicial officers of a State, or the members of the Legislature therof, is denied to any of the male inhabitants of such State, being twenty-one years of age, and citizens of the United States, or in any way abridged, except for participation in rebellion, or other crime, the basis of representation therein shall be reduced in the proportion which the number of such male citizens shall bear to the whole number of male citizens twenty-one years of age in such State.

Section 3. No person shall be a Senator or Representative in Congress, or elector of President and Vice President, or hold any office, civil or military, under the United States, or under any State, who, having previously taken an oath, as a member of Congress, or as an officer of the United States, or as a member of any State legislature, or as an executive or judicial officer of any State, to support the Constitution of the United States, shall have engaged in insurrection or rebellion against the same, or given aid or comfort to the enemies thereof. But Congress may by a vote of two-thirds of each House, remove such disability.

Section 4. The validity of the public debt of the United States, authorized by law, including debts incurred for payment of pensions and bounties for services in suppressing insurrection or rebellion, shall not be questioned. But neither the United States nor any State shall assume or pay any debt or obligation incurred in aid of insurrection or rebellion against the United States, or any claim for the loss or emancipation of any slave; but all such debts, obligations and claims shall be held illegal and void.

Section 5. The Congress shall have power to enforce, by appropriate legislation, the provisions of this article. [Adopted 1868.]

Article XV

Section 1. The right of citizens of the United States to vote shall not be denied or abridged by the United States or by any State on account of race, color, or previous condition of servitude.

Section 2. The Congress shall have power to enforce this article by appropriate legislation. [Adopted 1870.]

Article XVI

The Congress shall have power to lay and collect taxes on incomes, from whatever source derived, without apportionment among the several States, and without regard to any census or enumeration. [Adopted 1913.]

Article XVII

The Senate of the United States shall be composed of two Senators from each State, elected by the people thereof, for six years; and each Senator shall have one vote. The electors in each State shall have the qualifications requisite for electors of the most numerous branch of the State legislatures.

When vacancies happen in the representation of any State in the Senate, the executive authority of such State shall issue writs of election to fill such vacancies: *Provided,* That the legislature of any State may empower the executive thereof to make temporary appointments until the people fill the vacancies by election as the legislature may direct.

This amendment shall not be so construed as to affect the election or term of any Senator chosen before it becomes valid as part of the Constitution. [Adopted 1913.]

Article XVIII

Section 1. After one year from the ratification of this article the manufacture, sale, or transportation of intoxicating liquors within, the importation thereof into, or the exportation thereof from the United States and all territory subject to the jurisdiction thereof for beverage purposes is hereby prohibited.

Section 2. The Congress and the several States shall have concurrent power to enforce this article by appropriate legislation.

Section 3. This article shall be inoperative unless it shall have been ratified as an amendment to the Constitution by the legislatures of the several States, as provided in the Constitution, within seven years from the date of the submission hereof to the States by the Congress. [Adopted 1919.] [10]

Article XIX

The right of citizens of the United States to vote shall not be denied or abridged by the United States or by any State on account of sex.

Congress shall have power to enforce this article by appropriate legislation. [Adopted 1920.]

Article XX

Section 1. The terms of the President and Vice President shall end at noon on the 20th day of January, and the terms of Senators and Representatives at noon on the 3d day of January, of the years in which such terms would have ended if this article had not been ratified; and the terms of their successors shall then begin.

Section 2. The Congress shall assemble at least once in every year, and such meeting shall begin at noon on the 3d day of January, unless they shall by law appoint a different day.

Section 3. If, at the time fixed for the beginning of the term of the President, the President elect shall have died, the Vice President elect shall become President. If a President shall not have been chosen before the time fixed for the beginning of his term, or if the President elect shall have failed to qualify, then the Vice President elect shall act as President until a President shall have qualified; and the Congress may by law provide for the case wherein neither a President elect nor a Vice President elect shall have qualified, declaring who shall then act as President, or the manner in which one who is to act shall be selected, and such person shall act accordingly until a President or Vice President shall have qualified.

Section 4. The Congress may by law provide for the case of the death of any of the persons from whom the House of Representatives may choose a President whenever the right of choice shall have devolved upon them,

10. Repealed by the Twenty-first Amendment.

and for the case of the death of any of the persons from whom the Senate may choose a Vice President whenever the right of choice shall have devolved upon them.

Section 5. Sections 1 and 2 shall take effect on the 15th day of October following the ratification of this article.

Section 6. This article shall be inoperative unless it shall have been ratified as an amendment to the Constitution by the legislatures of three-fourths of the several States within seven years from the date of its submission. [Adopted 1933.]

Article XXI

Section 1. The eighteenth article of amendment to the Constitution of the United States is hereby repealed.

Section 2. The transportation or importation into any State, Territory, or possession of the United States for delivery or use therein of intoxicating liquors, in violation of the laws thereof, is hereby prohibited.

Section 3. This article shall be inoperative unless it shall have been ratified as an amendment to the Constitution by conventions in the several States, as provided in the Constitution, within seven years from the date of the submission hereof to the States by the Congress. [Adopted 1933.]

Article XXII

Section 1. No person shall be elected to the office of the President more than twice, and no person who has held the office of President, or acted as President, for more than two years of a term to which some other person was elected President shall be elected to the office of the President more than once. But this Article shall not apply to any person holding the office of President when this Article was proposed by the Congress, and shall not prevent any person who may be holding the office of President, or acting as President, during the term within which this Article becomes operative from holding the office of President, or acting as President during the remainder of such term.

Section 2. This Article shall be inoperative unless it shall have been ratified as an amendment to the Constitution by the legislatures of three-fourths of the several States within seven years from the date of its submission to the States by the Congress. [Adopted 1951.]

Article XXIII

1. The District constituting the seat of Government of the United States shall appoint in such manner as the Congress may direct:

A number of electors of President and Vice President equal to the whole number of Senators and Representatives in Congress to which the District would be entitled if it were a State, but in no event more than the least populous state; they shall be in addition to those appointed by the states, but they shall be considered, for the purposes of the election of President and Vice President, to be electors appointed by a state; and they shall meet in the District and perform such duties as provided by the twelfth article of amendment.

2. The Congress shall have power to enforce this article by appropriate legislation. [Adopted 1961.]

Section 1. The right of citizens of the United States to vote in any primary or other election for President or Vice President, for electors for President or Vice President, or for Senator or Representative in Congress, shall not be denied or abridged by the United States or any State by reason of failure to pay any poll tax or other tax.

Section 2. The Congress shall have power to enforce this article by appropriate legislation. [Adopted 1964.]

Section 1. In case of the removal of the President from office or his death or resignation, the Vice President shall become President.

Section 2. Whenever there is a vacancy in the office of the Vice President, the President shall nominate a Vice President who shall take the office upon confirmation by a majority vote of both houses of Congress.

Section 3. Whenever the President transmits to the President pro tempore of the Senate and the Speaker of the House of Representatives his written declaration that he is unable to discharge the powers and duties of his office, and until he transmits to them a written declaration to the contrary, such powers and duties shall be discharged by the Vice President as Acting President.

Section 4. Whenever the Vice President and a majority of either the principal officers of the executive departments, or of such other body as Congress may by law provide, transmit to the President pro tempore of the Senate and the Speaker of the House of Representatives their written declaration that the President is unable to discharge the powers and duties of his office, the Vice President shall immediately assume the powers and duties of the office as Acting President.

Thereafter, when the President transmits to the President pro tempore of the Senate and the Speaker of the House of Representatives his written declaration that no inability exists, he shall resume the powers and duties of his office unless the Vice President and a majority of either the principal officer of the executive department, or of such other body as Congress may by law provide, transmit within four days to the President pro tempore of the Senate and the Speaker of the House of Representatives their written declaration that the President is unable to discharge the powers and duties of his office. Thereupon Congress shall decide the issue, assembling within 48 hours for that purpose if not in session. If the Congress, within 21 days after receipt of the latter written declaration, or, if Congress is not in session, within 21 days after Congress is required to assemble, determines by two-thirds vote of both houses that the President is unable to discharge the powers and duties of his office, the Vice President shall continue to discharge the same as Acting President; otherwise, the President shall resume the powers and duties of his office. [Adopted 1967.]

Section 1. The right of citizens of the United States, who are eighteen years of age or older, to vote shall not be denied or abridged by the United States or by any State on account of age.

Section 2. The Congress shall have power to enforce this article by appropriate legislation. [Adopted 1972.]